Margret Müller

The World According To Israeli Newspapers

Medien und politische Kommunikation – Naher Osten und islamische Welt /
Media and Political Communication – Middle East and Islam, Band 25
Herausgegeben von Prof. Dr. Kai Hafez, Universität Erfurt
und Jun.-Prof. Dr. Carola Richter, Freie Universität Berlin
(in Nachfolge der gleichnamigen Schriftenreihe beim Deutschen Orient-Institut,
Hamburg 2000 bis 2005, Band 1 bis 10)

Margret Müller

The World According To Israeli Newspapers

Representations of International Involvement in the Israeli-Palestinian Conflict

Frank & Timme

Verlag für wissenschaftliche Literatur

HEINRICH BÖLL STIFTUNG

Die Forschungen von Frau Margret Müller wurden unterstützt durch die Heinrich-Böll-Stiftung.

FAZIT-STIFTUNG

Gedruckt mit freundlicher Unterstützung der FAZIT-Stiftung.

ISBN 978-3-7329-0286-6
ISSN 1863-4486

Zugl. Dissertation Freie Universität Berlin, 2015, D 188

Herstellung durch Frank & Timme GmbH,
Wittelsbacherstraße 27a, 10707 Berlin.
Printed in Germany.
Gedruckt auf säurefreiem, alterungsbeständigem Papier.

www.frank-timme.de

Acknowledgements

Thank you

... to my supervisor Prof. Dr. Barbara Pfetsch, for the support and liberty she gave me

... to my second examiner Prof. Dr. Moshe Zuckermann and my advisor Prof. Dr. Daniel Bar-Tal for their open ears and doors, investment of time and travel, advice, inspiration, and the long and fruitful discussions

... to my board of examiners Prof. Dr. Carola Richter, Prof. Dr. Alexander Görke, Dr. Annie Waldherr for their time and interest in my research and their constructive advice and criticism

... to Heinrich Boell Foundation, Einstein Foundation, and Fazit Foundation for the funding of this dissertation as well as for the funding of several research trips as visiting scholar at the Universities of Tel Aviv and Jerusalem, and inside the newsrooms of Israeli newspapers during crisis

... to my advisors and colleagues at Freie Universität Berlin, Hebrew University Jerusalem, and Tel Aviv University Jérôme Bourdon, Ifat Maoz, Zohar Kampf, Tamir Sheafer, Annett Heft, Keren Tenenboim-Weinblatt, Yossi David, Meital Balmas Cohen and Paul Frosh

Toda, Thank you, Danke

... to Tel Aviv to Dana M., Ruti, Yossi, Ayelet B. and Z., Danielle G. and Z., Alon, Asaf, Dana S., Matan, Tami, Birte, Hagar, Cecilie, Chava, Shira, Yasmin, Naama, Miri, and Omri

... nach Berlin an Mom und Pa, Astrid, Linda, Gal, Julia C. und N., Melanie, Iris, Sylvia, Wolfgang, Hannah, Jürgen, Kyra, Tatjana, Lukas, Felix, Simon, Hendrikje, Johannes, Paulie, Philipp (1-3), Ulla, Bettina, Julie, Marcel, Steffi, Ragna, Katrin, Sivan, Omer, Yaara, Nihad, Charlotte, Henrike, Ulrike, Lorena, Carini, Gincel, Rona, Mido, Frank und Ori

... in alle Ecken Deutschlands an Doreen, Rudi, Dominik, Elias, Hannah, Oma, Opi und Renate, Anne, Kerstin, Tabea und Nicole

... nach Münster an Simon, Christina, Simon L., Maren, Chrischi und Lydia

... an die humedicanerInnen Selin, Steffen, Raphael, Patrick, Ruth, Markus, Petra, Philipp, Linda, Steffa, Klaus, Irmgard, Hanna, Albrecht, Anja, Margret, Cindy, Judith, Kenneth, und unsere Partner auf den Philippinen, in CAR, Iran, and Vanuatu

... to other places: Leemor, Irad, Itay, Lira, Darren, Shira, Ori, Martina, Noga, Sobhi, Isabelle, Noa and Leny

for your help, support, and especially for the shared leisure time!

Contents

1 Introduction – Starting a Journey   **17**
  1.1 Media and Conflict Societies 18
  1.2 Research Gap and Questions 20
  1.3 Research Case – the Israeli-Palestinian conflict 21
  1.4 Aim and Structure of the Present Investigation 23
  1.5 Central Terms 25

I   Theory and Case   **33**

2 Theory – Ethos of Conflict in Mediatized Environments   **35**
  2.1 Socio-Psychological Infrastructure of Societies in Conflict 36
  2.2 The Ethos of Conflict 40
  2.3 The Struggle over Narratives 53
  2.4 Mediatization of Conflicts 55

3 Case – Israel and the World, the Gaza Flotilla and Israeli Media   **63**
  3.1 The International Community and Israel 64
     3.1.1 International Involvement 64
     3.1.2 International Media as a Battlefield over Narratives 68
     3.1.3 Israel's Political Position 73
     3.1.4 Israeli Understanding of its Position and Image 75
     3.1.5 Israel's Public Diplomacy 79
  3.2 The Development of the Israeli Ethos of Conflict 84
  3.3 The Israeli News Media 94
  3.4 The Gaza Flotilla Raid 101

4 Conclusions and Consequences for this Research   **113**
  4.1 Conclusion – Mutual Polarization? 113
  4.2 Research Question and Hypotheses 116
  4.3 Research Design 122

Contents

II Results of the Study 133

5 The Actors Involving Themselves   **137**
5.1 The Results in Short . . . 137
5.2 The United States – a True Friend and Partner? . . . 144
5.3 Europe – Connection and Alienation? . . . 151
5.4 The United Nations – An Ambivalent Relationship? . . . 156
5.5 Turkey – A Strategic Partnership Lost? . . . 160
5.6 The Gaza Flotilla Participants – the Direct Opponent? . . . 164
5.7 The World – Against Israel in Crisis? . . . 171
5.8 Russia and the Quartet on the Middle East – Uninvolved? . . . 173
5.9 The Actors and the Newspapers . . . 173
5.10 Conclusion . . . 174

6 The Actors' Involvement   **177**
6.1 The Results in Short . . . 177
6.2 Critical Involvement – "We Strongly Condemn..." . . . 185
6.3 Calling for Action – "Israel has to ... Immediately" . . . 188
6.4 Supporting Involvement – "We Support Israel's Right to..." . . . 191
6.5 Speechless Involvement – "..." . . . 193
6.6 Conclusion . . . 195

7 The Representation of Involvement and Actors   **199**
7.1 The Results in Short . . . 200
7.2 Defense of one's own Justness . . . 204
7.3 Friend or Foe . . . 207
7.4 Personalization versus Depersonalization . . . 216
7.5 Law and Order Versus Chaos . . . 217
7.6 Simplification Versus Complexity . . . 218
7.7 The Representations in the four Analyzed Newspapers . . . 220
7.8 Conclusion . . . 222

8 Discussion – Ending a Journey   **225**
8.1 The Major Findings . . . 226
8.2 The Limitations . . . 236
8.3 The Contributions of this Investigation . . . 237

Bibliography   **243**

Appendix A Tables   **263**

Appendix B Abstract   **265**

Appendix C The Codebook   269

Appendix D Gaza Crisis 2014   279

List of Tables

1   Examples of Terminology in the Israeli-Palestinian Conflict 71

2   Exposure of General Israeli Newspapers 97

3   Distribution of Time Periods in Content Analysis 125

4   Relevant and Coded Articles 127

5   Coding Scheme 129

6   Placement of Articles on Different Actors 138

7   Length of Articles on Different Actors 138

8   Institutional Background of Actors 139

9   Actors' Appearance in Newspapers 143

10   Framing of the Relationship to the Actors in Newspapers 144

11   Crisis and Routine Actors 174

12   Involvement and Period 178

13   Placement of Articles on Different Claims 178

14   Length of Articles on Different Claims 178

15   Topics the Claims Relate to 179

16   Claim and Framing of Actor 181

17   Claim and Framing of Relationship 183

18   Differentiated Framing of Claims 183

19   The Ethos of Conflict and the Represented Actors 200

20   The Ethos of Conflict and the Claims 201

21   The Ethos of Conflict in the Analyzed Periods 202

22   The Ethos of Conflict in the Newspapers 203

23   Actors' Appearance in Analyzed Periods 263

24   Framing of Actors 263

25   Framing of the Relationship to the Actors 264

26   The Actors' Involvement 264

27   Framing of the Claim 264

List of Figures

1	Interaction between International Actors and Israeli Actors	114
2	Actors' Appearance in Analyzed Periods	140
3	Framing of the Actors	140
4	Framing of the Relationship to the Actors	142
5	Framing of the Actors in Analyzed Newspapers	142
6	Cartoon on President Obama	147
7	American Sympathies for Israelis and Palestinians	149
8	Cartoon on Gaza Flotilla and International Media	168
9	International Involvement in Israeli Newspapers	180
10	The Actors' Involvement	180
11	Framing of Central Claims	182
12	Framing in Analyzed Periods	182
13	Involvement in the four Analyzed Newspapers	184
14	Cartoon on Hasbara and International Public Opinion	214
15	Narratives and Societal Beliefs of the Ethos of Conflict	222

Nomenclature

GFP	Gaza flotilla participants
Haggadah	The text telling the story of the Jewish exodus from Egypt read during Pessach.
Hasbara	Israeli Public Diplomacy
IBA	Israeli Broadcasting Authority
IDF	Israeli Defense Forces
IHH	Humanitarian Relief Foundation, Turkish NGO
Kibbuz	Collective communities, traditionally based on agriculture
MENA	Middle East North Africa region, includes all Middle Eastern and Maghreb countries
OCHA	United Nations Office for the Coordination of Humanitarian Affairs
OECD	Organization for Economic Co-operation and Development
PSC	protracted social conflict
Purim	Jewish holiday
Shabat	Seventh day of the Jewish week, friday evening to saturday evening, day of rest
UNESCO	United Nations Educational, Scientific and Cultural Organization
UNHRC	United Nations Human Rights Council
UNIFIL	United Nations Interim Force in Lebanon
UNRWA	United Nations Relief and Works Agency for Palestinian Refugees in the Near East
UNSCOP	United Nations Special Committee on Palestine

1 Introduction – Starting a Journey

> A conflict begins and ends in the hearts and minds of people, not in
> the hilltops.
>
> — Amoz Oz, Israeli Writer

Political conflicts can trigger intense international reactions. Following the deadly outcome of the Gaza flotilla raid in 2010, international response was enormous. Not only the supranational organizations, the allies and involved opponents felt obliged to comment – the reactions were global. The United Nations Secretary-General Ban Ki-moon stated: "I condemn the violence and Israel must explain". The NATO Secretary General expressed "deep regret", the African Union condemned Israel, Bolivia's Ministry of Foreign Affairs called the attacks "atrocious", Peru disapproved of the use of military force, the United States Secretary of State Hillary Clinton "support[ed] the United Nations Security Council's condemnation of the acts leading to this tragedy". Bangladesh expressed "shock", China condemned Israel, "Condemnation and deep anxiety [we]re being expressed in Moscow" and the European Union's President called the events a "clear and unacceptable breach of international law"[1].

How does a society that becomes the target of such an international storm of criticism react to these allegations? Given that most members of a society learn about these international reactions first through the media, questions arise about how the media interprets and contextualizes them. The following investigation examines in depth and breadth the manner in which these messages are conveyed and the degree to which they are imbued with the ethos of conflict and various conflict-related and or nationalist narratives.

When talking to Israeli friends or colleagues about the research subject of this investigation and explaining the goal of analyzing how Israeli newspapers represent international

---

[1] See for those and further statements:

http://www.aljazeera.com/news/middleeast/2010/05/20105316216182630.html;

http://english.cri.cn/6966/2010/06/01/1461s573834.htm;

http://www.theeastafrican.co.ke/news/-/2558/930300/-/pe18tiz/-/index.html;

http://unispal.un.org/UNISPAL.NSF/0/33913FBBAE6197C885257DDD006B615D;

http://www.nato.int/cps/en/natolive/news_63983.htm?mode=pressrelease;

http://edition.cnn.com/2010/WORLD/meast/05/31/israel.gaza.raid.reaction/index.html

involvement, a frequent and immediate reaction is along the lines of: "that is obvious – the whole world is against Israel!" This is uttered with various degrees of sarcasm.

But is such a representation really that obvious? Is the world, as mediated by Israeli newspapers to a domestic audience, simply "against Israel"? This thesis is based on the assumption that the situation is considerably more complex and that media representations vary in degree and manner across the spectrum of publications. Yet, why is this initial assumption, held by numerous Israelis from varied backgrounds, so prevalent?

The journey towards a deeper understanding of this complex interaction starts by identifying the impacts of long-lasting conflicts on the societies entangled in them, as well as their vision of their own world and the surrounding one (see Chapter 1.1). The role of the media hereby highlights central research gaps and raises pertinent questions (see Chapter 1.2). Within this examination, a particular society in conflict – in this case, Jewish Israeli society – and its complex relationship with other societies engaged in the conflict is introduced(see Chapter 1.3). Lastly, the aim and structure of the present investigation is illuminated (see Chapter 1.4) and central terms are clarified (see Chapter 1.5).

1.1 Media and Conflict Societies

Conflicts that last for years or generations have a tremendous impact on the societies entangled within them. The sacrifices demanded of the population and the personal costs of a conflict are far-reaching. At the same time, the focus of the overarching conflict leads to a situation in which basic needs are not met. For example, the needs for individual and collective safety and orientation (or nutrition and freedom of movement) fall by the wayside in the face of large-scale priorities such as defense. When these conflicts endure, communities adapt their lifestyle to the persisting conflict reality. Accordingly, societies develop enduring beliefs about themselves, their conflict reality, and their opponent. Those psychological adaptations are necessary to withstand the opponent, uphold a positive collective self-image and group loyalty, and develop a routine under the difficult conflict conditions. These societal beliefs serve as prisms for the interpretation of experiences. They are called *ethos of conflict* (see Chapter 1.5) and are found and perpetuated in cultural products such as newspapers, school books, theatre, literature etc. These beliefs do not only shape the perception of the conflict but also the perception of the external world and their relation to it.

Conflicts between societies do not occur isolated from the wider community of international actors (see Chapter 1.5), as societies continue to interact and interrelate with them throughout. International actors may either be involved directly or indirectly in the conflict itself or may involve themselves through concerted action or implication. This international *involvement* (see Chapter 1.5) also has an impact on how the conflict society views itself – on the society's understanding of its own position within that conflict and within the wider international community. Understanding this interaction is crucial for the members of these conflict societies, but also for political actors that take an active part. A central source of information and a key tool for understanding international involvement is to be found in mass media and its representation of the conflict. For the general population, media products provide an understanding of interactions with other societies, about international actors involving themselves in intra-societal affairs, and ultimately of the society's international standing. But in their role to mediate between societies, media actors must not be misunderstood as "objective" informants. On the contrary, they take a very active part in coloring this indirect interaction. Therefore, it is crucial to ask which role the media takes in representing international political actors and their involvement in a society's conflict situation. Within this interaction, media actors are at the intersection of several complex processes; the central ones are outlined in the following section.

With the increasing importance of mass media in *political communication*, often described as *mediatization of politics* (see Chapter 1.5), the relationship between mass media and political actors tightens and becomes increasingly complex. This is particularly true for more recent conflicts, which have been significantly mediatized. This results in a more shaded version of reality in which the fight on the ground is as important as the battle over its narration within media products (Wolfsfeld 2003). On the one hand, political actors have a great need to win this "battle over narratives", hence to exert control over media content. On the other, media actors are in great need of providing information in rapidly changing situations. Official state mouthpieces are often the only actors capable of providing prompt information that is considered reliable and managing this information with a considerable degree of professionalism. Because media actors need access to reliable information, they are compelled to avoid endangering their status as legitimate recipients of official information. This suggests a great dependence by media actors on political actors during times of conflict.

Nevertheless, when media actors cover foreign sources, they gain the possibility of incorporating external opinions on the conflict into their own coverage. This could present a possibility for independent information, and with it, alternating perspectives. In this context, representing international involvement poses an opportunity for media actors to liberate themselves, to a certain extent, from their dependency on official information and narratives. Orgad (2011) describes this as a tool for estrangement from the dominant or official national conflict perspective.

Another perspective regards the relationship between media actors and the recipients of their products. In the light of the structural constraints of media institutions within the political system, Dor (2005) advocates an independent interest of media actors in their recipients. Not only do they provide information and understanding through their narration of the world beyond the horizon of personal experience. In the framework of imagined communities (Anderson 2006), an implicit role of the media is to reaffirm the individual's self-perception and mediate between individuals and their imagined groups(Dor 2005: 94) that are also the consumers of the media products. The media reassures and gives a "sense of belonging"(Orgad 2011: 417) and connection, needed especially during conflict and crisis. Members of society expect media products to inform, and especially in conflict situations they are in need of this information to orientate themselves. In addition however, they want to be reassured of their understanding of the surrounding world and their place in it. In this sense, the media can and should be seen as part and product of its society (Caspi and Limor 1992) and as a tool of articulation and dissemination of a collective identity and (common) beliefs through "construction, production, and transmission of images, narratives, and myths" (Shinar 2005: 172).

1.2 Research Gap and Questions

Media actors in conflicts are torn between their need for information and the reliance on official sources to provide it, and their desire to inform their audiences and thereby provide orientation and belonging. Furthermore, media products are not mirrors of reality but constructed narrations within a field of different interests and hence *representations* (see Chapter 1.5) They themselves become part of the fight over narratives through the mediatization of conflicts.

1) The media plays a crucial role in *intra-societal mediation* – it provides orientation and a sense of belonging and understanding in the context of international involvement. The media is a member of the society and its discourses. As such, it constructs the narration of international involvement, interaction and society's standing through interpretation and contextualization (Sharvit and Bar-Tal 2007; Wolfsfeld 1997). In extensive research Bar-Tal outlines his framework of the ethos of conflict as a central part of societal ethos and discourse (see Chapter 1.5 and 2.2). A central indicator that beliefs are part of the ethos of conflict is their appearance in cultural products. The main source for the dissemination of those beliefs is believed to be the media, as Sharvit and Bar-Tal (2007) claim. However, there is not yet an empirical analysis to support this assumption.

2) The media plays a central role in *inter-societal mediation* as well. Recipients learn about the interaction of their society with other societies through media representations. These representations provide understanding and orientation on the inter-societal standing of the group. However, it is unclear whether those representations are shaped by the media's dependence on official sources and narratives or if they are used as opportunities for alternative narratives held by other societies. There is no empirical analysis on the role of the media in this setting.

Research questions The present investigation explores the stories that appear in a conflict society's media dealing with external actors' relations towards them: which narratives of the world are created, how is the relationship described and what does it say about the conflict society? In particular, the chapters in this investigation address the following questions:

How is international involvement in a conflict society represented in its daily newspapers?

1) The relationships of different international actors with the conflict society are assumed to be diverse. How are the external actors represented? Are there differences and if yes, why? What constitutes the differences?

2) The forms of involvement can differ. Is the character of the involvement relevant to the character of the representation?

3) The research on the socio-psychological consequences for conflict societies is strong. Nevertheless, it is unclear which role those consequences play in media representation. Do conflict beliefs and narratives play a role in the representations of international involvement?

4) Protracted conflicts are characterized by periods of relative calm and periods of crisis. Is the representation different, depending on the periods within the conflict? Are the society's media products different in their representations?

1.3 Research Case – the Israeli-Palestinian conflict

These questions will be explored in the case of contemporary Jewish Israeli society through content analysis of the four general daily Hebrew-language Israeli newspapers. Choosing the Israeli-Palestinian conflict as part of the Arab-Israeli conflict is particularly interesting, as it is one of the longest-lasting conflicts between societies in history. It is an intractable conflict that has strong implications on its societal members and their socio-psychological infrastructure. Furthermore, the Israeli-Palestinian conflict has, since its outbreak, been shaped by strong international involvement. These central factors define the suitability for the present investigation. However, any other intractable protracted or intractable inter-societal conflict could be subject to investigation according to these research questions (e.g., Russia-Chechnya conflict, Turkey-Kurdish conflict, Serbia-Kosovo conflict; see Chapter 1.5)[2].

The particular case chosen for the content analysis is the raid of the Gaza flotilla in 2010 as a crisis caused by a direct form of aggressive involvement on the part of several international actors, which itself caused intense international reactions. This period is

---

[2] So far, the adherence of the beliefs of the ethos of conflict is found to be dominant in different conflict societies, such as Kosovars, Serbs, Albanians, Croats, and Bosnians (MacDonald 2002), Hutus in Rwanda (Slocum-Bradley 2008), Greek and Turkish Cypriot (Hadjipavlou 2007) and Kurds (Uluğ and Cohrs 2014).

compared with the several weeks surrounding the crisis that are not shaped by a particular crisis and characterize routine periods within a protracted conflict.

Relevance The problem is summed up by Dowty (1999: 8) stating that: "Paradoxically, the Israeli public and media often display great sensitivity to external opinion even while denigrating its importance at the same time." First, there is de facto a high amount of external opinion; the lasting interest in the Israeli-Palestinian conflict is unparalleled. The conflict broke out under British Mandate following the partition of the Middle East after the First World War and increasing immigration of Jews from Europe. The decision for the partition of the territory of Mandatory Palestine into an Arab and a Jewish state was one of the early resolutions by the General Assembly of the recently founded United Nations in 1947. Ever since its foundation in 1948, the state of Israel has been engaged in numerous wars with its direct and indirect Arab neighbors as well as an ongoing conflict with the Palestinian population on the territory in conflict. These continue to split the allies of the conflict parties. Numerous international peace initiatives, governmental and non-governmental actors have attempted to resolve the conflict and countless UN resolutions have condemned either Israel or all conflict parties.

Moreover, the Israeli-Palestinian conflict stands alone in the degree of controversy and impassioned fervor it sparks in the minds of laypeople around the world, even those with no direct or indirect relation to the involved conflict societies. International actors of various backgrounds do not always occur as neutral mediators, but often as partial and biased. Across both the political sector and the non-profit sector, particularly in "Western" countries, this conflict evokes polarizing arguments for either side of the conflict. Individuals tend to form an opinion about the conflict that does not always correlate with a profound or informed understanding of it.

The conflict parties, however, are aware of the relevance of the fight over (international) sympathies and legitimization and engage in intense efforts to win support (Dor 2005: pp.105; Sheafer and Gabay 2009: 447; Shinar 2005: 177). However, in Jewish Israeli society, these efforts occur simultaneously with siege mentality – the conviction of being ultimately isolated and alone in a hostile world. Polls demonstrate that between 61 and 71% of Jewish Israelis are convinced that negative attitudes in Europe and the USA towards Israel will not change, regardless of Israel's actions. 39 to 56% are convinced that "the World is against Israel", and between 49 and 68% believe that criticism against Israel is rooted in antisemitism (Yaar and Hermann 2010a,b). Perceived isolation and alienation can lead to a state of mind that suggests that "The entire world is against us anyway, so what the hell, we'll do what we deem right"(Shinar 2005: 176). This attitude sums up the relevance of Israel's perception of its international standing and ultimately, the media representation, too, as it has a direct influence on decisions approved and legitimized during the conflict.

The relation between Jewish Israeli society and the international community serves as one example of the complex relationship between conflict societies and international actors that involve themselves in the conflict setting in manifold ways. The focus of this investigation is on the conflict society and in particular the media representation of international involvement. The analysis illuminates the understanding that members of conflict societies gain from media products about the international community and their relation to them. The focus is not on the actors that involve themselves in conflict societies – be it through research on soft or public diplomacy by international political actors, or research on peacekeeping, peace-making, and peace-building as central instruments of the United Nations in their involvement in conflicts.

1.4 Aim and Structure of the Present Investigation

The aim of this investigation is to explore and illuminate the characteristics of mediated representations of international involvement in a conflict society. The aim is to extract if and to what extent societal conflict beliefs play a role in these representations. Therefore, the primary goals of this investigation are as follows:

1) to create an instrument suitable for the content analysis of newspaper articles on international involvement. This instrument will be tested on Israeli newspapers, which are the focus of this research, but shall be equally adaptable to other conflict settings.

2) to contribute to the ongoing discourse on the societal impacts of intractable conflicts in particular societal conflict beliefs of the ethos of conflict that are expected to appear in cultural products such as the media. This is the first known empirical analysis of beliefs of the ethos of conflict in media products.

3) to further contribute to the illumination and understanding of factors that influence the national perception of international involvement in conflict societies. The analysis of media representation contributes to the understanding of the media and its shaping and orientation of social life (Orgad 2012: pp.82).

This investigation focuses solely on analyzing the mediated version of "reality". It is not the goal of this investigation to establish whether the media representations are "objective" or to evaluate their distance from "objective reality". Research on the relation between the media and "reality" has shown that mass media does not mirror the truth, but rather a biased, one-sided, vague part of it (Schulz 2008: 67). The understanding of reality itself relies upon its observers and therefore all attempts to describe it must be interpretations of their perception of it (Shoemaker and Reese 1996: 4). Whether one regards mass media's lack of proximity to "objective reality" as a bias due to journalistic political tendencies or as a structural problem of the media's need for simple narratives, objectivity shall be considered a journalistic norm, rather than a journalistic truth (Schulz 2008: 68). From this perspective, analyzing the representation itself is particularly interesting.

Research structure   The second chapter outlines the broad theoretical context with focus on the socio-psychological infrastructure of societies in intractable conflict and in particular the set of beliefs that comprise the ethos of conflict. This section will also illuminate how these beliefs relate to narratives and play a role in their construction. Narratives are an important part of media representations and are constructed through frames. The last part of this section elaborates on the mediatization of politics and in particular on conflicts that focus on the struggle over narratives.

The third chapter is devoted to the particular case of this investigation – Jewish Israeli society and its relation to the international community. One central argument of this study is that this relationship is characterized by mutual polarization. The first section introduces a framework to comprehensively understand the interest and investment and also the polarization of international actors in the Israeli-Palestinian conflict. As an example, the international media attention on the conflict and the ongoing debate on its biased polarization – to either side – is outlined. The second section introduces the other direction – that of Jewish Israeli interest in the international standing of Israel. The leading argument of a likewise polarizing view is based on arguably perceived and actual isolation that influences Jewish Israelis' understanding of themselves and their place within the world. As an example, the intense attempts by Israel to improve its image around the world through public diplomacy are introduced. In the third part the research on the Israeli ethos of conflict as well as the concrete case of the content analysis – the Gaza flotilla raid in 2010 – are introduced. The leading controversies surrounding the events are discussed. Furthermore some characteristics of Israeli media institutions are outlined.

The fourth chapter draws conclusions for the following investigation. It combines the lessons learned from both the theoretical framework and the background knowledge on the concrete case. The leading questions and hypotheses are thereby extracted for the following research. Furthermore it introduces the research design: the chosen method, the content analysis and the choice of research material, Israeli newspapers, and the period of investigation surrounding the Gaza flotilla raid in 2010 are outlined. The research plan, detailed decisions on relevant cases and the process of data collection and analysis are discussed. This includes the creation of a research instrument for data analysis, the codebook.

The second part of this research is devoted to the results of the content analysis. It is split into three parts: the analyzed actors, the analyzed involvement by these actors and the mediated representation. The findings indicate that the analyzed actors are represented in varying manner according to the perceived relationship with the international actors. Furthermore, the involvement by international actors as portrayed in Israeli newspapers is predominantly critical. While criticism is contextualized negatively, supportive involvement is represented as a reassurance of current Israeli policies. Promising is a form of involvement that demands concrete actions. The media representations are permeated by some of the societal beliefs of the ethos of conflict. They are found in several conflict-supportive narratives that dominate the media representations, especially during the times of crisis. These representations of the four analyzed newspapers vary only in one particular case. Finally, the contents of the thesis are summed up and discussed in the last chapter – the discussion. This closing discussion provides a cohesive understanding of the elements analyzed and draws relevant conclusions, as well as suggesting areas of interest for further research outside the scope of the present investigation.

1.5 Central Terms

This chapter introduces central terms for the present investigation. Those are classified in three sections.

- Media, Involvement, and Representation
  (Political communication, political actors, international actors, mediatization, representation, mediated reality, involvement, and claim)
- Society and Conflict
  (Social conflicts, protracted social conflict, intractable conflict, crisis and routine period, the Israeli-Palestinian conflict, ethnic groups, Palestine, Jewish Israeli society)
- Ethos of Conflict, Narratives, and Frames
  (Ethos of conflict, narratives, framing)

Media, Involvement, and Representation

Political communication – always an important part of politics – has increased immensely over the last decades. This is caused by an expansion of media products and available information. Furthermore, political actors professionalize their utilization of communication for their own needs with communication management. Politics mediatize and the changing power structure between politics and the media is one central topic of the increasing research field of political communication in the last three decades (Schulz 2008: 15).

Political actors can be collective or individual actors who act in a political role in their participation of reaching decisions on the distribution of power or resources. These actors can be parties, individuals, groups, parliaments, governments, supranational organizations and their members and representatives (Schulz 2008; Luhmann 1974), but also those who challenge them, such as groups of activists or civil right movements, interest groups etc. In their coverage of political events and issues and of activities of political actors, mass media acts as a political actor (Pfetsch and Adam 2008). They are referred to in this investigation simply as actors, often as *international actors*.

International actors are, in the context of this investigation, political actors who are not directly involved in the Israeli-Palestinian conflict (i.e., no states of the MENA region) but who take an active position (verbally or actively) in the conflict setting and societies. This regards primarily the members of the Quartet on the Middle East that are devoted to taking an active part towards a resolution of the conflict: the United States, the United Nations, Russia, and the European Union. South American, African, or Asian actors and Australia are not chosen explicitly, due to their low involvement as perceived in Israeli media.

Mediatization of politics relates to societal changes due to changes of mass media – media commercializes, stratifies and its products diversify, and societies increasingly depend on media products (Mazzoleni and Schulz 1999; Schulz 2008: 30). However, the role of mass media in giving orientation and creation of meaning also grows (Sarcinelli 1991). As Cottle (2006) argues, in mediatized times the contests over recognition and legitimacy or social change of the collective interest or identity are fought centrally in the arena of mass media.

This is especially relevant in insecure environments, in particular conflicts. Cottle (2006) coined the term of *mediatized conflicts*. Especially when the need for orientation is high, the battle over mediated narratives also increases – therefore in conflict and war mediatization intensifies (Lundby 2009).

Representations are the frames, images, contextualizations, explanations, and descriptions that construct meaning and thereby provide understanding of the world and its functioning (Hall 1997). *Media representations* are products of processes of this construction of meaning through signs by members of a culture (Orgad 2012: 17). An understanding of representation as a construction rather than as a mirror of something is particularly suitable for this investigation. It points out that representation is always selective in the particular description of a part of reality.

> We give things meaning by how we represent them – the words we use about them, the stories we tell about them, the images of them we produce, the emotions we associate with them, the ways we classify and conceptualize them, the value we place on them. (Hall 1997: 3)

Post-structuralist scholars challenge the notion of the existence of a "reality" or a "meaning" and consider meaning as "fluid, ambiguous, and contradictory (Gill 2007: 13). This approach would make research and evaluation of media representation impossible. However, it "highlights the immense power of representation, and underscores that representation is not an annex to reality, but its essence" (Orgad 2012: 25).

Stereotypes are characteristics about a person that are simple, easy to remember, and to grasp. It is widely recognized that they reduce a person or group to certain characteristics by exaggeration, simplification, and an often fixed manner (Hall 1997: 258). Stereotypes maintain a symbolic order, which draws lines between normal and deviant, acceptable and unacceptable, belonging and who is the "insider" and "outsider", what is the Own and what is the Other (ibid.).

Mediated reality in this context is used to describe the reality as it is represented in media products. It can be understood as an issue according to a certain media product.

Claims are the concrete forms of involvement, ascribed to the international actors in the present investigation.

The term *involvement* is chosen for the different forms of political activities international (political) actors conduct in a relation to the Israeli-Palestinian conflict or the societies entangled in it. These actions can be verbal or concrete physical forms of expressing opinions or evaluations of events, actors, or processes of the conflict; different forms of intervention; attempts to mediate between or influence the conflicted parties. Using the term involvement is preferable to the concept of intervention, due to the meaning the latter has in international politics as often concrete direct or indirect interference in the societal and political life, in particular in conflicts, often by violent means.

Society and Conflict

Social conflicts can be classified in numerous ways. Ethnic, religious, or political groups, societies or nations are in a relationship of social conflict with another group when they believe that their goals, activities and claims are not compatible with one another (Gray, Coleman and Putnam 2007; Kriesberg 2005: 66; Staub and Bar-Tal 2003: 711). This can happen when three preconditions are apparent: A sense of collective identity, grievance and a sense of suffering from an abuse of power by an adversary who is seen as illegitimate, while being convicted that affecting the other side would lessen their grievance (Kriesberg 2001: 374; Mauro 2011: 43). The conflict issues can be concrete and at times tangible – such as territory, resources, access to power or privilege. However, conflicts are often further rooted in intangible matters such as beliefs, values, and identity.

Azar, Jureidini and McLaurin (1978) provided the concept of *protracted social conflict (PSC)* , a violent and prolonged struggle between social groups over basic needs, such as acceptance, security, recognition or economic participation (Azar 1990: 93). Azar identified several characteristics of PSC: 1) The conflict is enduring for several generations. 2) The intensity and frequency of outbursts is fluctuating, since societies cannot bear intense phases continuously. 3) There is a strong spillover of the conflict into other issues, politics, security, but also education and culture are influenced by and subordinated to the conflict. 4) Equilibrating forces moderate the level of conflict. Those grow with the conflict, as the number of victims and destruction grows. Marginal topics (water, energy production and supply, agriculture) become salient problems of the conflict and both "constrain conflict and cooperation" (ibid.). 5) There is no end of the conflict in sight (ibid.).

The consequences of a conflict that has lasted for several generations and is nowhere near termination for the societies entangled in it are most suitably described as *intractable conflict.* Conflicts are seen as intractable when a range of indicators apply jointly. Kriesberg

(2005: 66) identifies the following criteria: 1) The conflict is protracted, meaning it lasts at least a generation. 2) The conflict is regarded by adversaries or observers as destructive and violent. That means not only armed actors but also civilians are suffering personally (from killings, destruction of property, being forced out of their homes and become refugees, atrocities committed). 3) Attempts by intermediaries and partisans to transform them fail, the conflicted parties view their goals as opposing without possible compromise. Perceiving the conflict as irreconcilable, the conflicted parties prepare for their continuation. 4) Thus, the conflicted parties make extensive investments on political, military, economic, psychological levels to deal with the situation (Kriesberg 2005: 66). Bar-Tal (2013: pp.36) adds three more indicators of intractable conflicts: 5) The conflict is total, meaning the goals are perceived as existential, be it tangible or intangible. 6) The conflict has a zero-sum nature. There is little room for compromise, since the goals, which are perceived as existential, can hardly be shifted by the conflict groups and the goals of the other group are opposing, therefore negated. This opens up a dichotomy in which one's own gain is the Other's loss and vice versa. 7) They are central in personal and public life. Both are constantly preoccupied with the conflict. That means, they can shape the personal feeling of safety or the media representations of different stories or the behavior of politicians (Bar-Tal 1998*a*; Bar-Tal, Halperin and Oren 2010; Staub and Bar-Tal 2003).

However, the degree of intractability can vary between conflicted parties and periods. They are likely to be subject of de-escalating and transformation efforts by conflict party members or external actors, and failed efforts of peacemaking often harden the positions (Kriesberg 2005: 68). Intractable conflicts are each unique, yet there are several types. Bar-Tal (2013: 27) distinguishes them first by their *societal implications*: Intra-societal conflict societies will live in one state (e.g., South Africa, Rwanda, Salvador). In a separatist conflict, societies struggle for or against independence of one part (e.g., Israeli-Palestinian conflict, Kashmir conflict, Chechnya conflict). In Intra-state conflicts, two states confront each other (Syrian-Israeli or Iraqi-Iranian conflict). A further distinction is the asymmetry (Mack 1975; Mitchell 1991) of conflicts: It describes the military, economic, and political superiority of one conflict side (e.g., Turkey, Israel, Russia), and the disadvantaged group without established institutions (e.g., Kurds, Palestinians, Chechens) or an asymmetry of access to resources of states (e.g., United States and Iraq or Russia and Georgia) (Bar-Tal 2013: 27). Intractable conflicts are traditionally regarded as unregulated (Deutsch 2005), but Gray, Coleman and Putnam (2007) identified persistent patterns "of institutionalized or even ritualized behavior" (ibid.: 1420) of destructiveness that becomes normal and resilient. They describe the institutionalization of behavior as a process of increasing adoption of certain behavior on which a social consensus exists.

Crisis and routine periods are understood as phases within intractable conflicts. As described above, the conflicts are enduring. However, there are phases of a low level of violence or extra-ordinary events (routine), and phases of violent outbreaks (crisis). See for the definition, especially for the content analysis, Chapter 4.3.

The terms protracted and intractable conflict are suitable for this investigation since they take into consideration the different calm (routine) and crisis phases a protracted intractable conflict can have. This investigation will analyze and compare both kinds of phases. Further, the emphasis on the duration of the conflict for several generations, its perception as existential, and importance for the personal life emphasizes the socio-psychological consequences such conflicts have on their societies which are central in this investigation.

The Israeli-Palestinian conflict is one of the most protracted and controversially disputed and analyzed since the Second World War. This is due to four reasons: It is the longest conflict since 1945, and a large variety of actors is involved (different size of countries, different ethnic groups, religions). Furthermore, there is variation in the level of violence, and there is a variety of the warfare (crisis, terrorism, civil war, guerilla, etc.). The Israeli-Palestinian conflict as part of the Arab-Israeli conflict is both an inter- , and an intrastate conflict. The core of the conflict are two ethnic groups – Jews and Palestinians (Mauro 2011: 42). An *ethnic group* is a group that shares a common identity which is perceived within and outside the group. There is homogeneity in either nation, religion, language, origin, culture, or history (Mauro 2011: 42). The Israeli-Palestinian conflict includes both, tangible issues and intangible matters, and involves high levels of violence and intensity. Therefore, the Israeli-Palestinian conflict can be understood as a multiform phenomenon that is hard to define due to its complexity. It is described as warfare, as deeply rooted, ethno-political conflict or warfare (Goertz and Diehl 1995; Maoz and Mor 1996) or, most suitably, as protracted or intractable social conflict (Azar 1990; Mitchell 1991). The Israeli-Palestinian conflict fulfills all characteristics of a protracted and intractable conflict. The termination of the Israeli-Palestinian conflict is – despite numerous peace initiatives – far, and more likely to be a gradual one than a sudden one. The conflict has survived several generations of conflicted parties. Therefore, there is an intensity fluctuation in order to be able to sustain the conflict. The conflict has spillover effects on other actions in the region and on an international level. The social component of this kind of conflict is very apparent; it shapes the society, its identity and its memory. This investigation focuses on the Israeli-Palestinian as opposed to the wider Arab-Israeli conflict. The term is more suitable than the general term Middle-East conflict that often relates to the same conflict but could also relate to so many others, especially recent crises in the region.

Palestine does not relate to the geographical region or the territory under British Mandate until 1948, but to the state accepted by the United Nations as non-member observer state in 2012. Its territories comprise the West Bank and the Gaza strip.

This investigation focuses on the *Jewish Israeli society* – as opposed to Israelis in general which include Palestinians with Israeli passports and other non-Jewish Israeli groups. This is mainly because the empirical investigation is conducted on the four Hebrew language newspapers in Israel, which centrally address the "mainstream" Jewish Israeli society. The author is aware of the further fragmentation within the Israeli society. However, a comparison of special interest newspapers (based on religion, language or migration origin) within Jewish Israeli society is not suitable for this investigation since it cannot give results about the ethos of the whole society[3].

Ethos of Conflict, Narratives, and Frames

The crucial beliefs societies form on their conflict reality comprise the *ethos of conflict* when they are institutionalized. These are beliefs in the justness of one's own goals, a positive collective self-image, the delegitimization of the opponent, beliefs in collective victimization, security, unity and patriotism of one's own group, and peace (see Chapter 2; Bar-Tal 2007*b*; Bar-Tal et al. 2008; Bar-Tal and Halperin 2011; Bar-Tal et al. 2012; Bar-Tal 2013; Halperin and Bar-Tal 2011; Oren, Bar-Tal and David 2004). They enable members to endure the conflict and bear high sacrifices, they are the basis for mobilization and solidarity within the group. At the same time, the beliefs reduce the readiness for compromises and harden thus the conflict. An indicator for the institutionalization of the beliefs of the ethos of conflict is their appearance in cultural products, such as the media (Oren 2009). They have been investigated and found in different conflict settings; however, the largest research corpus is conducted on the Jewish Israeli society (see Chapter 3.2). In its functions of explaining experiences and information, the ethos of conflict serves as a basis for *narratives* societies form on events of the present and past.

Narratives are stories with a plot, a beginning and an end that give meaning to things of the material world (Bar-Tal 2013). Individuals hold narratives that make sense of the reality within their mind. Groups as well form collective narratives on shared experiences. Bruner (1992) defines collective narratives as „social constructions that coherently interrelate a sequence of historical and current events; they are accounts of a community's collective experiences, embodied in its belief system and represent the collective's symbolically constructed shared identity" (Bruner 1992: 76). These narratives do not only exist in the mind of the group members, but find manifestation in the material world (in cultural products). They are lived and performed in the social interaction of the group, and

---

[3] Israels population comprises 7,9 million persons, ca.75% Jews and 20,5% Arabs (Central Bureau of Statistics. State of Israel 2012). Approximately 55% of the population are born in Israel. As Israel is an immigration country, most citizen are the second or third generation in Israel. Until the 1950s roughly 630.000 Jews lived in Israel (77% from Europe – Ashkenazi Jews). In the 1950s one million people immigrated to Israel, half of them originating in the MENA region (Mizrahi Jews). In the 1990s the second big wave of immigration comprised ca. 1 million people from the former Soviet Union, earlier roughly 100.000 Ethiopian Jews immigrated Israel. Integration has not always been easy and the different ethnic communities are still distinguishable (Smooha 2008). Besides, the segregation between Secular, Orthodox and National-Orthodox Jews is strong. About 42% of the Jewish population are Secular, 8% Orthodox (Haredi), 12% Religious, 38% traditional or half-traditional (Central Bureau of Statistics. State of Israel 2010). These numbers explain parts of the society's fragmentation.

     © Frank & Timme   Verlag für wissenschaftliche Literatur

contribute to the shared identity (Hammack and Pilecki 2012; Oren, Nets-Zehngut and Bar-Tal 2015).

Framing is the "process of culling a few elements of perceived reality and assembling a narrative that highlights connections among them to promote a particular interpretation" is called framing by Entman (2007: 164) in a definition that chooses the perspective of narrative building through framing. The emphasis on the decision-making process is stronger in this more popular definition of framing as "selecting and highlighting some facets of events or issues, and making connections among them so as to promote a particular interpretation, evaluation, and/or solution" (Entman 2004: 5). Wolfsfeld emphasizes on the construction of and reliance on narratives through framing by claiming it "can be understood as a process in which journalists attempt to find a narrative fit between incoming information and existing media frames concerning a particular topic" (Wolfsfeld 2004: 27). This also supports the assumption that framing is not undertaken independently, but within a society and within a media system.

Estrangement is understood as a representation that questions frameworks which are considered common-sense: "Estrangement refers to the ways in which media representations act as invitations to audiences to detach themselves from commonsensical conceptions of their lives in the national context" (Orgad 2012: 87).

Part I

Theory and Case

2 Theory – Ethos of Conflict in Mediatized Environments

> As we really and truly seek peace, we really and truly welcome you to live among us in peace and security. There was a huge wall between us which you tried to build up over a quarter of a century, but it was destroyed in 1973... Yet, there remained another wall. This wall constitutes a psychological barrier between us. A barrier of suspicion. A barrier of rejection. A barrier of fear of deception. A barrier of hallucinations around any action, deed or decision. A barrier of cautious and erroneous interpretations of all and every event or statement. It is this psychological barrier which I described in official statements as representing 70 percent of the whole problem.

> — Anwar Sadat, President of Egypt, in the Israeli Knesset November 20,1977

Conflicts, especially prolonged social conflicts and those perceived as intractable, are not only enduring due to technical incompatibilities between the conflicted parties but largely because of beliefs held by the conflicted parties that are established and fed by the conflict. The socio-psychological perspective of conflicting societies is in the center of the following chapter.

Kelman (2007: 64) outlines the following characterizations of this perspective as 1) process driven by collective needs and fears more than by rational and objective decisions; 2) an inter-societal process rather than only intergovernmental; 3) a process with multiple facets, and 4) an interactive process with escalatory, self-perpetuating dynamics. Thus it is established that socio-psychological factors are additions to genuine disagreements that play an essential role in the outbreak, perpetuation and continuation of conflict, and hinder resolution of conflicts. These socio-psychological barriers are numerous. Several approaches are proposed to describe those: cognitive and motivational processes are barriers in times of peacemaking as they lead to biased information processing, cognitive dissonance, loss aversion, optimistic overconfidence, naïve realism etc.(Bland, Powell and Ross 2012; Maoz et al. 2002). Another approach focuses on the collective emotional factors like fear and hatred that underlie conflicts (Cheung-Blunden and Blunden 2008; Gross, Halperin and Porat 2013; Halperin and Pliskin 2015). A third approach concentrates on the content, the societal beliefs on the conflict, the adversary and the own group (Bar-Tal 1998*a*, 2007*b*, 2013; Eidelson and Eidelson 2003; Halperin and Bar-Tal 2011; Kelman 2007) and is central in the present investigation.

Special attention is paid to the beliefs societies form on their present and past (see Chapter 2.2). This framework is based on the extensive work of Daniel Bar-Tal in this field, who developed and refined it in the last decades. Hence this part is mainly based on his work. Societal beliefs of the ethos (and the ethos of conflicts) shape collective narratives (see Chapter 2.3) that societies hold on events of the present and past. Those can become dominant, but are often challenged by other narrations and counter-narratives. They are disseminated, strengthened, and used in cultural products, such as media. Narratives are formed through frames, the perspectives taken on issues and events. So narratives are not formed unanimously by whole societies, they are challenged by different groups and actors have different interests to influence the dominant narrative or strengthen counter-narratives. Therefore, the question who constructs narratives in mass media coverage is discussed within the framework of mediatization of politics and conflicts in particular.

These developments of narrative construction do not occur unchallenged. Usually counter-narratives exist and hence the question arises who constructs the narratives in mass media coverage of political communication – media or political actors. This question is particularly important in times of conflict (see Chapter 2.4).

2.1 Socio-Psychological Infrastructure of Societies in Conflict

Societies that are entangled in conflicts over a long period need to develop a psychological infrastructure that enables them to endure these challenging circumstances. They experience stressful, challenging, and tough times characterized by uncertainty, threat, fear, heavy personal losses and high sacrifices. These situations alter in their intensity and have to be endured repeatedly and in intractable conflicts for several generations. This has strong psychological impacts on individuals as well as also on the societies as a whole. Bar-Tal (2007*b*) outlines a general framework on the *socio-psychological infrastructure of societies in intractable conflicts* as follows: The members of these societies have to adapt to three central psychological challenges: 1) Basic needs like knowing, safety, positive identity are deprived and need to be satisfied. 2) They need to learn to cope with stress and the costs of the conflict, and 3) they need to develop a psychological condition to sustain the conflict, withstand the adversary and still uphold a positive loyalty to the own group while remaining ready for sacrifice.

In intractable conflicts, the psychological adaptations to these challenges build a shared *socio-psychological repertoire* of societal beliefs, attitudes, and emotions (Bar-Tal 2007*b*: 1438). These are beliefs on the society in conflict, the rival and the violent conflict itself. Some factors indicate their *institutionalization*: When several generations grow up, live and die under conflict circumstances, share conflict beliefs, attitudes and emotions and hand them down to the following generations, hence they become part of the socialization of the group. Further, they are disseminated in the cultural products of the society, be it in films, theater, and literature. Public discourse is permeated by the beliefs and they are used in the education system, in media, and by political leaders.

When institutionalized, these *beliefs*, attitudes, values and emotions[4] build the *socio-psychological infrastructure*. The beliefs are very enduring, holding and enforcing them becomes an indicator for membership in this society. They serve as "prisms" for the way new experience and information is handled. To avoid cognitive dissonance, supportive information is by means of selective search, attention, storage, interpretation and dissemination processed very differently from contradicting information. To assure the maintenance of the socio-psychological infrastructure societies construct mechanisms such as censorship, sanctioning of critical voices as traitors etc. Still, this psychological repertoire can – in calm periods – become less salient, beliefs can change in content and centrality. Likewise they can be re-activated when violence breaks out again (See also Bar-Tal, Halperin and de Rivera 2007; Bar-Tal, Halperin and Oren 2010; Bar-Tal et al. 2008; Bar-Tal and Sharvit 2009; Gray, Coleman and Putnam 2007; Kelman 2007; Staub and Bar-Tal 2003: 712).

The Elements of the Socio-Psychological Infrastructure

The socio-psychological infrastructure of societies in intractable conflict contains three central parts that cover different areas as Bar-Tal (2007*b*: 1435) outlines: The *collective emotional orientation* is built through common emotions in society through experiences its members share. On another level, the beliefs of *collective memory* describe the coherent past of the society. The set of beliefs a society orms on its present to cope with the conflict is the *ethos of conflict*. All three components form the socio-psychological infrastructure and will be introduced in the following paragraphs. The focus in this investigation is on the ethos of conflict, since its beliefs are essential for the following investigation (see following Chapter, Bar-Tal 2007*b*: 1435). The socio-psychological infrastructure is part of a broader framework introduced mainly by Halperin and Bar-Tal (2011) analyzing socio-psychological barriers for peace. This includes also general worldviews, circumstantial and ideological beliefs and motivational, structural, and emotional factors. For further reading see: Bar-Tal and Halperin (2011); Bar-Tal, Halperin and Oren (2010); Halperin and Bar-Tal (2011).

Functions of the socio-psychological infrastructure   The socio-psychological infrastructure is the adaption to three psychological challenges of intractable conflict, especially during crisis phases. It answers deprived needs, gives mechanisms to cope and to withstand.

---

[4] Following Oren (2009), in the following the term belief is used for beliefs, values and attitudes. From here on beliefs are understood as the cognitive elements that define an understanding of an object or an action, attitudes are the feelings (positive or negative) of an object or action, and values are the understanding on how things should be.

In detail the socio-psychological infrastructure fulfills several functions in meeting those challenges as Bar-Tal (2007*b*: pp.1440) examines:

1) *Understanding of the conflict.* The coherent beliefs of ethos of conflict and collective memory help to explain events of the conflict. The confusing, stressful reality thus gains meaning and stress can be reduced.

2) *Justification of own acts towards the opponent.* Individuals need to hold positive beliefs upon their groups in order to identify with them. In conflict those groups harm other groups violently, destroy and kill its members. This could result in dissonance, guilt and shame. But the socio-psychological infrastructures of conflict societies serve~s as legitimization, logic and justification to hurting the "other" with excessive force. The opponent is held responsible for immoral acts against them. In this way, violence, atrocities and even genocide can be institutionalized while refraining from cognitive dissonance. This helps building and maintaining a positive social identity within conflict reality.

3) *Sense of differentiation and superiority.* The conflict groups are seen in dichotomous black-white pictures – therein the own group is glorified, righteous, superior. Responsibility for the conflict and negative attributions are solely to find within the opponent. Therefore, the own side is the only victim of the conflict itself and its events.

4) *Preparation of the society for violent acts of the adversary and difficult conditions.* In a sense members of a group are aware of threats of potential harm, they are confronted with. Expecting the worst can contribute to a certain level of predictability and thus stress reduction. Society members can still be surprised positively.

5) *Motivation for solidarity mobilization and action.* Just like penguins stand closely together to defend themselves against the cold, societies unite when opposed to a common threat or enemy. Fear and anger increase solidarity and the feeling of being one entity. Patriotism rises, and group members are more willing to endure sacrifices and to defend their group or to violently prevent possible harm to the group. Loyalty and mobilization are especially important for political leaders in need of support, particularly in conflict situation. A promising way to gain support for decisions and policies in conflict is the emphasis on threats onto national security or survival.

Collective memory Conflicts are shaped by the immediate and the long-term history. It is thus very decisive for societies how they keep their memories when in conflict. Memories of the same events can be numerous and contradict each other. This is why memory is constructed, cultivated and its re-/construction can serve political goals. For societies it is important to build shared memories over the history of collective experiences, for example the outbreak and course of the conflict. Beliefs of collective memory are those beliefs societies (here in conflict) share about the *past* of their society. Collective memory beliefs give a complete picture and meaning to the respective events and issues. Bar-Tal (2007*b*) outlines several characteristics: The narrated history is not objective but functional. It is constructed based on events in a biased, selective, distorted manner that serves the needs of the society's present existence, especially with the rival. The beliefs of collective memory are shared by society members and are considered as the true history of the group. This narration of history often permeate schoolbooks and official history-telling by the authorities. The rival group often upholds a contradicting understanding of this history and collective memories: "In short, the narrative of collective memories relating to an intractable conflict provides a black and white picture, which enables parsimonious, fast, unequivocal, and simple understanding of the history of the conflict" (Bar-Tal 2007*b*: 1436). The content touches four themes: 1) The outbreak and course of the conflict is justified; 2) the in-group is seen as positive; 3) the opponent is delegitimized; and 4) the in-group is seen as victim in societal beliefs of collective memory. History is often incorporated into the society's memory through collective commemoration. The choice of events, images, narration for the collective commemoration is often selective (Bar-Tal 2007*b*; Tint 2010: pp.240).

Collective emotional orientation   Collective emotions are felt by individuals due to their membership to a group. The emotions can be evoked by experiences some members of the group and is not necessarily shared by all the individuals. They can be felt through identification with the group. In intractable conflicts, several collective emotions arise, especially fear, but also hatred, anger, guilt, hope, and pride may appear (Bar-Tal 2007*b*: 1439). These collective emotions can be dominant and appear like a collective climate or mood. Kelman (2007: pp.82) emphasizes on the importance of collective climate and its effect on public opinion. The climate can be optimistic, pessimistic, angry, conciliatory, defiant, or resigned. This can change dramatically after strong incidents. Kelman's example is the assassination of the Israeli Prime Minister Yitzhak Rabin in November 1995 that put Jewish Israeli society into a state of shock and mourning and determinedness to continue with peace negotiations. This state was followed by terror attacks in early 1996 that changed public mood into wariness and less eagerness for peace negotiations. Further, Kelman (2007: 82) explains, public moods can be impacted decisively by strategic use of parts of collective memories. For example, drawing comparisons from current events onto collective traumata in order to evoke public moods, such as fear of annihilation or anger. Thus, public leaders on the one hand can shape public mood and opinion, on the other, they are bound to this public opinion and the dynamics it takes on its own. In intractable conflict it is more easy though to draw onto aggressive and escalating moods than on de-escalating ones (Bar-Tal, Halperin and de Rivera 2007; Bar-Tal 2007*b*) .

In sum,   this chapter introduces socio-psychological consequences that intractable conflicts have on the societies entangled in them. To endure the hardship of conflicts that last over generations, societies have to adapt their behavior, beliefs, memories, narratives, and emotions. Bar-Tal outlines those in the framework on the socio-psychological infrastructure of societies in intractable conflicts. It comprises the collective memory of a society, the collective emotions and the collective emotional orientation. The collective memory of a society entails the beliefs this group holds on their past. These selective, constructed beliefs give a meaningful narration on the past of the group. It is not objective but has functions that relate to the present. The collective emotional orientation describes emotions societal members feel because of their membership. In conflict, those are often fear, or hatred, pride, guilt, or hope. When dominant in a society they can turn into a collective mood. The ethos of conflict, as third part of the socio-psychological infrastructure is introduced in the following chapter. In general, the socio-psychological infrastructure helps societal members to understand the complicated conflict reality, to justify actions by the own group which enables them to sustain a sense of superiority, and remain motivated for solidarity and mobilization.

2.2 The Ethos of Conflict

The third part of the socio-psychological infrastructure in intractable conflicts, alongside collective memory and emotional orientation, is the ethos of conflict. It forms one part of the ethos of a society. The general ethos of a society is is seen by Bar-Tal (2013: 174) as an important part constituting the social identity of groups or societies. Social identity determines the being of a group. Members share similar notions of their memberships and the importance they ascribe to it. Only then the group exists and distinguishes from other individuals who may belong to other groups. This sense of belonging has social implications of shared beliefs and accepted behavior (Oren and Bar-Tal 2006). Oren (2009) defines the overall ethos of a society as the system of central beliefs, values and attitudes that most members of a society share about their present and future. The sum of the beliefs characterizes the society and connects its members[5]. Hereby the ethos gives orientation and meaning to societal life. That means that institutions, visions, concerns and actions by leaders of the society, as well as its members, are shaped, motivated, and justified by and within a given, accepted framework (Bar-Tal 2013: pp.174; Oren 2009: pp.2).

Beliefs constituting the ethos are enduring and develop over time. Hence, in societies entangled in prolonged conflicts beliefs on that conflict, the society in that setting and the rival evolve and form what Bar-Tal calls the ethos of conflict. According to him it is a holistic framework of eight central beliefs that are necessary for a society to function in conflict settings. The beliefs are: belief in the justness of one's own goal, opponent delegitimization, self-victimization, positive self-image, security, patriotism, unity, and

---

[5] Early works use the ethos as concept to investigate societies and their differences: See for example Epstein (1978) on several different societies and groups; and Mcclosky and Zaller (1987) on American beliefs in democracy and capitalism.

peace (Bar-Tal 2007*b*: pp.1438; Bar-Tal 2013: pp.174; Oren 2009: pp.6). The societal beliefs will be discussed in detail in this chapter.

Just as the overall ethos, the ethos of conflict serves as special orientation for societal members within the challenging reality of intractable conflict. Its simplistic one-sided understanding of situations gives meaning and justification to activities, serves as basis for solidarity and mobilization within the group. It enables its members to endure sacrifices, and cope with the conflict in general (Bar-Tal 2013). Exactly this is the crux of the ethos of conflict: Precisely because the conflict becomes bearable, a solution remains impossible. Solving a conflict is only possible after beliefs about one's own justness and victimization versus the illegitimacy of the opponents soften. Thus the ethos of conflict, as a major part in the socio-psychological infrastructure, serves as an epistemic basis for the continuation of conflicts (Oren, Bar-Tal and David 2004; Oren 2009).

Societal Beliefs of the Ethos of Conflict

The ethos of a society is constituted of beliefs that are shared by the majority of the society and serve as their common ground of self-understanding, communication, and actions. Common beliefs are important for groups just as personal beliefs are for individuals. Although individual and collective beliefs are enduring, collective beliefs generally stay longer due to the endorsing and validating of group members. They serve as "cognitive templates" or "prisms" that give interpretation and organization of shared reality and experiences, and are part of the societies' cultures[6] (Eidelson and Eidelson 2003: 182). These cognitions characterize the society and are part of what makes them unique. In fact, several of those beliefs of the ethos also constitute the collective memory. They underlie the emotional orientation and likewise generate emotions and set legitimate boundaries for expression of emotions. Oren (2009: 2) suggests the following criteria for beliefs to become central societal beliefs of the ethos: They are shared by a majority (Oren (2009) defines majority with 75%) of the society members over a long period in their actions and decisions, and are perceived as their common ground. They appear in public debates. Political and economic leaders use the logic of societal beliefs to justify and explain their positions and decisions. They appear in cultural products, rituals and ceremonies. They are passed down to the following generations. Still, the societal beliefs are usually not shared by the whole population. There usually exist alternating or counter-beliefs (Oren 2009).

Bar-Tal (1998*a*, 2007*b*, 2013) identifies eight central beliefs which are the basis for the present investigation. These eight beliefs can be divided into two categories: 1) *The core*

---

[6] Defining culture is difficult since it is such a broad concept and the understanding often depends on the background of the one defining it. This work is based on Triandis stating there is consensus on an understanding as "shared cognitions, standard operating procedures, and unexamined assumptions" (Triandis 1996: 407).

conflict themes. Three of the beliefs are core themes needed to maintain and justify the conflict and its goals: belief in the justness of one's own goals, delegitimization of the opponent, and self-victimization. 2) *General societal beliefs adapted to conflict setting.*The other five beliefs are necessary in all societal groups, but are adapted to the conflict setting and necessary to mobilize a society: positive self-image, belief in security, belief in patriotism, unity, and peace (Bar-Tal 2007*b*: pp.1435; Bar-Tal, Halperin and Oren 2010: 76).

In case these beliefs are not widely shared, a group will have difficulties to withstand the challenges of an enduring conflict. The introduction of the beliefs is based centrally on Daniel Bar-Tal's latest and comprehensive book in which he summarizes and refines his framework on socio-psychological foundations of intractable conflicts (Bar-Tal 2013).

Societal Beliefs about the Justness of one's own Goals

The belief about the justness of own goals is a crucial and basic motivator for groups entangled in conflicts. It is hard to mobilize groups when the goals do not appear as justified, legitimate and coherent (see System Justification Theory in Jost, Banaji and Nosek 2004). The justifications can be numerous (economical, ethnical, historical, religious, and national). The goals must be strong enough to mobilize, take into account high sacrifice, and be worth fighting for. Likewise, they serve as moral justifications for violent assaults on rivals (Bandura 2002: 103). Bar-Tal (2013) suggests that goals with this power are often considered "sacred". They are like moral institutions that can hardly be rationalized, but have to be protected by all means, even violent ones. Letting go of them is considered unethical and a slander of one's own values. These sacred goals need special justifications, which are usually religious or national-historical beliefs that touch the collective memories. These can be related to land, sites, or self-determination and freedom. Believing in the rightness and justness of these goals is the basis for a positive self-image, since when fighting for them, the group is still in line with its own moral codes (Bar-Tal 2013: 176). Bandura (2002) regards moral justification as one mechanism of moral disengagement. It "plays a key role in sanctifying violent means [...] In this process, destructive conduct is made personally and socially acceptable by portraying it as serving socially worthy or moral purposes" (McAlister, Bandura and Owen 2006: 142). Bandura outlines eight mechanisms of moral disengagement, three of them as central: moral justification, exoneration of social comparison and sanitizing language (Bandura 2002: 102). It enables upholding a positive and moral self-perception. Therefore, as Bar-Tal (2013) argues, the belief in the justness of these goals must be certain and clear. Otherwise doubts in the own goals are of high danger for the conflicting group since they will diminish the willingness to mobilize and to bear sacrifices. Believing that the own goals are just and worth to be fought for against another group that questions them goes along with denying the adversary just goals (Bar-Tal 2013: pp.176; on justification of the occupation see Chapter Halperin et al. 2010).

Societal Beliefs about the Delegitimization of the Opponent

Conflicting parties view each other as illegitimate in intractable conflicts in order to be able to harm each other while keeping a positive self-image and a feeling of morality. Delegitimization is understood by Bar-Tal as

> the categorization of a group, or groups, into extremely negative social categories that exclude it, or them, from the sphere of human groups that act within the limits of acceptable norms and/or values, since these groups are viewed as violating basic human norms or values and therefore deserve maltreatment. (2012: 30)

That means, the other group is perceived as a group that is so negative in its essence that it does not belong to the community of moral human beings anymore. Negativity and aggressive actions by the opponent are ascribed to the opponent's nature (be it religion, political system, ideology or character), and thus seen as inherent (Kelman 2007: 92).

There are several forms of delegitimization that Bar-Tal and Hammack describe: The de-humanization or demonizing of the opponent, the outcasting of the group from being part of moral societies, characterization with extremely negative traits, and comparison with other groups perceived as illegitimate. Ethnocentrism as well as conflict (especially when intractable) often serve as bases for delegitimization (Bar-Tal and Hammack 2012: 33). Bar-Tal argues that the term *enemy* implies the delegitimization of the opponent in intractable conflict. An enemy is seen as a threat, associated with negative labels and should be fought. Delegitimization of a rival group has several functions that are crucial in conflict setting according to Bar-Tal (2013: pp.182): 1) Delegitimization facilitates distrust and hatred of the rival group that is perceived as potentially dangerous and having bad intentions. That legitimizes a group to harm its opponent even with immoral means since the group itself is seen outside those moral boundaries.

> This implication is the essence of delegitimization and grants to this societal phenomenon its unique meaning: Psychological authorization to perform negative violent acts against the delegitimized groups, including mass killing, ethnic cleansing, and even genocide. (Bar-Tal 2013: 181)

2) Delegitimization of rivals exempts the own group from responsibility – of the outbreak and course of the conflict, the course of events, victims on the rival's side (they are responsible themselves due to their inhumanity) and in general violence conducted against the rival. In that sense, the delegitimization is also a part of moral disengagement (Bandura 2002). Bar-Tal (2013: 180) suggests it further frees groups from responsibility on the absence of a resolution of the conflict and of course of own victims and sacrifices. 3) Delegitimization therefore explains the outbreak, course and costs of the conflict and its continuation. 4) Thus, delegitimization frees society members from the danger of feeling guilt, shame, or dissonance. 5) Further, fighting an inhumane, immoral, illegitimate enemy

serves the positive feeling of the group and its belief in superiority. This is possible due to a classical mirror image – own violence is regarded as defense to the aggressiveness which is in the nature of the illegitimate adversaries (Bandura 2002). This process may seem extreme for individuals living in peaceful societies. It seems important to take into account that in conflict environment the direct interactions between civilians of the conflicting parties usually become scarce. Hence the only encounter remaining are consequences of violence conducted by the rival and the mediated information on the Other by the own environment. These two simple factors do enable and enhance mistrust and delegitimization over time (Bar-Tal 2013: 180).

Societal Beliefs about Victimization

When defining victimization of individuals, one can concentrate on the events that may cause it or on the psychological causes it may have on the individual. It can be seen as

> a mindset shared by group members that results from a perceived intentional harm with severe and lasting consequences inflicted on a collective by another group or groups, a harm that is viewed as undeserved, unjust and immoral, and one that the group was not able to prevent. (Bar-Tal et al. 2009: 229).

Victimhood beliefs can stand at the very beginning of conflict in which a group defines a problem and a specific adversary responsible for it; this can be used by leaders of those groups and lead to responses that can inflict the same beliefs in the Other.

Bar-Tal (2013: pp.187) states that, in a conflict setting in which one group considers itself and its goals to be just and moral, whereas the adversary is delegitimized, violence against the own group is likely to be perceived as immoral and unjust. This group will likely see itself as the victim. The (delegitimized) opponent is perceived as perpetrator who has immoral goals and uses immoral means. He or she is solely considered responsible for the often prolonged and repeated suffering. Therefore the reactions to the perceived injustice can range between feeling helpless or hopeless, self pity, guilt, loss of meaning or trust, low self-esteem, a tendency to blame, fear and anger. The negative emotions are directed towards the perpetrator and to those not granting the group victim status, whereas those emphasizing with the victim status are perceived positively. Hence the victim group may develop a need to prevent further harm, to restore justness or to revenge. The belief about collective victimhood corresponds with what Eidelson and Eidelson (2003: 186) describe as belief in vulnerability – the belief in potential or real threat. While the later concentrates on future atrocities, the first emphasizes those endured in the past. Thereby it is insignificant if the harm is experienced in long term, or individual cases, in present or in the distant past, since it remains accessible to the sense of victimhood through collective memory.

Volkan's introduction of "chosen traumas" is illuminating in that context. It is understood as "mental representation of an event that has caused a large group to face drastic losses, feel helpless and victimized by another group, and share a humiliating injury" (Volkan 1999: 46). While a group may not intend to be victimized it "chooses" to "mythologize and psychologize the mental representation of an event" (ibid.). A chosen trauma can be inactive for decades and be activated and change function following external factors, for example from an ideology of "glorified victimhood" to "entitlement for revenge", especially when the existence of the of the identity is threatened again. Reactivating the trauma serves as a bonding between the group members' identity (Volkan 1999: pp.46). Kelman (2007: 93) further emphasizes the tendency of societies to assimilate the understanding of the current experiences of victimization to historical victimization as part of the collective memories. This connection certainly enhances the perception of current victimhood.

In intractable conflict usually both parties consider themselves as victims of the opponent. This serves several functions according to Bar-Tal (2013: pp.188): it gives clarity in the complex conflict situation on responsibilities, this clarity helps coping with stress, it justifies violent reactions and mobilizes the group to defend itself or to restore justice, it gives a sense of moral superiority to the aggressive opponent, it supports solidarity between the group members and in general raises the identification with that group. Also, communicating this victim narration to the international arena is increasingly important: victims are perceived as morally superior, are granted international sympathy, legitimization, and real support. Further, victimhood protects from criticism. Therefore conflicted parties are more and more in a conflict over narratives, especially victim-narratives.

In general, as the conflict proceeds and each side suffers higher losses, the constant feeling of threat and thus the belief in victimization becomes a perception of the Self that can even survive the conflict. Conflicting societies often hold contradicting mirror images against each other (Eidelson and Eidelson 2003: 186). Basically both sides see each other in good-bad dimensions, positive attitudes are attributed to the own side and negative ones to the opponent. They will likely not be able to see and respect the opposing narrative with empathy, since the focus is on the own losses, and reduces feelings of responsibility for committed atrocities, and willingness to forgive (Schori-Eyal, Halperin and Bar-Tal 2014).

Societal Beliefs about a Positive Collective Self-Image

Just as individuals, societies also have a need to pertain a positive collective self-image. It is important to have a positive image of oneself in order to be able to live with feelings of guilt, shame or deep regret, for whatever reason they might appear. On the long run, a constructive handling of those feelings can be acquired when the individual assures itself to be a humane, worthy being, which is loveable and full of positive features (Eidelson and Eidelson 2003: 184). This is not very different for societies, especially those in intractable conflicts. By definition societies fight another group and inflict suffering on it in a wide variety of ways. This includes violating basic human rights, aggression, oppression, destruction, harm, killing, torture, rape of civilians, and much more. Bearing responsibility for these actions challenges beliefs in a positive identity of a society that hence need to be distinctive in order to withstand (Bar-Tal 2013: 190). Accordingly, groups might develop beliefs in superiority that Eidelson and Eidelson (2003: 184) describe as "the shared convictions of moral superiority, chosenness, entitlement and special destiny". It is based on beliefs of shared characteristics, achievements, and skills that can be based on present or past accomplishments and events. These beliefs are strengthened through comparisons with other groups that are perceived as lacking those capabilities.

Correspondingly, especially ethnic groups at conflict engage with great efforts in in-group solidarity, morality, civility, fairness, humaneness, trustworthiness, etc. A common tool to uphold a positive collective self-image lies in the ritualistic commemoration of chosen events to prove those values (Eidelson and Eidelson 2003). "Thus, groups involved in intractable conflicts engage in intense self-justification, self-glorification and self-praise, as well as moral disengagement" (Bar-Tal 2013: 190). Moral disengagement seems to be a precondition to be able to commit atrocities while upholding high standards (Bandura 2002). It might explain the paradox of war criminals, terrorists, Nazis that are described as loving parents while conducting horrible crimes against other humans in inhumane ways, and apparently without much cognitive dissonance.

A positive collective self-image fulfills several necessary and useful functions in a society in intractable conflict, as Bar-Tal (2013: 190) argues: 1) Only a group perceived as positive and valuable is worth fighting for and to endure the sacrifices this requires. 2) Feeling superior to the rival is necessary to fight and carry out violence against. 3) Remaining superior can legitimize, marginalize and rationalize violence and atrocities committed against the rival. 4) Believing in the positive spirit and the capabilities of the group to withstand and win the conflict is a precondition for mobilization. On the other hand, assumptions on false invincibility might cause unnecessary victims for the own group. 5) Maintaining and displaying a positive collective self-image is also important on the international arena. The latter extends support based on moral guidelines. In sum, a positive collective self-image is crucial for motivation mobilization, spirit and endurance of society's members, especially when excessive violence is used against the rival (Bar-Tal 2013: pp.190; Eidelson and Eidelson 2003: pp.184).

Collective Beliefs about Security

Security can become a dominant or the dominant theme in a society, its beliefs a central basis for argumentation, legitimization, and its institutions a determining power in intractable conflicts. Bar-Tal (2013: pp.192) outlines three elements that comprise the belief: The first element emphasizes the importance of security. Safety is one of the basic human needs according to Maslow's hierarchy of needs. This includes security of the body, health, property, employment, resources, morality and family. When these basic needs are not met, needs that follow safety such as love, esteem and self-actualization will be put behind and the first priority will be to restore safety (Maslow and Frager 1987). A second element are the factors that threaten personal and collective security, such as natural disasters, wars, terror, economic crises, loss of freedom, and political instability. Perceived or real threat leads to a sense of and belief in vulnerability that "has the potential to govern significant aspects of the group's internal life and its relations with other groups" (Eidelson and Eidelson 2003: 186). In times of conflict, security is threatened on several levels and often on a long-term perspective. A third factor are the means needed to (re-)establish security. The beliefs in vulnerability/victimhood can lead to strong calls for security and to hostility towards those powers that cause the vulnerability. It may provoke a group to preempt a threat by acting aggressively to assure safety[7].

Vulnerability beliefs hence result in security beliefs that become part of a society's ethos. Bar-Tal (2013: 193) proposes the following central parts: the identification of the source of insecurity (the rival), the necessity to change the situation (fight the rival), and the conditions needed (mobilization, motivation, sacrifices on a personal and political level that include restrictions of political, financial, economical and legal freedom). In this sense, beliefs about security have several functions: 1) They provide knowledge on the security concerns and provide a basis for coping with them. 2) Security concerns serve as legitimization for policies, decisions, and actions by leaders of different sectors. 3) They serve as motivators for mobilization, sacrifices, and may serve as basis for psychological coping with the means needed to maintain or restore security. 4) Security threats further serve as arguments for obedience and conformism. When security gains enormous meaning for a society, its institutions and members often become glorified and thus gain even more centrality as heroes of the group. This serves the moral, the motivation, and the willingness for personal sacrifices (like sending own children to the army) (Bar-Tal 2013; Eidelson and Eidelson 2003).

Societal Beliefs about Patriotism

Nations or ethnic group often hold patriotic beliefs. They serve as glue for the society and are characterized by a sense of belonging, solidarity, positive attitudes towards the group and pride. Patriotic beliefs are often shaped, promoted, and maintained by rituals. In intractable conflicts patriotism is essential. It serves as motivator and legitimization for sacrifices people take upon themselves for the sake of the society, even killing and the threat to die for the group. Patriotism is also a tool of mobilization (Kelman 2007: 85). Sacrifices for the group are often commemorated as patriotic acts. In times of crisis the definition of patriotism and patriotic behavior is often a very narrow. Often, aggressive, escalatory policies as response to posed or perceived threats on security or

---

[7] A need for these preemptive acts can be intensified when groups practice "catastrophic thinking" in which the worst case scenario appears as the logical, inevitable future. That is often the case when history is filled with traumatic experiences and genocidal initiatives. It may lead to fears of annihilation, but also assimilation and losing one's distinctiveness (Eidelson and Eidelson 2003: 186).

survival of the group are counted as patriotic. Conciliatory policies, thoughts or claims questioning or criticizing those "patriotic" policies are likely to be declared unpatriotic and traitor-behavior. Although those might be in the group's interest in the long run, they imply mistakes on the own side and a certain legitimacy of the opponent's claims. The members of the group are expected absolute loyalty for the behavior, policies and actions agreed to as loyal (Bar-Tal 2013: pp.196). Thus, "militancy and intransigence become the measures of loyalty" (Kelman 2007: 86).

Societal Beliefs about Unity

The need to conform to the beliefs agreed upon as patriotic is explained within the beliefs in unity of the group. These beliefs are based on the assumption that the society can withstand external threat only when the first is internally united. Therefore the common norms, values, and characteristics are emphasized. In times of conflict lacking unity is perceived as threat to the conflict goals and behaviors agreed upon as patriotic. Goals and courses of the conflict may be debated in peaceful times with a certain openness to critical questions. In conflict though, a society needs to function according to the goals and legitimate ways of fighting agreed upon. Accordingly, individuals or parts of the society claiming different possible courses to achieve a resolution or an alternating perspective on the opponent, pose a threat to the conflicting society, and are marginalized. Their claims endanger the motivation, mobilization, the other conflict beliefs and ultimately reaching the conflict goals agreed upon. Believing in the unity of the society and protecting it is also regarded as a treasure limited to the own group that is not granted to the opponent. The opponents masses are regarded as basically misled by their elites or the unity is artificial and kept alive by its leaders to keep the conflict alive. This too is part of conflict-mirror images (Bar-Tal 2013: pp.198; Kelman 2007: 93).

Societal Beliefs about Peace

Societies in conflict do hold strong beliefs on peace and their longing for it. Beliefs in peace serve as positive goals that are the ultimate longing of the groups within that conflict. These peace beliefs are wishes, longings, dreams and fantasies. They are enhanced and held up in culture, education, and politics and found in songs, theaters, rituals, school books and programs, speeches and conferences. Being a peace-loving society also serves as part of keeping a positive self-image within the collective, but also in contact with international actors. Peace beliefs are not beliefs on concrete steps a society should take to reach reconciliation and peace, including compromises and adjustments that are necessary, but a far dream (Bar-Tal 2013: 200).

Societal Beliefs of the Ethos of Conflict as Barriers to Peace

The socio-psychological infrastructure poses, as it is, a barrier to conciliation and peace (Bar-Tal, Halperin and Oren 2010: 97). Information flow is biased and distortive while alternative information that contradicts upheld convictions is prevented from being absorbed. The conflict reality becomes "bearable", hence the necessity for peace is reduced.

Accordingly, a society willing to pursue peace needs to undergo severe changes in beliefs and processes promoting conflict that Bar-Tal, Halperin and Oren (2010: pp.96) discuss. They outline several levels: Beliefs in peace have to be connected to concrete steps and policies towards compromise rather than be a far fantasy. Group loyalty needs to be re-defined to allow a debate over the courses of conflict taken and policies agreed upon. This enables critical questioning and the search for different responses to actions by the rival. The zero-sum thinking regarding the conflict as a central characteristic of intractable conflicts (see Chapter 1.5) has to be turned into a perspective in which all the parties involved in the conflict win. These are preconditions for negotiations that need readiness for sacrifices concerning the conflict goals and hence a re-thinking of the goals. Also, a commitment to a peaceful relationship with the opponent requires trust-building and re-shaping of mirror-images. Therefore, direct communication, tolerance and acceptance of the opposing beliefs of the Other are necessary (Kelman 2007). Apparently these are complex, painful, and challenging processes for societies to undergo. It is not in the scope of this work to write exhaustively on the possibilities to turn psychological infrastructures that are barriers to peace into catalysts of such and conditions in the infrastructure that enable a process of peace. But intense work on this is found in Bar-Tal, Halperin and de Rivera 2007; Bar-Tal 2013; Bar-Tal, Halperin and Pliskin 2015; Hameiri, Bar-Tal and Halperin 2014; Kelman 2007; Tint 2010 and on the media's role in peace process in Wolfsfeld 2004.

Ethos of Conflict in Research

The concept ethos of conflict was developed by Bar-Tal based on his experiences and research of the Jewish Israeli society, and the main research is conducted on different aspects of societal life in this conflict setting. Those studies on ethos of conflict in Israeli Jewish society are outlined in chapter 3.2 that introduces the case of the present investigation. Bar-Tal and his scholars repeatedly state the adaptability of the construct on other conflict settings internationally (Bar-Tal 2013). So far, the amount of international research on ethos of conflict seems limited and is introduced here.

Medjedovic and Petrovic (2013) analyze the relationship between the ethos of conflict, personality traits, social attitudes, and the respective evaluation of political parties in interviews with Serbian adults. They find a significant and the strongest connection between holding beliefs of the ethos of conflict and party evaluation. They further observe that the ethos of conflict creates a

> homogeneous, one-dimensional space of beliefs about the social group of people with whom there is long-lasting conflict [...] It is clear that this set of beliefs holds tension and hostility towards Kosovo Albanians, although the armed conflict was ended ten years ago. (Medjedovic and Petrovic 2013: 41)

People holding the beliefs of ethos of conflict tend to support parties with aggressive, non-compromising politics towards the Kosovo question. "Such attitudes are certainly an obstacle to the reconciliation between the Serbs and Kosovo Albanians" (ibid.).

Ulug and Cohrs (2014) analyze whether and to what extent society members hold the ethos of conflict in the context of the Kurdish conflict using Q methodology. They investigate whether the one-dimensional structures of the ethos of conflict "suggest greater unanimity in society members' understanding than there actually is" (ibid.: 1) and suggest that they can be based on several representations and be held to different degrees. In their study, 45 Turks, Kurds, and Arabs from the same region in Turkey were sampled. Their findings show that the viewpoints expressed are compatible with the ethos of conflict, and the beliefs shape the viewpoints in different levels. Still, since they analyze members of three different societal groups, there is variation in the way of representation of the conflict (who is seen as victim), which also depends on the ideological or opinion-based groups (ibid.: 16). They state that it "seems to be more subjective categorizations and identification [that determine what is meant by "one's own group"] rather than "objective" ethnic group membership that matters" (ibid.). Yet they admit that the great complexity and variety of viewpoints they found can be based on "lower intensity" of the conflict and less intractability than the Israeli-Palestinian conflict.

Hadjipavlou (2007) examines the beliefs within the Greek and Turkish Cypriot societies on the causes of conflict, their beliefs on themselves and each other and their beliefs in solutions. She conducted interviews with more than 2000 persons in both societies. Both groups believe that nationalism of the other side is a very strong contributor to the conflict. Moreover, "each community constructs the Other as the cause of their suffering and perceives their own side as not responsible" (ibid.: 335). Still both groups of interviewees believe their both groups' nationalisms perpetuate the conflict. Moreover, they are convicted their own leadership's mistakes perpetuated the conflict. However, they hold the Other's intransigence responsible. Another strong factor found is delegitimization of the other society by both communities. Hadjipavlou also emphasizes on the importance of split educational systems that share different narratives, celebrate own glories and traumas, construct enemy images and own patriotism. Most Cypriots from both sides believe this contributes to the conflict as well as they regard national symbolism and traditions as separating, contributing to the conflict and building on mistrust. The survey shows a great awareness of the Cypriot society on contributors to conflict perpetuation. The fact that nationalism and lacking communication are seen as conflict factors bears room for optimism and shows that the status quo appears not as the most satisfying solution. Still, victimization, delegitimization of the Other pertain and will take time and work to be overcome (Hadjipavlou 2007)[8].

The conflict supporting role of education, especially history education for the Cypriot societies, is further illuminated by Papadakis (2008). He analyzes historic school books before and after 2003 and shows how both societies are solely taught their "motherland" nations' history solely until 2003. In former books, narratives emphasize either Turkish or Greek nationalism that is seen as the only Cypriot identity. History is described in an ethnocentric way, accordingly the Other stereotyped. School books published after 2003 search for a more inclusive approach to both societies and a critical stance on nationalism. Although still ethnocentric, those books fit no narrative, let go of delegitimization, and positive self-images, and open space for internal differentiations and new identities that are diverse and open to change (Papadakis 2008).

Slocum-Bradley (2008) illuminates how in the context of the Rwanda genocide narratives distributed in the media ultimately legitimize actions against the Other. This is done through identity and legitimacy building that delegitimizes the Other and constructs conflict beliefs. He extracts different narratives about the delegitimization, the justness of one's own side, the positive collective self-image and about victimization. Delegitimization reached a point in which eradication of the Other became the logic reaction (Slocum-Bradley 2008).

Constraints of the Ethos of Conflict

The socio-psychological infrastructure, and in particular the ethos of conflict, should not be understood as the guideline to understanding conflict and conflict solution. The psychological perspective is one of the perspectives within a very complex and constantly changing setting of intertwined factors. It cannot explain conflict. The environments, leaderships, external factors, interests of involved or not directly involved actors lead to factual events and incompatible goals. These are factors that can hardly be influenced by psychological factors, but rather have an impact on them.

Another factor is that the debate on societal beliefs implies a very monolithic view on society. Humans hold different beliefs and behave different in reaction to one same event. Especially societies with diverse (ethnic) groups have several collective memories and belief systems that can be opposing each other and result from internal conflicts and misconceptions. But also other factors, like gender, education, religious, political and ideological beliefs lead to different positions regarding excerpts of reality and especially conflict reality and conclusions drawn from that. Ulug and Cohrs (2014) point out that the

---

[8] For further research on contradicting conflict narratives of Turkish and Greek Cypriots, see Papadakis 1998.

one-dimensional structure of the scale "may suggest greater unanimity in society members understanding of conflict than there actually is" (Ulug and Cohrs 2014: 1). It is true that despite the acknowledged diversity of societies and their fragmentation, there is a high pressure for conformity in times of crisis and a high tendency to silent dissent. However, one can conclude that the framework proposed has to be dealt with as one perspective on an aspect of conflict reality (Eidelson and Eidelson 2003; Ulug and Cohrs 2014).

In sum, this chapter introduces the concept of the ethos of conflict. It comprises eight central beliefs societies in intractable conflicts hold about their present. Those beliefs are held and shared by the majority of the society and manifest themselves in cultural products. They serve as prisms for interpretation and understanding of events and issues. The belief about the justness of one's own goals justifies actions necessary to achieve those goals. Believing in the justness of one's own group is necessary to mobilize and to bear sacrifices. Societal beliefs about the delegitimization of the opponent can be considered mirror images to the conviction of one's own justness. The adversaries are perceived as so negative, inhumane, immoral, and aggressive in their nature that violent action against them is considered legitimate. Societal beliefs about victimization ascribes the responsibility of the group's suffering to the adversary. These beliefs can be enhanced through connection with past experiences of victimization and through "chosen traumas" in which a group mythologizes the victimization. Victimizing beliefs may be used to argue for violent acts of revenge or preemption. Societal beliefs about a positive collective self-image are necessary to sustain a positive identity throughout the atrocities endured and committed. Positive traits and characterizations of the society are emphasized and upheld. Collective beliefs about security can become a dominant theme in a society at conflict. The personal and collective security is continuously threatened. Therefore, promising to restore safety legitimizes the use of force and policy decisions in different sectors. The need to restore safety mobilizes and enforces obedience and conformism. Societal beliefs about patriotism are positive beliefs the groups hold on themselves that motivate, mobilize and sometimes demand sacrifices. Societal beliefs about unity emphasizes on the importance to conform and to function. Societal beliefs about peace serve as positive goals of societies and are upheld like a fantastic treasure, however, without practical implications and a necessity to compromise. All those societal beliefs, while enabling the society members to sustain the conflict, hinder attempts to resolve the conflict. Only when these beliefs change, readiness for compromise and concrete steps to resolve the conflict rises.

2.3 The Struggle over Narratives

This chapter illuminates a way in which the societal beliefs comprising the ethos of conflict are found in the media representation of events and issues. It is argued that societal beliefs shape narratives that groups hold on past and present (see definition in Chapter 1.5).

Hammack (2014) suggests that humans comprehend their environment through narratives, "by clustering concepts, ideas, categories, characters, and events into a running dramatized storyline – provided to us through various forms of cultural construction, including the news media" (2014: 53). There are certain narratives that support the conflict reality in societies entangled in intractable conflict and there are always narratives that challenge them. Therefore there is a struggle over dominant narratives within the society and in the international arena. It is further argued that the media is one arena for this struggle. Narratives are formed and used through framing – decisions taken on what and how to represent issues.

These collectively held narratives can relate to specific issues, events, settings, or be master narratives that are holistic and complete comprehensive stories over parts of the collective identity, as Bar-Tal (2013) outlines. Their contents are rather what "should be" than merely describing what is. Master- or meta-narratives can be dominant in the whole society or shared by only parts of it. These narratives are anchored in societal beliefs of the ethos that in their "meaningful assembly provide a holistic story" (Bar-Tal 2013: 22) about collective identity and collective memory and hence social representations of both (Hammack and Pilecki 2012: 78). Dominant master-narratives and specific narratives about the present are building the ethos of societies and in conflict the ethos of conflicts. Dominant specific and master-narratives about the past build the collective memory of a society (Oren, Nets-Zehngut and Bar-Tal 2015: 217).

Conflict-supporting narratives In intractable conflicts, societies often form special narratives, described as conflict-supporting narratives by Oren, Nets-Zehngut and Bar-Tal (2015). These are communicated within the ethos of conflict and the collective memory. Being based on real events, they are selective and biased by promoting specific meanings and ignoring possible other perspectives. Oren, Nets-Zehngut and Bar-Tal (2015: 217) thus suggests that they entail at least one of the societal beliefs comprising the ethos of conflict. Hence, their functions are identical to the functions of the socio-psychological infrastructure of societies in intractable conflicts (see Chapter 2.1). Oren, Nets-Zehngut and Bar-Tal (2015: pp.220) observe several practices that lead to the construction of these narratives and are used by society members, leaders, and institutions: 1) Relying on supportive sources and ignoring of contradicting sources. These sources can be official governmental, chosen journalists, spokespersons, chosen eye-witnesses etc. 2) Supporting information is magnified and contradiction is marginalized. Events that suit the conflict-supporting narrative are discussed, especially when they concern themes such as the justness of one's own goals, a positive self-image, victimization and delegitimization of the rival. 3) Framing language is used in creation and telling of narratives. This practice is depictable in manifestations in cultural products, hence in media representations of events and issues and introduced below. 4) Contradicting information is ignored and suppressed. Oren, Nets-Zehngut and Bar-Tal (2015) suggest that these practices are used by gatekeepers of the society, leaders, scholars, and mass media. But they are also adapted in general by society members to avoid cognitive dissonance.

The struggle over narratives However they argue, narratives can be challenged by counter-narratives and different internal and external parts of the society. Therefore, there is a struggle over the hegemony of narratives. This struggle takes place in two central fields: the intra-societal and the international struggle. The first struggle over hegemony of conflict-supporting narratives within the society is mainly over control of information (through censorship, control of access), discrediting of counter information and those expressing them, monitoring, formal and informal punishment (e.g., of media institutions that do not comply), encouragement and rewarding (Bar-Tal, Oren and Nets-Zehngut 2014: 668). The struggle over international acceptance of the own narratives is important for the moral, diplomatic, or practical support of the society at conflict. Therefore these groups engage in great efforts to convince international leaders and publics of the justness of their conflict-supportive narratives (Oren, Nets-Zehngut and Bar-Tal 2015). For example, societies may control the access of foreign press, use third parties to disseminate their conflict-supportive narratives, or activate the own diaspora groups to promote their narrative about the conflict (Bar-Tal, Oren and Nets-Zehngut (2014: 669), see also Chapter 3.1.5).

Political communication as arena Actors, political issues, events, and messages are in a competition over media attention. This contest has two dimensions: the access to media agenda and the framing, the perspective taken on the reported events, issues, messages, hence the narrative that is constructed (Sheafer and Gabay 2009: 448). How are narratives built and enforced in mass media? Journalists are usually members of the society they write for. They have anticipations of their audience and are likely to share the beliefs, memories, emotions of the audience. Telling a story means to take decisions. What event, issue, message, actor is newsworthy and what is not? Where is information sought, and where not? Who is interviewed and who not? Where is the focus and where not? All these decisions, taken consciously or not influence what is told and how it is told – that means, the framing and hence the narratives that are constructed (Liebes 1997: 49; Wolfsfeld 2004: pp.15; Wolfsfeld and Sheafer 2006).

Framing Frames as defined in Chapter 1.5 have four functions according to Entman (2004; 2007): In a primary function they define the problem, define newsworthy issues, and thereby set the agenda. The following functions of framing are also described as second level agenda setting: Frames analyze causes and attribute responsibility. Furthermore, they convey moral judgment and in a fourth function endorse remedies or improvements. Frames can contain several of these functions and are then considered meta-frames. "All four of these functions hold together in a kind of cultural logic, each helping to sustain the others with the connections among them cemented more by custom and convention than by principles of syllogistic logic" (Entman 2004: 6). Frames give salience or importance to ideas and issues, activate schemes "that encourage target audiences to think, feel, and decide in a particular way" Entman (2007: 164). This influences the interpretation and preference of recipients and is called priming. It is the goal of strategic framing activities (Entman 2007: 165).

In sum, framing can be regarded as an interpretative pattern which is constructed through the choice of issues and the choice for or against certain perspectives and aspects in their coverage. Frames form narratives of issues of the present and past. While some of those narratives are held predominantly within a society, others challenge these. Therefore there is a struggle over narratives in democratic and free societies. The media is one arena of this struggle in political communication. Now, who is dominating this struggle – are political actors setting the agenda and the perspectives taking on it, or do they have to conform their agendas and frames to media constraints? Are journalists constructing the political communication or are they merely covering political issues and events relying on the narration and narratives of political actors? These questions are discussed in the following chapter.

2.4 Mediatization of Conflicts

As discussed in Chapter 2.1 and 2.2, conflict has great influence on the societies at conflict themselves. Their socio-psychological infrastructure, ethos, beliefs, narratives are shaped by the reality of enduring conflict. The media, as a part of social life, is also shaped by the societal situation.

But mass media itself has a particular and unique relation with conflict that has taken several developments and intensified during the last decades. In fact, media does not merely supply information on ongoing events of a conflict. Media has become a decisive factor in conflict and the courses it takes. Therefore "mediatized conflict" (Cottle 2006) is a popular and important term. To understand the complex relation between media and conflicts first the concept of mediatization is approached and the relationship between media and politics briefly sketched.

Mediatization of Politics

In general, mediatization describes a long-term process in which political actors and institutions adapt their public communication or even strategic planning and acting to the needs and constraints of mass media. Basis for mediatization is a factual independence of media from direct control by authorities, parties, or other institutions (Kepplinger 2002; Landerer 2013; Pfetsch and Mayerhöffer 2006). Mediatization is mostly discussed as mediatization of politics, but not restricted to it (see for example Peleg and Bogoch 2014: on mediatization of law). The central debate in research of mediatization surrounds the question who dominates the arena. Does media set the tone that political actors have to comply to or are understanding political actors in fact using mass media for their purposes? Mass media and politics are complex systems with their own logics and needs that will be introduced here to illuminate their interaction.

Media logic changes as mass media itself changes (Landerer 2013). The major change though is the privatization and profit orientation of the media, its factual independence from political parties, its technical developments and therefore multiple new types of the media (Kepplinger 2002: 973). Two strong developments are: diversification of organizations, formats, and media channels and concurrently concentration on several powerful big media institutions with international impact on several media channels. Hence, Landerer rightly claims that speaking of one "media logic" is over-simplifying complex diverse institutions into one entity (Landerer 2013: 243). Still, two main characteristics can be constituted for mass media in general (taken the simplification into account): Mass media follows an audience oriented commercial logic and mass media follows a normatively oriented public logic (ibid.).

The first *audience oriented commercial logic* bears several implications. Mass media ultimately has two intertwined needs: information and recipients (McQuail 2006). Therefore media engages in a constant competition over relevant "sellable" content, information, and formats in order to win the precious attention and monetary reward from their audiences (and advertisers) (Kepplinger 2002; Landerer 2013; McQuail 2006). The relevance of information is described in the theory of news values (Galtung and Ruge 1965; Pfetsch and Mayerhöffer 2006; Schulz 1976). Its basic assumption is that, among others, sudden, physical or culturally close events happening to relevant, mighty or prominent actors, in a surprising, negative, understandable, personalizable way, are highly valuable news. This relevant and newsworthy content thus is often oversimplified, dramatized, personalized, selective, biased, sensationalist, and generally emphasizing destruction more than construction (Kepplinger 2002; McQuail 2006). Other implications of commercial media logic lie in its organization, content gathering, own frequency (depending on channel and format) of research, construction and dissemination.

The second, *normatively oriented public logic* is shaped by beliefs and rules on how the media should report. This logic marks an ideal role that journalism in democratic societies should take. This idealistic role is to bring an independent voice to public debate that serves the public's right to know (Liebes 1997: 51). This role should be fulfilled by public service broadcast, and restricted by (public) institutions, assumptions on the needs of the recipients, the media institutions themselves or by the beliefs, and norms of the journalistic actors themselves on their role. However, the assumption of an independent "objective" media coverage is a myth (see Chapter 1). Any coverage is a representation based on the journalist's perspective, abilities, background and dependence within the journalistic and political system. Objectivity remains an unattainable goal for media actors that can shape the approach of political activity and its processing (Landerer 2013; McQuail 2006).

Political logic can be understood in two dimensions as well (Landerer, 2013). On the one hand, there is the *normative policy logic* on what politics should be about: decision making and implementation of those. This logic is in its essence independent from the media and more related to technocratic parties (Landerer 2013; Vowe 2006). The second, *electoral logic*, for example in democratic systems, can be seen as equivalent to commercial logic of the media. Both are *market logics.* Political actors need to campaign for support of their decisions and viewpoints, their party and person ultimately in order to get elected. Hence, political actors have an interest and need in shaping the political agenda in a way that will assure placement in the public debate and reach a wide audience. When interested mainly in winning elections, actors will be inclined to engage in conflict issues rather than substantial and complicated negotiations (Landerer 2013: 250). Thereore, when media coverage is dominated by commercial logic and political logic is dominated by electoral logic, both actors are engaged in a competition of the widest audience, be it recipients or the electorate (ibid.).

Interdependency Media and political logic are connected in shared spheres of action and dependencies. This leads to the question who is dominating the relationship. Several authors consider media and its commercial logic as the dominant system that political actors have to obey to. "Political communicators are forced to respond to the media rules, aims, production logic, and constraints" (Mazzoleni and Schulz 1999: 259). Strömbäck and Dimitrova (2011: 35) agree: "Media coverage is shaped by journalistic interventions, reflecting media logic, rather than the wants and needs of political institutions and actors, reflecting political logic." However, they see it as indicators for either media interventionism or mediatized content. According to Landerer (2013: 253), both political and media actors will emphasize sellable issues when market logic dominates their goals. He further concludes that professionalized media-competent political actors – knowing what to say how – "may have left private media companies more vulnerable to instrumentalization by political actors" (ibid.). However, while instrumentalizing the media to gain attention, political actors still adapt their content to media constraints and hence are not likely to engage in deep debates over context in such an attempt. Another perspective is found in Bennett's indexing theory (Bennett 1990). According to it, the media regards its role as limited by the legitimate range of viewpoints and debates, as established by political and social elites. This perspective understands the media as influenced by government (Hallin 1986; Herman and Chomsky 2002). The range of legitimate criticism rises when there is elite conflict regarding the issue. Wolfsfeld (1997, 2004) reflects on that in his concept of the relationship as a circle of interdependencies in his *political contest model.* He regards political environment as initiator of change that triggers change in the media environment, which in turn leads to change in political environment, depending on the level of elite consensus and competition among the political environment[9]. The media can advocate or amplify political impact, catalyze, or structure through narratives but they do mainly react to political initiatives (except for investigative journalism). Also Landerer (2013) supports the assumption of interdependence and a mutually beneficial struggle for attention of two very complex and intertwined groups of actors. Robinson (2001: 541) argues in his review on Wolfsfeld's model that it offers a starting point beyond a dichotomous perspective of the relationship of the media and politics in which either one dominates.

The consequences of mediatized politics are numerous and apparent in several developments in the political sphere: *1) Politics personalize.* The concentration is shifting from the party to the people representing it, especially in elections (Vowe 2006). *2) Politics professionalize their media management.* Individual actors need to acquire high media competency (i.e., the ability to make simple short statements rather than giving complicated explanations, or the ability to refrain from body language that can be interpreted in negative ways in TV). Parties and individuals have media advisers, media divisions and (should) engage in pro-active social-media activity (Kepplinger 2002; Pfetsch and Mayerhöffer 2006). *3) Events are shaped by considerations of commercial media logic.* There are events that occur "genuinely" without any connection to the media. Several events are not happening because of the media, but are adapted to media logic – for example party conventions – and thus classical mediatized events. Others are staged for the media – like press conferences. Other events exist solely to gain media attention – pseudo events (Kepplinger 2002; Pfetsch and Mayerhöffer 2006). *4) Contents are shaped by considerations of commercial media logic.* The emphasis is on symbols rather than on content of decisions and implementation, on simple, dramatic, negative, political attacks, conflict and sensational messages rather than on substance and background information (Pfetsch and Mayerhöffer 2006).

---

[9] Complementing is the "multigated" model of news gatekeeping by Livingston and Bennett (2003) differentiating between "reporter driven", "organizationally driven", "economically driven", and "technogically driven" news and the differing official involvement. Also Entman's (2003; 2008) "cascading activation" model proposes a differentiated view of actor's ascending powers to influence the framing of messages according to their position and ideas.

Mediatization of Conflicts

> War is the continuation of politics by other means
>
> — Carl von Clausewitz, 1832

The famous quote by von Clausewitz illustrates that conflict is continuing political inter-action and not replacing it. Thus, do the dynamics and interdependencies of the media and politics as outlined above apply in conflict situations?

Conflict logic and interests Conflicts themselves have undergone strong developments since the end of the Second World War. McQuails (2006) outlines the following: There are fewer conflicts between nation-states, or great powerful states directly, but series of conflicts with global strategic interests over values, ideologies, and resources in which great powers support or control different sides more or less in/-directly. The conflicted parties are often asymmetrical; the definition of terrorism often remains unclear and sometimes subjective. High-technologies have strong influence in the conduct of conflicts. They liberate audiences to a certain extent from images on the consequences of war. This kind of conflict needs good control over information politics and passive audiences (McQuail 2006: 108-114). He further argues that these new, complex, sometimes distant, asymmetrical conflicts over ideologies, humanitarian values, or resources need mobilization and support of the citizen, and the media is regarded as an instrument to gain it. Underlying is the assumption that the media gains access but can be controlled (McQuail 2006). Partially, conflicted parties gain great meaning only through the media, small conflicted parties in asymmetric conflict and especially acts of terrorism need media attention to fulfill their role (Liebes and Kampf 2004).

Assuming that conflict actors need media attention for mobilization and support and that conflict events are highly relevant content for media actors, it is argued that conflict actors like political actors adapt their narration to commercial media needs/logic (Robinson 2004). However, conflict actors do hold information that is highly needed by media actors, hardly accessible without them or not considered trustworthy. Conflict actors (for example PR apparatus of governments and military or militant groups) adapt through professionalized communication, strategic planning of conflict events adapted to media considerations. They further grant access to some media actors and not to others in form of interviews, embedding of journalists into battling groups, press passes (i.e. work allowances in the conflict area), press releases, conferences, etc.

Media logic and constraints For the media, war is not dysfunctional but a major event. War has always been a development boost for the media, be it in technological or economic means (see Dominikowski 2004: on the historical development of media and war relations). Conflicts have very high news value, they are full of immediacy, drama, conflict, negativity, personal stories etc. (See Galtung and Ruge 1965). Accordingly, conflicts have stronger news value than peace processes that are complex, long, calm and need to emphasize the legitimacy of the opponent's beliefs, suffering, priorities and own harm done (Wolfsfeld 2004). In this context Neiger, Zandberg and Meyers (2008) sum up three roles the media can take in conflict: It can define events, construct narratives, frame, and prime events .

However, the media is also constrained by fierce competition over news. The public needs and wants information on how its government or leadership functions and also how to take action for survival. Robinson (2004) doubts that technological and diversifying developments in mass media lead to more independence of media in those conflict contexts. He argues that although "any" information is available online, media actors rarely rely on unofficial sources; 24h-broadcasting leads rather to repetition, sensationalism, the impression of transparency while remaining superficial and refraining from substantial questions and background information.

But especially in conflict the public does not only demand information but also centrally orientation. During crisis phases societies tend to stand strong and united together and may even not want to know information or new narratives that conflict with existing beliefs and narratives. Ethnocentrism, especially during crisis, leads to emphasis of own righteousness and suffering, whereas the rival is reduced to the threat posing to the own society (Liebes 1997; Oren, Nets-Zehngut and Bar-Tal 2015; Wolfsfeld 2004).

Journalists of national media are challenged to reply to both needs. They concurrently confronted with the very challenging task to cover a conflict that affects their own people (including them), they are required to both professional detachment and to convey a message of closeness and belonging to their audience (Orgad 2009). Voicing opposition is very difficult, can even be sanctioned, and official (i.e., governmental) information is often the only source considered reliable. Yet, the decisions taken in exactly these phases are crucial, and the assumption of "national crisis" often leads journalists to rely on official sources and to more willingness to accept governmental restrictions (Liebes 1997: 51; Orgad 2009: 1; Robinson 2004; Wolfsfeld 2004: 39). Establishment sources are perceived as valid and credible and presented as "facts", whereas alternative information are perceived as less credible and presented as "versions or opinions" (Sharvit and Bar-Tal 2007: 214).

That inclines journalists to refrain from a critical watchdog role and narration that opposes hegemonial narration to an extent that could lead to their exclusion from the information circle for the sake of satisfying the need for information. Thereby the recruiting strategy by conflict actors leads to self-censorship and an internalization of elite-ideology, an influences the decisions on the narration of stories (Robinson 2004: 79). Both recruiting strategy and the need to be patriotic leads to a "rally around the flag", the adoption of categories of "us" versus "them" by media during crisis times and "political flak" – attacks on individuals that dare to criticize the official line. Although arguably simplified, the outlined interdependencies and mechanisms indicate why the media during conflict supports the hegemonic system and loses its critical distance, why national needs are assigned more relevance than the public mandate of the media. Hence, as Dominikowski (2004: 79) claims, the media is economically, individually, and thus structurally militarizable (See also Orgad 2009, 2011). McQuail (2006) explains this with Bennett's indexing theory (Bennett 1990). The legitimate range provides the frame for criticism or support of the conflict or its events. McQuail concludes on quite pessimistic tone that the media has no goal for itself but distributing what known sources are willing to give, chosen recipients are willing to hear, and pay for with money and attention (McQuail 2006: 117).

Interdependency Despite the dependency of media actors on information from official sources, also official political actors are dependent on the media. As stated, media attention is a necessary factor in conflicts. While the concrete role of the media in conflicts is debatable, it is accepted that media considerations have impacts on the strategy of the outbreak, course and actions of conflict (McQuail 2006; Wolfsfeld, Frosh and Awabdy 2008). Even further, Wolfsfeld (2001) claims that the fight over media and narrative supremacy is as important as the actual fight on the battle field. He illustrates that conflicted parties are in a contest over (inter-)national sympathy and support, which is often fought over the image of victimhood. This contest can even impact the conflicted parties' to strategic decisions, for example to restrain from responding to a violent attack to avoid damaging images. Or a conflict party may decide for low profile actions rather than big operations. In this perspective, the media itself appears as a weapon that professionalized conflict actors attempt to use it to their advantage (Witzthum 2002; Wolfsfeld 2001). An extreme form of the context for media attention can be seen in terrorism that gains its meaning and ability to both, implement fear in the wide target society and to cause the inner destruction of liberal values for "security reasons", only through media attention (Liebes and Kampf 2004).

In sum, mediatization does not simply describe the dominance of the media system and logic over the political system and logic or vice versa. It rather outlines a process of interdependence, both in mediatized politics and conflicts. Commercial logic of the media and politics have similarities that both can use for their gains. Political actors can use their knowledge over media needs and serve those. They usually initiate changes that the media reacts to, however control over the media developments is limited and can turn against them when their control over the political system shrinks and this appears as a new newsworthy event. In conflict settings, these dynamics are alike but not the same: From the perspective of media actors, conflicts are not dysfunctional as they bear high news values. Their audiences are in great need of information to orient themselves in a challenging situation. However, media competition over information is under special compulsions between 1) the need to get information that is centrally held by official actors, 2) the need to adjust to audiences' necessities, which is initially patriotic and supportive orientation, 3) and the normative obligation to remain independent and objective as members of the society.

The media is of high value for conflicting parties. It is a central platform to gain support for their cause – nationally and internationally. When understanding commercial media logic, they can use its information dependency to a certain extent and emphasize conflict beliefs and narratives. Sometimes national and international communication goals can be contradictory and strategy has to be accustomed. However, these considerations illustrate that recipients are in the highest need for information during conflict times, yet the likelihood to be well-informed is lower than in times of routine.

3 Case – Israel and the World, the Gaza Flotilla and Israeli Media

The theoretical considerations of the previous chapter are applied on a specific segment of the Israeli-Palestinian conflict, namely the interaction between Israel and international actors and in particular the mediated representation of it. Choosing the Israeli-Palestinian conflict as case for the present investigation is suitable for various reasons (see Chapter 1.3): it is one of the longest lasting conflicts. The conflict is protracted and considered intractable. Hence, the socio-psychological infrastructure and especially the ethos of conflict can be applied for the involved conflict societies and its appearance in media representation may be investigated.

This chapter aims to make sense of the very complex interaction between Israel and the Western world. One part is the international community that strongly involves itself in the Israeli-Palestinian conflict or sees itself strongly involved. The other part is Israel, which regards itself repeatedly as threatened and isolated from exactly this international community. Concurrently, both sides tend to polarize. How and why this is the case is illustrated in this chapter. A second aim is the introduction of the concrete cases of this investigation: research on Israeli ethos of conflict and characteristics of Israeli media, and the Gaza flotilla raid.

The first section (see Chapter 3.1) outlines the general context of the interaction between Israel and international actors with focus on the argued mutual polarization. The focus of this investigation is on political actors that are not directly involved in the conflict but involve themselves in various ways. The focus is centrally on European actors, the USA, Russia, and the United Nations (see Chapter 1.5). The chapter states that international interest in Israel and the Israeli-Palestinian conflict is elevated and seeks reasons for it (see Chapter 3.1.1). It proposes factors of identification that may lead to the polarization between international observers of the Israeli-Palestinian conflict and the conflict-involved societies. The interest, involvement and alleged polarization of one group – international media actors – is examined as an example (see Chapter 3.1.2). The Israeli side of this relationship is outlined first with focus on Israel's political international standing and image (see Chapter 3.1.3) and societal understanding of its international position that is largely shaped by collective memory (see Chapter 3.1.4) and is polarizing.

The second section concentrates in particular on the Israeli ethos of conflict, its historical developments and research on it (see Chapter 3.2). The characteristics and development of Israeli media and in particular newspapers are illuminated in the third section (see Chapter 3.3) and in the fourth in particular the events, implications and debates on the Gaza flotilla raid 2010 (see Chapter 3.4) as the chosen crisis event for this investigation. The consequences for the upcoming analysis both from this chapter on the specific setting and from the previous chapter on the theoretical considerations are outlined in the following Chapter 4.

3.1 The International Community and Israel

This chapter examines the relationship between Israel and the international community. It is lead by the argument that the relation is characterized by elevated interest and potential polarization on either side (see Chapter 1.3). The first part investigates the causes of the relevance and attention the international community pays to the Israeli-Palestinian conflict with focus on Israel. These causes further explain the potential to take a position on the conflict and to polarize into dichotomous categories of "pro-Israeli" or "pro-Palestinian".

This investigation focuses on media as battlefield over polarizing narratives. Hence, international media will be illuminated as an example for international interest and polarization in the above mentioned battle over narratives. This chapter will introduce some of the extensive research conducted on international media actors and their alleged bias to either side of the Israeli-Palestinian conflict as indicator of polarization.

The second part of this chapter introduces Israel's international political standing and image. This very complicated standing resonates with popular Israeli perception of its place in the international community that is largely influenced by Jewish history of persecution and isolation. Likewise, it leads to a polarized understanding of international attention up to categorizations of "with or against Israel". The relevant example for this is the importance Israel attributes to convincing the world of its standpoints through public diplomacy (see Chapter 3.1.5).

3.1.1 International Involvement in the Israeli-Palestinian Conflict – why does the Conflict Matter?

> Arabs and Palestinians are still a foreign affair. Israel is an interior one.
>
> — A Dutch Diplomat, Luyendijk and Middelhoek
> 2014

The Israeli-Palestinian conflict is one of the oldest still lasting conflicts (see Chapter 1.5). It certainly does not have the highest death rates, there are calm phases, it is located far away in the Middle East and not in Europe or North-America. Yet, most people in the western world know about it, and often have an opinion about it. The conflict activates people to take to the streets, participate in heated debates, be it online or in numerous events and demonstrations, engage themselves in NGOs, political or sympathy groups that defend either side of the conflicted parties. And there are think tanks and "monitor" organizations that study and report bias of actors, organizations and individuals to either side of the conflict (Shinar 2005: 176). Why is this conflict so interesting and why do people hold, defend and spread opinions about it?

This chapter proposes that different aspects of the Israeli-Palestinian conflict connect to the beliefs and identification of individuals around the globe and therefore have the potential to engage them emotionally and practically. In this argumentation, their standing towards the conflicted parties can tell something about the so called "active bystanders" themselves.

The author and journalist La Guardia outlines the following reasons for international interest in the Israeli-Palestinian conflict in an interview with the BBC: the religious, the socialist, anti-colonial connection, and its role in the conflict between the "West" and Islam (Mansel 2014). These factors are integrated and expanded with more aspects that are considered relevant for identification with Israel in particular and the Israeli-Palestinian conflict in general:

1) The religious connection: The land of Israel/Palestine is one, if not the center for the three monotheistic religions Christianity, Islam, and Judaism. It is hence known to believers around the world as a place they feel a connection with. This varies between mere knowledge and the strong belief in the land as "holy" and "promised" and a certain sense of ownership.

2) History of persecution, mentalities, and responsibility: The Zionist call and later movement was Theodor Herzl's answer to persecution of Jews in Europe. Several conclusions can be drawn from the fact that arose in Europe. 2a) Europeans and in particular Germans discriminated, persecuted, murdered, and burned Jews over centuries, setting new standards to inhumanity. Others refused to grant refuge to those endangered by the unprecedented persecution. Thus, Germany, Europe and the international community hold responsibility either as persecutors or as bystanders refusing to help to the necessity for a Jewish save haven. The chosen form of which became the nation state of Israel. 2b) The Holocaust as the climax of this persecution is considered a catalyst of the foundation of the state of Israel. 2c) Many Israelis have European roots. They do not only share a history and collective memory of persecutors and persecuted, but also culture, value orientation, and often languages – at least in the first generations of immigrants. The connection to Palestinians arises for those considering them as victims of second degree of the persecution of Jews and the Holocaust. Europeans share history with Jews and perceived or real responsibility for the foundation of the state of Israel. Therefore the conflict may lead to a very special consideration and sense of connection to the Israeli-Palestinian conflict of the former persecuted Jews in the supposedly safe country. 2d) The international approval of the Partition Plan of Palestine and hence the foundation of Israel at the United Nations General Assembly in 1947 marks the first great and international decision of the institution's members and concurrently the strong international involvement and positioning towards the state from its beginning on. This too can lead to a sense of connection and responsibility.

3) Connection to pioneering: The Zionist project and its settlement of the land has been from its beginning on a socialist project, especially the *kibbuzim*, agricultural collective communities, symbolize the socialist spirit. The settling and cultivation of the supposedly empty land has parallels to the pioneering of North America through Europeans. Both countries were not empty but populated and both pioneer nations share great sets of beliefs surrounding the emancipation of conquering the land and cultivating it.

4) Connection of ideas on the conflict: The Israeli-Palestinian conflict as well has several characteristics that foster identification. 4a) It is an anti-colonial struggle. In this perspective Jewish Israelis are seen as colonialists. 4b) The conflict is identified as cultural conflict between the West (Israel understood by non-Israelis as a Western society) and the East. It has become identified as a conflict of the Western world against Islam and as a war against terrorism. 4c) The conflict was asymmetric from its beginning on. A clear distinction of "David versus Goliath" is possible but the allocation is in the eye of the beholder (Israel considered as David relates to the young, unequipped, small state of Israel against all the Arab states; or Israel considered as Goliath relates to the military superior and powerful state of Israel against occupied Palestinians), whilst either way observers tend to identify with whomever they perceive as David.

5) Political connection to the conflict: Israel/Palestine are located very strategically within the Middle East, connecting several Arabic countries to the sea, connecting Africa and Asia. Military (nuclear) power can control or endanger many surrounding states that have numerous natural resources and political power.

Consequences – international involvement and polarization   These are some of the factors that can explain the relevance and connection of this conflict to international actors and individuals. While not being complete at all, these factors may explain 1) why the international community is strongly involved and involving itself in the Israeli-Palestinian conflict and 2) why it is often polarizing in its judgment of the conflicted parties.

On 1) As indicated in the factors above the Israeli-Palestinian conflict is in its essence a conflict with elevated international involvement. There are numerous examples for that: 1a) Jews came to Palestine largely as refugees and immigrants from Europe and Russia starting in the late 19th century until the 1950s. Following the 1948 and 1967 war, the

Palestinian population became refugees in the neighbor states. 1b) The conflict broke out under British Mandate, the Partition of Palestine was decided by the United Nations. 1c) The first wars between Israel and its neighbors split the international community (within the blocs of the cold war) to one or the other side. 1d) International involvement became apparent later in numerous peace-initiatives by diverse actors and governments. 1e) There are countless proposals for the "solution" of the conflict by different actors. 1f) The Israeli-Palestinian conflict plays its more than proportional role within the debates and decisions of the United Nations (see Chapter 5.4). An example for the international attention paid to the conflict is the amount of media coverage (see Chapter 3.1.2).

On 2) These factors bear the potential for polarization of the conflict since they serve as connections to the identification of individuals. In a way, the perspective one takes on these issues defines the position one takes on the Israeli-Palestinian conflict. For example, opinions on the USA and its policies, on colonialism, the understanding of the Holocaust and its consequences for perpetrators and victims alike, the perception of responsibility, the understanding who is David and who Goliath, the religious standpoint etc. often define the position taken on the Israeli-Palestinian conflict. Taking into consideration the centrality, controversy and explosiveness of these issues, neutrality or disinterest is often no option when it comes to the Israeli-Palestinian conflict. It may explain the potential of diverse actors to identify completely with the cause and narrative of one conflict party and engage in fierce fights to convince opponents.

Examples of "activated bystanders" are numerous. Solidarity movement groups of both sides ("pro-Israeli" and "pro-Palestinian") are found in every sector of religious, educational, national, and regional life in the western world[10]. They organize demonstrations, especially during crisis times and engage actively in "educational" work to convince the assumed opposing side of their arguments and possible desinterested people. One of the most continuous battlefield in the international arena is the media. But also other institutions and actors are emotionally divided into sections of "biased" and "unbiased" meaning pro-XY or anti-XY (Mansel 2014).

As an example for international polarization and the debate about it, the international media attention of the Israeli-Palestinian conflict is introduced here. Additionally it is

---

[10]Examples for pro-Israeli support groups: "Christians United for Israel" is the largest US-based pro-Israel organization; "Stand with Us – Supporting Israel around the World" is based in the US and emphasizes on campaigns in High Schools and Universities; "The Friends of Israel Gospel Ministry" is an international evangelic christian solidarity group; "Conservative Friends of Israel" are supporters of Israel within the Conservative party in Great Britain; "Friends of Israel" is an initiative of notable individuals under the leadership of former Spanish Prime Minister José María Aznar to defend Israel's right to exist; "European friends of Israel" is a group of members of the EU parliament that support a strong relationship between Israel and Europe. The most popular pro-Israel lobby groups in the USA are: AIPAC and J-Street.

Examples for pro-Palestinian support groups: "the BDS movement" calls for boycott, divestment and sanctions against Israel; "The Palestine Freedom Project" supports grassroot Palestine solidarity groups internationally and coodinates the activities; "Palestine Solidarity Campaign" is a British solidarity group.

considered the counter-part of the later analyzed Israeli media attention of international involvement.

3.1.2 International Media as a Battlefield over Narratives

> The blogosphere and the new media are basically a war zone in a battle for world opinion.
>
> — IDF-spokeswoman upon launching the IDF-YouTube Channel , Mazmudar 2012

When conflicted parties try to win international public support, the media is a central arena. The battle over international support has several actors: On the one hand are the conflicted parties, for whom international media is just another battlefield, the one over international support and sympathy. Their fight is hence over influence and manipulation to shape supportive narratives, ultimately through delegitimization of the Other and self-victimization of the own side (Wolfsfeld 1997, 2001). On the other hand, for actors of international media institutions the conflict is highly relevant due to the conflict's generally high news values (see Chapter 2.4) and the high attention paid to this particular conflict (see Chapter 3.1.1). The following section introduces the attention the media pays to the Israeli-Palestinian conflict, characteristics of the coverage, and the multiple debates and investigations focuses on whether media institutions are biased towards one of the conflicted parties.

Media Attention to the Conflict – The Over-Reported War?

> Jews are news
>
> — dictum

The Israeli-Palestinian conflict has gained elevated media attention since its beginning until today. The amount of media attention paid to Israel-Palestine is apparent in the work force assigned to it. German correspondents build the 4th largest group of correspondents in Israel after Europe, North America and Russia (Hahn, Loennendonker and Schroeder 2008: 144). The whole continent of Africa has just a few more foreign correspondents stationed than Israel. The Israeli "Foreign Press Association" has more than 480 members (FPA Israel 2014). For comparison, the German "Foreign Press Association in Germany" has 400 members (VAP 2014). In this perspective it is not surprising that Segev and Blondheim (2013) find in their study of news sites in 12 countries in 2009 to 2010 that Israel and Palestine are the 5th and 6th most salient countries, just following the USA, China, Great Britain and the Iran. In the Arabic speaking countries and Iran Israel/Palestine are intact the most salient countries. In general Israel and Palestine are mostly found in the top news and world news section. Differences are that Israel is more often found in the "world news" section due to its conflicts with Iran or Turkey as well as in business articles ,whereas Palestine is never found in business categories but in "culture" and entertainment.

The high salience in international media is explained in the conflict's newsworthiness. The conflict does not cease to make a good story. Shinar (2005) argues that in reporting the Israeli-Palestinian conflict "facts are often made to fit familiar paradigms for the sake of a good story" (Shinar 2005: 176). The thoughts of a recent podcast by the BBC, reflecting on its own coverage of the Israeli-Palestinian conflict in the last decades, illuminates what has been perceived a good story (Mansel 2014): It began with the conquering and cultivation of the supposedly empty land while opposing over-powerful enemies. The Jewish settlers met various news values and make up sympathetic heroes. Of special relevance is their transformation from the victims of persecution and Nazi-Germany to active fighters for freedom and self-determination. The founding of the state of Israel shortly after the Holocaust made a positive story out of a horrible, unbearable truth. In the 1950s, BBC coverage was characterized by fear of Arab nationalism, while Israel was seen as European enclave, admired for its construction of Kibbuzim. Palestinians were either portrayed as distant threat or victims, without getting an own voice. Israel was clearly seen as the David versus the Arab Goliath (Mansel 2014).

This perception slowly changed after Israel surprisingly won the Six-Day-War in 1967 and gained control over the West Bank. The early international euphoria changed into narrations of occupation, oppression, and neo-imperialism. The dealing of Israelis with the West Bank, the construction of settlements and the prolonging control over Palestinians changed the narrative. Palestinians gained attention only as terrorists (for example in the Munich massacre in 1972 or the kidnapping of a plane in 1976). The BBC described the Lebanon war in 1982 as a tipping point. Images of Israeli jets bombing Beirut and defenseless populations changed the perception of "David and Goliath". In the late 1980s, during the First Intifada stone throwing Palestinian teenagers were confronted by the Israeli army that appears increasingly as an occupying power (Mansel 2014). Shinar describes the sharp switch of "David and Goliath" in media presentation with expectations international publics have on Israel: "Against a historical image of Jewish weakness in the Diaspora, some assume that the use of power by a Jewish state has been both unexpected and difficult to accept by the media" (Shinar 2005: 176). Still, presentations of Israeli and Palestinian victims are very different. While Palestinians are mainly shown with images of crying and shouting women, stories of Israelis are personalized (the name, age, picture are published details about their life given) and thus enabling more identification (Langenbucher and Yasin 2009: 259;Shinar 2005: 177).

There is another journalistic factor summed up perfectly by a correspondent interviewed by Langenbucher and Yasin (2009): "No place like here." For (war) correspondents, covering the Israeli-Palestinian conflict offers an attractive working field not only due to its reliable continuation of newsworthiness but also due to comparably comfortable living conditions. Israel offers the comforts of a Western-oriented society, with hot weather and beaches. The area of conflict is very small, hence every conflict-point is easily reachable without having to live directly in conflict areas – the West Bank or Gaza – and access is generally granted (besides cases in which the IDF declares areas as "military zones" and bans media personnel from it). Despite censorship, the societies are quite open, people on both sides are well-trained combatants in the battle over narratives and know to speak in quotable manner. Correspondents usually live in Israel and do not have tofly in when major crisis occurs. That also causes a high need for work, hence news. This factor is mentioned especially by those ascribing bias to journalistic coverage of the conflict. Still, this argument, while being part of the overall picture, falls short of explaining the media relevance of the Israeli-Palestinian conflict.

Media Covers the Conflict in a Biased Way – but Whose Bias?

The combination of conflict actors that are eager to influence international media of its narratives and numerous international media actors that are eager to get stories makes a perfect combination for a mediatized conflict and fights over narratives. In their extremes, media narratives are contrasting. Actions are displayed as either self-defense or aggression; actors as either oppressors or victims; Israel either as democracy or as state-sponsored terrorism (Shinar 2005: pp.176). These examples introduce the debate over alleged bias of international media institutions when covering the Israeli-Palestinian conflict. It is an intense and long-lasting debate, used itself as a weapon in the battle over narratives. In the Israeli-Palestinian conflict, the battlefield of narratives is complicated, since its narratives have different terminologies and it is just too easy to mistakenly use terminology that supports either side of the conflicted parties and implies dissent with the Other (see examples in the Table 1).

As apparent in these examples, it is hard to cover the conflict without using terms that might lean to either side or be misleading. Is it a sign of balanced media coverage to give both perspectives the same time and space or should any asymmetry be taken into consideration? In a circle of violence, which side should be presented as acting and which as reacting? A journalist for the Christian Science Monitor is quoted: "[it] is a place where on both sides there is somehow an assumption that if you're not 100 percent for us, then you're an enemy. So, neutral and objective coverage is something that's not regarded as a virtue" (Trudi Rubin in Ghareeb 1983).

Research on the representation of the Israeli-Palestinian conflict in media coverage

An example for the "bias" debate are numerous studies on the international coverage of the Israeli-Palestinian conflict. Some of them and their results will be introduced here.

Table 1 – Examples of Terminology in the Israeli-Palestinian Conflict

Term I	Term II	Term III
West Bank	Judea and Samaria or Disputed territories	Palestine or Occupied territories
Barrier	Security or Separation Fence	Apartheid-Wall
Extremists, vigilantes	Terrorists	Martyrs, Freedom Fighters
killed, died	Neighbourhood	Settlement
	murdered	lynched, slaughtered
	retaliation, response	attack
	Israelis but only relating to Jewish Israelis	Israelis relating to all Israeli citizen
	Arabs relating to Palestinians (in denial of the existence of a Palestinian people)	Israeli Palestinians relating to Palestinians with Israeli citizenship

Especially media actors with international outreach are often judged for their bias – for example the BBC. After an internal unpublished investigation claiming no deliberate bias (Segev and Blondheim 2013), Downey et.al. (2006) find in their report on the BBC coverage "biased terms" that lean to both sides, such as "occupation" for Israel and "terrorists" for Palestinians. Furthermore, Israeli sources than Palestinian sources are used. Barkho (2008) examines the strategy and practice of the BBC in its coverage of the Israeli-Palestinian conflict and finds that while editors are aware of the difficult terminologies of the conflict but the chose vocabulary reflects on the asymmetry of the conflict. Barkho concludes that in the Arabic BBC service both Palestinian and Israeli casualties are trivialized and in the English service Palestinian casualties are undermined. In a further discourse analysis Richardson and Barkho (2009) find that in their dissemination of arguments from each conflict party, the BBC represents the authority-based argumentation of the Jewish Israeli side stronger.

Philo and Berry (2004, 2011) conduct extensive content and audience studies on news in British television (BBC and ITV). They find a pro-Israeli bias due to the lack of historical context given on Palestinians and more emotionalization of Jewish Israeli victims. They argue that the Palestinian perspective is accounted for but not the Palestinian side. They attribute both biases to easier access to Jewish sources and more identification with Jewish Israelis by international journalists. As the introduced studies show, the interest in the BBC coverage of the Israeli-Palestinian conflict is high. However, while all these investigations find a pro-Israeli bias (with emphasis on different aspects) the BBC is perceived in Israel as Pro-Palestinian (see Chapter 7.3).

Werder and Golan (2002) compare the newspaper coverage of Israeli elections in Western newspapers and find that the media representation depends on the relationship between the countries. Ibrahim (2003) analyzes the influences of individual influences of journalists and organizational routines in news production on the representation of the Israeli-Palestinian conflict. She finds in interviews with former and current correspondents in the Middle East that financial pressures, group thinking and crisis journalism perpetuate distortive and stereotyping coverage of Arabs. Other factors are censorships imposed by IDF or Palestinian authorities. The influence of the personal background on the representation however remains unanswered.

Deprez and Raeymaeckers (2010, 2011) study the coverage of the First and Second Intifada in Flemish newspapers. They find that too little background and context is given, but also that in Flemish newspapers the Israeli-supported terminology is used less than the Palestinian-supported terminology. Palestinian victims are more individualized than Israelis. However, whereas in the first Intifada Palestinians were described as victims, during the second Intifada Israelis are seen as victims.

Zelizer, Park and Gudelunas (2002) analyze the coverage of the conflict in the New York Times, the Washington Post, and the Chicago Tribune. They find terminology that is closer to the Israeli perspective than to the Palestinian perspective. Kalb and Saivetz (2007) analyze the coverage of the Lebanon war 2006 in the Arab, British, and US-media. They find that the Arab and in parts the Great Britain media represent Israel as the aggressor whereas the US-media supports Israel. Oehmer (2010) studies German newspapers and finds that Israel is seen both as the main aggressor and as the main victim. Segev and Miesch (2011) study the coverage in five countries and several newspapers and classify them all as very critical of Israel, especially the British newspapers. The Italian media is the most sensational of all the analyzed, while the French and Swiss media are more neutral. The different results of various studies on bias of the international media illustrate a great interest for international perception of the Israeli-Palestinian conflict, an assumption of bias, and different findings as to who is biased.

In sum, the section illustrates that the international media pays great interest to the Israeli-Palestinian conflict and the debate whether it is biased is a central part of it. There are numerous investigations on bias of international media finding bias leaning to either side. The existence of these investigations demonstrates the interest in bias over the Israeli-Palestinian conflict, the challenge to go about it in a balanced manner, and the importance for the conflicted parties to influence the international communities of their narrative. The last section introduced how the entangled societies go about it in social media (see further Chapter 3.1.5).

3.1.3 Israel's Political Position – Isolated and Alone or Local Power?

In the light of high international media attention, involvement and polarization, the question of Israel's international standing is central. Complicated as it is, it serves as basis for polarizations in either direction. Is Israel the small country surrounded by enemies longing for its annihilation, with mostly not very reliable Western partners that are often antisemitic? Or is Israel a regional colonial power, a base of the Western World within the Middle East? Assumptions of this kind can be the outcomes of polarized standpoints. This section analyzes Israel's political standing and its image in international surveys. Most of the following data is taken from a recent report by Sharon et al. for Molad, the Center for the Renewal of Israeli Democracy, on the issue (Sharon et al. 2013: 16).

Israel is isolated geo-politically Firstly, it is the only Jewish state. Second, it is surrounded by neighbors that did not (partially until today) accept the UN-decision to establish the state of Israel, and fought several wars with it, boycotted it and supported Palestinians in various ways. Economic consequences include limited, secret and risky trade with neighbors, but mostly dependence on maritime and air transport; limited tourism and no possibility to benefit from regional growth and regional cultural events. Political consequences include the opposition from Arab states in international institutions; lacking affiliation with a regional group (e.g., was Israel in no working group within the UN until accepted into the "Western European and Others Group" in 2000). The standing improved with established relations with Egypt, Jordan, the end of the boycott in the Oslo Accords, but did not end the regional isolation (Sharon et al. 2013).

Israel concentrates its strategic relations on the West – in the early years predominantly on France and later on the USA. The main trade markets are Europe and North America, both with free trade agreements. Israel is partner at the World Trade Organization of the World Bank, the International Monetary Fund and since 2010 member of the OECD. Israel is a privileged neighbor of the European Union. On the other hand Israel has no free trade agreements or memberships within Asia. Israel's main security support comes from the USA that see Israel as "Non-NATO-ally" and grants it information, equipment, coordination and high financial assistance ($3 billion, plus the Iron Dome system) (Sharon et al. 2013: 18) . The United States protect Israel in the United Nations through its veto-right[11]. The security cooperation with European actors is limited to significant discounts for weapons. But the cultural cooperation is stronger, Israel

---

[11]Between 1972 and 2011, the United States vetoed 202 Security Council resolutions, 49 of them were directed against Israel (condemnations of policies on Palestinians and calls for evacuation of the occupied territories) and nine called for Palestinian right to self-determination (Sharon et al. 2013: 60). Details under "US vetoes at the UN Security Council" from 1972-2002 at: http://www.phon.ucl.ac.uk/home/geoff/UNresolutions.htm [accessed October 20, 2014].

is integrated in European sports and events such as the Eurovision Song Contest due to the lack of regional affiliation. This reflects on and perpetuates the western orientation of Israel's dominant culture, economics, security, diplomacy despite its location in the Middle East (and a significant population that stems from that area). Israel is thus regionally isolated, but not internationally (Sharon et al. 2013: 18).

Israel's diplomatic standing is complicated due to its conflict reality   Despite its orientation towards western countries and institutions, its conflict situation has negative consequences on its integration in institutions and bilateral relations. The KOF Political Globalization index 2012[12] shows that in both parameters Israel lags behind most countries of its regional reference group (e.g., Egypt, Morocco, Tunisia, Jordan). A membership in NATO is bound to conditions that are not reachable in the near future (a peace accord, a membership request from both Israelis and Palestinians, and the approval of the UN-security council) and would not make sense, since Israel cannot access most areas of NATO operations (Sharon et al. 2013: 26). Israel did not ratify the five conventions of the UNESCO for full membership due to tensions on the West Bank and East Jerusalem. Not only in international institutions, but also in bilateral relations, the course Israel chooses within the conflict and its perception pose severe challenges.

Problematic matters are human rights violations by Israel, its policies towards Palestinians. Main legal disagreements concern the legality of the occupation of the West Bank and the blockade on Gaza. This basic disagreement leads to numerous condemnations of Israel, calls for the halt of settlement construction, display of disappointment by EU or US-leaders, lost patience or support. After hopes for peace in the 1990s and the Second Intifada in the early 2000s, the responses chosen such as the separation barrier, the blockade of Gaza, reenforced settlement construction, several wars on Lebanon and Gaza, restrictive and ethnocentric laws, the relations with Europe and the USA especially with the Netanyahu administrations are complicated. A recent example is the recognition of the Palestinian Authority as "non-member-observer-state" in the UNESCO with a very strong majority of 138 votes in favor, 9 against and 41 abstaining in 2011 (Keane and Azarov 2012). Israel's response, to construct within the E1 zone gained even more criticism as it would finally split the Palestinian areas in the West Bank and render any nation-state-building impossible. Another example is the halted process of granting Israel special partnership with the EU following the Gaza war 2008-09 and the EU-guidelines published in 2013 that distinguish between Israel and settlements, restricting any agreement with institutions that are active within Palestinian territories (Sharon et al. 2013: 30)

---

[12]The KOF index is based on the globalization index for the Foreign Policy magazine. It is calculated annually for 181 countries and uses broad, comprehensive sets of data. In 2012, Israel is 58th on the Political Globalization Index out of 181; 29th of the 34 OECD states. This number dropped dramatically, in 2014 Israel is 99th on the Political Globalization Index. The components of the ranking are: Embassies within the country, membership in international organizations, Participation in UN security Council Missions, International Treaties (Dreher 2014; Sharon et al. 2013).

Israel's international image is poor   International polls based on interviews with citizen often show a more dramatic picture in which Israel has a very negative image. Two examples are the Anholt Nation Brands Index and the BBC world poll. The Anholt Nation Brands Index (now: The Anholt-GfK Roper Nation Brands Index) measures the reputation of nations through polls on 20.000 people in 20 countries (on 50 countries). It claims upon its inclusion of Israel in the quarterly Index in 2006 that Israel has the most negative image ever measured and reaches the bottom of almost each question (in total place 36 of 36). Israel is perceived as behaving the least responsible in areas of international peace and security. It is ranked amongst the last places interviewees would want to work in, live in, visit or feel welcome in. The report concludes that "the political aspects of the country's image appear to be contaminating perceptions of other areas of national interest which, in theory, should be entirely unrelated" (Anholt 2006: 5). The BBC conducts a yearly poll on 24 countries and the influence these are perceived to have by others. For several years, Israel ranked on the fourth last place, meaning its influence was mainly seen as a negative, just a bit less negative than North Korea, Iran and Pakistan. This has improved several points on the scale between 2013 and 2014, but remains at the last position. Especially European countries perceive Israel as having a negative influence, whereas Russia and Turkey perceive it as less negative than before (Globescan, Pipa 2014).

Results like those raise the question why Israel is seen as extremely negative. A possible answer lies in deeply rooted antisemitism within many societies. Israel might furthermore be judged differently from non-democratic societies because it is a democratic state (at least to the Jewish Israeli population[13]) with proclaimed Western values and an adherence values such as human rights. Moreover, Israeli policies and events regarding the Israeli-Palestinian conflict have a constantly high news value (see above) and the continuous media coverage may contribute to the formation of opinions. However, the polls regarding Israel's international image support the above-mentioned polarization.

3.1.4 Israeli Understanding of its Position and Image – Is there an Eternal Enemy?

The previous chapter shows that international media attention is high and often polarized. At the same time, Israel's political standing is complicated because of the conflict and its image is very negative. How does a country cope with that? Just as individuals care for their image, so do politicians, governments and countries for their international standing (Straughen 2011).

The leading argumentation is that Israel engages in public diplomacy but that it has a special meaning and value in Israeli society. This is indicated by several reasons: 1) As

---

[13]Shinar (2005: 179) describes Israel as "internal democracy for Israeli Jews, manipulative democracy for Israeli Arabs, and no democracy for Palestinians."

outlined above, Israel's international standing is complicated. It is the only Jewish state and not affiliated to its regional bloc but rather in conflict with some neighbors. Israel aspires to meet and keep international Western standards but is challenged to meet those norms due to the conflict reality (Sofer 2004: 3). 2) Israel's special attitude towards the international community and hence the efforts to shape its image are found in Jewish tradition, the long history of Diaspora, persecution, and beliefs stemming from those. Both Israel's political and economic standing and its history shape a very special kind of public diplomacy, *hasbara that* is introduced in the end of this chapter.

To understand the Israeli attitudes towards the international community and hence its policies towards it, a closer look at Jewish history and politics is necessary. Jewish life in the Diaspora has been characterized by holding heritage of Jewish law and a deep sense of secrecy towards the outside world. Lots of patterns and normative institutions arose from the position of living as minority in often hostile environments. That lead to high in-group solidarity, self organization, a strong sense of a shared fate based on a strong distinction between Jews and non-Jews (Dowty 1999: 8).

History of segregation stemming from within   Jewish tradition and religious practices are deeply rooted in compliance with numerous day-to-day practices, prayers and holiday customs. They serve the segregation and ultimately the survival of Jewish people in Diaspora for several thousand years. The practices include a special diet, the prohibition of intermarriage and strict religious rules that define everyday routines. The separation of Jewish people is often referred to as people made to "dwell in loneliness" (Bar-Tal and Antebi 1992*a*: 634; Bar-Tal and Antebi 1992*b*: 253).

History of segregation stemming from the outside world   The Jewish Diaspora separation of the people since the destruction of the Second Temple in Jerusalem 70AD is characterized by a long history of discrimination, hatred, anti-Jewish and antisemitic hostilities, persecution, restrictions, forced conversions, pogroms, and the climax in the Holocaust. Accordingly there is an external segregation on behalf of the outside non-Jewish world. It is perceived as hostile or at best ignorant or indifferent, and self-reliance is seen as the only answer towards it. Anti-Judaism and antisemitism shape Jewish experience in Europe more than anything else (Pardo and Peters 2010). Even before, according to biblical tradition, the history of the people of Israel is shaped by destructive wars, slavery, attempts to destroy the people, and diaspora. Hence, there is the fundamental religious belief in an eternal enemy ready to destroy the nation of Israel that exists and changes in every generation. It is called *Amalek*[14]. One source is found in the *Haggadah* prayers read at *Pessach* "For more than once they [other nations] have risen against us to destroy

---

[14]Amalek was the "First Born of a Mixed People" – Esaus son out of wedlock – who since the Exodus of the Israelites from Egypt seeks their destruction. His power rises whenever the Israelites do not follow the commandments (Mueller 2009: 2). Although comparisons to Amalek are prominently used in

   © Frank & Timme   Verlag für wissenschaftliche Literatur

us; in every generation they rise against us and seek our destruction. But the Holy One, blessed be He, saves us from their hands". Remembering and loathing the cruelties done by Amalek is a *Mitzwat Azeh*, a law of deed remembered in the *Shabat-* and *Purim* readings (Mueller 2009: 3). Antisemites and the Nazis, as for some the Palestinians or Iran are hence one phase within an endless line of Amaleks.

The belief in Amalek is not reduced to the religious sector but very alive in political argumentation. A prominent example is Prime Minister Netanyahu and his comparisons of changeable rivals with Amalek. Beinart (2015) lists the following examples: In 2010 Netanyahu says in Auschwitz "We won't forget to be prepared for the new Amalek, who is making an appearance on the stage of history and once again threatening to destroy the Jews"; 2015 in US-Congress, comparing the regime in Iran to Haman, "Amalek's genocidal heir from the Book of Esther and to Nazi-Germany "The days when the Jewish people remained passive in the face of genocidal enemies, those days are over." One commandment of action (Mitzwat Azeh) is to remember Amalek and his actions[15] and is part of the great role collective memory of persecution takes in Jewish identity (Mueller 2009: 2).

Zionism was and is regarded as the answer to the continuity of Amalek, Anti-Judaism and antisemitism. The movement arose in the late 19th century from the understanding that orthodox Diaspora-Judaism would always be subjected to Anti-Jewish hatred. Secularization or assimilation offered also no possibility for emancipation since the European societies were increasingly antisemitic. It aspired for a change in Jewish history in hostile environments and sought an escape from segregation (Dowty 1999: 3). Instead it connected to ideologies of socialism, nationalism, liberalism, and disconnected from what was perceived as weak and shameful Diaspora Judaism, while seeking for a "New Jew", a strong, self-sufficient Jew able to cultivate the land and defend him-/herself (Zuckermann 2009: 45). By building a nation-state in a "land without people for a people without land" (Zionist slogan) the people sought to emancipate as human beings and liberated themselves from discrimination and persecution. However, neither was the land empty of people, nor did the foundation of the state of Israel lead to peace and the end of persecution. "It is a stunning irony that the state founded to solve the age-old problem of Jewish insecurity has itself been plagued by chronic insecurity" (Dowty 1999: 4). Surrounded by hostile Arab states, the young state of Israel again finds itself alone amidst the internal and external threats to national and personal survival that are, for example expressed literally by Arab leaders as intention to destroy Israel (David 2012; Teitelbaum and Segall 2012).

---

contemporary Politics, from a religious perspective it is debated whether Amaleks action is reduced to biblical days (See for example Rabbi Sachs http://www.rabbisacks.org/face-evil-beshalach-5775/).

[15]An annual reading on Purim, the holiday to remember the genocide that was avoided by Esther, is Deuteronomy 25:17-18: "Remember what the Amalekites did to you along the way when you came out of Egypt. When you were weary and worn out, they met you on your journey and attacked all who were lagging behind; they had no fear of God."

Internal and external segregation lead to a sense of isolation Merom (1999) argues for a sense of exceptionalism that derives from the sense of being abandoned while maintaining a strong in-group identification. Besides the argued exceptionalism, Dowty (1999) emphasizes a deep sense of isolation in a hostile world, reinforced through the history of persecution, the Holocaust, the lacking international response, the loneliness in facing the neighboring Arab states ready and willing to conquer the just founded state of Israel in 1948. During the following decades and their crises and wars this sense only strengthened. Every crisis is seen as a threat to the very survival of the state. The real threat and subjective threat have merged, leading to a strong focus on security as a central belief of the society (see Chapter 3.2) but also to mistrust of the international community. The United Nations is famously called "UM-Shoom" (UN-nonsense) by David Ben Gurion, and the Arab-Palestinian-Israeli conflict is often not seen as rooted in objective disputes over territory and sovereignty etc. Contemporary criticism, hostility, or terrorism is interpreted within the framework of Jewish history, predominantly the Holocaust but also the general history of persecution and hence often polarized as acts of antisemitism (Dowty 1999: 6). Arian (1995: 27) concludes:

> even mainstream Zionist parties still tend to reject a geopolitical explanation of international conflict and persist in analyzing the Israel-Arab conflict in the spirit, and often in the lexicon, of the persecution suffered by Jews in most European countries and in some of the countries of the Muslim world.

This can be extended to perception of international involvement in general. And in this sense, objective threat and isolation is magnified by subjective reality.

The sense of isolation leads to siege mentality Bar-Tal and Antebi argue in 1992 that the reactions of Jewish Israelis towards international actors in times of crisis can be understood within the context of siege mentality, the conviction that "the world is hostile toward them and no one will make any special effort to save them in a case of disaster" (Bar-Tal and Antebi 1992*b*: 253). Differing from the societal beliefs comprising the ethos, this is a temporary state of mind that can be activated during crisis, and weakened when these conditions change. Dowty emphasizes the temporary character and calls Israel an "interrupted society" that closes up during crisis but goes back to individualism after crisis and rejects the idea of siege behavior. Still, both do not contradict each other (Dowty 1999: 8). Bar-Tal and Antebi also find that certain groups tend to hold siege mentality stronger than others, especially religious people and people with hawkish political positions.

Siege mentality implies and leads to mistrust, and a high sensitivity towards information that might show negative intentions, and the tendency to perceive ambiguity as supporting the expected negative intentions. The tendency is to rely on oneself and even use drastic measures to ensure survival. A basic perception of international criticism is based on the conclusion that the world has lost moral grounds to criticize Israel after not preventing the Holocaust (Bar-Tal and Antebi 1992*b*: 264). The ultimate consequence of the siege mentality is that Israel has to defend itself by all means, since there is no "back-up plan" to rely on. The fear over the existence of the state of Israel, the fear over annihilation, the fear to be "thrown to the sea" by Arab neighbors is real and deeply rooted in historical experience and "catastrophic thinking" (see Chapter 2.2). The assumption of a siege mentality in Jewish Israeli society is supported by surveys of the Peace Index[16] that show that between 61% (December 2010) and 77% (August 2010) of Jewish Israelis believe that the negative attitudes of Europeans and Americans towards Israel will not change whatever course Israel decides to take within the conflict. 39% (December) to 56% (August) are convinced that the "world is against Israel"; and 49% (December) to 68% (August) believe that criticism on Israel is rooted in antisemitism (Yaar and Hermann 2010*a,b*). The difference between the surveys in August and December indicate that siege mentality is perceived stronger following a crisis than in routine times. The August survey was conducted just two months following the Gaza flotilla raid that lead to strong international reactions and criticism (see Chapter 3.4). In comparison, the numbers in December show a less strong adherence of siege mentality.

In sum, Jewish history and culture is characterized by a dual isolation. From within it derives from customs and tradition requiring segregation from non-Jewish people. From outside it stems from discrimination, persecution, and segregation by non-Jewish people. The historical experience and its political continuation led to a sense of isolation in a hostile world and to siege mentality. In this sense, daily politics are at least partly evaluated in the light of historical and collective memory. Siege mentality, with its perpetuation in contemporary perception of international involvement leads to polarization of the latter into categories of "with or against Israel". Two of the relevant implications touch 1) the way public diplomacy is approached and conducted (see following section); 2) the way policies regarding the conflict are perceived. Perceived isolation can lead to a chosen isolation in which Israel disconnects from caring for its international standing and does what it deems right (Shinar 2005: 176). This illustrates the relevance of media representation of international involvement.

3.1.5 Israel's Public Diplomacy – A Country Explaining Itself by all Means?

One part of the complex interaction between Israel and the Western world are Israeli attempts to influence its international standing. In a setting of mutual polarization (see Chapter 3.1.1 and 3.1.4), Israel engages in enormous efforts to improve its international image. Israeli public diplomacy is a part of the struggle over narratives conflict societies

---

[16]The Peace Index is a survey conducted monthly by the Guttman Center for Surveys within the Israel Democracy Institute. It monitors Israeli public opinion regarding the Israeli-Palestinian conflict (See www.peaceindex.org).

engage in over international acceptance (see Chapter 2.3). 2) It shows the meaning the international image has for Israel. 3) It illustrates the Israeli part of polarization of the Western world and efforts to influence it. 4) One of the central arguments regarding the negative international image of Israel (see Chapter 3.1.3) is that Israel repeatedly fails in its public diplomacy. This section illustrates that the Israeli public diplomacy is pro-active and the efforts to explain Israel to the world are sophisticated.

Countries engage in efforts to shape their image through public diplomacy (Gilboa 2008*a*; Mor 2006; Nye 2008). It is understood as "efforts by the government of one nation to influence public or elite opinion in a second nation for the purpose of turning the foreign policy of the target nation to advantage" (Manheim 1994: 132). A widely discussed channel of public diplomacy is media. Mediated public diplomacy (Entman 2008; Gilboa 2001; Sheafer and Gabay 2009; Sheafer and Shenhav 2009; Sheafer et al. 2014) "involves shorter term and more targeted efforts using mass communication (including the internet) to increase support of a country's specific foreign policies among audiences beyond that country's borders" (Entman 2008: 88).

Public diplomacy has a special name in Hebrew that reflects on the perception of its task. It is called *hasbara*, a term that can be translated as "explanation". This shows a very limited, defensive approach of public diplomacy reduced to justification and self-explanation (Sheafer and Shenhav 2009; Shenhav, Sheafer and Gabay 2010). There is a great debate on the role and effectiveness of Israeli hasbara in Israeli public, the media, and the academic world. A very popular assumption in Israel underlying the debate is that Israel's international image would be much better if only Israel could explain itself properly (Sherman 2012). Accordingly, the debate on the hasbara apparatus is often polarized and politically motivated. „It is customary to blame Israeli diplomacy for many lapses and deficiencies: its lack of foresight and long-range planning, a susceptibility to impulse and crisis exigencies, and a paucity of originality and inventiveness" (Sofer 2004: 1). Strong criticism towards hasbara is sometimes connected to emphasis on the internationally biased, distortive and hostile attitudes towards Israel that hasbara has to overcome but fails to do. A strong example is Gilboa, who emphasizes in his comprehensive critique: 1) the lack of a strategy and coordination of messages, 2) the financial resources 3) strong competition on behalf of the sophisticated anti-Israeli public diplomacy (Gilboa 2006: 1). Sofer (2004) and Sheafer and Shenhav (2009) support this criticism and search for reasons within the history of Jewish politics that are characterized by suspicion of foreign powers and hence suspicion of public diplomacy. They call for a general change of attitude away from explaining actions and towards planning policy strategically and suitable for international interaction[17] and pro-active creation of events and building of relationships. Just as some criticize the failure of a weak and short-sighted hasbara, others glorify the

---

[17]An example: Instead of explaining why tanks were positioned at a place one should ask if positioning the tanks there is advisable when taking public opinion into account

Israeli hasbara apparatus as a huge machine that pro-Palestinian efforts have no chance against (Erdem 2011).

The fields of hasbara activity Following a critical report by the State comptroller in 2007, the apparatus underwent a reform that changed the situation. Greenfield (2012) investigates the Israeli hasbara for the think tank Molad, the Center for the Renewal of Israeli Democracy, based on seven indicators for effective public diplomacy: central coordination and management of messages, informal public diplomacy, branding, long-term cooperation, multi-dimensional media strategies, dynamic crisis management of messages and strategic targeting of populations). Their report is based on governmental sources and examples of hasbara activities will be introduced in the following (Greenfield 2012).

All national hasbara activities are now coordinated directly by the "National Hasbara Forum" that is subordinated to the Prime Minister (the coordination includes the IDF, police, Ministry of Foreign Affairs, Ministry of Defense, governmental media departments, and the Ministry of Public Diplomacy and Diaspora affairs). It establishes standards for dynamic/suitable messages, spokespeople, material, training, delegations for all bodies, and coordinates production and distribution of messages (Greenfield 2012: pp.28).

A central part of the activities is *informal hasbara*, since official messages are limited to diplomatic structures. Numerous initiatives engage the general public, volunteers and youth in Israel and abroad. One project is "We are all Ambassadors". It aims at organizing Israelis speaking foreign language to talk to the foreign media during crisis situations. Prominence was gained by the *"Masbirim"* (Explaining Israel) project that equips traveling Israelis with arguments, information on history, politics, demography and rhetorical skills (body language, proper listening) to actively defend Israel's image abroad (masbirim.gov.il). The campaign includes booklets distributed at the airports, workshops for tour guides, clips in television, radio and internet (Eichner 2010; Greenfield 2012; Hershkovitz 2011). This campaign was criticized for promoting right-wing opinions that are not consensus and an "imaginary country" (Livneh 2010; Associated Press 2012).

A focal point are the messages in *social media and talkbacks* – therefore volunteers and high school students are trained to post arguments supporting Israel in the social media or in European news sites and online surveys. Other projects activate students on campuses of universities to organize events, and educate Jewish students from around the world in Israel ("birthright" trips). Other in-official activities of hasbara include founding straw-companies that can pursue diplomatic goals free from constraints (Greenfield (2012: pp.38); Ravid 2010)[18].

---

[18]Especially in crises in the last years, the media battlefield has increasingly extended to social media which both, Hamas and IDF use extensively. Whereas the Lebanon war 2006 was called the most blogged war (and hence a milestone for intense conflict-communication outside mainstream media), the Gaza conflict 2012 is the first war announced on Twitter by the IDF. The analysis of Twitter success is simple when studying the prominence of either side is the contest over popular hashtags (#Israelhates versus

Branding of Israel's the attractiveness is given high attention. The budget was raised from 10 million ILS to 100 million ILS (about 2 million € to 20 million €). The activities are mainly online and central messages include the Israeli environment, science and technology, arts, diverse populations, lifestyles and support of people in need. The branding includes trainings for journalists to aid them identify with these values, organization of parades, exhibitions, and cultural events abroad. In this light diaspora communities gain new meaning, since they are assumed to have national impact. Seminars are held in critical communities, trainings conducted to build "Zionist leadership in the Diaspora", material produced adapted to needs of different organizations. This is a milestone in the complicated relationship between Israel and the Diaspora (Shefler 2012). Again volunteers (students and retired people) are engaged for translation and production of web pages. Pro-Israeli lawyers are trained to deal with "delegitimization against Israel", meaning attempts to discredit Israel internationally and legally. Special attention is gained by the attempts to brand Israel as a gay-friendly place (and refuge for Arabs within an intolerant Middle East), a tactic often referred to by opponents as pink-washing (Bohrer 2014; Greenfield 2012; Associated Press 2012).

There is further a *multidimensional communication strategy* that has several levels (the daily coordination with foreign media, coordination of messages for foreign and local media in Israel and abroad, Arab media, and media spokespeople). It includes strong presence in social networks by the different Israeli institutions (army, ministries, embassies, diplomats) and again in-official messages on blogs and news sites to counter anti-Israeli messages (Greenfield 2012).

Crisis management is dynamic and is updated in monthly meetings with several advisers, monitoring sites to identify crises. There is a "virtual situation room" engaging several thousand volunteers during crisis times to communicate online. One goal is specific targeting of senior actors of governments, organizations or media institutions. Hence, business, academic and religious elites are invited by Israeli governments to tours in Israel (Jansezian 2011; Greenfield 2012).

The authors of the Molad report conclude that hasbara has undergone an effective reform. What has been criticized as re-active "explanation" of policies and events after they happened is turned into a pro-active multifaceted and sophisticated public diplomacy. Based on these outlined seven factors for effective public diplomacy Greenfield (2012) concludes that hasbara has undergone a strong reform, from re-active to pro-active multifaceted and sophisticated public diplomacy. Accordingly, he argues against a connection between the negative image of Israel and the often blamed failures of the hasbara apparatus as

---

#Israelloves (Sacharoff 2011). Although the Israeli government launched large and professional social media campaigns it clearly lost the war over online sympathy in the Gaza crisis 2014 as the hashtag #GazaUnderAttack was used in 4 million Twitter posts compared to 170,000 for #IsraelUnderFire (Rudoren 2014).

> It is difficult to find any nation, even those embroiled in long-term conflict situations that trains civilians to take part in hasbara messaging for its policies while abroad, or that sends groups of young citizens to advocate its position on campuses worldwide. It is no less difficult to find other nations that enjoy such well-developed, global support on institutional, communal, and private levels, especially in North America and Europe.(Greenfield 2012: 52)

Assuming a strong and pro-active hasbara apparatus that answers to the above mentioned criticisms raises questions why Israel's image did not improve? Shinar (2005) claims that Israel was not successful in convincing of its arguments of "anxiety", the "never again" motif, its respect for human rights. Pfeffer (2012) argues, debating "the hasbara problem" is an excuse that cannot replace policies that are compromising Israel's image. The Anholt Nation Branding Index (Anholt 2006) in its special analysis of Israel's image shows how nations can brand their images by defining their products and marketing it to very well-defined audiences. Still the author argues that the effects could never be measured:

> This is surely because all countries, at some level, get the reputation they deserve – either by things they have done, or by things they have failed to do – and it is astonishingly naïve to imagine that the deeply rooted beliefs of entire populations can possibly be affected by advertising or public relations campaigns unless these campaigns truthfully reflect a real change in the country itself. With questions of national image, both the problem and the solution always have far more to do with the product than with the packaging. (Anholt 2006: 5)

He concludes that sophisticated and diverse repetition of the argument fail to convince, but also be counterproductive. People mistrust foreign powers that try to convince of their policy. The only effective way is a change of the political direction, and faced with this option, unpopularity is the cheaper price to pay (ibid.).

In sum, this chapter aimed at making sense of the very complex interaction between Israel and the Western world. The complexity is apparent in opposing tendencies that are interrelated. One part is the international community that strongly involves itself in the Israeli-Palestinian conflict or sees itself strongly involved. The Israeli-Palestinian conflict comprises numerous factors for identification (historical, religious, political, etc.) that may lead to opinionated and polarizing involvement. This is apparent in the high international media coverage of the conflict and the ongoing debate on their alleged bias. The other part is Israel, which regards itself repeatedly as threatened and isolated from exactly this international community. Its international standing is complicated by its conflict reality and the efforts to improve its image are very high.

Concurrently, both sides tend to polarize. International actors and individuals judge the conflict and its parties, and the claim of neutrality is often judged by others or themselves in categories of "pro-Israeli" or "pro-Palestinian". Israel at the same time, while denigrating the relevance of the international community polarizes its place in it into categories of "with or against Israel". Underlying are historical experiences and the resulting assumption of isolation and loneliness. Israel further engages in enormous efforts to "explain" itself, its intention and what it believes is misunderstood.

3.2 The Development of the Israeli Ethos of Conflict

It is one of the central aims of this investigation to analyze the adherence of the ethos of conflict in Israeli newspaper representations. The concept of the ethos of conflict as part of the socio-psychological infrastructure of societies in conflict is introduced in 2.1. Most of the research on the societal beliefs comprising the ethos of conflict is conducted on the Jewish Israeli society, hence it is possible to use a variety of studies explaining its development over the last decades, its specifications, functions, and permeation into cultural products. In preparation of the first analysis of the ethos of conflict in media this section introduces the current Jewish Israeli conflict ethos, based on the state of the art.

The overall ethos of the Jewish Israeli society includes beliefs in democracy and . Both are part of the declaration of Independence ("Israel is a Jewish Democratic state"). There is serious debate until today whether and declared Democracy contradict or complement each other. Especially the belief in is easily connected to the core beliefs of the ethos of conflict: about victimization, the justness of one's own goals, and the delegitimization of the rival. That means the own goal to claim and cultivate the land and to an own Jewish state is regarded as justified. At the same time Palestinian goals to a Palestinian state on the same territory may appear as illegitimate and hence hostilities by them seen as unjust and hence the own group victimized by Palestinian aggression (Oren 2009: 14).

Societal beliefs are very enduring. As the example of Israel's history and the development of Jewish Israeli beliefs illustrates, they may change over time. Reasons for changes in the ethos of conflict can be events or developments that contradict the existing beliefs or emerging beliefs that contradict each other. This creates a cognitive imbalance that groups can cope with by denial, cognitive differentiation, adjustment or change of the belief (Oren 2009). Beliefs cease to be societal when they are not shared anymore, do not serve the leaderships' justification and do not appear in cultural products. This may have an impact on the course of conflict when beliefs of one's own justness and ability to sustain the conflict change as well as beliefs on the threat posed by the opponent. In this case, societies are ready for a change in the conflict. As the following parts illuminate, in Israeli history, these developments take time and are related to policy changes (Oren 2009: 4). Oren investigates the development of Israeli societal beliefs based on polls, their appearance in cultural products and political platforms. She outlines the relations and contradictions between beliefs and strategies and their development over four phases, from 1967 until the 21st century. The following elaborations are based on her findings and supported by Bar-Tal and others (Bar-Tal 2007a; Bar-Tal, Halperin and Oren 2010; Oren and Bar-Tal 2006).

Phase I from 1967 to 1977 This first analyzed phase characterizes the peak of the intractable conflict. Just after winning the 1967 Six Day war Israel is isolated and surrounded by rivals and begins the occupation[19] of a whole people in the West Bank and Gaza with all its costs (Halperin et al. 2010). The Yom Kippur war in 1973 and its difficult experience of a surprising attack by several neighboring countries had a deep effect on Israeli society and politics. Oren (2009: 15) finds that the beliefs of the ethos of conflict were held very strongly. That means, they were shared by at least 75% of the Jewish Israeli society, used by the leadership to explain its policies, found in the narratives of cultural products and education material. A strong basis is the belief in the right of Jewish people to settle in Israel () – although the borders of the territory served as source of great controversy in this decade and the following. The existence of a Palestinian people and hence their claim to a state of their own was still denied. Palestinians and Arabs were presented in cultural and educational material in a stereotypical negative simplistic way and delegitimized and held responsible for the conflict. Beliefs regarding the threat to Israel and the priority of establishing security were high as well as beliefs on being the victim, while glorifying Israel, a very abstract belief in peace, patriotism and unity. Oren argues that the 1967 war was perceived as a moral and humane act of self-defense. Throughout the decades the army's conduct is described within the framework of its "purity of arms", and often the term "shooting and crying" (based on a book) was used to emphasize the moral dilemmas of Israeli soldiers. Central contradictions in this phase are 1) the negation of a legitimate opponent and an abstract, dreamy belief in peace; and 2) beliefs in security (and necessary violations of liberties through censorship), 3) the justness of the occupation of Palestinians and 4) beliefs in democracy. These contradictions were dealt with mainly through denial. Israel was perceived as strong enough to withstand the Palestinian threat, thus the need for peace and also ripeness for a peace process was not very high (Bar-Tal, Halperin and Oren 2010; Dowty 1999; Halperin et al. 2010; Oren 2009).

Phase II from 1977 to 1987 The Yom Kippur war had deep after-effects on the society. The Labor party, in power since the establishment of the state, proved ineffective and corrupt. It was time for a change. In 1977, the Likud party came into leadership for the first time. Another central event for the conflict is the visit of Egypt's Premier Sadat and the end of Israel's isolation in the region. The society became more pluralistic and less

---

[19]In international law, occupation is a formal procedure between an occupying force and an occupied population. It is temporary, the occupant is not allowed to induce permanent changes into the territory, it is an unplanned product of military activities, hence regarded as military occupation. In practice, for the Israeli-Palestinian Conflict, this is a long-term status. It is more accurately defined as "effective control of a certain power (be it one or several states or an international organization), over a territory which is not under the formal sovereignty of that entity, without the volition of the actual sovereigns of that territory"(Benvenisti 2012: 4). Prolonged occupation (longer than 5 years) raises questions regarding the intentions of the occupier and as suggested by (Halperin et al. 2010) has socio-psychological implictations for occupying societies.

attached to the parties that were central in the foundation of the state (Caspi and Limor 1999: 169; Doron 1998). In polls, movies, school books and party platforms Palestinians were increasingly accepted as a nation in the 1980s and -90s (Podeh 2002). Oren outlines that Arabs were less viewed as one group, peace beliefs become more realistic in character and connected to concrete steps such as negotiations and compromises. Patriotism was less important and the overall ethos was less present in statements by the leadership and cultural products. Still there were contradictions: The belief in the goal of the Arabs to eliminate Israel persisted and coexisted with modified peace beliefs that were perceived as politically possible. These contradictions were addressed by a distinction between those Arab nations "willing to eliminate Israel" and those Israel could possibly draw peace agreements with. In this way, cognitive differentiation helped addressing these contradictions. Oren concludes that due to Israeli remaining beliefs in superiority in the conflict with the Palestinians there was no need to solve the conflict and the status quo appeared as most desirable (Oren 2009).

Phase III from 1987 to 1993   began with the outbreak of the First Intifada, which came as a shock to many Israelis that lost the belief in Israeli supremacy. Beliefs such as patriotism, delegitimization and siege mentality – the fear to be alone in the world – are less apparent. Jewish Israelis are less opposed to a Palestinian state after the Intifada (70%) than before (90%). The fears of Arabs wanting to eliminate Israel also decrease further, likewise beliefs in victimization; there was a greater ripeness to accept a solution of two states and in general to accept a Palestinian partner to talk to (Yassir Arafat) as representative of Palestinians. The violence during the First Intifada, and especially the perception of soldiers versus stone throwing youngsters, gave rise to deep contradictions between the beliefs in democracy and the justness of one's own goals, and security. Further contradictions were the beliefs in peace, democracy, a greater Jewish Israel, the belief in democracy, and the Jewish majority of the state. There was greater awareness of these contradictions and they were dealt with by willingness to give up territories (the West Bank). There was less belief in Israeli superiority after the experiences of the First Intifada. Moreover, continuing the conflict appeared risky and costly and the status quo lost desirability, and the feeling of threat decreased. These developments lead to a stronger ripeness for peace and higher chances to achieve it as apparent in the Peace Process started in 1993 (Oren 2009: 17).

Phase IV from 1993 to 2000   indeed was characterized by prospects of hope due to the Oslo peace process and further weakened beliefs of conflict. The belief in peace was the strongest, and perceived as something that could realistically be achieved. Almost two third of the Jewish Israeli population accepted the option of a Palestinian state and beliefs delegitimizing Palestinians weakened accordingly (Oren 2009: 17). However, even in this phase, the beliefs in the peace process were still unrealistic, as they ignored the issues most pressing to the Palestinians, especially the refugee problem.

The Societal Beliefs since 2000

This calm and hopeful phase ends harshly with the failure of the Peace talks in Camp David 2000 and with Premier Minister Ehud Barak famously stating that there is "no partner for peace". Shortly after that the Second Intifada breaks out. It lasts until 2006 and is characterized by severe violence and constant threat. Ever since, the conflict has taken only stronger turns towards intractability. That led to a depression and return of societal beliefs comprising the ethos of conflict. Some of the beliefs have changed in content though. Bar-Tal, Halperin and Oren (2010: pp.79) argue that the majority of Jewish Israelis accepts the plan of a Palestinian state[20] . However, beliefs that the West Bank is core Jewish land are held by the majority of the population and strengthened by politicians. This is combined with a reluctance to recognize or accept the Palestinian narration of the conflict[21]. More than that, most Jewish Israelis do not think that Israel is responsible for any suffering of Palestinians in 1948 through the establishment of the state of Israel and the high amounts of land Palestinians lost[22]. The reluctance to recognize Palestinian narratives or responsibility for their suffering can rationalize the unwillingness to give up land perceived as core Jewish land (the West Bank and Jerusalem) or to accept refugees from 1948 and 1967, two major Palestinian demands for a two-state-solution (Bar-Tal, Halperin and Oren 2010; Halperin et al. 2010; Peri et al. 2005).

In general, the image of Arabs by Israeli Jews worsened again and went back to considering them as one entity[23] . Palestinians are perceived as having no respect for human life and are characterized as dishonest by the majority of the Jewish Israeli society[24]. This goes

---

[20]The results of the Peace Index show that 58% of Jewish Israelis support the establishment of a Palestinian state in November 2008 (Yaar and Hermann 2008*b*). In March 2008, 68% support a two-state solution (Yaar and Hermann 2008*a*). In 2009, 62% of them recognize the existence of Palestinian people Yaar and Hermann (2009*b*)

[21]The majority of Jewish Israelis (55%) regards the West Bank as "liberated territory" and not as "occupied territory". That is supported by the observation that 57% believe the borders should not be based on the Green line(Yaar and Hermann 2008*a*).

[22]The majority of Jewish Israeli (56%) denies being even partially responsible for suffering caused to Palestinians by the 1948 war. This includes the refugee problem (Yaar and Hermann (2009*a*))

[23]The joint Israeli-Palestinian opinion poll in 2006 reveals that 78% of Jewish Israelis agree with the statement: "The Muslims in the region will never accept the existence of the state of Israel"(Shamir and Shikaki 2006).

[24]In 2000, 78% of Jewish Israelis believe that Palestinians have little or no regard for human life and therefore continue to use violence, despite the high casualties. Even 86% believe knowing that Israel values life high enforces the Palestinian violence in order to erode Israels power to resist. (Yaar and Hermann 2000) Bar-Tal and Halperin found the same numbers in 2008 (Bar-Tal, Halperin and Oren 2010: 82).

along with the conviction that Palestinians want no peace and the belief that Arabs want to eradicate the state of Israel[25](ibid.).

The beliefs of victimization become very strong after 2000. The second intifada is characterized by many suicide bombings and high numbers of civilian deaths on the Jewish Israeli side. Taking into account that the majority of Jewish Israelis do not accept the Palestinian conflict narrative and perceive their own actions as justified, the violence conducted against them is regarded even more unjust and the intifada is regarded as caused solely by Palestinians[26].

Further, the perception of victimization includes not only being the victim of attacks by Palestinians. It extends to feeling victimized by the Palestinian leadership for forcing Israel to kill Palestinian civilians by fighting it (due to the alleged Palestinian lack of respect for human life) (Bar-Tal, Halperin and Oren 2010: 84). An example is the citation by former Prime Minister Ehud Olmert following the Gaza war in 2009 in which 1000 Palestinians were killed:

> Israel, which withdrew from the Gaza Strip to the last millimeter at the end of 2005 – with no intention of returning – found itself under a barrage of missiles. Hamas violently took control of the Gaza Strip and began attacking the communities in the South more intensely. Hamas's methods are incomprehensible. It placed its military system in crowded residential neighborhoods, operated among a civilian population which served as a human shield and operated under the aegis of mosques, schools and hospitals, while making the Palestinian population a hostage to its terrorist activities, with the understanding that Israel – as a country with supreme values – would not act. The external Hamas leadership, which lives in comfort and quiet, continued to set extremist policies while ignoring the population's ongoing suffering and out of a conspicuous unwillingness to ease its situation [...] I also wish to say something to the people of Gaza: even before the military operation began, and during it, I appealed to you. We do not hate you; we did not want and do not want to harm you. We wanted to defend our children, their parents, their families. We feel the pain of every Palestinian child and family member who fell victim to the cruel reality created by Hamas which transformed you into victims[...] Your suffering is terrible. Your cries of pain touch each of our hearts. On behalf of the Government of Israel, I wish to convey my regret for the harming of uninvolved civilians, for the pain we caused them, for the suffering they and their families suffered as a result of the intolerable situation created by Hamas.(Olmert 2009)

Olmert clearly considers Hamas fully responsible for all the suffering of Gazan civilians and emphasizes the morality of Israel as well as its moral superiority, while being victims of Hamas in having to conduct war.

Beliefs about the positive collective self-image and feeling of moral superiority are a major driving force. Bar-Tal, Halperin and Oren (2010: pp.85) outline that not only do Jewish Israelis feel that they are morally superior, as they are not responsible for the conflict, but also due to their willingness to resolve it. The readiness to a two-state-solution and

---

[25]The INSS polls in 2007 and 2009 indicate that 44% of Jewish Israelis believe that Palestinians want peace . Furthermore, 71% believe that the ultimate goal of Arabs is to eradicate the state of Israel in 2009 (results quoted in Bar-Tal, Halperin and Oren 2010). According to the Peace Index, 63% believe that Palestinians would destroy Israel if they could (Yaar and Hermann 2008*b*).

[26]Halperin and Bar-Tal (2011) show that 81% of Jewish Israelis agree that „Arabs have repeatedly forced war, despite Israel's desire for peace" (Halperin and Bar-Tal 2011).

painful compromises is accompanied by the deep conviction that the Palestinians are not willing to work towards peace and thus are no partners. Ignoring the Palestinian narrative contributes to that feeling, since thus their compromises will not appear as such. The positive self-perception is also connected to strong beliefs in Israeli security and military supremacy are connected to a positive self-perception.

The beliefs about security supremacy are followed by the dominant belief that Jewish Israelis can endure the conflict longer and is in better shape than the Palestinian society (Bar-Tal, Halperin and Oren 2010: 85). This factor also reduces the need to end the conflict immediately[27]. A strong and capable security system is regarded as necessary. Extremely positive characterizations are attributed to the Israeli Defense Forces as center of the society, and especially its moral and factual superiority[28]. Serving in the army and volunteering for it remains important, refusal is regarded as egoistic and even as treason (Bar-Tal, Halperin and Oren 2010; Oren and Bar-Tal 2006).

Beliefs of Peace on the other hand, are not regarded a priority to the society anymore and are exchanged by mistrust and pessimism (Yaar and Hermann 2008*a*). Rationalizations include the perceived inability of Palestinians to live democratically and a lacking partner for a peace process – Yassir Arafat was not considered a partner, Abu Mazen is perceived as not strong enough and the overall violence contributes to the pessimistic outlooks of the prospects. As described above, the willingness for peace is again more of a lip-serving longing that has no practical implications, and is not connected to necessary concessions such as ending the occupation (Bar-Tal, Halperin and Oren 2010: 86; Zuckermann 2012: 87).

There is a strong contradiction between the willingness for peace and compromise, accepting the Palestinian's right to a state of their own and the mistrust of their willingness to compromise for peace and feeling superior to them. The chosen strategy of coping with these contradictions is the conclusion that it is in Israel's hands to change the context unilaterally. The withdrawal from Gaza and the construction of the wall or separation fence can be regarded as consequences (Bar-Tal and Sharvit 2009; Halperin et al. 2010).

Societal beliefs regarding the occupation of Palestinians Jewish Israelis hold beliefs that justify the beginning and later the sustaining of the occupation. The beginning in 1967 is explained as a preventive act amidst the hostility surrounding Israel and as liberation of East-Jerusalem and the whole territories of Judea, Samaria (West Bank), Gaza, the Golan Heights, and Sinai. Further explanations are security-related and aimed at creating buffer-zones to keep attacks on Israel away from civil populations. These

---

[27]The Peace Index in October 2007 indicates that 63% believe the Jewish society is doing better than the Palestinian society (Yaar and Hermann 2007)

[28]The War and Peace Index in April 2009 reveals that 81% of Jewish Israelis regard Israel's greatest success in the military-security sphere and 91% trust the IDF. Only 57% trust the Supreme Court (Yaar and Hermann 2009*a*)

became very central rationales. Later, the argument that Jewish Israeli settlements in these territories became so numerous that the point of no return has been reached, were raised. Continuing the occupation was interpreted as serving peace, because the occupied territories could later be returned to Palestinians in exchange for a peace agreement. Keeping peace as the ultimate goal, the territories serve as a land to return for something. The generally very negative perception of Palestinians serves the justification of the occupation. Especially in the first decades when Palestinians were not seen as an entity but simply referred to as "Arabs", they were hardly regarded as occupied. In this light, both acts of resistance and actual acts of terror will be framed as terrorism (Halperin et al. 2010: 65).

The term "enlightened occupation" is used especially by parts of Jewish Israeli society that do not believe that the West Bank is core Israeli land. The term is meant to describe and emphasize the positive, moral manner of occupying, and the positive effects the occupied enjoy in economic, social, and cultural ways. It is a way of white-washing to keep a positive self-image. Apparently the enduring occupation challenges the society's collective positive image. These difficulties are dealt with by defense mechanisms to avoid contradictions with moral values that the behavior of the group poses (Halperin et al. 2010: pp. 65).

Palestinian societal beliefs   To understand the ethos of a conflict society it is important to consider the the contradicting – often mirroring – ethoses with the rival society and the way they touch the characteristics of the identity of the societies. It illustrates the contribution of the beliefs to the intractability of the conflict. Three of the societal beliefs are on both sides directly contradicting.

1) Beliefs about the justness of one's own goals are conflicting based on the claim for the same territory and hence the basis of the conflict. Palestinians regard themselves as the true and native inhabitants. Their goal is a Palestinian state and one of the conditions is the return of Palestinian refugees. The Zionist movement and the establishment of the state of Israel is seen as the last occupying force in a long line of historical occupation of this land that caused large refugee groups and the rise of a national consciousness. The beliefs in the justness of one's own goals is strong: In 1999, the majority of Palestinians wanted a Palestinian/Islamic state in the entire territory (Oren, Bar-Tal and David 2004: pp.139).

2) Beliefs delegitimizing the opponent are just as strong as in the Jewish Israeli society. While Jewish Israelis regard Palestinians as violent, dishonest and unintelligent, Palestinians hold the same beliefs regarding Jewish Israelis, but with a different distribution[29]. Jews are seen as aggressors wanting to destroy Palestine. is regarded asa colonialist, imperialist

---

[29]Jewish images of Palestinians in 2000: violent 68%; dishonest: 51%; weak: 35%. Palestinian images of Jewish Israelis: violent:94%, dishonest: 81%; weak: 23% (Oren, Bar-Tal and David 2004: 145).

movement and sometimes compared with Nazi movements. In polls, Palestinians differentiate between the Israeli government that they perceive as not wanting peace and the people that they do believe long for peace (Oren, Bar-Tal and David 2004: pp.145). Another strong mirror belief of delegitimization is the mutual denial of the national identities and national movements of each side by each other (Kelman 2007: 93).

3) Beliefs about collective victimization. Just as Jewish Israelis, also Palestinians see themselves as the sole victim of the conflict. Jewish Israelis are regarded as the aggressors to whom Palestinians react. The major suffering was inflicted on them during the wars of 1948 and 1967 in which Palestinians had to flee their homes and lands. This connects to the historical belief in victimization that is anchored in the numerous foreign invasions and occupations of the territory. This near and far history is seen with sorrow and as tragical history of a nation that is forced to live under occupation and in refugee camps (Oren, Bar-Tal and David 2004: pp.148).

Complementing the consensual mirror beliefs, Gayer (2012) identifies contested beliefs in both societies. There are struggles between "particularistic nationalist identities" that long for critical debate, peace and a partner on the one hand, and "liberalistic national identities" that hold up the societal conflict beliefs on the other. Both the mirroring beliefs between both societies and the opposing beliefs within each of those societies build inner fences and walls that are not easy if impossible to overcome. People perceiving themselves as just victims can hardly compassionately listen to a contradicting narrative (Bar-Tal 2013; Gayer 2012; Oren, Bar-Tal and David 2004).

Studies on the Ethos of Conflict in Jewish Israeli and Palestinian Society

The *relation between the eight beliefs* comprising the ethos of conflict has been studied by several scholars. Bar-Tal, Sharvit, Halperin and Zafran constructed a 16-item scale to test the adherence of the ethos of conflict and found that the beliefs while being unique have each their own function. Combined, they all complement each other and form a "holistic perspective on the conflict context" (Bar-Tal et al. 2012). Gopher interviewed Israeli Jewish adults using a larger 48-item scale and identified three core beliefs of the ethos of conflict: The beliefs about the justness of one's own group, the beliefs about victimization, and the beliefs about the delegitimization of the rival. He further found a correlation between beliefs about security and patriotism. Security threats often lead to higher beliefs in patriotism and the willingness for self-sacrifice (Master's thesis, see Bar-Tal 2013: 201; Oren 2009: 14). Fuxman (2012) also emphasizes the important connection between patriotism and security in his dissertation. He conducted interviews with Jewish Israeli high school students on their prospects of becoming members of the

Israeli Defense Force. In this context the connection of patriotism and security seems obvious.

Two studies reflect on *the functions of the societal beliefs* comprising the ethos of conflict. The first study is also based on the above mentioned (see Chapter 2.2)16 item scale. Jewish Israeli undergraduate students are asked to fill out scales regarding their Jewish identity and standpoints on concrete policies. The researchers find that beliefs of the ethos of conflict serve as prisms for interpretation of new information on the conflict and for the judgment of policies. The readiness for compromise is reduced by those beliefs (Bar-Tal et al. 2012). This is supported by a study by Bar-Tal et al. (2008). They let Jewish Israelis with different political standpoints interpret images showing Jews and Palestinians in different power and aggression positions. They also find that the level of adherence to the ethos of conflict strongly influences interpreting and processing new information in the conflict reality (Bar-Tal et al. 2008). The effects of adherence of the ethos of conflict beliefs on selective information processing is studied by Porat, Halperin and Bar-Tal (2015). They find that individuals holding the ethos of conflict high tend to avoid new contradicting information.

Halperin and Bar-Tal (2011) conduct a survey among Jewish Israelis to validate their model of socio-psychological barriers to peace (see Chapter 2.1). They find that the general worldviews have an impact on openness and support for compromise to reach peace. Also societal beliefs of the ethos of conflict, especially victimization and delegitimization, are highly connected to openness for compromise. Circumstantial beliefs have an impact on support for compromises but not on openness. They see their framework supported and conclude that conflict starts in the mind and will also end there through infliction of beliefs that motivate to re-evaluate held convictions (Halperin and Bar-Tal 2011).

One indicator of societal beliefs comprising the ethos of conflict is the frequent *appearance in cultural products*. There are several investigations on societal beliefs in school textbooks (Bar-Tal 1998*a,b*; Podeh 2002) that find strong support for societal beliefs within those educational books, throughout the years, grades, and topics. Security is the belief relied upon the strongest, followed by positive self-image and victimization. Nasie and Bar-Tal (2012) investigate the articles young Palestinians write for a youth magazine in three time periods and found that articles dealing with the conflict show societal beliefs of victimization, patriotism, and the emotion of hope. They also find a relationship between periods of peace, hope, violence, and calm and the amount of societal beliefs expressed.

In sum, this chapter illuminates the permeation of the ethos of conflict in Israeli (and Palestinian) society, its developments, functions, and relations. From a historical perspective, the interdependence between changes in societies and political, environmental developments and events and hence beliefs comprising the ethos of conflict become apparent. The latter can change over time in intensity, character and content. When the conflict is perceived as tractable, beliefs diversify; there are developments of ideology to pragmatic solutions, less holding of security beliefs as top priority, more possibility for self-criticism instead of idealization. There exist more, differentiated images of Arabs and Palestinians and the society is able to bear a less unified outlook hence more diversity of viewpoints. Still, the ethos of conflict is easily re-adapted when violence re-occurs (Oren and Bar-Tal 2006).

3.3   The Israeli News Media

> To understand Israeli society and Israeli politics, you need to
> understand Hebrew printed media
>
> ———————————————————————
>
> Noam Sheizaf, +972 Magazine

The present chapter gives an overview of Israeli newspapers that are, as a part of Israeli society, dependent on societal developments. The Israeli media landscape has special characteristics for several reasons: it is very young, very small, and constantly more or less entangled in conflict coverage dependant on routine or crisis phases.

A first notable characteristic regards the recipients – *Israelis are news obsessed*. Shinar (2005: 171) states: "one of the most-observed secular rituals in Israel is reading, watching, and listening to the news". Public radio daily broadcasts four hour long news magazines. The TV-channels 1,2, and 10 have each three daily newscasts of 30-60 minutes followed by longer magazines, all of which are held "holy". The high interest in news can be understood when taking the continuing conflict reality into account. Perceived danger to personal and collective security leads to a high need for orientation and to survey the environment (see Chapter 2.2). News therefore are regarded as a "national addiction" (Shinar 2005: 171). Furthermore, Tenenboim-Weinblatt (2014: 414) categorizes the Israeli news media as a hybrid case based on the combination of interventionist tendencies with some level of political parallelism and a liberal market-oriented journalism that follows journalistic professional ethos at the same time. The leading elements of those characteristics of the Israeli news media landscape are illuminated in the following with a short introduction of their historical roots Later, the four leading Israeli daily newspapers are introduced and characterized in depth as they are the source for the upcoming content analysis.

Characteristics of Israeli Media

Historical connection between the media and the political environment   The Zionist movement arose in the late 19th century (see Chapter 3.1). The party-like system formed within local European structures had branches in Palestine that built the infrastructure for immigrating Jews and the foundations of the state of Israel. That involved, among others, housing, jobs, health system, clubs, and insurances, and newspapers. These newspapers were fully owned and controlled by the political parties. They served as direct communication arm and active instruments in the "nation building" and socialization of heterogeneous immigrant groups and in Zionist education (Doron 1998). Each party owned a newspaper and its popularity reflected the party structure (for example Davar by the Labor Zionist Mapai; Al Hamishmar by the Socialist Party; HaBoker by the Centrist General Zionist; Herut by the right wing bloc; KolHaam by the Communist

Party). Private newspapers like Haaretz, Yediot Aheronot and Maariv were not central yet but also published within the accepted Zionist narrative (Doron 1998: 168).

The control or cooperation of the media and the political environment is apparent in three characteristic institutions, namely 1) the Editor's committee, 2) the military censorship, and 3) the late founding of only one, state controlled, television channel (Caspi and Limor 1999; Doron 1998: 168).

The *Editor's Committee* was a briefing of the editors in chief of all the Hebrew newspapers and the Jerusalem Post by either the Prime Minister or a top official/cabinet minister on military and security issues. One goal was to inform on classified information in order to preclude its publication. This forum allowed the government to regulate the public agenda and to avoid sensitive or embarrassing information becoming public. The media and the government acted rather in concert than as two separate entities. The *military censorship* was accepted by the public, governmental and communication elites since the state of Israel was at danger. In fact, David Ben Gurion, Prime and Defense Minister (1949 to 1965), was in charge of security, intelligence, military and hence in control of any sensitive information and its publication. Further, self-censorship in security matters was internalized. A third characteristic of the close control of the state of Israel over the media was *the late introduction of television* into the Israeli media sphere. While radio was state controlled and intensely used for nation-identity-building and integration of different communities, television was perceived as mis-education and started only in 1968 under the control of the government appointed Israeli Broadcasting Authority (IBA) (Caspi and Limor 1999; Doron 1998). All Israeli radio stations are accountable to the Israeli Defense Forces (IDF) or to the Israeli Broadcasting Authority. The senior positions of the latter are held by political appointments often close to the prime minister (Sharvit and Bar-Tal 2007: 212).

Especially in the first decades of nation-building and the state of Israel the media was not an independent sector, but a mobilized institution with close ties or even under control of the government in nationalizing, secularizing, and building Israeli life. Moreover, Israeli media not only played a strong role in connecting the members of the "imagined community" through reassurance, a sense of security, coherence, and belonging (Orgad 2011: 404), it actually commits to creating that imagined Zionist community. The media addressed its role of social responsibility by addressing the needs of the diverse ethnical backgrounds, by forming and communicating the "proper Hebrew" and "proper vocabulary", by communication and establishment of Zionist values, construction of myths, and narratives.

Commercialization and intensifying competition over a limited market   As already discussed above (see Chapter 3.2) the Israeli society changed substantially in the 1970-80s as did the conflict. Party press was not able to adapt to changed needs of a liberalizing, diversifying society. The long-existing private press, being more flexible, filled the gap and dominated the market since the 1990s. Journalists held collectively bargained contracts until the mid-1980s, as with the rise of private press individual contracts and freelance journalism arose (Meyers and Cohen 2011: 8). The previously very restricted and effective Editor's Committee was enlarged to broadcasting, senior editors, and journalists. The bigger circle eventually diminished its status and hence influence. Criticism and competition became increasingly legitimate (Doron 1998: 8).

The market's weight changed substantially. The commercialization and competition internationally grew stronger in the beginning of the 21st century with vast changes, technological developments, globalization, and diversification. Consumer interest and behavior changed, attention became an increasingly precious and rare good, more and more media actors competed over less attention. An example are the advertizing budgets: In 2004 to 2010, the print share decreased from 50% to 31%; the TV share increased from 35% to 42%, and the internet share rose from 3% to 16% (Caspi 2011). Newspapers continued with cutbacks, constraints, less employees (under higher pressure to serve not only print, but also online and often tablet), higher time pressure and consequences for the quality.

Pseudo-pluralism   The limited market of the small country lead its media actors into strong competition. Broadcasting underwent a crisis, the IBA weakened due to mismanagement and calls for deregulation, electronic media grew fast, satellite broadcasting started in 2002 (Shinar 2005). Today, Israel has four Hebrew general interest newspapers, namely Yediot Aheronot, Maariv, Haaretz and since 2007 Israel Hayom. As discussed below they are engaged in fierce competition that only two papers seem to survive. Of all the party newspapers only four orthodox religious papers remained. Apart from those, there is foreign language and Arabic press and local newspapers that are mostly owned by the general newspapers and added as regional supplements on Fridays (Caspi and Limor 1999: 37). In Israel, cross ownership is not forbidden. Hence, media pluralism is further limited due to media conglomerates of a limited number of actors that hold the biggest media formats in online, print and broadcasting. This eventually limits the choice of ideas, thoughts and opinions.

In sum,   As introduced, the Israeli media landscape is a hybrid case combining democratic norms and relatively free information flow and some authoritarian rules to regulate the media (partially inherited from the British Mandate) remaining in practice. Military censorship, the Editor's Committee, the Israeli Broadcasting Authority are examples of these regulations. If these regulatory instruments were applied fully, Israeli media would not be independent. This is not the case, regulations are not implemented and relationships are mainly informal. However, ignored laws cannot guarantee democratic function of the media (Foreword by Galnoor in Caspi and Limor 1999: 37). In the context of the present investigation the characteristics of the Israeli media landscape suggest a close relationship between the media and authorities during crisis times and a high adherence to official narratives. This is based on the conclusion that media actors are in practice independent from control. However, not only military censorship, but also self-censorship and regulations that may be applied at any given point, and a very small media landscape with a low number of media conglomerates reduce the independence of journalists.

The Four General Israeli Hebrew Daily Newspapers

The four main Israeli newspapers today are Haaretz, Maariv, Yediot Aheronot, and Israel Hayom. Data on circulation is hard to find, more information is published on exposure (see Table 2).

Table 2 – Exposure of General Israeli Newspapers (in Percent)

	Yediot Aheronot		Maariv		Haaretz		Israel Hayom	
Year	Week	Weekend	Week	Weekend	Week	Weekend	Week	Weekend
2001	48.8	62.8	26.8	35.6	9.1	11.4	–	–
2007	38.4	50.7	17.0	21.9	7.4	8.4	founded	–
2010	34.9	43.7	12.5	16.1	6.4	7.4	35.2	35.7
2014	34.5	38.0	3.2	8.0	4.8	6.8	39.8	34.0

(see Gilboa 2008*b*; Katz 2011; Kelner 2014)

Yediot Aheronot has been the most popular newspaper since the 1970s until 2010. It was founded in 1939 by Nachum Kumarovas as an evening and afternoon newspaper. Yediot Aheronot came into major crisis when its senior editorial staff, headed by the editor in chief left to open a new paper, Maariv, in 1948. The main conflict was over a profitability orientation of the owners of Yediot Aheronot and a service orientation by the editorial staff. Yediot Aheronot adapted to the new situation of losing its senior staff by training of new journalists that helped adapt to changing needs and hence journalistic standards like more vibrant, colorful look, shorter articles with limited information and simple language. The paper kept its orientation towards profitability. That led to a pluralistic coverage that is open to different political views to attract as much readers as possible (Caspi and Limor 1999). Its format is tabloid but its content is in fact "crossbreed", meaning there are literary and arts columns, national and security issues are covered at length. Still there are soft news, human interest and entertainment stories. The headlines can be sensational (Caspi and Limor 1999; Dor 2004: 6). The writers comprise some respected analysts and reporters (ibid.). The newspaper is owned by the Mozes family and is published by Arnon Mozes and owned by the Yedioth Aheronot Group. This group owns parts of the influential commercial TV station "Channel 2", the Cable TV company "Hot", several specialized or local newspapers and magazines (Dor 2004: 6). Generally, the newspaper's orientation can be seen as centrist, conservative on military and security issues, more liberal with regard to civil questions. Yediot Aheronot is "the voice of the middle class Israeli". It is, despite its decade-lasting competition with Maariv and the latest competition with Israel Hayom (see below) still the strongest media institution in Israel, not at least due to the dominance of the semi-independent online news portal "Ynet", the most successful of its kind in Israel. In general, Ynet is the second most popular internet page following Google in Israel (Caspi and Limor 1999: 81; Lipson and Cohen 2008; Sheizaf 2010). Despite the competition with Israel Hayom Yediot's exposure rose up to 37.6% on weekdays in the first half of 2012 from 34.8% in the second half of 2011 (Abarbach 2012).

Maariv   was first published by the former senior staff of Yediot Aheronot, led by Ezriel Carlibach, in 1948. The newspaper was founded as a cooperative, owned by a publishing company, the Nimrodi family, and the journalists hold controlling stakes. The editorial board remains autonomous from the owners. Maariv strives for more serious, sober coverage than Yediot Aheronot. The newspaper was based on high journalistic standards, reliable information, and quality commentary. It aimed at addressing a readership that was characterized as having higher socio-demographic profile than Yediot-readers. Today, Maariv owns several local newspapers (Caspi and Limor 1999; Dor 2004) .

Maariv and Yediot Aheronot became more important in the first decades of the Israeli state, especially with the decline of the party press. Maariv led the competition until the 1970s but its complex financial structure and high journalistic standard and restricted editorial consensus complicated changes according to modern needs of recipients. Yediot appeared more capable of adapting to different tastes and needs of recipients. Its profit orientation allowed a high variety of political views. The latter remained dominant for about forty years and used its advance in sales and advertisement for better service, high-profile journalists and coverage from abroad. The competition led the two evening newspapers to publish gradually earlier until they turned into morning papers and subscription became possible (Caspi and Limor 1999).

In 1990, Maariv changed its strategy from deep sober analysis to a strategy of similarity of format, appearance, content, and the "crossbreed" format of Yediot Aheronot. Both newspapers were sometimes hard to differentiate, using big banner headlines, large pictures, and having similar sections and supplements. This strategy could not halt the downward spiral and Maariv further lost advertisements and readers, leading to its deep financial crisis in the 2000s and changing ownerships. In 2010 Zaki Rakib bought 50%, one year later Nochi Dankner bought Maariv, but the newspaper continued to struggle and was soon unable to pay its staff. With deep cuts in staff and content the newspaper was sold to Shlomo Ben-Zvi, the owner of the national religious newspaper Makor-Rishon in 2011. The goal was to unify both papers. In 2014 the paper was sold again to Eli Azur, who holds shares of English language Jerusalem Post, Sport1 and Israel Post, a newspaper distributed free of charge at supermarkets (Sheizaf 2012; Kershner 2012).

Haaretz is the oldest private newspaper, founded in 1918 with sponsorship from the British military government and soon taken over by a group of Zionists from Russia. In 1937, Salman Shocken acquired the newspaper and his son Gershom became chief editor until 1990. The family owned the paper until 2006, when the German DuMont Shauberg acquired 25%. In 2012, Leonid Nevzlin bought 20% (5% from DuMont and the rest from Shocken), leaving Shocken with 60%. Haaretz is published in Hebrew and English. The English version contains the international edition of the New York Times, the Herald Tribune. It is the most prestigious publication in Israel and defines itself as "paper for thinking people". Its layout, coverage, and political leaning differ from the other newspapers. It is published in broadsheet format, the language is restrained, it is focused on deep analysis rather than on large images and headlines. The newspaper has a liberal, non-nationalistic editorial policy. In security matters, Haaretz follows a dovish line, meaning it opposes the occupation of the Palestinian territories. Haaretz gained its elitist image due to its journalistic standards and high-profile readers, who tend to be educated, influential, mostly western born. Despite its very low circulation, it is important due to its influential readership. Haaretz is regarded as a mediator between the different elite-sectors of economy, politics, and culture (Caspi and Limor 1999; Dor 2004; Sheizaf 2010).

Israel Hayom entered the market in 2007. This tabloid newspaper is distributed free of charge, but keeps an appearance of journalistic standards. This is possible due to complete financial backing from Sheldon Adelson, an US-billionaire known for his support for Republican politicians and Prime Minister Netanyahu (Tenenboim-Weinblatt 2014: 414). Since 2010, the newspaper surpassed Yediot Aheronot as the most read newspaper among the Jewish Israeli population (see Table 2). In 2009, the newspaper started publishing a weekend edition that also became almost as popular as Yediot Aheronot (Sheizaf 2010).

A shaking market Israel Hayom shook up the Israeli press and media market, limited as it is due to several reasons: The newspaper does not follow a financial agenda. Due to its financial backing the paper is not dependent on income through sales and advertisement. Israel Hayom does not need to compete over advertisers, but offers advertisement prices that are far below what the other newspapers can offer. Israel Hayom is a free newspaper, surpassing any possible sale price for the other newspapers. That mean, not only do the other newspapers lose recipients, they also cannot compete with the low prices Israel Hayom offers for commercials. Furthermore, Israel Hayom has a political agenda. Sheldon Adelson supports Republicans in the US and is an open supporter of Prime Minister

Benjamin Netanyahu (Kershner 2012). An early study in "The Seventh Eye"[30] finds that indeed, Israel Hayom downplays events that are not advancing a positive image of Netanyahu and upscales events that support him and the Likud party (Rada 2008). A political agenda that is financially secured, meaning not market dependent, is to the very least a catalyst in an anyway competitive and limited market. The results are easily observed in the rapidly shrinking readership of the anyway struggling Maariv and Haaretz. In this context, it is notable that Israel Hayom was printed at Haaretz' printing house until 2013 (rumors said this saved Haaretz from bankruptcy) and later purchased Maariv's printing house. The severe crisis of the newspaper market has a new peak in 2014 as the Minister of Interior announces that Maariv and Haaretz are no longer considered as "highly popular" newspapers acknowledged by the government. Instead, Israel Hayom and Israel Post (another newspaper distributed free of charge at supermarkets and lacking any journalistic significance) were added. The Israeli newspaper market thus comprises one sold paper, Yediot Aheronot, and two freely distributed papers, Israel Hayom and Israel Post since 2014 (Kelner 2014). Besides the trend of newspapers circulated free of charge there is an emerging market of economic journalism in Israel (Haaretz publishes the daily economic The Marker, Yediot Aheronot publishes the daily economic Calcalist) (Nossek 2009). The competition between freely distributed newspapers and established newspapers with an economic agenda increases the general competition over content and readers (ibid.). Just as the earlier assumptions on the characteristics of the Israeli media, also the Israeli newspaper landscape in particular suggests that the competition leads to conformism in the media coverage.

Online strategies All the newspapers developed strategies to cope with the new internet opportunities and challenges. Haaretz used the internet first and created a new page with innovative format covering entertainment, culture and information, called Walla. The page is very successful in Israel, but Haaretz sold it to the telecommunication company Bezeq. Besides, Haaretz also has an independent team for its online page in Hebrew and English. The strongest online news site is Ynet, sister company to Yediot Aheronot (Caspi 2011). Ynet has an independent staff and is the most important page in Israel. The page was hit 25 million times by 1.5 million users after the Gaza flotilla raid. Ynet is very interactive, has extensive talkback sections, live coverage of events and 24/7 coverage. So is Haaretz, but its online contents are not free of charge without limit. Following Google, it is the second most used website in Israel (followed by Walla). Maariv's online page was very hesitant and did not succeed to compete. Israel Hayom publishes its complete paper

---

[30]The Seventh Eye Journal "Promoting media responsibility and accountability" is a Hebrew Online platform by and for Israeli journalists on their profession. Media coverage is debated, evaluated, and questions are discussed. It is a project of the Israel Democracy Institute. See: http://en.idi.org.il/projects/israeli-society/the-seventh-eye-journal.

online (ibid.). In sum, also in the online market Yediot Aheronot is more successful than other newspapers and further established its crossmedia position.

3.4 The Gaza Flotilla Raid

This investigation focuses on the media coverage of international involvement surrounding one particular event, the Gaza flotilla raid in 2010. The choice of this event is based on the following reasons: 1) The event happened recently. 2) The conflicted parties of the event are not Israelis and Palestinians but the Israeli army versus international individuals seeking to break the Gaza-blockade in a clear position against Israel's policies. The direct conflict group are therefore international actors involving themselves. On the one hand this event is therefore extraordinary and on the other hand suitable to investigate on Israeli media perceptions and representations of international interference. 3) While the concrete events during the raid of the flotilla remain largely unclear, the international reactions were strong and mostly very critical. 4) The event is still regarded a decisive point in Israel's international relations and standing, especially with Turkey, but also other Western countries.

The present chapter illuminates the central controversies about the raid of the flotilla based on international and national reports, and introduces the international reactions. Last, the Israeli hasbara efforts regarding the events are presented.

Investigating the Events of the Gaza Flotilla Raid

The events that took place on the raid of the flotilla bound to the Gaza strip on the night between May 31 and June 1, 2010 are discussed highly controversial and some details remain unclear and open to speculation. The main controversies are: The reasons for the flotilla bound to Gaza – is the blockade of Gaza legal and what is its humanitarian impact on the Gazan population? The legitimacy of the Gaza flotilla members – are they peace activists or terrorists? The events of the raid of the Gaza flotilla – who attacked and who defended? Several inquiries tried to answer these questions and their findings are introduced following.

Several investigations were conducted to investigate the events. An Israeli IDF probe led by Maj.Gen.Giora Eiland (Ret.) investigated the operational decisions and concluded that the commando had the right to self-defense. It regards the underestimation of the passengers on the Mavi Marmara as the main mistake committed by the Israeli Navy (Migdalovitz 2010: 7). Prime Minister Netanyahu established an inquiry headed by retired Supreme Court Justice Jacob Turkel to investigate the lawfulness of the blockade on Gaza and the actions of the flotilla members. This inquiry did not investigate military personnel. The investigation was coordinated with the United States, who requested an international component. The Turkish Foreign Ministry did not consider this sufficient and warned it would review its relations with Israel if an international commission was not set up (Migdalovitz 2010: 9). The Turkel Commission finds that the blockade on Gaza is legal and the suffering of the population in Gaza is proportionate to the prevention of arms supply to Hamas (Craig 2011: 283). In contrast to these findings is the report of the Turkish government that was published in April 2011. It was headed by senior officials of the Turkish Office of the Prime Minister, the Ministy of Justice, the Ministy of Interior, the Ministry of Foreign Affairs and the Under-Secretariat for Maritime Affairs. The inquiry finds the blockade of Gaza and the raid of the flotilla by the Israeli navy illegal. The actions of the Israeli soldiers are described as "well-planned attack", as "excessive disproportion" and the soldiers as "brutaliz[ing] and terroriz[ing] the passengers" in the Turkish report (Turkish National Commission of Inquiry 2011: 4). The UN Secretary General Ban Ki-moon, announced an international investigation headed by Geoffrey Palmer. It was published in September 2011. The "Report of the Secretary-General's Panel of Inquiry on the 31 May 2010 Flotilla Incident", chaired by Sir Geoffrey Palmer (Palmer et al. 2011) is the main source for the following description of the events. It is based on the information gathered by the Turkish and the Israeli governments in their own reports and evaluations and therefore displays the three standpoints of Israel, Turkey and the UN. This is the report considered closest to an objective investigation on the complex events and opposing viewpoints.

Debate I – The legality of the sea blockade on Gaza   In 2005, Israel withdrawed from Gaza in an unilateral step and its control over Gaza remained in the form of border control. A year later, Hamas won the legislative elections of the Palestinian Authority. Hamas was and is regarded as a terrorist organization by several countries, the European Union, the United States and Israel. Foreign aid to Palestinians by these countries was halted after massive pressure from Israel. Others, like Turkey and Arab states, regarded Hamas as legitimate and democratically elected group. A unity government with Fatah which lead all previous governments, failed and ended in a forceful takeover of Gaza by Hamas in 2007. Fatah took the West Bank and restored international relations. Furthermore, an Israeli soldier, Gilad Shalit, was captured in 2006 by Hamas militants. In response Israel imposed a tight land, sea, and air blockade in 2007 to prevent the movement of weapons, terrorists and money, and to stop rockets and mortars that were fired from the Gaza strip into Israel. This was justified as a means to pressure Gazans to release Gilad Shalit. Another intention was to turn the Gazan population against Hamas as life in the West Bank is easier. Only products meeting "humanitarian needs" were allowed, but products with possible "dual use" (like construction material or agricultural fertilizers) and numerous products were prohibited as "luxury goods" such as chocolate, coriander, coffee (Strand 2015). Rather the opposite happened: the isolation of the area and the following wars strengthened Hamas' control. During the Gaza war in 2008/09

Israel destroyed much of Gaza's infrastructure, more than 1,000 Palestinians were killed and the blockade was further tightened (Migdalovitz 2010: 1).

In the context of the Gaza flotilla, the naval blockade is relevant as it was the attempt of the flotilla organizers to break it. It was imposed in January 2009 (Buchan 2011: 210). The debate surrounding the legality of the naval Gaza blockade is based on the San Remo Manual (International Institute of Humanitarian Law 1995). It outlines conditions for lawful sea blockades and considers them illegal if they have excessive effect on the population and if the purpose appears to be restricting the population's access to goods needed for survival (Buchan 2012: 266). The manual is used by all three Commissions as a basis of their argumentation. Spelman (2013), in reviewing all three positions on the legality, concludes that Israel complies with four of five conditions of the San Remo Manual, despite the failure to specify the duration and extent of the blockade. The fifth condition, the humanitarian situation is difficult to establish. Spelman "accepts that the civilian population of the Gaza strip is clearly suffering as a result of the naval blockade and the Closure Policy" (Spelman 2013: n.p.) but she cannot conclude if that is caused by the blockade only and hence cannot draw conclusions on the lawfulness of the blockade. The Palmer Commission regards the naval blockade as lawful and in compliance with international law, since the conflict is defined as an "international armed conflict." Israel left control of the Gaza Strip in 2005, and according to Israel's Supreme court did not exercise "effective control". The Israeli Turkel Commission also claims that the blockade fulfills customary international law requirements in notification, effectiveness, and enforcement (based on San Remo Manual) and does not accept claims of a humanitarian crisis (Palmer et al. 2011: 27, 38).

However, the Turkish National Commission of Inquiry does not view the Israeli naval blockade on Gaza as lawful, but regards it as a tool of political and economic warfare (Turkish National Commission of Inquiry 2011: 78). The Commission criticizes it as disproportionate and aggravating the humanitarian crisis in Gaza. Further, the lacking transparency over allowed and prohibited goods for import and the inconsistency of interceptions of vessels bound to Gaza (before 2009, at least six vessels entered) is denounced (Palmer et al. 2011: 14). It views the blockade as illegal, since blockades can only be imposed on a state in international conflict, and Israel does not regard Palestine as state or the conflict with Hamas as international. Furthermore, the blockade of occupied territory is not possible. The Commission also claims that Israel did 1) not notify the "duration and extent", 2) publish a list of allowed goods or 3) enforce the blockade consistently as required by customary international law. Hence the Turkish commission concludes that the blockade is not reasonable, proportional or necessary and that it is a collective punishment of the Gazan civilians and therefore breaches the Fourth Geneva convention (Palmer et al. 2011: 15; Turkish National Commission of Inquiry 2011: 116). Buchan (2012) adds another perspective to the debate on the legality that regards the fifth point of the San Remo Manual which requires the conflict to be an international armed conflict. This is not the case for the conflict between Israel and Hamas, because Hamas is not a state (ibid: pp.267).

Notably, the question of the humanitarian situation determines the lawfulness of the blockade. Israel maintains that there is no humanitarian crisis. It considers itself fulfilling its humanitarian law obligations in i.e. supplying goods essential for survival. The IDF also publishes weekly reports of goods imported into Gaza. Still, the suffering of the Gazan population is undoubtable. Just in April 2010 the Humanitarian Monitor of OCHA reported of tripled numbers of poor people according to an UNRWA survey since the beginning of the blockade in 2007. In 2010, 300.000 families lived in abject poverty (unable to secure access to food, purchase basic items). Altogether, 700.000 refugees in poverty are part of the

> immense challenges facing humanitarian and human development assistance providers [...] in the Gaza strip. A decade of socio-economic decline, caused by the politics of closure and blockade, have shattered livelihoods, eroded the productive base and impoverished ordinary people. (OCHA 2010)

The report concluded that there is disproportionate damage of the blockade on the civilian population. Still, there is no evidence that starvation is the purpose of the blockade and it is hard to establish if military gain and civilian suffering are disproportionate (according to Paragraph 102 (b) of the San Remo Manual on International Law Applicable to Armed Conflict at Sea, See International Institute of Humanitarian Law 1995; Spelman 2013). This is intended, as Dov Weissglass, adviser to former Prime Minister Olmert stated famously in 2006: "It is like a meeting with a dietician. We have to make them much tinner, but not enough to die" (Benn 2006). Weissglass refused the statement later (Sofer 2006). It however illustrates the fine line chosen for the blockade and hence its controversiality. The intention of the blockade is to increase hardship of life but not to starve a people. Hence, the Palmer Commission finds, contrary to OCHA, that the blockade is not a tool of collective punishment and therefore lawful (Migdalovitz 2010: 1; Palmer et al. 2011: 27). (Buchan 2012: 273) contests the conclusion of the Palmer report that the humanitarian consequences are not excessive and concludes that the lawfulness of the naval blockade will remain debated. Undoubtedly, the intended hardship of life in Gaza has increased severly after the war in 2014 and it is questionable whether sustaining life is possible in the area.

Debate II – the composition of the flotilla participants   The 2010 flotilla is not the first attempt to breach the naval blockade imposed on Gaza but the largest, most "successful", and well-known one[31]. The flotilla was initiated by the Free Gaza Movement that is based in Cyprus and operates internationally, rooting in the International Solidarity

---

[31]Earlier attempts to breach the blockade of Gaza included 1.300 activists trying to enter Gaza on New Year's Eve 2009, carrying only little humanitarian goods. They were stopped. The Free Gaza Movement

   © Frank & Timme   Verlag für wissenschaftliche Literatur

Movement that aims at ending the occupation of Palestinian land. After several attempts to breach the blockade, the movement cooperates with the IHH in 2010, a controversial humanitarian aid organization based in Turkey (see below). The flotilla comprised six vessels, three of them set sail between May 22 and May 29 2010 in Turkey, the others in Ireland and Greece. They joined 30 miles south of Cyprus. All together, approximately 700 passengers from 40 different countries were aboard. Among them were members of IHH, other NGOs and journalists, authors, politicians and others. One of the vessels, the Mavi Marmara had 29 crew members and 546 passengers on it, the others less than 20 each. They carried 10,000 tons of supplies. The Palmer report questions whether all the passengers were civilians motivated by genuine worry for Gaza and whether the amount of passengers was necessary to supply humanitarian goods. It further alleges that a "hardcore group" of 40 IHH activists boarded as personnel of the ship and did not undergo security screening (Palmer et al. 2011: 30).

The IHH, while declared a humanitarian aid organization that has ties to the International Red Cross and consultative status with the UNESCO, is controversial, since among operations in 100 countries, it also supports Hamas. Israel outlawed it in 2008, the USA did not. However, IHH is part of an umbrella-group of charity organizations created by Hamas that the USA has designated a terrorist group (Migdalovitz 2010). The flotillas carried 10.000 tons of humanitarian supplies and, according to the Turkish Commission, no weapons and they were screened prior to boarding by the departure ports. The Israeli Commission comes to different findings – it reports to have found weapons and combat equipment, flares, rods, axes, knives, tear gas, gas masks, protective vests and night vision goggles. Although not finding firearms the Commission believes their existence could have been possible (Palmer et al. 2011: 15, 30). Buchan (2011: 240) questions the balance of powers as the Israeli military with automatic weapons was superior to those basic weapons which could also be considered basic boat equipment.

Debate III – the intentions of the Gaza flotilla The Turkish Commission refers to the flotilla as "convoy" and regards its intentions as solely humanitarian delivery of aid to the people of Gaza. Therefore the Turkish Commission regards the flotilla as "humanitarian vessels" that are as such protected under humanitarian law. The Israeli Commission also views the main goal of participants as humanitarian, but adds that the leading organization, IHH, is a "humanitarian organization with radical-Islamic orientation" that supports radical Islamic terrorist organizations including Hamas. It further claims that the flotilla participants have no right to ignore the blockade no matter if they accept it as legal or not (Palmer et al. 2011: 16, 29). While the Palmer Report accepts that most of the flotilla participants came motivated by concern for Gaza, it also questions the objectives of the leading organization IHH (ibid.).

---

sent boats to Gaza since 2008 with small amounts of humanitarian aid. Some were successful. The group Viva Palestina tried breaking the blockade three times in 2009 (Sørensen and Martin 2014: 88).

Debate IV – preemptive steps taken to avoid violence The Turkish Commission claims that prior to the events on the flotilla, both the Israeli and Turkish governments reached an understanding that the vessels would change their destination if necessary and not force to breach the blockade and that Israel would use restraint and refrain from violence. The Israeli Commission claims diplomatic efforts were made to prevent the departure and proposals to Turkey were not accepted (ibid.).

Debate V – the boarding and take-over of the vessels The vessels were in international waters, 72 nautical miles from the coast when the Israeli navy took over. The Israeli Navy communicated first at 10.30 p.m. May 30, 2010 and asked for identification and destination of the vessels. Following, the captain was warned by the Israeli naval forces to change course since Gaza was under blockade. The vessels responded that in international waters they could not be directed for another course. The Palmer Report argues that still on international waters, the Israeli Navy boarded the vessels on the night of May 31, 2010 from helicopters. No use was made of other measures to stop the ships (Palmer et al. 2011: 52). Boarding the biggest vessel, Mavi Marmara, violent confrontation broke out as some passengers resisted the boarding in an organized and violent manner.

The Turkish Commission reports that the Mavi Marmara did change course at 11:30 p.m. towards the coast of Egypt. The vessels received calls by the army but no demand to "stop, search, and visit" the boats. Starting at 2:00 a.m. on May 31, 2010, the vessels were shadowed by the Israeli navy. Communication with them or with satellite was no longer possible. Passengers describe rising anxiety and fear during this time (Palmer et al. 2011: 18). The Israeli Commission reported that the course was not changed. The Turkish report claims the Israeli forces attempted to aboard the vessels at 4:32 a.m. without prior warning with speedboats and then with helicopters. The army fired stun and smoke grenades, paintball guns, rubber bullets and live fire. Even before boarding two passengers were shot. Although changing the course to open water, and while still being in open water the naval frigates forced the convoy to turn back towards Israeli waters. The Israeli report shows a different picture, in which an attempt to board from the two speedboats failed due to violent resistance of some of the passengers on the Mavi Marmara. When descending from helicopters "flash bang" stun grenades were thrown, but no shots fired. The Israeli Commission further stresses that, while there was a high amount of preparation for the operation by the political, military and intelligence sectors, the chances of violent opposition were not anticipated and not taken into consideration (Palmer et al. 2011: 31).

According to Turkish reports the passengers of the Mavi Marmara "panicked and acted in self-defense to prevent the IDF personnel from boarding the vessel. Passengers threw plastic bottles, waste bins and chairs at IDF personnel attempting to board from the speedboats, and physically overpowered the first three soldiers to rappel onto the vessel from the helicopters but no guns or other weapons were used" (Palmer et al. 2011: 20).

The Israeli Commission reports of extreme violence meeting the descending soldiers from the first helicopter. "They were shot at and attacked with clubs, iron rods, slingshots and knives" (Palmer et al. 2011: 32). Within 15 minutes, soldiers descended from two more helicopters and another 15 minutes later from speedboats. In this time it is reported that they "partially secured the roof and lower decks, restrained and handcuffed the passengers, and completed a take-over of the bridge" (ibid.). There is no information on how they got control over the violent attackers when being the minority. Thus the Turkish Commission claims there was excessive force used by the IDF, and individuals that did not threaten Israel were attacked and weaponry was disproportionate. Nine passengers were killed, five of them shot at close range. The Israeli Commission does not support the Turkish claim that passengers acted in panic and self-defense but rather states that their violence was organized and they were armed with weapons, including firearms. The shooting by the soldiers was in response and nine soldiers were wounded, two received bullet wounds. The nine passengers killed are described as activists or volunteers in IHH or other Turkish Islamic organizations (Palmer et al. 2011: 21, 32).

The Turkish Commission reports of severe mistreatment after the takeover and during the detention of the flotilla members, while the Israeli commission reports of immediate evacuation of wounded people and their resistance. The Turkish Commission concludes the actions were illegal since no ship can be boarded in the high seas without consent, but Israeli Commission regards the attempt of breathing the blockade as justification for capturing and enforcing the blockade. Turkey regards the blockade as illegal and the vessels as "humanitarian vessels", and the violence as unnecessary and disproportionate (Palmer et al. 2011: pp. 21).

In sum, the legality of the Gaza flotilla, the composition of the flotilla members and the events on the Gaza flotilla raid remain partially unclear and controverial. The UN Palmer-Report concludes that "it unfortunately may never be possible to fully establish precisely what occurred" (Palmer et al. 2011: 54). Nine Turkish passengers were killed, several of them with multiple shots, at short range or from behind. Many passengers were severely wounded. All the passengers were deported to Israeli prisons, and as the UN-Palmer-Report found, "there was significant mistreatment [...] this included physical mistreatment, harassment and intimidation..." (ibid.: 66). The controversial debates and the different conclusions drawn from them illustrates the basis for the possible polarizing perceptions of international actors and Israel in this concrete subject. Therefore, despite the lacking clarity of the blockade and the controversial Gaza flotilla incident and its members, it evokes unambiguous, intensive, and polarizing international reactions and exactly the opposing reactions in Israel. This incident has had a lasting impact on Israel's international standing.

International Reactions on the Gaza Flotilla Raid

Israel's actions were condemned almost globally. The UN Secretary General Ban Ki-moon condemned the action and called for a thorough investigation. The UN Human Rights Council voted for an independent international inquiry of the events of the flotilla. The UN Security Council formed a compromise statement that regretted the lost life

> resulting from the use of force during the Israeli military operation in international waters against the convoy sailing to Gaza. The Council [...] condemns those acts which resulted in the loss of at least ten civilians and many wounded [...]. (United Nations Security Council 2010)

The Council further supports the UN Secretary General's call for a "prompt, impartial, credible and transparent investigation conforming to international standards". Further, with "grave concern over the humanitarian situation" the Council calls for "a regular flow of goods" and to pursuing a two-State solution.

The formulation chosen by the Council of the European Union sound alike: "The EU deeply regrets the loss of life during the military operation in international waters against the Flotilla sailing to Gaza and condemns the use of violence." The Council calls for an "immediate, full, and impartial inquiry" with credible international participation and for "immediate, sustained and unconditional opening of crossings for the flow of humanitarian aid, commercial goods and persons" and for a solution that addresses "Israel's legitimate security concerns including a complete stop to all violence and arms smuggling into Gaza" (Council of the European Union 2010).

The events had an immediate impact on Israel's diplomatic relations with some countries: Nicaragua broke the relations, Ecuador and South Africa recalled their ambassadors, and many Israeli ambassadors were called in for protest. Russia and China called for an opening of Gaza's border crossings. For the United States, the diplomatic handling of the events was particularly tricky. It has close and strategic ties with both countries and needed to find a path to keep both (Migdalovitz 2010: 9). Hence, the President's reactions were very cautious:

> The President expressed deep regret at the loss of life in today's incident and concern for the wounded. The President also expressed the importance of learning all the facts and circumstances surrounding this morning's tragic events as soon as possible. (The White House 2010)

The Secretary of State Hillary Clinton said: "Turkey and Israel are both good friends of the United States." She confirms their work with both countries in the aftermath of the events and her support of the UN condemnation and "in the strongest terms" its call for an investigation. Clinton "supports an Israeli investigation that meets those criteria." She continued to state that the situation in Gaza is unsustainable and unacceptable. Israel's legitimate security needs must be met, just as the Palestinian's legitimate needs for sustained humanitarian assistance and regular access for reconstruction materials must also be insured. Clinton concluded on the US-commitment to a two state solution (CNN video,

2010). David Cameron, the British Prime Minister called Israel's actions "unacceptable". While confirming the commitment to Israel's security called on Prime Minister Netanyahu to lift the blockade and to react constructively to "legitimate criticism" (The Telegraph 2010). The spokesman of the German Chancellor Angela Merkel said to both Israel and Turkey:

> Every German government has always recognized and supported the right of Israel to defend itself but this right must of course be within the boundaries of proportionality. [...] At first glance it does not look like this basic rule was adhered to. (Deutsche Welle 2010)

The French President Nicolas Sarkozy condemned "the disproportionate use of force" (cited in Migdalovitz 2010). And the Turkish foreign ministry spoke of "irreparable consequences" for the relations of both countries: "By targeting civilians, Israel has once again shown its disregard for human life and peaceful initiatives. We strongly condemn these inhumane practices of Israel" (Deutsche Welle 2010).

Israeli Hasbara following the Gaza Flotilla Raid

The rapid and most likely unforeseen events on the Gaza flotilla challenged the Israeli hasbara apparatus to act fast in explaining the events to national and international media and publics. Mazmudar (2012) outlines the efforts of the Israeli public diplomacy to shift the blame from the IDF towards the flotilla participants through construction of a narrative in which negative public perception diffuses. Two elements are central for the Israeli strategy during and after the flotilla incident to gain information supremacy: First, the communication capabilities of the flotilla participants are cut. The participants are hold in detention and their media material is confiscated. And second, the IDF publishes its own edited footage that contains captions to direct audience understanding (like "soldier being hit with metal rod" (Philo and Berry 2011: 382). Some hours after the deadly incident, the IDF published several YouTube clips that showed night-vision footage taken by Israeli soldiers of the raid, which attempted to show the violence of the flotilla members and the way Israeli commandos were being attacked when boarding the ship from the helicopter. The most popular clip shows Israeli soldiers being beaten while boarding the ship from the helicopter. The clip is filmed with night-sight camera and relevant events are circled. The video includes monochrome, infra-red images of the abseiling. These images became the most prominent visualization in the first days following the incident, because the flotilla participants were detained and their media equipment confiscated (Archibald and Miller 2012; Mazmudar 2012). Further, the IDF published pictures and videos of knives and other weapons found on the Mavi Marmara (Migdalovitz 2010) and later videos of the radio transmission between the flotilla and the Israeli Navy, and humanitarian aid delivered to Gaza. The main claims of Israeli public diplomacy were: 1) There is no humanitarian crisis, 2) the actions against the flotilla were last resort actions, and 3) the flotilla members were terrorists and their sympathizers.

There is no humanitarian crisis   The rejection of a humanitarian crisis was communicated even before the raid, when journalists were taken on tour to Gaza to show them the open restaurants, and afterwards in public statements (Mazmudar 2012). An example is Prime Minister Benjamin Netanyahu: "There s no humanitarian crisis in Gaza[. . .]. There is no shortage on food. There is no shortage of medicine. There is no shortage of other goods" (Israel Ministry of Foreign Affairs 2010). This narrative opposed the narrative of the Free Gaza Flotilla movement that claim to bring humanitarian aid to Gaza where people suffer (Sheffer 2014: 141). Mazmudar (2012) concludes the Israeli narrative is not successful, because the public knows about the humanitarian situation and the message is inconsistent with other messages; e.g., Israel's transfer of humanitarian aid and cooperation with international aid organizations.

Raiding the flotilla was a last resort action   According to the Israeli perspective, alternatives would have been possible in advance. Netanyahu said "we made several offers – offers to deliver the goods on board of the flotilla to Gaza after a security inspection. Egypt made similar offers. And these offers were rejected time and again" (Israel Ministry of Foreign Affairs 2010). Hence Israeli boarding of the vessels was the regarded the only possible reaction to the flotilla's breach from the blockade. Mazmudar (2012) sums up that this narrative is not successful because no real threat by the flotilla on Israel was detectable in the videos published ahead of the operation, but rather readiness to board the ships.

The flotilla participants are terrorists and their sympathizers   The claim that the activists were terrorists was based on the assertion that a sponsor organization, IHH, is a terrorism funding organization and supports Hamas. Hence Netanyahu declared them members "of an extremist group that has supported international terrorist organizations and today supports the terrorist organization called Hamas [. . .] These were not pacifists. These were not peace activists. These were violent supporters of terrorism" (Israel Ministry of Foreign Affairs 2010). While the night-camera clip might support this narrative, IDF videos of activists leaving the ships show middle-aged people, diverse people. The Gaza flotilla participants consider themselves activists for human rights and the Palestinian people, therefore also this narrative opposes the Israeli narration (Sheffer 2014: 142). Prior to the flotilla incident the Israeli media described the flotilla participants as activists, including journalists, parliamentarians, writers etc. Furthermore, their deportation three days after the incident argues against this claim. A third perspective questions this narrative as inconsistent: it is difficult to understand why armed soldiers of the IDF are surprised by a mob of untrained activists armed with knives and household items (Mazmudar 2012).

Concluding thoughts   As the largely negative international reaction illustrates, Israel did not succeed to convey its narratives to the international audiences. "Israel did not adequately manage the situation nor did they appeal to the international, multicultural audience to which they were speaking" (Sheffer 2014: 145). The problem was not lacking or unprofessional hasbara, but unsuitable narratives. Israeli hasbara is again pre-occupied with sophisticated and intense explanation of actions after they were conducted. Considering pro-active public diplomacy might have led to different decisions. Both sides conducted poor decisions: The Israeli choice to board the "Mavi Marmara" is questionable and shows a lack of military strategic planning. It is unclear whether the flotilla members foresaw the consequences of their actions provoking the military of a state upholding a naval blockade with hundreds of individuals including some with high readiness for violence. The choices made by the Gaza flotilla participants to resort to violence are questionable as well. It can only serve the goal to prove Israeli violent re-/action. However, questions regarding the goals of the flotilla remain unanswered. And whether their gain was worth the cost of losing nine lives (Zuckermann 2012: 84)?

4 Conclusions and Consequences for this Research

The aim of this section is to connect the information gathered so far and derive the conclusions for the present investigation from them. Following, the research question and the hypotheses are derived from the conclusions.

4.1 Conclusion – Mutual Polarization?

Summary of Chapter 2 and 3 The *theoretical background* (see Chapter 2.1) introduces the psychological impacts, (intractable) conflicts have on societies involved in them and how they might impact the media coverage. Societies develop a *socio-psychological infrastructure of conflict* (see Chapter 2.1) that comprises collective memory, a collective emotional orientation and societal beliefs of the *ethos of conflict*. The latter is central for this investigation and hence introduced in depth (see Chapter 2.2). These beliefs help societies to sustain the difficult conflict conditions. However, they also reduce the readiness to compromise and thus cultivate the conflict. The ethos of conflict serves as basis for *narratives* (see Chapter 2.3) that societies form on events of the present and past. *Conflict-supportive narratives* based on the beliefs of the ethos of conflicts are biased and highlight certain aspects of an issue while suppressing others. Within mediatized politics in general and conflicts in particular narratives become a battlefield themselves (see Chapter2.4). This battlefield is characterized by the interdependence of its actors. However, in conflict settings the media is under several constraints that make it particularly vulnerable to lose its independence.

The *research case* of the present investigation is the relation of a conflict society, namely the Jewish Israeli, to and within the international community. A central assumption is that this relation is based on *mutual polarization*. The international community pays disproportionate attention to the Israeli-Palestinian conflict and in particular to Israel (see Chapter 3.1.1). A relevant example for high international involvement and polarization is international media attention towards the conflict and the ongoing debate whether it is biased to either side (see Chapter 3.1.2).

Israel's factual position within the international community is complicated. While geographically quite isolated, Israel is integrated in the Western community. Still those relations are complicated by the conflict reality and in international polls Israel is perceived very negatively (see Chapter 3.1.3). Hence, Israel exerts considerable efforts to influence its standing and image. An indicator for that is the continuous internal debate regarding Israel's public diplomacy (see Chapter 3.1.5). At the same time, Jewish Israeli self-perception and collective memory of Israel's international standing is also characterized by polarization, segregation and fear of annihilation, perceived and real isolation that may lead to siege mentality (see Chapter 3.1.4). This perception has impacts on political decisions, since the ultimate consequence of perceived isolation may be: "If Israel is alone, it can do as it believes to be right." This however, could lead to material isolation.

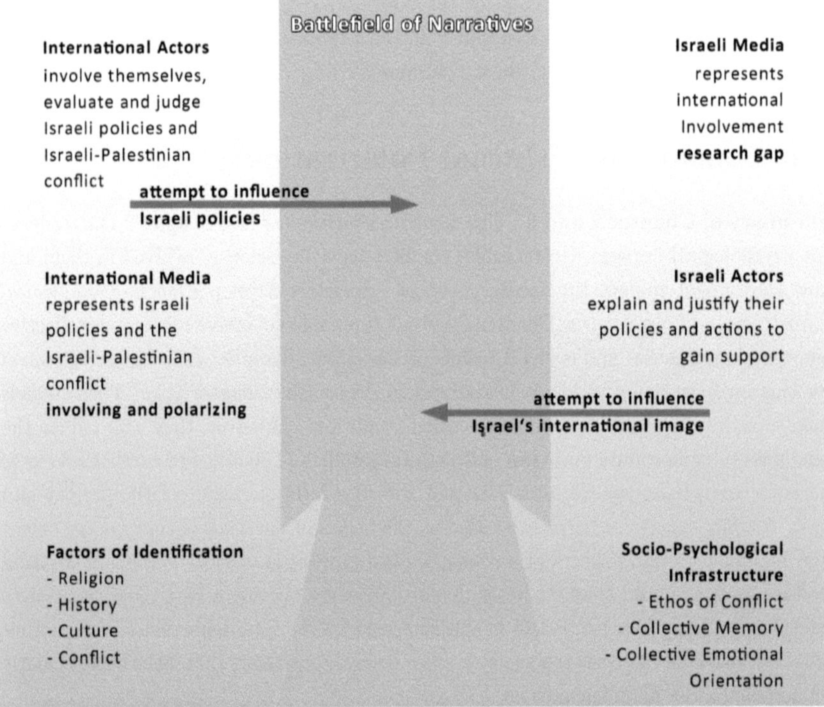

Figure 1 – Interaction between International Actors and Israeli Actors

Conclusions International and Israeli actors interact within a battlefield of narratives. As illustrated in Figure 1, each side contributes beliefs and assumptions on the Self and the Other to the battlefield of narratives. The Jewish Israeli perspectives of a conflict society are characterized by beliefs of the ethos of conflict, beliefs of collective memory and collective emotional orientation. These have an impact on the narratives they form on themselves when interacting with international actors as well as on the narratives they form on the Other. They furthermore influence the perception of the overall interaction, Israel's standing and image within this setting. Concurrently, international perspectives towards Israel are characterized by factors of connection and identification with either conflict party. Those factors can be religious, cultural, historical, political standpoints, or values. These as well influence the narratives formed and the perceptions on the interaction. Thereby each side's underlying concepts have an impact on the interaction, the understanding on it and on decisions of own actions.

The above *interaction between the actors* is based on these underlying factors. 1) In the direction from Israel to international actors, Israeli official actors seek to gain support and attempt to influence Israel's international image through efforts in hasbara. Thereby Israeli actors explain Israel's policies to win support in international media and ultimately international populations. International media pays considerable attention to the conflict, and its factual or perceived polarization is under intense debate. In this way international media polarization and Israeli hasbara efforts interact in a battle over narratives and ultimately the fight between poles. 2) In the direction from international actors to Israel: International actors are involving themselves seeking to influence the conflict parties and populations. Their involvement is again represented to the Jewish Israeli populations mainly through Israeli media.

Desiderates While the direction from Israeli actors towards international (media) actors is investigated and studied (see Chapter 3.1.5 and 3.1.2), the opposite direction from international actors towards Israeli media is not yet clear. How is international involvement presented and perceived? It is the aim of this research to pursue a central aspect of this question – the presentation of international involvement to Israeli citizen in Israeli media.

As illustrated (see Chapter 1 and 2.4), the media is both a central mediator between international actors and a target society and hence a central source of information for recipients in those societies worldwide. During conflict times the external perspective offers an opportunity for self-distanced perspectives. At the same time, national media institutions are part of their societies and mediators between their members, whom they confirm in their beliefs about themselves and provide with a "sense of belonging" (Orgad 2011: 417). However, the media plays an important role in creating distance by reporting "the world" that might negate and disturb the national narratives. Especially in conflict, when the pressure to conform and attachment rises, it is challenging for national media to find a proper distance between independent coverage yet the expectation not to report from "outside the society" (see Chapter 2.4; Orgad 2009). Accordingly, it can be expected that the representation of international involvement in Israeli media includes not only the narrative of the sender but also the beliefs and narratives of the recipient society, in this case Jewish Israeli. Therefore the analysis of media content can lead to conclusions both regarding the information recipients of media content receive on international involvement and in some ways on this society itself.

Research in this field is currently scarce. Segev (2010) finds in his comparison of international news sites and their coverage of international actors that Israel has the highest Local Salience Index: In almost every second article (47%) Israeli newspaper articles refer to Israel itself (16% in Germany). In this analysis, the USA appears as a strongly dominant international actor in Israeli news sites, more than twice as frequently mentioned as the following Iran and Palestine. Segev shows that Israeli news sites are largely self-absorbed and grant only little space to international events in general. However, his study is reduced to the appearance of of international actors in Israeli media and does not provide any information how the actors appear in Israeli media.

Orgad (2009; 2011) analyzes how international actors are represented in Israeli television news during the Gaza crisis 2008/09. Her leading question is whether it is used as tool for estrangement. She finds that the television coverage rarely used opportunities for estrangement from the official narrative by covering external actors. The findings indicate three versions of estrangement: Either the "foreign vocabulary" is adapted that offers a different perspective, or foreign images of Gazan suffering are displayed, or criticism by international actors is voiced that gives a possibility to see the events through the eyes of the Other. All three versions were rarely used as tool for self-distancing but rather contextualized as proof for the hostile international community and siege mentality. Orgad concludes that the "Israeli political system and culture do not allow meaningful expression of self-distance" (Orgad 2011: 412). Orgad's analyses (2009; 2011) are illuminating for the present investigation and offer valuable insights on the constraints of national media during conflict (See above). However she does not provide empirical data. Her analysis remains episodic. There is no comparison between crisis and routine phases within the Jewish Israeli society. There is no thorough analysis how the representation is constructed, which narratives are used. There is no differentiation between the involving actors and their claims.

The present investigation however goes further and aims at a thorough analysis how international involvement in a conflict society is represented in its media products. The case is the Israeli newspaper representation of international involvement surrounding the events of the Gaza flotilla in comparison to calmer phases before and after the crisis (see for choice of case: Chapter 1.3, and for choice of analysis: Chapter 4.3).

4.2 Research Question and Hypotheses

It is the aim of this research to investigate the representation of international involvement in the Israeli-Palestinian conflict in Israeli newspapers within the context outlined above and summarized in Figure 1. The central research question (RQ) of the present investigation is:

How is international involvement in the Israeli-Palestinian conflict represented in Israeli daily newspapers?

This question leads to the following sub-questions:

1) Is there a difference between crisis and routine times in the representations?

2) Are the actors and their claims represented differently?

3) Are the representations influenced by societal conflict beliefs?

4) Are representations different among the Israeli newspapers?

To answer these questions, hypotheses are developed on the basis of discussed concepts and on a pretest on Israeli newspapers. This combination of deductive and inductive hypothesis- and later category-building is recommended by Früh (2011: 72). While deductive "basic-knowledge-based open category-finding" and gradual refining can extract the variety and complexity of features, only inductive approaches can show missing categories. First, based on basic knowledge and the state of research, presumptions and categories were built. They were tested, selected, specified, supplemented, and refined during category building based on empirical findings of the sample survey on a representative cross section of the material under investigation (ibid.: pp.77, for procedures of the present investigation see Chapter 4.3). Based on these first findings, hypotheses were developed to translate the research question into several testable statements. In the following the hypotheses will be introduced and the underlying background outlined.

Representations of the Actors

The basic assumption is that actors are perceived differently in Israeli newspaper coverage based on the relationship with the respective actor. That implies that President Barack Obama is contextualized differently than the Secretary-General of the United Nations Ban Ki-moon, because the relationship with the United Nations is complicated whereas the relationship to the USA is strong and positive (see for example Gilboa 2008*b*).

H_1 The investigated actors are represented differently. Actors are represented in a polarizing manner of "with or against Israel".

The hypothesis is based on the previous elaborations in Chapter 3.1 and in particular the outlined concept of siege mentality (see Chapter 3.1.4). On the one hand, the Israeli-Palestinian conflict "enjoys" high international attention, and is controversially discussed (Shinar 2005: 176), and actors easily polarize in categories such as "pro-Israeli" or "pro-Palestinian". On the other hand, Jewish Israelis tend to categorize actors, nations, and institutions into one or the other extreme and in doing so polarize in "friend" or "foe" dualisms. Therefore, the representations of international actors expected to be not only different in general but also through polarization in dichotomous categories of "with or against Israel". H_1 is tested in the content analysis by combination of the appearance of actors with their representation and the representation of the relationship.

Representations of the Involvement

As illustrated above, international involvement in the Israeli-Palestinian conflict is polarizing (see Chapter 3.1). Therefore it can be expected that involvement appearing in Israeli newspapers is polarizing, either supportive or critical, i.e., voicing criticism, of Israeli policies and actions. Accordingly, it is assumed that this involvement is represented in different manners.

H_2 The claims by the actors are represented differently. The involvement is either supportive or critical. Supportive involvement is contextualized positively and critical involvement is contextualized negatively.

This hypothesis is based on the assumption of mutual polarization introduced above and on the pretest that showed different representations on different forms of involvement. Further, the pretest has shown the need for another category of involvement that does not focus on past events, but calls for future actions. It will be coded separately. All this indicates that the focus on past or future has implications on the framing. To test H_2, the appearance and character of the claims (supportive/critical) and their focus (focus on past events versus focus on future events) is analyzed within the representation of the claims and the representation of the actors, and other factors.

Representations and the Ethos of Conflict

This hypothesis is based on existing research on the ethos of conflict in Israeli Jewish society. As introduced in Chapter 2.2, the beliefs comprising the ethos of conflict are a product of societies coping with the reality of intractable conflict (Bar-Tal 1998*b*, 2007*a*,*b*, 2013; Bar-Tal, Halperin and Oren 2010; Bar-Tal, Halperin and de Rivera 2007; Bar-Tal et al. 2012; Nasie and Bar-Tal 2012). It has been studied and repeatedly proven that the Jewish Israeli society developed and holds a strong set of beliefs that constitute the ethos of conflict (see Chapter 3.2). Societal beliefs are expected to appear in cultural products, particularly in the media (see for example Sharvit and Bar-Tal 2007).

H_3 Israeli newspaper representation of international involvement is permeated by beliefs of the ethos of conflict that are found in narratives.

The assumption is that social identity is mediated through societal beliefs. Sharvit and Bar-Tal (2007: 204) state:

> In the case of a society involved in an intractable conflict, the media helps disseminate and consolidate the beliefs that form the ethos. Accordingly, societies that are engaged in an intractable conflict tend to enlist the media in the societal effort of coping with the conflict, and in some cases the media enlists in this effort at its own initiative. (2007: 204)

Bar-Tal occasionally accentuates his arguments with newspaper headlines or parts of news items. Sharvit and Bar-Tal (2007) describe the Israeli media during the Second Intifada, but although they draw conclusions on the media's conduct during this phase and on the occurence of the ethos of conflict they do not specify which media products were analyzed, in which period, and with which instrument. Their assumptions remain vague and very general. That means, a systematic empiric research on media and ethos of conflict could not be found yet. H_3 is tested by analyzing the appearance of the eight beliefs of the ethos of conflict (see Chapter 2.2). To find out aspects triggering the appearance it will be tested with the other categories (e.g., newspaper, period, actor, claim, etc.) in addition to the eight beliefs.

Difference between Crisis and Routine Periods

The impacts of intractable conflicts on societies entangled in them are discussed in Chapter 2.2. The beliefs and narratives societies hold about themselves are apparent in cultural products such as the media. As outlined, conflicts are mediatized and the formulation of narratives to contextualize events constitutes a battlefield just as the conflict itself (see Chapter 2.3). Intractable conflicts are protracted and therefore characterized by relatively calm phases (called here "routine" since the general conflict is still ongoing) and phases of violent outbreaks (called crisis phases) (see Chapter 1.5). Therefore also media coverage in times of crisis and routine is expected to differ.

H_4 The appearances and representations differ between times of routine and times of crisis. In general, the representations of the analyzed actors and their involvement are expected to be more negative in crisis times than in routine times.

This hypothesis is based on existing research of (Israeli) media coverage in times of crisis. It is the aim of this investigation to test these concepts on the context of international involvement and its representation in Israeli media. Several mechanisms characterize media coverage in times of crisis and will be briefly outlined here. External conditions with impact on the coverage, especially in war times, are e.g., censorship, self-censorship, and the media's heavy dependence on official sources, such as the military and government (Liebes 1997). At the same time, the public relies on news during conflict timeseven more than during times of relative routine.

The relevant framing mechanisms in times of crisis can be put into two general categories – the coverage of the Own, the "dominant" group, versus the coverage of the Other, the rival, as part of the media's tendency for ethnocentric reporting of crisis, starting with the journalists' ethnicity (in this case usually Jewish Israelis), the narrative and language, and the dependency on official sources from the own side (Rinnawi 2007; Wolfsfeld 1997, 2001; Wolfsfeld, Frosh and Awabdy 2008).

The coverage of the own and dominant side is easily characterized by a "rally around the flag" syndrome and often fulfills a role of mobilization. Ethnocentric information flow and mobilization leads to "victims mode of reporting" (Wolfsfeld 2003). In this mode, own victims are highly personalized, emotionalized and dramatized. This is contextualized by ethnic solidarity and demonizing of the adversary. Thereby, concentrating on several details helps to prevent concentration on the bigger context (Liebes 1997; Wolfsfeld 2003). Violence exerted by the own side is downplayed and legitimized (Wolfsfeld 2003), while the consequences remain unclear – the dirty side of the conflict is "disinfected" and the adversary and consequences of violence are excised (Liebes 1997). In cases of exaggerated violence, the "defense mode" of coverage applies, characterized by a low level of emotionalization, a non prominent, analytical, and intellectual coverage in the news. Victims on the adversary side are depersonalized and sometimes the blame for their situation is assigned to the adversary itself (Wolfsfeld 2003). They and their actions are delegitimized in their goals, demonized, dramatized, stereotyped, and equalized in their power through mystification (Bar-Tal 1998a; Liebes 1997; Rinnawi 2007).

Based on this research it is assumed that in the following investigation the representation of international actors and their involvement is more negative in crisis than in routine times. First, it can be assumed that more critical claims are found in crisis times, and second that their framing is more polarizing, the narratives are expected to be closer to official lines and beliefs of siege mentality might be held stronger. To test H_4 the investigation period is split in a crisis period surrounding the Gaza flotilla raid and two surrounding routine periods (routine A and B). The appearance, kind of involvement and framing of the actors, relationship, claim and appearance of societal beliefs of conflicts is compared between the three periods.

The Representing Newspapers

As outlined in Chapter 3.3 the four newspapers differ in their tradition, political leaning and format. This could indicate that the newspapers differ in their representations of international involvement. However, as also shown in the chapter and in Chapter 2.4, there are some implicit limitations to the Israeli media such as a pseudo-pluralism, military censorship, self-censorship and authoritarian regulations that may be implemented at any time that might decrease pluralistic media representations. The content analysis will investigate whether the newspapers are different in their representations on one particular issue.

H_5 The newspapers' representation of international involvement differs according to the respective political line.

This hypothesis is supported by research on Israeli newspaper coverage during conflict times and findings on editing patterns. There are different results so far. Dor (2005) claims representations of conflict phases (he studied Operation Defense Shield in 2002) differ in the newspapers. While Maariv mostly supports the official government line, and seeks collective support and coherence, Yediot Aheronot longs for collective support and consensus while criticizing the government. Haaretz offers a variety perspectives (Dor 2005: Chapter 3; 6). Dor's research on the outbreak of the Second Intifada shows similar results (Dor 2004). Khalil Rinnawi, on the other hand, did not find any difference between the newspapers coverage (Yediot Aheronot and Haaretz) in his study on delegitimization of Israeli-Palestinian protests during the second Intifada (Rinnawi 2007: 177). Nevertheless, both agree that framing of news can be achieved inter alia through manipulation of salience attributed to information, for example through formulation of headlines, leads, the positioning and size of an article, and through positioning and size of the article (Dor 2004: 9; Rinnawi 2007: 152). The H_5 is tested by analyzing the four newspapers with all the other categories.

4.3 Research Design

> "Begin at the beginning," the King said gravely, "and go on till you come to the end: then stop."
>
> — Lewis Carroll, Alice in Wonderland

After introducing the research questions and hypotheses this chapter demonstrates the path taken to construct the research design and conduct the actual analysis. First, the content analysis, the chosen sample, the period and the procedure of data collection are outlined. Second, the development of the research instrument, measures, and tests are discussed and further the instrument itself introduced. Last, the analysis itself is described.

Chosen Method – Content Analysis

The research question on the representation of international involvement in Israeli media naturally asks for a content analysis rather than any other research method, since the content of media products is the main interest. Content analysis has proven to be one of the most effective methods to analyze media coverage and is widely used in the media and communication studies. There are different definitions of content analysis and its capabilities. A classic definition by Berelson (1952: 18) understands content analysis as "a research technique for the objective, systematic, and quantitative description of the manifest content of communication". Though classic and widely used, several parts of Berelson's description of content analysis is not useful for this study, as the goal "objectivity" can not be reached, solely "quantitative" analysis is too restrictive, and the material is not considered "manifest" as it still is perceived different by different recipients. Werner Früh's definition is more useful here:

> The content analysis is an empirical method for the systematic, inter-subjectively comprehensible description of content and formal characteristics of releases, mostly with the goal of an inference based upon such interpretive issues on external situations. (Früh 2011: 27, translated from German)

Früh (2011) implies a different understanding of communication, which cannot be analyzed objectively and is not manifest, but contains information that is interpreted by the recipient. In this sense, objectification is achieved through a systematic and inter-subjectively comprehensible approach to the object of study. Rather than focusing on the impossible goal of "objectivity", Früh concentrates on traceability and shifts the focus onto the instrument, here the codebook which has to enable different coders to obtain similar results. Furthermore, the reduction of content analysis to quantitative methods was not made by Früh.

Rössler (2005) proposed the term "standardized content analysis" to avoid ambiguous distinction between quantitative and qualitative approaches. Früh (2011: 39) also argues that in content analysis, the frequency and character of "qualitative" features is measured. Thus, quantifying measuring requires qualitative analysis, and a combination of approaches is common (ibid.: 38). Merten (1983) further explicated the correlation between content and context – again not reducing it to quantitative measures. "Content analysis is a method for inquiry of social reality, in which conclusions from features of a manifest text are drawn on non-manifest contexts" (Merten 1983: 102, translated from German). In this sense, Atteslander (2003) concludes the use of content analysis as

> a method of data collection for detection of social circumstances. Conclusions can be drawn through analysis of a given content (e.g. text, image) describing the context of its creation, the intention of its transmitter, and on the effect on its recipient and/or on the social situation. (Atteslander 2003: 238, translated from German)

Atteslanders understanding goes very far, as its focus is not merely on the description of the content but on drawing conclusions on the directly or indirectly involved society, the recipients, and the media actors. Although one aim of the investigation is to test the adherence of the ethos of conflict in Israeli newspapers it is out of the scope of this analysis to draw direct conclusions on the effects this has on recipients. The focus is first on the analysis of what recipients "receive" when consuming newspaper content. Following Frühs (2011) understanding of content analysis, it contains an interest in selection and classification that is actually a searching strategy (Früh 2007: 78; 134). Creating such a searching strategy is challenging, it starts with the choice of articles and continues with the operationalization (see below). A central task of content analysis is to reduce complexity (Koch 2012: 147) for the classification of media phenomena in the data material into a nominal scale. The loss of information is what enables winning a larger perspective on structural characteristics and comparability (Früh 2007: 35; 42). To achieve results that can be generalized, the process needs to be intersubjective. This requires disclosure of the procedures, complete, distinct categories and clear rules for coding.

In the present investigation a quantitative content analysis is conducted. That means, characteristics of the text are collected in a closed system of categories (Koch 2012: 148). The term is used because of the chosen closed categories, although the categories are derived from the text material in a qualitative pretest. Closed categories allow for a greater amount of text material to be analyzed. The next sections outline the procedures. The chosen case, the Israeli-Palestinian conflict and in particular Jewish Israeli society, is introduced earlier (see Chapter 1.3, 3.3, and 3.4). In the following sections the chosen sample, investigation period, the chosen international actors whose involvement is analyzed, and the procedure of data collection and the final sample are introduced. The procedure of creating the codebook and the final product and last of conducting the analysis is outlined.

Chosen Media – The General Israeli Newspapers

The chosen media for this analysis are newspapers. Though their printed circulations are in decline, they still are an important source of information for leaders, general public, and in "forming foreign images and influencing the character of international relations" (Pardo and Peters 2010: 81). In contrast to television or online news sites, newspapers are published once a day. Hence, the pressure to publish is comparably low and allows more time for interpretation and contextualization. Moreover, in a society as news-dependent as the Israeli society, one can assume that newspaper do not actually "break the news", but deepen, analyze and describe what is already known through radio, television and online news. In the present investigation the central question is how international involvement is represented, contextualized (See 4). Central hypotheses regard the representations of actors, their involvement, and the narratives used for that. Therefore, analyzing newspapers is the right choice as they can be expected to focus more on contextualization than on mere news-reporting.

The focus is on the overall Jewish Israeli society. Therefore the four Israeli Hebrew daily printed newspapers directed at the general Hebrew speaking population are chosen: Israel Hayom, Yediot Aheronot, Maariv, and Haaretz. Although the newspaper market has changed since 2010, these four newspapers were the relevant Israeli newspapers at the time (for changes of the newspaper market in 2014, see Chapter 3.3). Other newspapers with specified target groups inside the Israeli society, be it based on religious beliefs (e.g., Jewish orthodox, Chassidic or traditional; Muslim; Christian; Bahai), ethnicity (e.g., Russian, Arabic or Anglophone population), or special interest (such as economics) are not part of this analysis. The focus of this investigation on general mainstream newspapers derives from the research question. It aims at the representations that derive from narratives and beliefs of the overall Jewish Israeli society. For those, mainstream press is expected to give generalizable answers answers regarding the dominant beliefs and narratives within media representations in Jewish Israeli society and not solely in stratified groups within the society.

Chosen Investigation Period – Surrounding the Gaza Flotilla Raid

The sample of items for this investigation is chosen deliberately and not in a random sample since it is a case study. The chosen case is the Gaza Flotilla raid on May 31, 2010 (see Chapter 3.4). To ensure comparability between routine and crisis times three months surrounding the events (April 15 to July 15, 2010) are analyzed.

Splitting of the investigation period for comparison   The period of three months is split in three phases of roughly a month each. The first and the third period are times of relative routine whereas the central weeks (surrounding the events of the Gaza Flotilla raid) are a period of crisis. The distinction between the periods was initially cut between months (month 1 routine; month 2 crisis; month 3 routine). After collection of the data, this distinction was adapted to the research material that suggested different lenghts of the periods.

In the context of this research a *crisis period* is defined as a period characterized by negative, violent incidents that cause multiple and prominent coverage of international involvement. The chosen indicators are at least three relevant and coded articles appearing on the first ten pages of the analyzed newspapers for more than two days in a row. Hence, a *routine period* is characterized by a lack of a negative, violent incidents that causes multiple and prominent coverage of international involvement for more than one day. Yet, if no more than three coded relevant articles appear on the first ten pages and they are not related to a violent, negative incident, this indicates routine. The distribution of periods as it evolved from the research results is illustrated in Table 3.

Table 3 – Distribution of Time Periods in Content Analysis

Routine A	Crisis	Routine B
April 15 to May 26, 2010	May 27 to June 14, 2010	June 15 to July 14, 2010

Routine A represents the time before the Gaza flotilla raid. Routine B might differ from phase A due to the strong impact of the Gaza flotilla raid on Israel's international standing. The crisis period starts before the raid of the flotilla. The Gaza flotilla raid was no surprising event, media coverage prior to the raid was preparing for it. As the coverage intensified, a sense of crisis was created in the last days prior to the raid on May 31. The periods are compared with each other and their proximity is considered an advantage. Since the period of crisis is embedded in the periods of relative routine, one can expect external influencing circumstances in the newspapers and media-sphere, the political environment, and socio-political constitution, etc. to be almost the same in the three phases.

Chosen Actors

The investigation focuses on international actors that are not directly involved in the conflict setting but are economic, cultural, political partners that involve themselves in the conflict setting. As described in section 3.1.3, Israel has strong relations with Europe and North- America and since its foundation sought for inclusion into international organizations. An alliance of countries and institutions particularly relevant to Israel as partners that aim to impact the Israeli-Palestinian conflict is the Quartet on the Middle East. Its members are the European Union, Russia, the United Nations and the United States of America. Aside from Arabic countries, these comprise the countries and supranational institutions that are centrally involved in efforts to interfere in the Middle

East conflict. Therefore it is particularly relevant to investigate how their involvement is perceived.

Due to the chosen period of investigation surrounding the Gaza flotilla raid in 2010, Turkey and the Gaza flotilla members are added as investigated actors. Furthermore, another group of actors emerged during the pretest since a lot of articles write about "the World" and its attitudes towards Israel, or summed up "international involvement", meaning general western actors. This group is called "unspecified Western actors".

Criteria for Article Selection

The criteria for selection of articles are the following: 1) newspaper articles in Israel Hayom, Yediot Aheronot, Maariv, and Haaretz 2) published in the week and weekend edition are scanned in 3) the general section (excluding sections such as culture, literature, sports, economics, travel, shopping or weekend supplies) for relevant articles.

Relevant are any articles that contain 4) naming or referring to a nation, institution, or actor belonging to the Quartet on the Middle East, Turkey, or the members of the flotilla bound to Gaza in 2010, 5) in which the actor/s address an issue of the Israeli-Palestinian conflict; Israeli politics and policies through verbal or real action; 6) or articles in which the author discusses the relationship between the actor and Israel 7) in the headline, sub-headline or first sub-section.

Data Collection and Sample

Israeli newspapers are not listed in the database LexisNexis. Therefore, the relevant articles had to be searched manually. The databases of the analyzed newspapers were used for the collection of relevant research material according to the indicators declared above. The author was granted access to the internal databases of Yediot Aheronot, Maariv, and Haaretz. Yediot Aheronot and Maariv have a local database in their newsrooms. There they keep a pdf-version of the printed newspaper. Therefore all the newspapers in the analyzed period were screened on the computers of the publishing houses and articles found relevant were saved from there. The database of Haaretz works solely as a searching engine, therefore the newspapers were screened manually at a library archive in Tel Aviv. Relevant articles were then downloaded from the online database. Israel Hayom publishes its printed newspapers also online and keeps an open database, therefore no special granting of access was necessary. Overall, 861 relevant articles were identified.

Due to research economical reasons the amount of the 861 articles had to be reduced. First every fourth and then every second article per newspaper was selected. As the table shows, between 45% to 49% of each newspapers' articles were chosen that are between 81 and 115 articles of each newspaper. Thereby the amount of selected article was balanced with the percentage chosen of each newspapers total amount of relevant articles to avoid a strong imbalance between the newspapers (see Table 4).

Table 4 – Relevant and Coded Articles

Newspaper	Relevant articles (N=861)	Coded articles (N=400)	Coded articles in %
Israel Hayom (IH)	257	115	45
Haaretz (HA)	217	100	46
Maariv (MA)	167	81	49
Yediot Aheronot (YA)	220	104	47

The amount of articles was weightened with their percentage to ensure balance between them. This approach was chosen over coding strictly the same amount of articles per newspaper as it would lead to an imbalance of chosen articles per newspaper. Altogether, 400 articles, meaning roughly every second relevant article of the investigated period, were coded. The following section gives an overview over the process of coding and the coded variables. Each article is given an ID that identifies the newspaper (MA = Maariv; HA = Haaretz; YA = Yediot Aheronot; IH = Israel Hayom) the date of publication, and the page of publication (for example: IH_2010_06_03_002) and as such appears in the following chapter.

Instrumentation – Creating the Instrument

The chosen instrument to analyze the relevant articles that deal with international involvement in the Israeli-Palestinian conflict is a codebook. The codebook is a system of categories to measure the relevant parts of the research material (Rössler 2005: 93). The categories shall be disjunct, i.e. not overlap and without omission, exclusive and not include more or less than the research material. In this manner, an exhaustive category system can be built which structures and limits the room of meaning for the classification of the research objects (Früh 2011: 86). No literature was found on such an analysis on the media representation of international involvement in a conflict society. Therefore, a new instrument had to be created. Based on the theory, the beliefs of the ethos of conflict were to be tested. They were adapted from the scale used by Nasie and Bar-Tal (2012) in a content analysis on articles written by Palestinian children on the setting of this investigation. The formal categories were also clear before the pretest (newspaper, date, actor, etc.). The categories for the representation of the involvement were created and refined through thorough pretesting.

First phase – creation In a pretest of 20 random articles chosen of the total corpus of relevant articles were analyzed in depth. This first qualitative coding was based on what

Früh describes as "empirically guided category building" (Früh 2011: pp.156) in four steps: 1) selection and reduction of text parts related to the research question, 2) summarizing of these text parts, 3) abstraction and designation of those parts, and 4) reference back to theory and hypothesis. Based on the theory and the hypotheses (see Chapter 4) the following questions were leading in stage 4 of the category building:

1) Who is the international actor?

2) What is the actors' central claim?

3) How is the claim framed?

4) How is the actor framed?

5) How is the relationship between Israel and the actor framed?

6) Are there societal beliefs of the ethos of conflict?

These questions were addressed at the reduced, summarized and abstacted text parts of the first 20 texts and lists categories built from this. On the base of this process a first codebook was created, discussed, and refined. This draft codebook comprised a very detailed list of categories regarding the central questions.

Second phase – refining In the next phase 100 articles were coded based on the draft codebook to test whether the coding gave valuable results. The range of results was very broad which makes comparable results difficult. Clearly, the variables had too many categories. In the next phase the draft codebook was modified and refined. First the existing categories were re-evaluated based on step three and four of Früh's empirically guided category building as described above. Then the new codebook was reviewed with experts and scholars in the relevant fields (political communication, political psychology, Israeli-Palestinian conflict, and statistics). In a third step the codebook was tested again on the first 100 articles. After a review of those preliminary codings with a statistician the codebook was finalized and ready to use for the content analysis.

The Codebook

The final version of the codebook (see Appendix C) contains several sections (see Table 5). Not all the variables can be outlined here in detail, but the relevant and complex ones are introduced in the following.

Formal variables (01 to 06) The first set of variables comprises the formal factors of the article. Those regard the coder, the ID of the article, its date, the page of publication, the newspaper, the amount of words, and the format of the article. The size of an article is measured by amount of words rather than by physical size since the newspapers in general have very different appearance.

Table 5 – Coding Scheme

Section	Variables
Formal variables	ID, coder, investigation period, date, newspaper, page, amount of words, article format
Actor and involvement	Main actor, institution, Gaza flotilla participant, citation, topic, claim
Representation	Framing of the claim, framing of the actor, framing of the relationship
Mechanisms of representation	Contextualization, impact enhancement, further mechanisms
Ethos of conflict	Societal beliefs of the ethos of conflict

The actors and their involvement (07 to 11b)   First, the *main actors* in the articles are coded. As explained above, these are European actors, Russia, Turkey, United Nations, United States, unspecified Western actors, the Quartet on the Middle East, and the Gaza flotilla participants (GFP). The next variable asks for the *institutional background* of the actor. This is seperated into: governmental (any institution related to government, opposition, authorities), the media, NGO, unclassified individuals (this is coded when the actors are described as a group of demonstrators, musicians, citizen etc. not related to media, NGO or government), or not specified. Following the *appearance of citations* by the actors within the article is coded. It is considered an indicator of estrangement from the own narratives and personalization of the involving actors if they are quoted directly and not merely paraphrased in their involvement.

The next category regards the *central topic* the claim relates to. This variable was kept very general. Either the claim related to the Israeli-Palestinian conflict in general (e.g., settlements, negotiations, nuclear weapons, the gaza blockade, or terror attacks), to the Gaza flotilla (e.g., intentions, expectations, preparations, the raid, the outcomes, or the aftermath of the raid), or to the relationship between Israel and the actor.

The final variable asked for the main *claim* of the actor in the article. The claim is the central message by the international actor to Israel (in the interpretation of the journalist). This message can be an action, a statement, a behavior. All of them can be sorted into four general categories: they can either be critical (e.g.,"X condemns Israel's ..."), supportive (e.g., "X supports Israel's..."), refrain from a judgment of present and past policies (e.g.,"X demands..."). A last option is the lack of a claim by the actor (e.g., when merely the relationship between the international actor and Israel is discusssed by the journalist).

In a second step the direction of the claim was established: Either it relates to existing or past policies (e.g., "X supports/condemns Y") or it relates to future events the actor wishes to happen (e.g., "X calls for ..."). Both the direction and the character of the claim establish eight different forms of involvement. An involvement can be supportive and related to current or already past events or policies (e.g., "X supports Israel's right to defend itself") or relate to the future (e.g., "X supports Israel's plan to investigate the events on the flotilla"), criticism related to the past (e.g., "X condemns Israel's actions during the raid of the flotilla") or criticism related to the future (e.g., "X criticizes the plan to stop the flotilla"). It can also refrain from a judgment with focus on present and past (e.g. "both parties ..."), or refrain from a judgment with focus on the future (e.g., "X calls for an investigation"). After the coding and the analysis, in chapter 6, four main forms of involving were formed of these eight possibilities: supportive and critical involvement, calls for action, and articles without claims

The representation of the actor, the involvement, and the relationship (12 to 14)   Each of these variables is constructed alike. There are separate questions whether there is *framing of the actor/involvement/relationship*. This can be either positive (yes/no); and/or neutral (yes/no); and/or negative (yes/no). Separating these questions on the general character of the frames allows multiple answers. That is intentional because it is possible that an article has multiple frames – for example negative and positive frames on a certain actor (e.g., "the actor is a supporter" and "the actor lacks understanding for Israel"). This is regarded as indicator for a debate on either the claim, actor, or relationship. Each evaluation of a framing is supplemented by examples that are not used for statistical analysis but for orientation of the coder and later for the discussion of the results (for example "negative framing of the involvement" has subcategories: "Negates Israel's policies", "illegitimate", "counterproductive on path to peace", "not important", "exaggerated").

Positive frames of the claim can be: "the claim is in agrement with Israel's policies", "the claim is helpful on the path to peace", "the claim is important". Neutral frames of a claim are: "the claim is worth a discussion", "the claim is balanced". Negative framing of the claim can be: "the claim negates Israel's policies", "the claim is unacceptable", "the claim is counterproductive on the path to peace", "the claim is not important".

Some examples for positive framing of the actor are: "the actor is a supporter of Israel", "the actor understands Israel", "the actor is legitimate", "the actor is pro-Israeli". Neutral framing of the actor can be: "the actor is unbiased", "the actor is uncommitted". Negative framing of the actor is for example: "the actor is biased", "the actor lacks understanding for Israel", "the actor is a terrorist", "the actor is responsible", "the actor attacks Israel".

The framing of the relationship is positive when these frames appear: "the actor is a friend", "the actor is a partner", emphasis on the cooperation, "the relationship imporved", "the relationship is strong". Neutral framing of the relationship can be: "the relationship is nonpartisan", "the relationship is uncommitted". Negative framing of the relationship can be: "the actor is an enemy of Israel", "the actor is no partner", emphasis on a confrontation", "the actor is not relevant for Israel", "the relationship worsened or is in a crisis". Another possible framing is the emphasis on the relationship as complex.

The contextualization (15 to 17) Following several *mechanisms of framing* are listed. These appeared in the pretests and their spreading is tested. First the contextualization of the claim is categorized either as embedded in wider contexts or as concentration on details. A second variable categorizes whether the impact of the claim is enhanced or softened by the journalist. Indicators for enhancement are: the repetition of an argument, repeated emphasis on the consequences of an issue, repeated emphasis on the importance of the actor. Indicators for softening of the impact can be: downplaying of the impact ("it could have been worse"), downplaying of the relevance of the actor.

In a third variable known frames are listed. A further frame is "law and order versus chaos" (see Chapter 4) in which the involving actor is described as destroying the order (disorder news) while Israel is described as restoring order (order news). Gans (1980) described order and disorder news and Wolfsfeld, Avraham and Aburaiya (2000) adapted it to the Israeli-Palestinian conflict. The concept of siege mentality is introduced in 3.1.4 and coded when the international actor is described as attacking Israel that is isolated and alone. Another frame is "with or against Israel" (see Chapter 1.3, 3.1.4, and 4), which categorizes the international actor in polarizing manner. Another possible framing is the "personalization of the rival" which appears when the rival is described with human traits, named, his/her intentions are described.

The ethos of conflict (18 to 25) The last section entails the *beliefs of the ethos of conflict* (see Chapter 2.2). The eight categories and descriptions are adapted from a previous study by Nasie and Bar-Tal (2012). Delegitimization is coded, when the actors or their actions are attributed with negative, inhumane characterizations. Victimization of the own group regards the information the text gives on Israel, emphasizes unjust experiences by Jewish Israelis (e.g., harsh international criticism, attacks, etc.). This includes beliefs regarding a hostile world. The belief in security is coded when either threats to Israeli security or the protection of security are emphasized. The justness of one's own goals regards the emphasis on Jewish Israeli goals and actions to achieve them as right. That includes the right to exist and settle in Israel. National Unity is based on the support of the society, the leaders, and their goals. Patriotism includes the pride and loyalty to Israel. Beliefs in peace are coded when its relevance, importance or nature is emphasized or when it is used to argue for or against something. Positive in-group image includes all the descriptions of positive characterizations of Jewish Israelis.

Procedures

The research material was collected and coded in summer 2013. While the main corpus of the material was coded by the author, four native Hebrew speakers coded some of the articles to ensure that language was not a factor in the coding. All four coders were trained at length in several meetings, through an intensive introduction of the codebook, and by several test codings together and separately. The coders could not be paid therefore the amount they actually coded comprises only 53 articles. Because their work was important centrally to test the accuracy of the author's coding, those articles were coded by both the author and the coders. The codebook comprises 100 items, and in the differences between the author and the coders were never higher than 5 items of these 100 variables. In these cases of differences, those were discussed and the codebook refined. The rest (347 articles) was coded solely by the author.

The coding process was conducted as follows: In a first step the coder double-checked the relevance of the respective article. Then the categories of all variables were filled in an Excel-Sheet. The coding refers to all the words of an article, accordingly frame elements are coded both from the content of the article (the author's words) and from citations the journalist chose to mention within the article. Several variables are not part of the statistical analysis and were answered in free writing for qualitative purpose and to follow up on the answers given. All the coding is documented in a large Excel-Sheet that serves as good basis for basic analysis and was converted into an SPSS-compatible file where most of the analysis was undertaken.

Statistical tools The statistical tests were conducted in SPSS 21.0. The statistical significance (p) is set at $\alpha=.05$. Different types of hypothesis tests were used. To analyze the dependency between to nominal scaled variables *chi square* (χ^2) was used. The chi square test compares the expected numbers under the assumption of independency and the observed data and provides a measure of the discrepancy. A low level p-value inidcates a high dependency of the two variables. If the p-value is smaller than α the assumption of independency was rejected and the two variables were associated.To analyze the dependency of the mean of ratio scaled variables X on a nominal variable Y one of two different tests was used. If X is normally distributed for each value of Y, a T-test was conducted, otherwise a Mann-Whitney-test was conducted. Again, a low p-value indicates a high dependency of the means of the means on variable Y. Ony tests regarding the variable "page" and "amount of words were tested this way. To test a sample on normal distribution, Shapiro-Wilk-Test was used. Holding the null hypothesis that the variable is normally distributed, it is only discarded if the p-value is smaller than α.

Part II

Results of the Study

This second part of the thesis introduces, contextualizes and discusses the results of the study designed in the previous chapter and conducted accordingly. The following chapter introduces the results on the appearance and representation of the analyzed actors and contextualizes them with relevant literature (see Chapter 5). Chapter 6 analyzes the differing forms and representations of involvement by those actors (see Chapter 7). The third and central chapter discusses central narratives in representing international actors and their involvement.

Every chapter starts with a section introducing the relevant results that are then outlined in detail. The related tables are introduced either in this section or the appendix. All the numbers are rounded to zero decimal points. The sections discussing the results are enriched with episodic examples of articles to illustrate the quantitative results.

5 The Actors Involving Themselves

The international actors analyzed in this investigation are the members of the Quartet on the Middle East, namely the European Union, Russia, the United Nations and the USA. Because of the chosen research period surrounding the Gaza flotilla, the Gaza flotilla participants and Turkey were added as actors. Furthermore, another category evolved in the coding – the category of unspecified Western actors, relating to an undefined number of general Western actors (see Chapter 4.3). Since there are not enough articles on Russia and the Quartet on the Middle East as such, both have been excluded from the following evaluation as explained in detail below. Analyzing the appearance and representations of these actors tests hypothesis H_1. It states that investigated actors are represented differently and in a polarized manner.

First, the relevant results of the content analysis regarding the appearance, personalization, placement, and representation of the actors are listed. Second, the results are interpreted separately for the respective actors by contextualization of the results with literature on the relationship.

5.1 The Results in Short

This section lists the results. They are contextualized and discussed in the following sections.

Appearance of actors All six actors appear in Israeli newspapers in different frequency (see Figure 2). The United States are the main international actor in 151 of the 400 analyzed articles. Turkey, Europe, and the Gaza flotilla participants (GFP) follow with 63 to 57 articles each. The next group of unspecified western actors (Unspecified) appears in 47 of the coded articles. Articles on involvement by the United Nations are less frequent than on the other actors with a total of 22 articles. There is a significant difference in the actors' periods of appearance ($p = .000$). While European actors, United Nations, and the USA appear continuously throughout the three periods, the other actors Turkey, GFP and Unspecified are referred to more often, or almost exclusively, during the crisis period (see actors and their appearance in detail in Table 23 in Appendix A).

Table 6 – Placement of Articles on Different Actors (in Pages)

	Europe (n=57)	UN (n=22)	USA (n=151)	Turkey (n=63)	GFP (n=60)	Unspecified (n=47)
$\bar{n}$	11.2	8.5	8.6	9.8	8.9	11.6
σ	9.0	7.7	7.8	7.3	8.5	9.9

$\bar{n}$ = average value, σ = standard deviation

Table 7 – Length of Articles on Different Actors (Amount of Words)

	Europe (n=57)	UN (n=22)	USA (n=151)	Turkey (n=63)	GFP (n=60)	Unspecified (n=47)
$\bar{n}$	317.5	347.8	388.3	347.8	416.4	386.1
σ	136.7	167.4	225.2	147.6	258.2	167.6

$\bar{n}$ = average value, σ = standard deviation

The placement and length of articles Both, the pages and the length of the articles on the different actors do not differ considerably. Explorative data analysis shows average values between page 12 on European and unspecified Western actors, page 10 on Turkey, page 9 on Gaza flotilla members and page 8 on United Nations and United States. A nonparametric test (Mann-Whitney U test) reveals significant differences between European actors and the USA ($p = .045$). As the table (see Table 6) shows, the standard deviation of the pages is very high. That is a reason for the non-significant differences between the articles' placement. The average word count of the articles (see Table 7) is also analyzed by explorative data analysis. The average values of articles on Gaza flotilla members are highest with 416 words, followed by United States with 388 words, unspecified Western actors (386 words), and United Nations (359 words). Shortest are articles on the European Union with 318 words and on Turkey with 347 words on average. A nonparametric test (Mann-Whitney U test) of the European actors versus all the other actors results in a significance of $p=.016$. That means, articles on European actors are significantly shorter than those on other actors and significantly on rearer pages than those on the USA.

Institutional background of actors The actors are ascribed to significantly different institutional background (see Table 8). The institutions are coded in five categories: members of the government, members of the media, members of NGO's, unclassified individuals, and not specified. As introduced in chapter 4.3, government refers to all members of governmental institutions. Western unclassified individuals are those described as lose groups of civilians (demonstrators, musicians), but not affiliated to an NGO, a government or the media. not specified is chosen when the actor is not described at all as belonging to an institution. When covering the USA, 80% of the articles refer to its government. The reference to the government is lower when covering European actors

Table 8 – Institutional Background of Actors (in Percent)

	Europe (n=57)	UN (n=22)	USA (n=151)	Turkey (n=63)	GFP (n=60)	Unspecified (n=47)
Government	47	55	**80**	38	2	9
Media	2	–	6	–	–	**13**
NGO	2	–	1	3	**13**	–
Individuals	19	18	3	10	**50**	21
Not specified	30	27	11	49	35	**57**
Total	100	100	101[1]	100	100	100

$\chi^2(30, N = 400) = 218,956, p = .000$ [1] rounding error

(47%) or those of United Nations (55% refers to the Secretary General). Articles on Turkey deal with its government in 38% of the times. Media actors are most frequently named when referring to unspecified Western actors, but only in 13% of those. Non-Government organizations are not mentioned very frequently, but appear in 13% of the articles on Gaza flotilla members. The category Unclassified individuals is most frequent when covering the Gaza flotilla members in 50% of the articles on them. No specification of the actor is most frequent when articles cover the unspecified Western actors, this is the case in 57% of the articles on them.

Quotes by the actors There are significant differences between the actors and the amount of articles in which they are quoted ($\chi^2(5, N = 400) = 16,967, p = .005$). The percentage of articles with citations of actors is highest when European (56%) or US-actors (52%) are covered. Turkish actors are quoted in 42% of the articles. The least frequent are quotes in articles on the United Nations (23%), GFP (30%) and unspecified Western actors (38%).

The framing of the actors The amount of frames found in articles on the analyzed actors differs (see Figure 3; and Table 24 in Appendix A). The amount can be seen as indicator for more intense discussion of the actors and their actions. The highest amount of frames per article is found in articles on the United States (on average 2.6 per article) the second group consists of Turkey, United Nations and Europe with roughly 2 frames per article. Unspecified Western actors follow with 1.7 and the Gaza flotilla participants receive on average only 1.4. As indicated above (see Chapter 4.3), the occurrence of several frames in one article is perceived as an opportunity for a variety of opinions within that article's representation – if there is only one frame, it can be only either positive, neutral, or negative.

The framing of the actors is either negative or positive but rarely neutral. In general, actors are not often framed in a positive manner but with significant difference ($p = .000$).

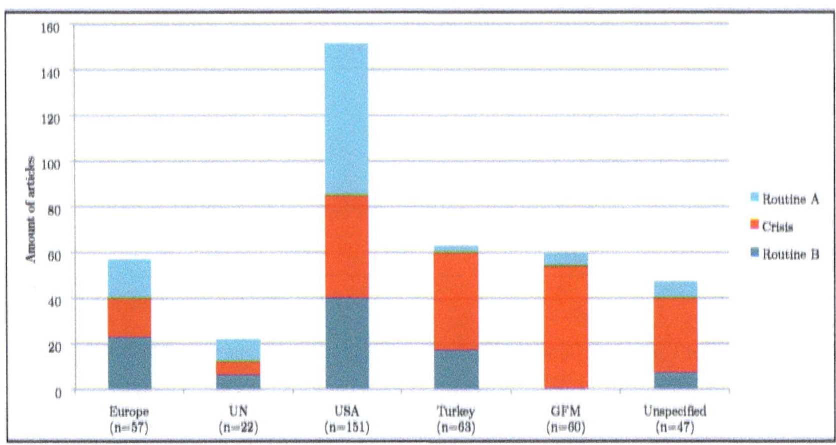

Figure 2 – Actors' Appearance in Analyzed Periods
$\chi^2(10, N = 400) = 109,368, p = .000$

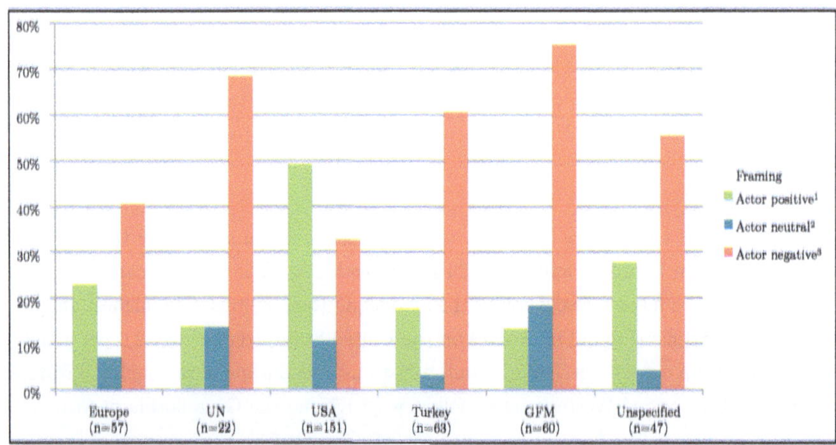

Figure 3 – Framing of the Actors (in Percent)
[1] is $\chi^2(5, N = 400) = 42,514, p = .000$
[2] is $\chi^2(5, N = 400) = 10,938, p = .053$
[3] is $\chi^2(5, N = 400) = 41,706, p = .000$

The one actor with high amounts of positive framing is the United States; every second article (49%) contains positive frames on the USA. More than half of those articles emphasize the importance of the United States, almost 30 articles either the legitimacy of the actor or its supportive character. Less frequent is the description of the actor as understanding of Israel or as pro-Israeli. The other actors are rarely framed positively, in between 28% (unspecified Western actors) and 13% (Gaza flotilla participants) of the articles. If they are framed positively, it is usually for their importance to Israel or since they are seen as legitimate.

Neutral framing of the actor, for example as unbiased, nonpartisan, or uncommitted actor is even less frequent and is not significant ($p = .122$). The Gaza flotilla participants gain some of this neutral framing, when their diversity is described in every sixth article discussing them, but in general it is very rare.

Negative framing of the actor is very common and found in every second article. Europe and the United States are framed negatively in 40% and 32% of their articles. Respectively this implies that percentages are much higher in articles covering Turkey, unspecified Western actors, and GFP. The unspecified Western actors are framed negatively in 55%, followed by Turkey (60%). Most negative framing receive the Gaza flotilla members in 75% of their articles. Most frequent is the framing of the actors as attackers, followed by the frame "anti-Israeli or antisemite"[32], framing the actor as hypocritical or biased.

The framing of the relationship   between Israel and the actor in general is not very frequent (see Figure 4; and Table 25 in Appendix A). Only every fourth article contains any evaluative information on the relationship. The relationship is framed positively and with significant difference ($p = .000$) mainly when covering involvement by the United States (in 54% of the articles). Only the relationship to European actors (23%) and Turkey (22%) also gains positive framing. Neutral framing is almost absent. The highest amount of negative frames of the relationship ($p = .000$) is ascribed to Turkey. In two out of three articles (63%) that is the case. The relationship to Europe is framed negatively in 28% of the articles, to unspecified Western actors in 23% and to the United Nations in 31% of the articles on them. That means, the relationships in general are described less frequent than the actors themselves, however, the relationship to the USA is considered frequently as positive, and the relationship to Turkey is considered as negative frequently. Both indicate an importance ascribed to debating this relationship as is interpreted in the following chapters.

The actors in the different newspapers   The actors appear in similar frequency in the newspapers, however they are contextualized differently.

---

[32]The terms antisemitism and anti-Israelism are not misunderstood as adressing the same issues, however they are often used interchangeably in Israeli media and therefore coded in one category (see for a detailed discussion Chapter 7.3).

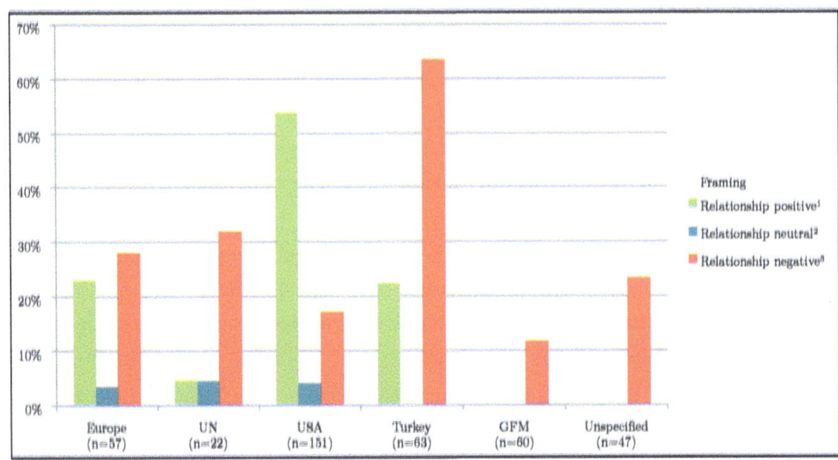

Figure 4 – Framing of the Relationship to the Actors (in Percent)
[1] is $\chi^2(5, N = 400) = 100,227, p = .000$
[2] is $\chi^2(5, N = 400) = 6,890, p = .229$
[3] is $\chi^2(5, N = 400) = 57,980, p = .000$

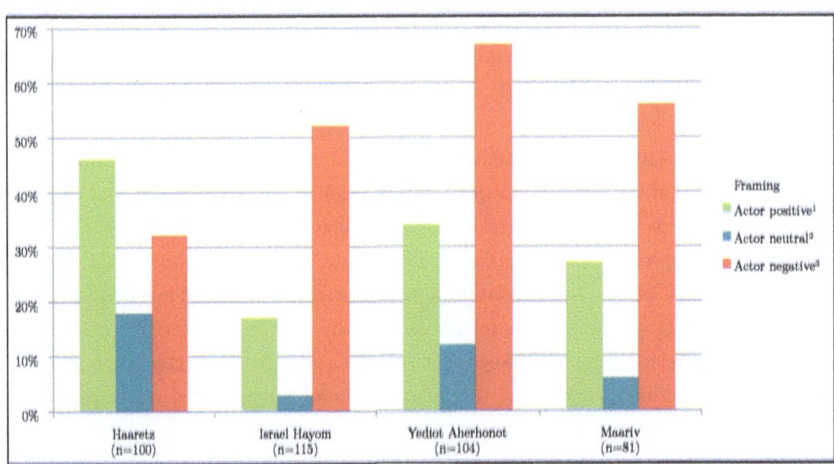

Figure 5 – Framing of the Actors in Analyzed Newspapers (in Percent)
[1] is $\chi^2(3, N = 400) = 22,848, p = .000$
[2] is $\chi^2(3, N = 400) = 16,301, p = .001$
[3] is $\chi^2(3, N = 400) = 15,908, p = .001$

　　　© Frank & Timme　Verlag für wissenschaftliche Literatur

Table 9 – Actors' Appearance in Newspapers (in Percent)

	Haaretz (n=100)	Israel Hayom (n=115)	Yediot Aherhonot (n=104)	Maariv (n=81)
Europe (n=57)	12	10	18	17
UN (n=22)	10	6	4	1
USA (n=151)	43	42	30	36
Turkey (n=63)	17	17	14	15
GFP (n=60)	10	13	21	16
Unspec. (n=47)	8	12	13	15
Total	100	100	100	100

$\chi^2(5, N = 400) = 20,078, p = .169$

The distribution of *actors' appearances* is not significantly different ($p = .169$, see Table 9). Thus, the differences are minor. Haaretz and Israel Hayom cover US-involvement slightly more than the other two papers. The GFP appear most frequent in Yediot Aheronot (21% of the total coverage of international actors) and comprise only 10% of Haaretz' coverage of international actors. The UN appears in 10% of the analyzed articles in Haaretz, and even less in the other newspapers.

However, the *representations of the actors* are significantly different ($p = .001$, see Figure 5). The most frequent positive framing appears in Haaretz (in 46% of the articles), followed by Yediot Aheronot (in 34% of the articles). Actors are the least frequently positively framed in Israel Hayom (17%). There is a significant difference between Israel Hayom, Maariv and Yediot Aheronot ($p = .013$), the latter two contain more positive framing[33].

Neutral framing in general is rare, but used in 18% of the articles in Haaretz. But also the differences between the three newspapers excluding Haaretz are significant ($p = .030$), because Yediot Aheronot contains 12% of articles with neutral framing[34].

The actors are most frequently negatively framed, mostly in Yediot Aheronot (67%), but also Maariv (56%) and Israel Hayom (52%) frame the actors negatively in more than every second article. Haaretz is different with negative frames of actors in only every third article (32%). The significant differences are only between Haaretz and the other three newspapers that do not vary in their amount of negative framing[35]. This indicates that the actors' representation in general varies significantly between the four newspapers, negative framing of the actors is significantly different in Haaretz than in the other three newspapers.

The *representations of the relationship* to the actors do not differ significantly among the four newspapers (see Table 10). The relationships are framed positively in 20% to

---

[33] χ^2 on Israel Hayom, Yediot Aheronot, Maariv excl. Haaretz is $\chi^2(2, N = 300) = 8,670, p = .013$
[34] χ^2 on Israel Hayom, Yediot Aheronot, Maariv excl. Haaretz is $\chi^2(2, N = 300) = 7,042, p = .030$
[35] χ^2 on Israel Hayom, Yediot Aheronot, Maariv excl. Haaretz is $\chi^2(2, N = 300) = 493, p = .782$

29% of the articles. Neutral framing of the relationships is very rare, it is found in total in nine articles, therefore there is no significant difference between the newspapers. Negative frames on the relationship are more frequent (107 times in total), but also not distributed significantly different among the newspapers, each newspaper has negative frames of the relationship in 24% to 34% of the articles.

Table 10 – Framing of the Relationship to the Actors in Newspapers (in Percent)

		Haaretz (n=100)	Israel Hayom (n=115)	Yediot A. (n=104)	Maariv (n=81)
Relationship positive[1]	Yes	27	24	30	27
	No	73	76	70	73
Relationship neutral[2]	Yes	5	–	2	1
	No	95	100	98	99
Relationship negative[3]	Yes	34	23	24	26
	No	66	77	76	74

[1] is $\chi^2(3, N = 400) = 1,142, p = .767$
[2] is $\chi^2(3, N = 400) = 6,656, p = .084$
[3] is $\chi^2(3, N = 400) = 3,729, p = .292$

5.2 The United States – a True Friend and Partner?

The representation of the United States shows that the country is perceived in a very prominent and positive manner in Israeli newspapers. Although the relation with President Barack Obama is not perceived as solely positive, the intense and special relationship of the United States and Israel reflects in its media representation. Several patterns of representation are striking for the United States: The USA appears a lot and continuously and in a personalized manner, it is presented in a positive way, mostly as supportive, important and pro-Israeli. The relationship is seen as very strong, special but also complicated. These patterns will be introduced, supplemented by examples and some background on the actual relations between Israel and the United States.

The United States continuously appear in a prominent manner in Israeli newspapers   The amount of appearance of the United States' involvement in Israeli newspapers is with 151 articles is 2.5 times higher than the following actor Turkey with 63 articles. The involvement is continuous throughout the three phases of routine and crisis and higher in the first routine phase than in the crisis phase (Routine A: 44%; Crisis: 30%; Routine B: 26%). The high amount of continuous appearance indicates the importance of the USA and its involvement for Israel (see below).

The degree of personalization is very high   The USA is specified more often than other actors. And, more than any other actor the articles refer to the government (80%) and the media (6%). Every second article (52%) contains citation by a US-actor. These numbers are higher than for other actors with whom less interaction with the government is covered and who are quoted less.

The *mediated reality* (see Chapter 1.5) conveys an image of a strong governmental, official relationship. There is not much interaction with other sectors in the USA. 1) and 2) are regarded as first indicators for the importance ascribed to the relationship between the USA and Israel.

The USA is in general framed positively   In general, the USA is ascribed the highest amount of frames per article (2.6). The other actors are framed less (2.0 – 1.4 frames per articles). The USA is framed positively in every second article (49%) much more often than any other actor (14% to 28%). Most frequent are the following two frames:

a) The United States is important to Israel. The emphasis on the importance (44 articles, 59% of the articles with positive frames) and legitimacy (28 articles, 38% of the articles with positive frames) of the US is conveyed in the majority of articles on the US. Numerous are the news articles and comments discussing in depth the expectations, relations, outcomes and implications before and after meetings of President Obama and Prime Minister Netanyahu, e.g., most articles around their meeting on July 6, 2010. Meetings with other leaders are usually covered in one article only. As is later discussed, proposals and calls by US-actors are debated in depth (see Chapter 6). In approaching talks between Israelis and Palestinians the United States are clearly presented as leading responsible mediator (e.g., YA_2010_05_02_004, HA_2010_04_26_15, HA_2010_05_07_30).

b) The United States are pro-Israeli and support Israel's causes. If framed positively, the USA is described as pro-Israeli in 18% (14 articles) and as supportive in 40% of the articles with positive frames (29 articles). An example are articles on US-citizen prominently defending Israel "against the worldwide tirades", for example in an article on an interview of former Candidate for Presidency, McCain in Fox News with an "pro-Israeli" interview: "The IDF soldiers acted in self-defense" (IH_2010_06_04_005b)[36]. These supportive articles contain a high amount of citations

The relationship with the United States is presented as important and strong

It is framed positively in more than every second article (53%). That is slightly more than positive framing of the US itself. Very frequent are emphasizes on the importance (44 articles) and strength (18 articles) of the relationship, the cooperation between both states is highlighted in 33 articles and the character defined as friendship in 21 and partnership in 33 articles. Repeatedly, US-actors are quoted in their "commitment to Israel's security",

---

[36] All the examples taken from the analyzed texts are translated by the author

and the assurance of the "deep bond between the states" (YA_2010_05_31_025B). An example is the coverage of the leaders' meetings in July 2010. In an article on page two of Israel Hayom the two first paragraphs focus on Obama's declarations of sympathy and belief in the strong relations, refusals of any crisis and in quotes like "I believe in him [Netanyahu] from the moment I met him, even before the elections" (IH_2010_07_07_002a). Also Maariv prominently collects the compliments by Obama: "That is a wonderful new chapter in our relationship", "The relationship between Israel and USA is unbreakable and will last forever" (MA_2010_07_07_02b). Another indicator for the importance of the friendship is the attention paid to personal stories, for example the family visit of the White House Chief of Staff Rahm Emanuel. The activities, restaurant visits, trips, interactions with Israelis, intentions and prominently the son's *Bar Mitzwa*[37] are covered closely (for example MA_2010_05_17_006; MA_2010_05_23_006). Another example are episodes such as "Obama spontaneously appeared" in a meeting of the Security Minister and Security Adviser of both states (YA_2010_04_27_06) or articles on the fact that "Obama called Netanyahu". These examples indicate the importance ascribed to personal aspects of the relations, to details, and to connecting aspects.

Still, the relationship is presented as complicated The relationship is not without complications, and described as such in 39 articles. President Obama is perceived with ambivalence, especially his efforts in the Middle East and his partially critical attitude of Israel's policies. Hence, nearly one third (32%) of the articles on the USA contain negative framing of the actor, arguing the actor is hypocritical (16 times) or lacks understanding (14 times). Those articles almost completely relate to the US-government. The perception of President Obama proposing solutions or demanding changes from Israel while lacking understanding for the context of the Middle East is illustrated in Figure 6. The cartoon is published during the Gaza crisis 2014, following a demand for ceasefire. It is rejected strongly through emphasis on Obama's misconception of the Middle East. In general, the Obama administration is perceived as more critical and distanced towards Israel than the predecessors (Waxman 2012: 72).

An article in Maariv (MA_2010_07_07_05c) sums up the problematic perception of the relationship with President Obama in Israel: He is described as seeing potential in the Middle East to advance his chances of becoming a great American President. But the relationship with Israel is shaped by misunderstandings – Netanyahu did not understand Obama's vision and new priorities in the Middle East and Obama did not understand the challenges and perspectives of living in the Middle East. An interesting "turning point" is the mentioned meeting in July 2010, in which authors discuss the "warm" meeting after a period of "cold" relations: "This is not because they suddenly fell in love with him [Netanyahu]: The White House decided to change the tone since they conclude that with

---

[37]Ceremony celebrating a boy's coming of age.

Figure 6 – Cartoon in Israel Hayom on President Obama
Shlomo Cohen's Daily Cartoon. July 31, 2014 in Israel Hayom

hugs they will get more out of Netanyahu than with pressure and humiliating ceremonies" (YA_2010_07_05_28). But the author claims that Obama's warm embrace comes at a price of expectations of Netanyahu to approach peace talks and differing positions on the Two-State-Solution remain. Another indicator is that more frequent than descriptions of the "friendship" and "partnership" is the emphasis on the "importance" of the relations – a more pragmatic approach (see Chapter 7.3). However, these articles discuss the relationship, differences, and expectations in deeper ways than relations with other states.

The findings indicate that the Israeli media represents the US-involvement very differently from other actors' involvement and regards the relationship and the actor itself as more positive than the other actors. These findings indicate that the representation of US-involvement in Israeli newspapers is a reflection of the relationship between Israel and the United States. This relationship is without doubt very strong and also very exceptional. The United States is the most influential actor outside the Middle East in striving for peace in the region (O'Donnell 2008). It does not cease to repeat its commitment to Israel's security, while Israel regards itself as an outpost within the Middle East for its strongest ally and necessary patron. However, the results further show that the relations are nevertheless not without complications.

Background of the Relationship

Historically, this relationship has not always been as strong. In 1948 the Truman adminis-tration was ambivalent towards Israeli independence. President Truman supported the partition in the last minute, while George C. Marshall, then Secretary of State, opposed the planned recognition of Israel (Lieber 1998; Sharon et al. 2013: 20; Spiegel 2014: pp.16) . In the first years of the young state, France was Israel's strongest ally, mainly in shared opposition to Egypt's Gamel Abdel Nasser. The fragile relationship between the USA and Israel came into crisis when the USA opposed Britain, France and Israel and pressured Israel to withdraw from the Sinai Peninsula that it captured from Egypt in 1956 (Khalidi 2009: 3). The US-policy change started during the second Eisenhower administration in 1958. The relationship with the USA improved and deepened slowly, especially after the Six Day war (1967), the Yom Kippur war (1973) and the peace treaty with Egypt (1979) (Lieber 1998; Little 2008: pp.79). Israel was a strategic asset during the Cold War when the Arab states were backed by the Soviet Union and both superpowers equipped their allies with increasingly sophisticated military equipment. Due to the superpower's rivalry within the Arab-Israeli conflict, none of the peace initiatives was fruitful and numerous crises [38] produced superpower confrontation and exacerbated the conflict (Khalidi 2009: pp.24, 84, pp.117). Khalidi argues, peace was simply no priority for the powers (Khalidi 2009: 30, pp.80, pp.114). Following the end of the Cold War and the disappearance of the Soviet Union as dominant player in the area, the United States engaged in the Middle East with confidence. Prominent is (among the leadership of a coalition against Iraq in the Gulf War in 1991) the initiation of the the Arab Israeli peace conference in Madrid in 1991 that led to the Oslo Accords in 1993. The American efforts at a resolution of the Israeli-Palestinian conflict manifested its role as its peace-broker (Khalidi 2009: 7) and the permanent fixture of the relationship to Israel in US foreign policy (Little 2008: 78).

The source of this special relationship is widely debated. Critics seek reasons in domestic politics and the arithmetic of elections. Indeed, Jewish voters are important in key states (New York, Illinois, and California), however, their total population numbers are very low. There are lobbying groups such as the American Israel Public Affairs Committee (AIPAC). However, the lobby impact is low compared to other groups and frequently overestimated[39]. Supporters base the relationship on calculated geopolitical factors, such as the strategic alliance during the Cold War (Little 2008: 78). Indeed, Israel appeared as the only reliable pro-Western asset in a region torn by crises (Lieber 1998). Leo and Terlizzi (2014: 1084) argue for mutual strategic interest: Israel sought a partner for military assistance, while the United States sought a partner in the Middle East . Little (2008) concludes that

---

[38]Including the Suez Crisis in 1956, the Six-Day War in 1967, the Egyptian-Israeli War of Attrition 1968-70, the Yom-Kippur War in 1973, the Lebanon War in 1982 (Khalidi 2009: 84).

[39]See the interactive reports on organisations and their contributions to US-politics by the Center for Responsive Politics at opensecrets.org

careful examination of the ambivalence and informal alliance that emerged between the
United States and Israeli during the fifty years after 1945 reveals that, more often than not,
both simple arithmetic and differential calculus were at work. (2008: 78)

The strength of the relationship between Israel and the USA is further rooted in several
proclaimed powerful bonding aspects. Both states claim the same strategic goals for the
Middle East: Both want to prevent nuclear proliferation Iran, want to counter other powers
in the region maintaining ballistic missiles and weapons of mass destruction, both want to
fight Islamist-inspired terrorism in the Middle East, and promote pro-Western regimes,
such as Jordan (Little 2008: 114; Waxman 2012: 74). The USA claims, a stable Middle
East is in its national interest, therefore it conducts attempts to resolve the Arab-Israeli
conflict, ensures Israel's security (see below), and secures a free flow of oil. Both want to
limit Iranian influence. Both, Obama and Netanyahu repeatedly state the shared values,
namely democracy and freedom. The bond is not restricted to the establishment, but
supported by strong affiliations of both countries' populations (Sharon et al. 2013). As
Figure 7 illustrates, sympathies of US-citizen for Israelis are higher than for Palestinians.
Particularly high are the sympathies of US-Republicans. Practical characterizations of
this relationship today are:

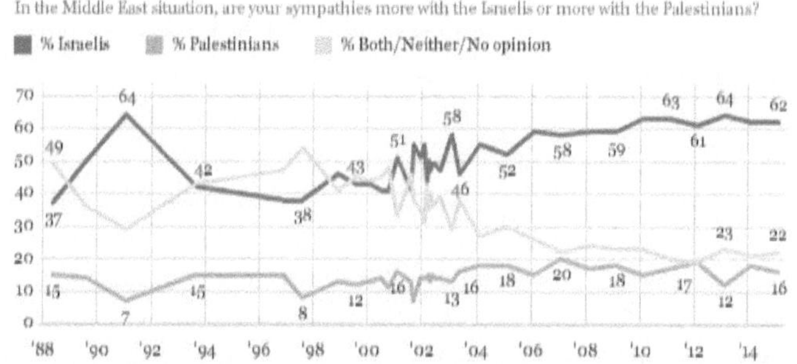

Figure 7 – American Sympathies for Israelis and Palestinians
annually conducted polls by Gallup (Saad 2015).

1) *The diplomatic relations.* The United States play a key role in every step of the
Arab-Israeli peace process from the 1970s on (Lieber 1998). However, the role of the USA
for Israel manifests itself not only in its military and economic power, but also in the
inability of other powers to fill that role, and furthermore, the understanding that the
USA will not allow Israel to be defeated. In this sense, the USA are on the one hand the
accepted protector of Israel, but at the same time, for Israel this relationship is without
alternative. An example is the essential role the USA plays at the United Nations Security
Council for Israel through numerous vetoes of resolutions criticizing Israel (Mearsheimer
and Walt 2006).

2) *Material support:* Israel is the recipient of the largest amount of foreign assistance
from the USA between 1976 to 2004 (Sharp 2009). It started in 1952 with $86 million,

and stayed low ($13 million in 1967), but increased after the 1967 war to $76 million in 1968 and quickly to $600 million in 1971. Between 1974 and 1997, $75 billion were paid to Israel and it became the largest recipient of aid. This ranks at $3 billion direct aid, one-fifth of the US foreign aid budget.

3) Security relations. The largest part of this budget is military assistance. Israel is granted benefits other recipients do not receive, it may use some of the assistance for research and development in the USA and 26% for purchases from Israeli military manufacturers (Sharp 2009: 3). Accordingly, the rest of the military assistance is purchased from US defense equipment. Therefore, this "aid" has strong economical benefits for the USA. This military comes with a certain dependency, in exchange for policies and with the power to withhold services if Israel does not comply (Bapat 2011). The USA hence is Israel's guarantor of its security in political, military, and financial terms (Lieber 1998: 13) which leads to a reliance and dependency of Israel in the USA.

Another perspective on the relations is prominently offered by Mearsheimer and Walt (2006). Their publication caused huge debate, was fiercely criticized and at times declared antisemitic. Mearsheimer and Walt (2006) argue that the USA has no strategic benefits from a close relationship with Israel since the end of the Cold War. On the contrary, they claim that the alliance to Israel complicates the US-relationship to the Arab world. They dismantle the arguments of an alliance based on shared values, the US-support for Israel as underdog in the region (Israel is the strongest military power in the Middle East largely due to US-military aid), and of support for Israel as only democracy in the Middle East (the democracy is reduced to Jewish citizen and the USA has stable relationships with dictatorships as well). Mearsheimer and Walt contend that AIPAC's lobby work prevents US-politicians from exerting pressure on Israel and is the base for US-behavior against its best interests (ibid.). It is hard to believe that the USA would act against its strategic interests with high political and financial costs solely to satisfy a particular lobby group. However, the question remains, whether the relationship is still in the best interest of either party. Little (2008) concludes that "neither side can agree whether Israel should be America's partner or merely its proxy" (2008: 115): While the American side believed that the military and economic leverage may force Israel to certain policies, the Israeli side believed in its military capabilities and the Jewish voters and lobby to withstand the pressure which turned Israel for the USA either into a strategic asset or a diplomatic liability.

Waxman (2012) adds that the strategic interests of both actors are the same but their understanding how to achieve those differ, especially regarding the Israeli-Palestinian conflict, the Iranian nuclear program, and the Arab Spring. Undoubtedly the relationship between Israel and the USA is complicated and characterized by disputes and signs of crises and disagreement between President Obama and Prime Minister Netanyahu. However, the alliance between both states is strong and stable, as it is grounded in strong strategic, financial, economic, cultural, and security relations. This reflects in the analyzed Israeli media representation in which the USA appears differently from all the other actors.

5.3 Europe – Connection and Alienation?

All articles referring to either the European Union, to several European states or a specific European state are subsumed under the category "Europe". Most frequent are articles covering either several European states together, Europe as such or the European Union (13 articles). Some articles deal with only one European state separately. In this category Germany is most frequent with 11 occurences. France, Great Britain, Ireland and Spain are covered five times each, the other European countries even less than that. Due to that strong stratification, it is coded within one category. Moreover, Europe is perceived as one unit in Israel culturally, historically and in its political relation to Israel[40].

Europe appears continuously Altogether, European actors appear in 57 articles. Compared to the other relevant actors, this is not a lot considered that Europe consists of many countries. Articles on European actors appear continuously throughout the three periods and a bit stronger after the crisis (Routine A: 30%; Crisis 30%; Routine B: 40%). In more than half of all the articles the involved European actor is quoted. The amount of specification of the institutional background of the European actors is also average compared to the other actors. Almost half the articles relate to governments (47%), one fifth cover individuals and 30% are not specified. These numbers put Europe just in between the US with much more government and Turkey much less government concentration. Articles on Europe appear comparably on rear pages and with lower word count. The placement suggests a lack of importance ascribed to the actors.

The framing implies an ambivalent perception of European actors and the relationship towards them. There is positive framing of European actors in every fifth article (23%) as important, understanding or supportive; but there is more negative framing in 40% of the articles, mainly as being anti-Israeli or antisemite or being hypocritical (see examples in Chapter 7.3). Hence, also in its framing Europe is seen as less positive than the United States and less negative than the others. The relationship is also framed both positively (23%) and negatively (28%) .

One example for the framing of Europeans in an ambivalent way, both as important and as hypocritical is an article warning of a "developing deep crisis in the relations between Israel and Germany" (YA_2010_07_13_024b) in Mid July 2010. The reason is a

---

[40]Several papers and studies on Israeli perceptions of Europe/the EU show distinct and complex images that Israelis connect to Europe while considering it as one unit (Harpaz and Shamis 2010; Pardo and Peters 2010: pp.69).

resolution adopted by the German parliament that holds Israel responsible for the events of the flotilla raid, calling for an independent investigation and demanding the end of the Gaza blockade: "In days of most severe political and economic crisis suddenly all the parties in the Bundestag succeed – from the radical left, the former Communist to the Pietiest Conservatives – to find a topic that unites them all: one-sided and irrelevant criticism of Israel [...] This is a cheap populist decision." The journalist underlines this judgment with the fact that the Bundestag did not condemn the persecution and systematic murder of Kurdish people by the Turkish government. He holds Israel responsible for taking "its friend for granted" and for neglecting the importance of explaining Israeli policies and positions in German media. The author thus warns that the relation has to be taken care of and Germany has to be told its borders (YA_2010_07_13_024b). While the relationship is perceived as important, the criticism is seen as hypocrisy, as it is only against Israel and not against Turkey or other pressing issues, and not legitimate. The solution is seen in hasbara/public diplomacy.

Background of the ambivalent relationship

Sharon et al. (2013: 23) indeed describe this ambivalence of the relations characterized by emotional and moral identification but also resentment. The basic argument is that the perception of Europe is characterized by feelings of belonging and resentment alike: There are political, economical, and also historical-cultural ties between the EU and Israel that indicate a strong and positive connection. However, Europe is not perceived as essential by Israeli population and decision/policy makers. Aside from the European foreign policy a reason lies in the perception of Europe as anti-Israeli in its strategic policies and of the deep roots of antisemitism in Europe (Pardo and Peters 2010: 91). These arguments will be outlined here.

The connection   The positive historical connection is grounded in the fact that many of the founders of the Zionist movement and almost half the Jewish Israeli population (47%[41]) has European origins and thus many cultural values are shared and upheld with great affinity. The Zionist secular ideology itself is clearly a product of late 19th century European political and social thought (Harpaz and Shamis 2010; Sharon et al. 2013: 588). The immigrants brought their culture, education, and knowledge, which largely shaped the function of the young state in various levels (architecture, law, medicine, education, culture, and so on, see also Chapter 3.1.3).

On an economic, scientific, and cultural level, there are intense and unique relations, since Israel is an associated member of the EU. In 2007, Israel asked for an upgrade at the EU that grants its full integration to the economic and security mechanisms. The

---

[41]see Statistical Abstract of Israel, 2009, CBS: http://www.cbs.gov.il/reader/shnaton/templ_shnaton_e.html?num_tab=st02_24x&CYear=2009

upgrade was approved after a long debate in 2009, and is significant, since it was decided unanimously and no other country received such an integration to the EU. It was, however frozen during the Gaza operation Cast Lead in 2009 and remained closed due to Israel's policies in the occupied territories. This had strong financial consequences and has been a significant loss for Israel's economy but also to its political relationship (Sharon et al. 2013: 27).

Despite the frozen upgrade, there are intense cultural, economic, and scientific relations based on several agreements. The most important agreements are introduced briefly Pardo and Peters (2010: Chapter 3): Israel is member of the Euro-Mediterranean Partnership (EMP, Barcelona Process) which had a positive effect on the EU-Israel relation during the peace process in the 1990s. In this context in 1995, the EU-Israel Association Agreement (it took effect in 2000) laid the foundation for a free trade of industrial goods and liberal trade of agricultural products, cooperation in research, development, tourism, transportation, and so on. (Harpaz and Shamis 2010; Pardo and Peters 2010). Israel was the first non-EU state within the EU Research and Technological Development Framework Programme. In 2005, the "EU-Israel Action Plan" was adopted to intensify political and security cooperation that was widened to further EU initiatives and was basis for enhancement of the relations in general. For both sides, economic, touristic, scientific and cultural exchange is positive and important. Nearly one third of Israel's export goes to Europe, whereas 37% of the import are from the EU (in 2009), thus the EU is Israel's most important trading partner. The European Neighborhood Policy was also inaugurated in 2003 and grants neighbor states with "shared values" economic, political, and social privileges (Pardo 2009: pp.57). These programs are basis for further agreements Israel signed with the European Union (Harpaz and Shamis 2010: 596; Pardo 2009: 52; Sharon et al. 2013).

In 2013, the EU published guidelines that distinguish between Israel and the settlements. Agreements between Israel explicitly excluded institutions and organizations in the Territories. The Israeli response was very harsh, Prime Minister Netanyahu described it as dictation of the borders, then Minister of Economics Bennett called it "an economic terror attack" but despite strong pressure the guidelines were issued on time (Sharon et al. 2013: 51).

The EU commitment to involvement in the Israeli-Palestinian conflict is rising. In several aspects, the EU is taking part in security issues and fought hard to be part of the diplomatic efforts towards the peace process. The EU is one of the biggest donors to Palestinians and leading security trainings for Palestinian police. Between 2005 and 2007, the EU Border Assistance Mission monitored the operations of the Rafah border crossing (it became inactive after the Hamas takeover). Following the Second Lebanon war, the EU provided 7.000 soldiers to the UNIFIL mission in southern Lebanon (Harpaz and Shamis 2010; O'Donnell 2008).

These cultural, political and economical connections indicate strong relations between Europe and Israel. The findings of a series of studies by Pardo and Peters (2010: 73) and the Konrad-Adenauer-Foundation on perceptions of Europe within the Israeli society supports the connection between Israel and the EU. They find that the majority of Israelis (69% – 70% of Israeli population) supports joining the EU and indeed believes the EU is important. Half of the decision and policy makers interviewed by Pardo and Peters believe the EU will become a superpower, but still see the USA as the best power to maintain stability and peace (Pardo and Peters 2010: 73).

The resentment   A further major and repeated finding by Pardo and the Konrad-Adenauer-Foundation is that good relations to the EU are not essential for Israel (Pardo and Peters 2010: 73). There are several political reasons. In 2009, 56% of the respondents prefer US-involvement in the Middle East over EU involvement, 34% believe the EU involvement prevents the peace process. Asseburg (2003) criticizes the role of the EU in the Israeli-Palestinian conflict already in 2003 as "too little and too late", particularly since

> the European approach has not taken [the continuing occupation] sufficiently into account: it [European aid] has been one of post-conflict peace-building – as if there were n continuing conflict, occupation or mobility restrictions hampering economic development, reconciliation and institution-building. (Asseburg 2003: 177)

Pardo and Peters (2010) further argue that Europeans and Jewish Israelis in general have different perspectives on nationalism, security, and international law, and they have disagreements over priorities, interests and strategies in the conflict. The EU often has difficulties to find a common policy regarding the conflict. It is often left condemning but failing to take concrete action. The perception remains that the EU uses its economic power to reach political goals in its rhetoric, but in practice is less strict. This discredits its capability to take a constructive role in the region. One of the challenges for European actors, especially the EU is to act faster and more coherently (Pardo and Peters 2010). O'Donnell (2008: 31) as well agrees that EU claims are confused or washed out of content, and its credibility suffers from that. Therefore O'Donnell argues for a constructive role the EU can offer in strengthening the Israeli security environment and feeling. She suggests training of Palestinian security forces and deployment of international peacekeeping forces, although it is questionable if Israel would agree to the latter. Furthermore she suggests the EU could "offer deeper bilateral relations. In exchange for a settlement with the Palestinians" within the Neighborhood Policy, so Israel could enjoy participation in the European market without full membership at EU institutions.

But possibly the major factor for the negative perception of the EU role in the Middle East is related to the historical connection of antisemitism in Europe and especially the Holocaust. Europe is the place where Jews were persecuted, slaughtered and had to flee from; the place that made necessary as the only possibility for Jews to a self-determined live free of persecution. Hence, the foundation of the state of Israel in 1948 cannot be separated from Europe and ultimately the Holocaust. As such, the Holocaust until today is central in Jewish Israeli collective memory and identity (Harpaz and Shamis 2010: 589). It has strong implications on Israel's foreign and security policy, and the real and perceived threat by its neighbors as discussed above in the Chapters 2.2 and 3.1.4. Therefore, when European-Israeli relations are debated, past and present are intertwined. Pardo and Peters outline the strong conviction of Jewish Israelis that Europe is anti-Israeli and biased in its Middle East politics. The reason is seen as antisemitism. Therefore, the represented critical involvement by European actors is perceived as illegitimate since Europe has disqualified itself from having a critical voice. When European actors then base their criticism on values such as human rights, peace, liberty, and respect for international law this is perceived with bitterness (Harpaz and Shamis 2010: 600; Pardo and Peters 2010: 71). Harpaz and Shamis (2010: 604) conclude that

> the effectiveness of Normative Europe in the Middle East depends, *inter alia*, on the ability of the EU to take cognizance of the multifaceted and somewhat incoherent perceptions of Normative Europe held by the 'other' (in our case, in Israel) and on its ability to adjust its normative agenda and rhetoric accordingly.

The adaption of a more cautious, self-reflective approach with higher sensitivity of history is advised and should be accompanied by a stronger allignment of practical assistance and rhetorical statements (ibid.).

In sum, the representation of European actors in Israeli newspapers is characterized by ambivalence. In several features (placement, quotes, amount of articles) it is average compared to the other actors, but articles are shorter and on rear pages. The relationship is almost equally presented as positive and negative. This apparent ambivalence mainly based on intense relations, shared history and interests, but also different standpoints regarding the Israeli-Palestinian conflict and deeply rooted mistrust of Europeans who are perceived as antisemitic, hypocritical and in general anti-Israeli. The co-existence of these realities explains the results found for European actors in the analysis.

5.4 The United Nations – An Ambivalent Relationship?

Also the perception of the United Nations (UN) is characterized by ambivalence. This ambivalence stems, as is shown here, from different reasons, but it is not very different in its outcomes. From UN perspective the foundation of the State of Israel is one of the first big decisions in 1947. Ever since, the UN involves itself frequently and strongly in the Israeli-Arab and Israeli-Palestinian conflict with questionable double standard. From Israeli perspective its standing within the UN is complicated due to its geo-political situation. This reflects in the media representation. The UN is considered as not important and negatively biased.

The UN is important in the foundation of the state of Israel In 1946, one year after the foundation of the United Nations, the Palestine Question was brought before the institution. At that time, Jews held 20% of the cultivable, 6% of the total land, and their population was half as large as the population of the Palestinian Arabs (Smith 2001: pp.190). To answer the question, the United Nations formed a committee that investigated and recommended solutions – UNSCOP with participants from eleven countries. Their report called for an end of the British Mandate and independence of Palestine with different proposals for the character of the new state. The Partition Resolution in favor of a Jewish state next to a Palestinian one needed a two-third majority in November 29, 1947 and won surprising 33 to thirteen countries with ten abstentions (ibid.). The question of Palestine/Israel was one of the first ones the UN debated and decided upon. In a first attempt to find a solution to the conflict between Arabs, Palestinians and Jews, now Israelis the UN was decisive for the founding of the state of Israel and for the initial partition of the land. The conflict resolution is still ongoing (Abraham 2012: pp.83).

The UN is strongly involved in the conflict with questionable double standard
Numerous resolutions from different UN-institutions regard the Israeli-Palestinian conflict, however their impact remains low. The UN Security Council addresses Arab-Israeli conflict in 131 resolutions from 1967 to 1989. Most prominent and determining is Resolution 242 issued by the Security Council following the Six Day war in 1967. This resolution is still the official framework of peace negotiations (Philo and Berry 2011: 51). In an attempt to consider both Arab demands for return of the territories and Israeli demands for secure borders in return, the resolution calls for a "just and lasting peace in which every state in the area can live in security" and "withdrawal of Israel from territories occupied in the recent conflict" (Security Council of the United Nations 1967). It further demands an end of belligerency, but sovereignty and independence for every state and a just solution for the Palestinian refugees (Security Council of the United Nations 1967; Smith 2001: 306).

However, since 1967 the United Nations Security Council has not taken any significant action to address and resolve the Israeli-Palestinian conflict since 1967. Israel's relationship with the United States protects Israel from critical condemnations as every fourth US-veto concerns Israel in 1972 to 2011 (see Chapter 3.1.3). Since the end of the Cold War, only one US-veto did not relate to Israel and Palestine(Leo and Terlizzi 2014: 1081).

The General Assembly is blamed to single Israel out in an "overt politicized way", meaning that several groups or blocs seek for a political aim within the UN (Freedman 2013: 175). Becker et al. (2015) find that of 1676 resolutions taken in the UN General Assembly between 1990 and 2013, 480 resolutions involve Israel, directly or in relation to neighbors. Of those, 88% criticize Israel (Israel is criticized 422 times, followed by South Africa (59 times), USA (39 times) and North Korea (38 times). In 2013, the UN General Assembly adopted 21 resolutions regarding Israel, and four regarding other countries (one resolution each regarding Syria, Iran, North Korea and Myanmar).

The controversial[42] United Nations Human Rights Council (UNHRC) is blamed to single Israel out disproportionally (Johnson and Mack 2014) with the consequences that other serious human rights violations are not considered due to limited time at the Commission sessions (Freedman 2013: 44). The UNHRC has so far condemned Israel in almost half its country-specific resolutions (46%) (Franck 1984; It Is Apartheid 2014; UN Watch 2013).

Clearly, the involvement of the UN in the Israeli-Palestinian conflict is disproportionate[43]. On the one hand the institutions of the United Nations are preoccupied with Israel more than with any other state regarding its human right violations. On the other hand, the USA protects Israel from further and binding condemnations within the Security Council. Both these facts serve as basis for allegations on bias and questionable alliances, either of the international community "against Israel" or of the United States "with Israel".

From the Israeli perspective the conflict complicates Israel's membership status Israel was not a member of any working group within the UN system until 2010 when it joined the Western European and Others Group (WEOG). This strategic relation with Western Europe helps Israel to partially overcome its geopolitical isolation within the UN. The three groups with high numbers are the Arab states (22), the Organization of Islamic Cooperation (56), and the non-aligned states (118). These groups strive to limit Israel's participation and influence on international levels. The new membership in the WEOG, while being an important step in the direction of a full partnership in the UN, is limited to activity in UN organizations in New York, excluding those in Geneva. And for the first time, Israel can submit and circulate proposals, and its standing in sub-organizations is upgraded. Israel is not part in all the sub- organizations, for example UNESCO, the international cultural diplomacy institution. It has five conventions of which Israel ratified one in 1954 and signed one in 1972. The low involvement in UNESCO is based on disagreements regarding the West Bank and particularly East Jerusalem. Especially, when the Palestinian Authority was introduced as "State of Palestine" and joining the 1972 Convention on the Protection of World Cultural and Natural Heritage, Israel froze its membership payment in opposition but remained a member (Sharon et al. 2013: 13-41). In November 29, 2012, the Palestinian Authority was further accorded status of a "non-member observer state" at the UN General Assembly by 138 countries in favor, 9 against and 41 abstaining votes despite massive lobbying campaigns in advance. Israel

---

[42] Hug and Lukács (2014) find that especially countries with a blemished human rights record draft and submit resolutions. The voting preferences are determined by the human rights record and less by the level of democracy of the country. European countries systematically lose in controversial votes. Hug and Lukács (2014) suggest that the defects of the preceeding institution UNCHR are not mended with the newly founded UNHRC. The first institution lost its credibility as it was politicized, particularly by countries with poor human rights levels to blame other states.

[43] See for a full record of Security Council Resolutions, Security Council Presidential Statements, Secretary-General's Reports, Secuirty Council Letters, Security Council Meeting Records, Secuirty Council Press Statements, General Assembly Documents, Human Rights Council Documents related to Israel/Palestine: http://www.securitycouncilreport.org/un-documents/israelpalestine/

reacted by announcing the construction of settlements in the E1 area of the Palestinian territories which would finally cut the West Bank in two parts. Israel repeatedly and continuously ignores or criticizes the numerous Resolutions and Condemnations regarding the Israeli-Palestinian conflict. They are declared anti-Israeli and the fact that the Israeli-Palestinian conflict is the issue of many Resolutions the regarded as proof of the UN's bias. This complicated relation between Israel and the UN is reflected in the media representation in this analysis.

The United Nations do not appear prominently in Israeli newspapers The most popular and frequent description of the United Nations in Israel is "UM-Shoom" ("UN-Nothing" – a persiflage to the irrelevance of the UN), a term David Ben Gurion coined first (Zuckermann 2010: 25). Considering the impacts the United Nations had on the foundation of the state and the continuation of the conflict, this might be surprising. Yet, it suits the perception of "siege mentality" – of Israel being ultimately alone in the world. The denial of the importance of the UN can be perceived as a response to that. This reflects in the newspaper analysis. Most outstanding is the small number of articles about the UN, whereas the other analyzed actors appear between 50 and 60 times in the chosen period, the UN appears in 22 articles. There is no increase in its involvement during the crisis period, quite the contrary, most articles appear in the first phase (Routine A: 46%; Crisis and Routine B each: 27%). Half of the articles (54%) specify the actor as a leader within the UN (General Secretary or Security Council). 27% of the articles do not specify the institution or actor within the UN refers to. The placement and length of the articles is average among the other analyzed actors. The actors rarely gain their own voice; only 23% of the articles contain a quote, which is the lowest amount of all the analyzed actors. That means that the UN does not appear frequently and if it appears in newspapers then not on the first pages or in long articles. The formal factors indicate that the UN is not considered a very important actor for Israel.

The newspaper representation is predominantly negative Only three of the 22 articles contain a positive framing of the actor, but 15 articles contain a negative framing of the actor. More than half of those consider the UN as attackers (8) as hypocrites (6), or as biased (5). The perception of a biased UN was prominently expressed by former Prime Minister Yitzhak Shamir in 1988: "The UN, the world court, international arbitration, or international conference – it's always against us" (quoted in Dowty 1999: 8). That means, in the rare cases of its appearance the UN is not represented positively.

The relationship is mentioned rarely One third of the articles (32%) contain negative framing of the relationship. One article contains a positive framing of the relationship. That is a very small number. Only Gaza flotilla participants and unspecified Western actors receive less discussion on the relationship. In addition to its scarce appearance and the negative representation there is also not much positive representation regarding the relationship.

In sum, the findings of this analysis indicate that the UN is not presented as the opponent but certainly not as an important actor. The UN is, while being the institution deciding on the foundation of the state, is presented as being irrelevant (UM-Shoom). That is supported by the results of this content analysis, since the UN appears rarely in Israeli newspapers and in the rare cases of appearance the UN is represented negatively and the relationship is, if mentioned, seen as negative. Concurrently Israel is the subject of a disproportionate amount of resolutions and condemnations, be it due to its breach of international law or general bias of UN member states. The rare appearance of the UN in newspapers, combined with framing it as hypocrate and biased can indicate a perception of the UN as not relevant for Israel or even opposing it.

5.5 Turkey – A Strategic Partnership Lost?

The relationship between Israel and Turkey has reached a peak of a gradually growing crisis in the analyzed period. Therefore, first the background of the positive strategic relation in the 1990s and the phase of slow deterioration beginning in the 2000s that led to the Gaza flotilla crisis between Israel and Turkey is introduced, before analyzing the media representation of Turkey.

Background of the Relationship

Early low-key relations Turkey was the first Muslim state to recognize Israel in 1949. For Israel, Turkey has always been an interesting strategic partner, due to its human, geopolitical, and material resources, and the shared similarities as Non-Arab nations in the Middle East. Its early foreign policy "periphery doctrine" led Israel to seek for connections with those Non-Arab nations in the Middle East (Turks, Persians, and Kurds). Still, its diplomatic efforts to intensify relations remained unsuccessful for several decades. During the Cold War era, Turkey's foreign policy was a balancing act between its ties with the United States on the one hand; and historical and religious ties to the Arab and Muslim neighbors as well as dependence on their oil production on the other hand. Therefore Turkey held somewhat friendly but low-key relations with Israel (Arakelyan 2013).

Strategic partnership After the Cold War era, Turkey found itself lacking strong alliances while being surrounded by unstable neighbors Syria, Lebanon, and Iran. It seeked to counter security concerns and the Iran-Syria axis by striving towards a strategic partnership with Israel as the latter just starts the Oslo Peace Process. Both countries share similarities in their Western alliances, their striving towards a NATO-membership, and their "sense of otherness" as Non-Arab States in the Middle East. Hence, in 1993, both countries established extensive trade relations, military and security cooperation agreements. The military coordination was upgraded in 1996 and superior to the civilian partnership between the governments, since Turkey needed military technology and Israel geo-strategic depth. Turkey became one of Israel's key military allies. For the region, these relations had a positive impact: Arab states realized they can use the connection with Israel through Turkey. Hence, Turkey gained weight through its involvement in the Arab-Israeli peace process and Israel gained influence within the region (Arakelyan 2013; Dag 2013; Ulutaş 2010a).

Slow deterioration through opposing policies This phase of close strategic ties gradually changed and deteriorated in the 2000s. Arakelyan (2013: pp.39) outlines the development: While the Israeli-Palestinian conflict entered a new phase of intractability with the Second Intifada in 2000, the Turkish government changed with the moderate Islamic Justice and Development party taking power in 2002. The latter led to a new, more pro-active foreign policy approach of "zero problems with neighbors". Turkey thus sought for stability, economic integration, and a more dominant position within the Middle East. In this context Turkey established a cordial cooperation with Syria, Iran, Georgia, Russia and Iraq, and strived towards ending the animosity with Armenia and Cyprus. While Turkey sought to influence unstable nations and states through engagement and cooperation, Israel chose the opposite approach by trying to isolate those. Therefore, opposing Europe, the USA and Israel, Turkey defended accepting Hamas as democratically elected party and thus preempting a connection to the Iran-Syria-Hezbollah axis. This cooled the relations between Israel and Turkey (Dag 2013: 32). Further, in seeking closer ties to Arab and Muslim nations, Turkey increasingly criticized Israeli behavior in the Israeli-Palestinian and -Arab conflict. The stagnating Oslo Peace Process, the Second Intifada, the construction of settlements, the Lebanon war and the Gaza blockade were directly decrimental to the Israeli-Turkish relations. Still, Turkey is active as mediator, for example in indirect negotiations between Syria and Israel in 2008 (Arakelyan 2013: 41).

The relationship entered a phase of crisis in 2009, beginning with the Gaza offensive of which Turkey was not informed (nor was Egypt) and perceived it as an affront of its mediation initiatives. Turkish leaders responded harshly to Israel's increasing efforts to change the situation in Gaza. The increasing mistrust and lacking confidence corresponded with anti-Israeli sentiments and demonstrations in Turkey and an inflammatory rhetoric by Turkish Prime Minister Erdogan and lacking sensitivity on the Israeli side. Joint military exercises were canceled; Turkish and Israeli politicians accused and humiliated each other publicly and prominently in several incidents (Zuckermann 2010: 47). This development gained Turkey increasing support in the region, while Israel became increasingly isolated and was taken by surprise. In this context, the Gaza flotilla incident marked an unprecedented low and a turning point in the relations. Turkey responded with inflammatory and harsh rhetoric, recalled its ambassador, demanded Israel to take responsibility, pay compensation and apologize publicly. The later publication of the Palmer report led Turkey to expel the Israeli ambassador and to sanction Israel for refusing to apologize (Arakelyan 2013; Ulutaş 2010*b,a*).

The Findings

The context of the relationship between Israel and Turkey is reflected in the media representation of the latter. As the investigation shows, Turkey appears in newspapers in relation to the crisis and its significance for Israel is debated. Although it is negatively represented, highlights of Turkey's importance for Israel do appear.

The mediated involvement by Turkey is strongly crisis related   More than two third (68%) of the articles appear in the crisis period, but also after the crisis in Routine B (26%) Turkey still appears in newspapers. That indicates that the debate or crisis with Turkey lasts longer than the crisis with the Gaza flotilla participants that appear in no articles after the crisis. The amount of articles on Turkey (63) is alike the amount of articles on European actors (57) and GFP (60).

In this crisis, the role of Turkey is debated intensely   Most striking in the framing is the intense debate of the relationship between Israel and Turkey. It is discussed more often than the relationship to any other actor. Every fifth article (22%) describes the relationship as positive and almost two third (64%) describe it as negative. This is the highest percentage of negative framing of the relationship for all analyzed actors. Almost all of those frames concentrate on the worsening and crisis of the relationship. This indicates both a turning point of the relationship and in importance ascribed to it (See below). Turkey is represented negatively in nearly two of three articles (60%). The following patterns are prominent:

1) *Turkey has attacked Israel and is responsible for the crisis.* This is the most frequent form of negative framing (30% of the articles contain frame "Turkey attacked" and 13% contain the frame "Turkey is responsible"). A popular explanation of the events ascribes the responsibility of the crisis to President Erdogan's foreign policy, his reaching out to Iran and "other enemies of Israel". Haaretz:

> A period like this shows the true character: [...] In recent months, Erdogan escalated his attacks on Israel, but now he has come clean and is indeed threatening to join Mahmud Ahmadinejad. The Turkish prime minister makes it clear that he is not only no friend of Israel but also an ally of its enemy. (HA_2010_06_07_15)

2) *Turkey is anti-Israeli, hypocritical and biased.* These forms of delegitimization (they appear in 24% of the articles each) are discussed in chapter 7. An example are references to the atrocities committed by the critics themselves in the same article: Erdogan is

described as "the man who represents the state that committed genocide on the Armenians and currently persecutes the Kurds" (HA_2010_06_07_15). Another example is found in Israel Hayom, citing Israeli academics that "condemn" the "hypocrisy" of the Turkish government at length and its policy towards Israel's enemies. They advise the Israeli government to acknowledge the genocide committed against the Kurds, and demand from Turkey to give up disputed areas with Syria and Cyprus (IH_2010_06_09_07). Again, this argumentation delegitimizes Turkey by calling its government hypocritical – thus illegitimate in its demands and focuses on Turkey as committer of genocide and country with its own disputed areas. This argumentation shall divert attention from the criticism itself. This fallacious argument ad hominem is discussed in Chapter 7.

The degree of personalization   Almost half the articles do not specify any background or institution and then often simply relate to "Turkey" as one entity. However, another large part (38%) concentrates on the Turkish government. Length and placement of the articles is average compared to the other actors. Quotes are found in 43% of the articles, hence still more often than in articles on Gaza flotilla participants and unspecified Western actors, but less than European or American actors. In its formal representation (length of articles, amount of articles with quotes, specification of institutional background) Turkey does not stick out in comparison to the other actors. The numbers are just about average among the other analyzed actors.

There are articles that emphasize Turkey's importance for Israel   Despite the negative framing, nearly one fifth of articles frame Turkey and the relationship to it positively (17%), and argue for its legitimacy and importance. For example, an article in Haaretz (HA_2010_06_18_06) discusses in detail the possible negative effect of a crisis on the close security cooperation. The journalist dates the beginning of the crisis to the Gaza war in 2009, "still the warm relationship between the armies continued." The journalist regards the relationship as endangered due to the flotilla raid and Erdogan's demand for an Israeli apology. But although "the Turkish army is [...] interested in keeping the good relations with the IDF despite the tensions between both governments [...]", Turkish relations will determine their fate and might improve only after election of a "less Islamist government". The responsibility for crisis and its ending is solely seen in the Turkish governments course (HA_2010_06_18_06).

A very short note in Israel Hayom quotes the Israeli Minister of Industry and Trade, Benjamin Ben Eliezer, emphasizing the "strategic interest" of good relations with Turkey that should be kept "at any cost" (IH_2010_06_27_9b). The "strategic interest" is elaborated on in a column in Yediot Aheronot:

> But we need, we have to cooperate with Turkey. Turkey. Yes, this vile little Turkey with the huge modern army, which actually means our State. Without it we are almost blind. That's true, in many senses Turkey is 'our State's eyes.' The Turkish are vile,

> Muslim, fundamentalist, Israel-haters, but throughout the decades we have been able to
> cautiously walk on and among the glowing coals of their wonderful restaurants, all included[44].
> (YA_2010_06_01_008)

While enforcing negative images the importance of Turkey is enforced. A more cooperative and two-sided angle is chosen by an article in Yediot Aheronot two weeks later regarding secret talks between the states to calm the situation down even during the days of crisis. After describing the danger of a further deterioration of the relationship, Erdogan's words are reported extensively in a meeting with the rabbi Froman expressing "disappointment in Netanyahu's government and that it was a pity it is so tough and not well thought-through, but stressed that he had nothing against the people of Israel and especially not against the Jewish people." The journalist continues to express that Erdogan misses Ehud Olmert as Prime Minister and is disappointed with Shimon Peres. The article ends with a comment by the Israeli translator of the meeting: "Now I am more relaxed. Erdogan wants peace in the Middle East. Overall, a very positive message" (YA_2010_06_13_009). The journalist emphasizes a very personal, warm side of Erdogan, and strongly stresses on the importance of Turkey for Israel. Still, those articles are rare, since most articles concentrate on the delegitimization of Turkey and the intentions and actions of its policy-makers.

In sum, the representation of Turkey in Israeli newspapers clearly reflects on the crisis between two countries on the verge of losing their strategic partnership. The coverage is intense in the crisis period but also continues afterwards. The framing is negative, holding Turkey responsible for the crisis, disapproving of its changing foreign policy. The criticism expressed by Turkey is declined as hypocritical and Turkey's own moral conflicts are emphasized. Striking is the high amount of framing of the relationship, especially of its worsening due to the crisis. This indicates the importance ascribed to this crisis.

5.6 The Gaza Flotilla Participants – the Direct Opponent?

As outlined above (see Chapter 3.4) the Gaza flotilla participants are the direct opponent during the analyzed period. Their attempt to breach the naval blockade on Gaza was halted by Israeli naval forces and ended in violent and deadly clashes. In total, 60 articles of the 400 analyzed articles deal with the Gaza flotilla participants (GFP). That is roughly the number of articles on Europe (57 articles) or Turkey (63 articles). Taking into consideration that the Gaza flotilla participants were relevant just for a very short period of crisis, the number comparable to Europe and Turkey indicates that the crisis had a high meaning for Israel.

---

[44]Turkey was a popular destination for all-inclusive holidays for Israelis before the crisis.

The GFP are represented in a de-personalized manner   A de-personalized representation is considered as one in which the actors remain vague, there is no description of their background and they are not quoted in the article. The individuals cannot be identified as such in this form of representation. A de-personalized representation allows for numerous alternative narratives about the actors, as no background is provided for them. Three findings support this assumption: the origin and institution ascribed to the GFP and the amount of direct speech found. Nearly half of the articles (43%) do not indicate where the GFP come from. Ten articles (17%) concentrate on European GFP (five of those describe the Irish participants of a vessel arriving later and peacefully, two articles deal with German GFP). Fourteen articles (23%) describe the members as Turkish, ten (16%) indicate that the GFP come from various nations. That leaves 26 articles (43%) without any mention of the GFP's origin. The high number of articles without any mention of an origin of these GFP indicates that they remain vague, impersonal.

The second indicator for the low level of personalization is the low ascription of institutional background. In 13.3% of the articles, the GFP are described as members of non-government organizations (either the Free Gaza Movement or the IHH); in 50% they are "unclassified individuals" (this category includes all descriptions of individuals as demonstrators, musicians, not affiliated civilians, etc.) and in 35% not specified at all. It means that in more than four fifths, the GFP are not described as members of an organization or a movement or specified in any other way.

A third indicator is the low rate of articles including quotes by GFP: only 30%. Except for the United Nations, every other analyzed actor is quoted significantly more. Inserting quotes into an article is always based on the choice of the journalist writing the article. However, it poses an opportunity to give a perspective on the events that differs from the overall narrative. Quoting the direct opponent is a possibility for estrangement from the general narrative that is rarely chosen in Israeli newspapers (see Chapter 4).

The three indicators show that the GFP remain vague and non-personal. In most articles, neither is an origin described nor an institutional background of the GFP introduced nor a quote inserted in the article. This vagueness of the description of the GFP contributes to an overall distance from them and leaves room for interpretations following official narratives. An example is the naming of the flotilla. Netanyahu is repeatedly quoted saying: "This was not a boat of love; this was a boat of hate" (YA_2010_06_03_004). In comparison, naming them as "Pro-Palestinian activists" (HA_2010_05_28_02; YA_2010_05_28_003) is neutral. Frequent and less neutral are descriptions as "Gaza lovers", "peace" activists or "humanitarians" – always in quotes to emphasize the disbelief in the GFP's intentions (IH_2010_05_30_002; HA_2010_06_07_15). The often lacking description of an origin, institutional belonging or quote indicates a de-personalized representation of the Gaza flotilla participants.

The GFP are represented prominently and negatively The representation of the Gaza flotilla participants is the least positive and most negative of all analyzed actors. Only every tenth article (13%) contains positive framing. All those cases are considered positive framing through an emphasis on the legitimacy of the actors. The GFP are described in every fifth article as a diverse group.

The amount of *negative framing* in the articles is striking: Three quarters (75%) of the articles contain negative framing of the GFP. For comparison, the total average of all articles with negative framing is 49%. In general the amount of framing the GFP receive is the lowest of all actors with 1,4 frames per articles and indicates a simple evaluation and little debate or discussion. These findings indicate that the GFP are represented very negatively and very unambiguously, with rarely more than one frame. Frequent negative framing of the GFP includes:

1) *The GFP are illegitimate, terrorists and anti-Israelis.* This kind of framing is the most popular. In nearly every third article , the GFP are framed as illegitimate (28%) and anti-Israeli or antisemite (27%), in 36% of the articles the GFP are named terrorists. These frames are very absolute in their meaning and leave no room for doubt on the actor's character. The actors are delegitimized (see also Chapter 7.3). An example is found in Maariv (MA_2010_06_10_08b): "Who but us remembers that there existed a Turkish terror flotilla [...] in which Israeli soldiers defended themselves and their country, killed nine red fascists, warmongers, from the bloodthirsty modern school of Islam." The journalist attributes de-humanizing traits to the GFP. Therefore killing them is considered an act of self-defense. This form of delegitimization is very total and efficient as links of terror, Islam and bloodthirsty evoke very clear reactions in a society that experienced terror attacks of various kinds for decades.

Another article in Israel Hayom is characteristic for the contextualization of the GFP within the greater network of terrorism, by connecting IHH to the Muslim Brotherhood. A member of the latter is quoted, claiming the organization would not stop the Jihad as long as Zionists existed (IH_2010_06_03_011a). This framing suggests that the flotilla is part of a well-known movement and a larger call to destroy Israel. Calling for Israel's destruction can be expected to strongly resonate within Israeli Jewish society as it directly addresses the insecurity over the very existence of the state of Israel and the beliefs in an eternal enemy (see Chapter 3.1.4, 7.3 on "Amalek"). Another aspect of the framing of the GFP as terrorists is found in Haaretz:

> The incident [...] was nothing more than a run in the long war against international terrorism. The terrorists will be defeated in this war despite their PR-people, and the good-hearted people around the world that in their innocence support the terrorists for the mistaken belief that they are freedom fighters that righteously use terrorism as a weapon. (HA_2010_06_07_15)

Again, the flotilla raid is contextualized within the greater war on terror (and hence many possible questions are made obsolete) but further, this sentence highlights two more aspects: Those not identifying the "terrorism-frame" are described as naïve and the media aspect of the events is mentioned.

2) The GFP attacked the Israeli soldiers and are responsible for the events on the flotilla. The framing of the participants as attackers is most frequent and found in two third (65%) of all articles. In 18% they are explicitly described as responsible for the events. Ascribing the responsibility of the events solely to the GFP frees Israel from any responsibility. A drastic, but typical example for a) and b) is found in an article in Yediot Aheronot on June 1:

> The soldiers did not encounter peace activists but a wild, armed and murderous terrorist group, who started to lynch the Israeli forces, for the cameras. Terrorists tried to kill the Navy soldiers with their bare hands. Beat them up until they bleed and throw them from a great height to their death. The soldiers, lacking any choice, defended themselves bravely and under impossible conditions and succeeded heroically to meet the purpose of the operation and cause the minimal amount of deaths on the other side. (YA_2010_06_01_019)

In the eyes of the journalist, the image is clear: The GFP are terrorists, aggressors, and attackers of the the helpless soldiers who had to defend themselves. The journalist does not illuminate what lead to the assessment of the GFP as terrorists. This example, as several examples above illustrate the connection between delegitimization of the actor and victimization of one's own side: The opponent is described in drastic delegitimizing and de-humanizing forms and at the same time the Israeli soldiers killing those opponents are described as defending themselves against a lynch, against terrorists, etc. In this description, the responsibility for the outcomes lies solely in the hands of the flotilla participants.

3) The GFP seek publicity to damage Israel's international image. This framing is found in four articles describing the GFP as "biased" and in every fifth article (20%) as "hypocritical". It also appears in articles before the flotilla raid itself. Haaretz reports on May 28, 2010: "The Israeli army's estimation is that the flotilla members intend to arrive at Gaza in daylight, to document the raid of the Israeli navy and to present Israel in the international media as aggressive and violent state" (HA_2010_05_28_02). They further believe that negative images will hardly be avoidable since raiding the ship organized by IHH will end up entangling the Navy soldiers in violence (ibid.). It is noteworthy that this article was published two days before the raid – and apparently violence is a possibility in the eyes of the journalist. The cartoon in Figure 8 is also published before the raid, it illustrates the perception of the Israeli army that is trapped between two bad options, eating a fishhook – the Gaza flotilla – or being eaten by a bigger fish – the international media.

After the raid, an article in Yediot Aheronot enhances the argument of the raid for publicity: "The flotilla participants started to lynch the Israeli forces, in front of the cameras" (YA_06_01_019). Here the violence is described as "lynch" and the intentions reduced to the fight for images in international media.

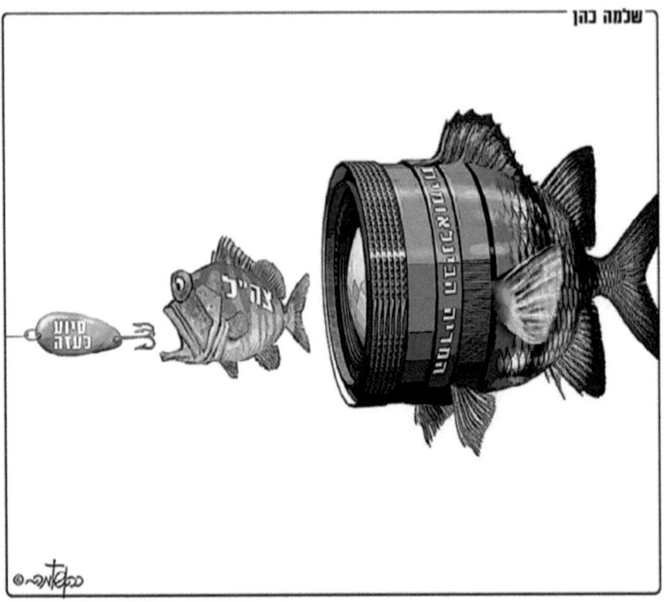

Figure 8 – Cartoon in Israel Hayom on Gaza Flotilla and International Media
'Flotilla to Gaza' (on the fishhook) 'Israeli Defense Forces' (yellow fish)
'The International Media' (big fish)
Shlomo Cohen's Daily Cartoon. May 27, 2010 in Israel Hayom

Another perspective of this framing of the GFP as seeking publicity is apparent in an article on German members of the Parliament and flotilla participants, titled sarcastically "Over there they are heroes." It describes their return to Germany as follows: "This is the big hour of politicians without any importance, Human right workers that nobody has known until now, shifters imbued with religious and ideological hatred against Israel" that finally receive the attention "they looked so much forward to". The GFP here are not framed as terrorists but as unimportant people catching a publicity-wave on the anti-Israeli atmosphere (YA_2010_06_02_014). An article in Israel Hayom emphasizes the "war over images":

> The multiple cameras [at a press conference] reminded us that soon a new [fighting] front on the image will open [...] In the modern war, it is not clear what is more important – the missiles or the cameras? [...] Israel will win the operation when it hinders the flotilla from reaching Gaza [...] and our Turkish friends with hundreds of activists from around the world shall win the media battle. (IH_2010_05_30_002)

This paragraph illustrates not only the dilemma for the Israeli authorities (see below) but also the fourth framing pattern:

4) GFP are as strong as Israelis are. This is reached through equalization of media and military power and war-vocabulary. Both are found in Yediot Aheronot (YA_2010_05_28_003):

     © Frank & Timme   Verlag für wissenschaftliche Literatur

"The Pro-Palestinian activists have a not less efficient weapon: cameras" Later, the author adds cell phones to the list of weapons. Using war-vocabulary by describing the flotilla participants as war opponents, and their cameras as equally dangerous weapons, equalizes the GFP in their power to Israel and lets them appear no less strong or dangerous than the Israeli army. Liebes describes this framing mechanism in conflict coverage – as "equalization" of an enemy to legitimize the use of force by the own group (Liebes 1997; see also Chapter 7.2).

Examples: exceptional articles on the GFP that offer possibilities for estrangement Despite a majority of articles following the above-mentioned framing patterns there are articles that offer a different perspective. Those articles either portray participants of the flotilla, quote them, display their diverse backgrounds, or outline their intentions. A week before the raid, an article in Yediot Aheronot describes the flotilla participants in their diversity, quotes a (Israeli Jewish) participant affirming the non-violent approach and details the aid material aboard (YA_2010_05_23_004). While the journalist shows no sympathy for the interviewed participant, the flotilla participants are represented as individuals, their intentions are explained within their narration.

On the day after the raid, an article on page two in Maariv offers the perspective of the flotilla participants, describes their diversity (parliament members, Holocaust survivors, Nobel Prize winners), quotes a participant describing the events of the night, "Dramatic calls" sent to European States to intervene and to prevent Israeli takeover, and an organizer claiming: "Two Israeli navy ships are onto us. We call all lovers of freedom in the world to protest against the Israeli aggression. We are in international waters and Israeli navy ships threaten to attack us" (MA_2010_05_31_002). The violent events after takeover probably occurred after the editorial deadline. However, covering the developments of the flotilla from the perspective of the flotilla members on page two is remarkable. In this article they do not appear as a faceless, vague group that is intending to hurt Israeli soldiers physically or Israel's image through images of violence. This article describes another perspective, in which the GFP represent themselves as anxious victims.

Two days after the raid, both Maariv and Yediot Aheronot publish articles on the adventurous trip to the headquarters of the IHH. Both articles are very personal and emphasize the danger of "entering a lion's cage". The Maariv journalist emphasizes his fear to be identified as Israeli. He meets a Palestinian at IHH and quotes his perspective at length:

> This organization supports Gaza's citizen with food and clothes and assists those that lost their houses because of you [...]. For you [Israelis] all the Palestinians are targets. You shot people that were on the flotilla and just wanted to bring assistance to Gaza. The situation in Gaza is very hard, there are lots of hungry people. (MA_2010_06_02_008)

This ambivalent and human picture of the people in the IHH-headquarter is very rare. The journalist continues to describe the absurdity of his connection with the Palestinian as two people from the same place abroad with very differing but co-existing narratives. Although the article is framed within the fear of being a Jewish Israeli within the IHH headquarter, the journalist offers the perspective of the rival, outlines the ambivalence of the conflict and its absurdity.

An article in Haaretz quotes the novelist Henning Mankell, a flotilla participant, at length on his intention to sue Israel in Den Haag, for raiding a ship in international water and his doubt whether to continue publishing in Hebrew. Furthermore a member of the German Bundestag that was on the flotilla is interviewed, seeing her responsibility as member of a German Parliament and Germany's history to call Israel to avoid violating Human rights of another people. She considers the behavior of the flotilla members as "self defense" (HA_2010_06_04_09).

These articles are examples for a representation that Orgad (2012: 87) calls estrangement, "a symbolic process of distancing national audiences from their own narratives, culture, politics and history". While it is difficult, particularly for national media to convey the message of the opponent in a time of crisis, these articles serve as examples for such opportunities, even during a time of crisis.

In sum, the representation of the flotilla participants is permeated by several characteristics. The coverage clearly falls into the crisis period and the GFP are perceived as threat and enemies. That is reflected by their representations: The participants remain very de-personalized, anonymous, voice- and faceless. Many articles refrain from describing their origin, and institutional background and from citing them. The coverage of the flotilla participants is prominent, they appear as often as Turkish or European actors but with longer articles. The framing of the flotilla participants is more negative than of the other actors. It is based on several frames that add up to a whole narrative. The GFP are described as attackers and as responsible for the violent outcome of the raid. They are contextualized as motivated by hatred towards Israel and the aim to hurt Israel's international image by forcing it into a publicity disaster.

Why could six vessels and 700 participants be perceived as such a threat and why was it necessary to present them in such negative manner? Sørensen and Martin (2014) argue that the Gaza flotilla participants posed a dilemma of two bad choices for the Israeli authorities. Either let the vessels arrive and unload their cargo in Gaza at the price of giving in to pressure and losing the blockade's deterrence effect, or stop the vessel and risk violent outcomes and a public relations disaster. Either way, the GFP seem to either gain their goal of reaching Gaza or publicity for their cause. Hence the arenas of conflict were the sea and the media. In their analysis of several cases in which activists pose a dilemma for authorities Sørensen and Martin (2014) outline an important continuum of these cases – a contest over narratives between authorities and activists: The activists frame their action as positive and constructive (deliver humanitarian aid to Gaza). Authorities can choose to either adopt that positive framing or contest it through framing the activists as provocateurs or law-breakers (Sørensen and Martin 2014).

The challenge of explaining what is wrong in sending humanitarian aid may lead to the necessity of extra-negative framing of the Gaza flotilla participants. The dilemma approach supports assumptions why describing the Gaza flotilla members as terrorists may seem a solution in the contest over framing. However, as illustrated above, there are also representations that offer a different perspective in which the GFP are represented as individuals, are quoted, and their intentions are outlined.

5.7 The World – Against Israel in Crisis?

The category unspecified Western actors is coded when the article's author refers not to one relevant country or institution, but to various countries at the same time. This category appears in total 47 times. Articles where it is used refer either literally to "the world" (66%) or to "them", meaning a number of western countries. This category is only chosen when it is apparent that the countries referred to are the studied countries of this research, not for example "the Arab Nations". An example for "the world" is: "The pressure from the leaders of the world for an international investigation rises" (IH_2010_06_07_01). An example for an unspecified "them" is an article on international news after the flotilla raid: "Watching the foreign news [...], in the foreign television things look less bad" (MA_2010_06_03_26). The focus is not on one media institution but on western media in general, later Bloomberg, France24, BBC, CNN, and Sky News are introduced as examples. The leading argument regarding unspecified Western actors is that they appear in a clear dichotomy of "us" (Jewish Israelis) versus "them" (the world). Moreover, despite their lacking closer description They remain vague; these articles appear during crisis times, and they are framed negatively.

Unspecified Western actors remain vague in their representation   Their institutional background is not specified in 57% of the articles. In 12% the articles relate to international media, 8% specify the governments of those countries, but the vast majority relates to "them" as a non-specified group of actors. In these articles, 38% contain quotes by any actor; the United Nations and GFP have less quotes, the other actors more (see in results above). As indicated above, the category Western actors relates to an unspecified group of actors, therefore also their institutional background is not restricted.

Unspecified Western actors appear in crisis   70% of the articles with unspecified Western actors are published in the crisis period. That is clearly the time period in which it is important "how the world sees Israel" and the time in which a dichotomy of "the world" versus "Israel" is established. In crisis times it is particularly important to win international support but also to gain orientation on the international standing (see Chapter 2.2 and 1). Therefore articles on those two issues are important. On the other hand, this vague description of "them" or "the world" amplifies convictions of siege mentality (see Chapter 3.1.4).

These unspecified Western actors are framed negatively In 55% of the articles, negative framing and two major categories can be identified:

1) They are against Israel and attack Israel. The framing as "anti-Israeli" or "antisemite" appears in every fourth article on these actors. Frames on "them" attacking Israel appear in 17% of the articles (see Chapter 7.3).

2) They lack understanding, are biased and hypocritical. Each of these frames appears in about 17% of the articles. An example is found in an article in Yediot Aheronot on international media coverage of the flotilla raid, titled "The coverage in the World – distorted image". The article describes in detail that "only one news agency distributes images of the lynch on the soldiers", while the others "hide those images". It argues how the agencies "procrastinated" images showing the "lynch" on the soldiers on purpose and deliberately did not acknowledge their reliability. The text is accompanied by images of newspaper front pages titled "almost all the newspapers of the world attack Israel" (YA_2010_06_02_011). The dichotomy is clear: International media is described in angry tone as a single powerful, yet deliberately biased entity that is attacking Israel. An article in Israel Hayom from the same day is headed "The world already passed the sentence" and opens asking "Why was it to be expected that the world's newspapers present the Israeli army as pirates taking over an innocent ship and not as soldiers that were hit". It describes in detail how international newspapers blame Israel and hold it responsible for everything (IH_2010_06_02_15). In this description, the world is biased and Israel the scapegoat. Two articles quote Prime Minister Netanyahu in the first lines of articles: "The state of Israel is under an international attack of hypocrisy" (MA_2010_06_03_005; YA_2010_06_03_004). Still, there is positive framing in 27% of the articles. An example for positive framing of international criticism as justified is found in Yediot Aheronot (YA_2010_05_16_25) titled "Alone, based on our faults". It reacts to criticism by an unspecified group on the thorough security screenings at Ben Gurion airport for non-Israeli citizen. The journalist defends the criticism as justified and explains that Israel became a control- and security-obsessed state, which he reasons using the conflict reality. Nevertheless he accuses Israel for having lost its ability for self-criticism. This article is an example for international criticism framed positively and taking the international perspective as a chance for self-critical coverage.

In sum, both the existence of 47 articles on "the world" or "them" involving themselves in the Israeli-Palestinian conflict and the representation of "the world" indicates the existence of a dichotomous "us" versus "them" perspective and what Bar-Tal and Antebi call "siege mentality" (see Chapter 3.1.4). The description of these actors remains vague and generalized as they appear predominantly during the crisis period. They are often described as prejudiced and attacking Israel. Still, Gaza flotilla participants are represented more negatively. The difference is the form of involvement: While the Gaza flotilla participants involve themselves as active opponents, the Western actors are involved centrally in statements. Moreover, the ultimate goal is not fighting unspecified Western actors but belonging to them. Therefore, the representation of unspecified Western actors can rather be understood as alienation than as direct opponents. The existence of this category supports the assumption of siege mentality as part of the representation of international involvement. It is discussed in Chapter 7.3.

5.8 Russia and the Quartet on the Middle East – Uninvolved?

The Quartet on the Middle East and Russia are excluded from the analysis. The initial research also searched for articles regarding Russia and the Middle East Quartet. But the amount of articles on both is so low that these were excluded from the analysis. Both appear in five and three articles respectively during the whole period. This is not based on a total lack of interaction. Official sources show that there is interaction between Russia and Israel: Russia condemned the events of the Gaza flotilla and called for an investigation (Ministry of Foreign Affairs 2010*b*) and its Foreign Ministry reports of several official interactions during the investigated period, the Russian Foreign Minister Sergey Lavrov talked twice with Israeli Foreign Minister Avigdor Lieberman on the phone (May 13 and 18, 2010) and visited Israel and the Palestinian Territories (29.06.2014) (Ministry of Foreign Affairs 2010*a*). The Quartet on the Middle East published an official statement on June 21, 2010. Immediately after the flotilla incident Tony Blair, the Quartet's Representative published several statements and his visit to a Gaza crossing was reported by the Office of the Quartet Representative (Office of the Quartet Representative 2010). Hence the question remains why both Russia and the Quartet do not appear in Israeli newspapers.

5.9 The Actors and the Newspapers

The results (see Chapter 5.1) show that the appearance of the different actors in the four researched newspapers does not significantly vary. Haaretz, as the liberal intellectual newspaper, and Israel Hayom, as the right-wing freebee, publish slightly more articles on the USA. Yediot Aheronot on the other hand publishes most articles regarding the Gaza flotilla participants.

The newspapers do, however, differ significantly in their evaluation of the actors. Haaretz' representations contain the most positive and neutral frames on the actors and the least negative frames. In its representation of actors, Haaretz is focused on continuous involvement by the USA and the UN and the representation is rather balanced or positive. In contrast, Israel Hayom frames actors in the least positive manner. Although Haaretz and Israel Hayom publish articles on the same actors, they evaluate them differently. This might be due to different political intentions. Haaretz is known for its balanced coverage, which explains a tendency for positive and neutral evaluation of international actors and for concentration on continuous involvement. Israel Hayom on the other hand serves the central goal to promote the Likud party and in particular Prime Minister Netanyahu (see Chapter 3.3). That might alter the agenda. Maariv and Yediot Aheronot as newspapers that are predominantly dependant on street sales appear with the highest numbers of negative framing of the actors. However, the differences between the newspapers can only be sufficiently discussed when taking the representation of involvement into account as is done in the next chapter (see Chapter 6).

5.10 Conclusion

This chapter sums up the main lessons learned so far regarding the representation of the analyzed actors in mediated reality in Israeli newspapers. In general, the following tendencies have become apparent: 1) Actors are represented differently in "crisis" and "routine" periods. 2) The United States are represented very differently from all the other actors. 3) There is a category solely for siege mentality.

Table 11 – Crisis and Routine Actors

Routine actors		Crisis actors	
USA	UN Europe	Turkey	Gaza flotilla Unspecified western
trustworthy partner	ambivalent relationship	lost strategic partner	opponents

1) The difference between "crisis" and "routine" actors. The analysis of the different actors shows that actors' appearance and representation differ due to the general time of their appearance (see Table 11). Routine actors appear throughout all three periods. Those are the USA, Europe and the UN. Articles about them are published throughout the whole analyzed period. Crisis actors appear predominantly during the crisis period. Those are Turkey, Gaza flotilla participants and unspecified western actors. The central difference is the continuity: Routine actors seem to be of importance to Israel at all times, whereas crisis actors are not relevant in routine times. Yet the differences in their representations are striking: Crisis actors are presented in a more negative way. In articles on crisis actors there are hardly several frames that might possibly contradict each other and give a diverse persective. In general, there is only one negative frame per article. All three crisis actors are described as attackers and as hypocrites. Still, there are differences between the three crisis actors. Whereas GFP and Unspecified are framed negatively and impersonally and appear as direct opponents, Turkey's role seems more complicated. Turkey, while clearly a crisis actor, does not appear in a solely negative manner. The relationship to Turkey is discussed intensely and its importance repeatedly emphasized. This indicates that Turkey is perceived as an actor in a transition – in respect to the background of the relations one can conclude that there is a severe crisis in a relationship that is considered strategically important and necessary. GFP as the adversaries in this crisis do not exist as actors in routine times. First, the GFP acted as ad-hoc group that does not exist anymore after the raid, second its relevance for Israel ended with the raid. There are numerous articles that cover not a particular international actor but an unspecified group of international "Western" actors or the "World" involving itself in general. These articles are a clear crisis phenomenon that indicates both a crisis that triggered a strong international involvement, but also that in Israeli media, the "Israel versus the world" perspective is predominantly a crisis phenomenon.

The routine actors USA, UN, and Europe appear continuously and in a balanced manner throughout the analyzed periods. They are framed less negatively and are personalized more often. This indicates that these actors do in general play a role in Israel which is not dependent on certain events. Still, there are differences between Europe and the UN on one hand and the USA on the other hand. Europe and the UN are not referred to as positively as the USA, and they are less personalized. There is negative framing, for example as hypocrites. In general, the relationship to Europe and the UN is ambivalent. Both are perceived with reluctance and as biased against Israel. The USA appears differently (see next subsection).

2) The difference between the USA and the other actors. The United States are represented very differently from all the other actors. The USA appears more often than all the other actors, is personalized more often, both in the amount of articles with quotes and the concentration on government actors. The articles about US-involvement contain a higher number of frames that are more frequently positive. The USA is predominantly described as important, legitimate, pro-Israeli and supportive. The relationship is also described as important. This is reflected also in the coverage of personal stories and articles debating the complicated relations. These results show the clear concentration on the USA as a trustworthy partner, friend and supporter. Israel and the USA are connected through shared values, interests, and policies. In mediated reality, the USA is described as the sole honest counterpart and the only international actor without a negative bias against Israel.

This is alone accounted for by the reliance on the USA and the perceived isolation from any other international entity.

3) There is a category solely for siege mentality. The appearance of the actor category unspecified Western actors opposing Israel as a tool for siege mentality will be debated in chapter 7 which focuses on the patterns of representation. The appearance of this actor category indicates a "world against Israel" perception during crisis.

The findings of 1) and 2) support the assumptions of hypotheses H_1 and H_2. In mediated reality of the Israeli newspapers, representations differ greatly between crisis and routine times and different actors appear. During crisis times, not only the adversary, the GFP in this case, become visible in newspapers but also a perspective of "the world versus Israel". These "crisis actors" are contextualized in a more negative way than routine actors who appear independently from the crisis and are also described less negatively. The previous chapter also shows that there are larger differences in the representation between the different actors than between "crisis and routine" actors. The USA is covered with high frequency and very positively as friends and partners. More ambivalent is the contextualization of Europe and the UN who also appear continuously, but less frequently and positively than as biased against Israel. The crisis actors differ as well – the GFP and Unspecified are framed very negatively and as attackers, as is Turkey. But in the coverage of the latter there is frequent debate regarding the relationship and an emphasis on its importance. The category of crisis and routine actors found in this chapter is under scrutiny in the further analysis to evaluate if this distinction can be upheld also regarding the forms and contextualizations of the involvement.

6 The Actors' Involvement

This chapter illuminates the different forms of involvement by the analyzed actors as represented in the Israeli newspapers. As described in Chapter 4.3, the involvement is operationalized as a so-called claim which can be a direct action or statement, but also a claim ascribed to the actor by the author. Two levels were coded, namely the character of the represented claim (supportive, critical, no position, no claim) and its direction (related in existing or past policies, related to future events the actor wishes for). The resulting eight different claims are too stratified to give significant results. Therefore in the present analysis claims relating to the future are subsumed into one category; "call for action". This is suitable, as the actor explicitly calls for an action in the future and thus shifts the attention from "evaluating" past and present policies to a future policy deemed suitable. A fourth category comprises articles in which there is no claim by the international actor (but merely the relationship is discussed) and articles in which the actor has a claim but a neutral one. In both, the actor is not represented as taking a position. Therefore, both forms of involvement are counted as being within the same category.

Hence the four relevant categories of claims for the further evaluation are: support, criticism, call for action, and no claim. First, all relevant results of the involvement are introduced briefly. In a second step the different forms of involvement are discussed in detail.

6.1 The Results in Short

The appearance of the involvement   Criticism is the most frequent claim by international actors in Israeli newspapers (see Figure 9), it appears in 183 articles (46%), followed by call for action in 93 articles (23%), support in 63 articles (16%) and 61 articles without a claim by the actor (15%). There is a significant difference in the appearance of the involvement and the crisis and routine periods (see Table 12). Clear forms of crisis involvement are criticism (64%) and articles without claim (53%). Supportive involvement appears strongest in routine A (41%) and B (37%), calls for action appear equally in period routine A and the crisis period (38%) and less in routine B (25%). Each claim is discussed in depth in the following chapters.

Table 12 – Involvement and Period (in Percent)

	Criticism (n=183)	Call for action (n=93)	Support (n=63)	No message (n=61)
Routine A	18	38	**41**	26
Crisis	**64**	38	22	53
Routine B	19	25	**37**	21
Total	101[1]	101[1]	100	100

$\chi^2(6, N = 400) = 41.242, p = .000$ [1] rounding error

The formal appearance Average pages (see Table 13). Call for action appears on average on page 7, criticism on average on page 11. In between are supportive claims that appear on average on page 10 and articles without a message that occur on page 9 on average. These results are not normally distributed as explorative data analysis shows, therefore a Mann-Whitney-U test was conducted. There is a significant difference between the average page of criticism and call for action ($p = .000$), however a no significant difference between support and call for action ($p = .054$).

Table 13 – Placement of Articles on Different Claims (in Pages)

	Criticism (n=183)	Call for action (n=93)	Support (n=63)	No message (n=61)
$\bar{n}$	10.9	7.0	10.0	9.5
σ	8.9	6.6	8.2	8.0

$\bar{n}$ = average value σ = standard deviation

Table 14 – Length of Articles on Different Claims (in Amount of Words)

	Criticism (n=183)	Call for action (n=93)	Support (n=63)	No message (n=61)
$\bar{n}$	371.3	383.9	360.0	382.5
σ	187.3	183.9	269.3	190.1

$\bar{n}$ = average value σ = standard deviation

Average word count of the articles (see Table 14). The longest articles are those without involvement (383 words average) or calls for action (384 words average). Supportive involvement can be found on average in the shortest articles with a 360 word average. These average numbers are not normally distributed, therefore a Mann-Whitney-U test was conducted that revealed that there is no significant difference between criticism and call for action ($p = .525$) and no significant difference between supportive involvement and call for action ($p = .176$) in the length of the articles. That means there are no significant differences in the average word count of the articles.

The formal appearance of the claims is not significantly different, both in page appearance and in word count. The only significant difference is between critical claims that appear in articles on rear pages and calls for action that appear on earlier pages. The high standard deviation of each claim in article length and page explain these results.

The highest amount of *quotes* is found when the actors are supportive (65%). The least amount of quotes is found in articles without central claim (26%). Critical claims (43%) and call for action (46%) are alike. These differences are significant ($\chi^2(3, N = 400) = 19.262, p = .000$).

Table 15 – Topics the Claims Relate to (in Percent)

	Criticism (n=183)	Call for action (n=93)	Support (n=63)	No message (n=61)
Gaza flotilla	**51**	30	10	30
Israeli-Palestinian conflict	24	**60**	29	10
Relationship actor-Israel	25	10	**62**	**61**
Total	100	100	101[1]	101[1]

$\chi^2(6, N = 400) = 112.873, p = .000$ [1] rounding error

Also the *topic* the involvement is related to differs significantly (see Table 15). Critical involvement is strongest when related to the flotilla (51%), calls for action refer to the conflict itself in 60% of the cases, support is to two thirds (62%) related to the relationship as well as articles without claim by the actor (61%). These results are discussed in the next sections.

The actors' involvements are different (see Figure 10, and Table 26 in Appendix A). Except for the USA, all actors appear in Israeli newspapers as predominantly critical. Three quarters of the articles on the GFP contain those critical claims, followed by Turkey and unspecified Western actors with 64% critical claims. The routine actors UN and European actors are almost equally frequently critical with 59% and 60% respectively. The USA is presented very differently in Israeli newspapers with only 14% of the articles stating a critical claim.. The dominant US-claim is a call for action (40%). The discussion of these numbers follows in the next sections.

The framing of the involvement is most of the time significantly different. The positive and negative framing of claim, actor, and relationship differ significantly. However, neutral framing of the relationship and the claim is rare and not significant ($p = .346$) (see Tables 16; 17 ; and 27 in Appendix A). As Figure 11 illustrates, the framing of critical involvement is predominantly negative, whereas supportive involvement is framed predominantly positive. Calls for action are framed in a more balanced way, meaning there are more neutral frames and an equal amount of positive and negative frames.

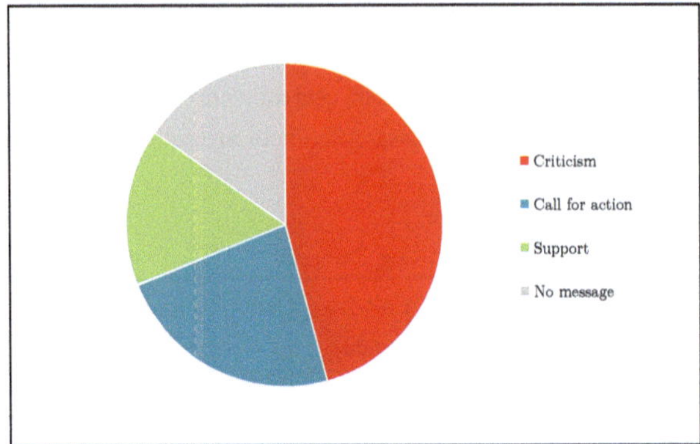

Figure 9 – International Involvement in Israeli Newspapers

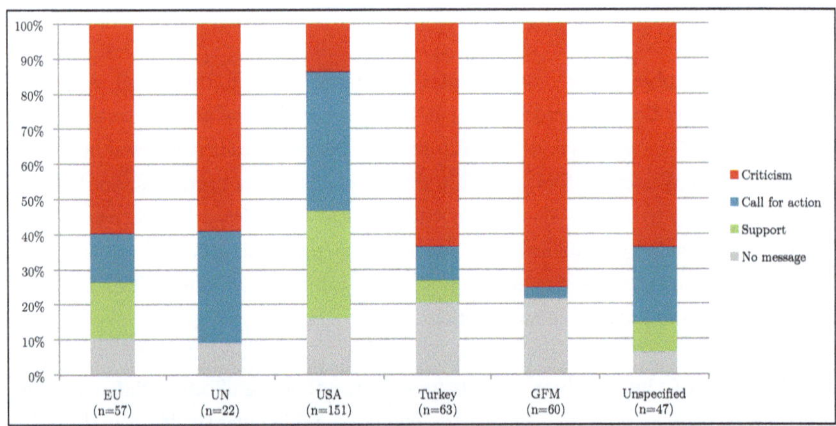

Figure 10 – The Actors' Involvement (in Percent)
$\chi^2(15, N = 400) = 136.922, p = .000$

The *period* itself has an impact on the framing. As outlined above there is more critical involvement during crisis times. The representation is different during the crisis period as well. There are almost twice as many frames during crisis periods than in the routine periods (crisis: 378; Routine A: 254; Routine B: 209). But while most frames are proportionally less frequent, negative framing of the actor, which comprises in routine times (A and B) 18% of all frames, comprises 30% of all frames in crisis (see Figure 12).

Also the *amount of frames* varies according to the character of the involvement. Call for action receives the highest amount of frames (2.7 frames per article), support follows with 2,4 frames per article, articles without claims receive 2 frames per article and criticism the least with 1.7 frames per articles. The amount of frames within an article is regarded an indicator for the amount of debate attributed to actors and their involvement. Only when there are at least two frames (e.g., actor framed positively, and actor framed as negatively; or actor framed positively, and claim framed positively or negatively; etc.) can there be a possibility for a debate or a variety of opinions. In articles with only one frame it is clear that there is only one perspective provided (e.g., actor is negative; or actor is positive; etc.).

This assumption is supported by the results (see Table 18). The tests illustrate that most articles ($n = 238$) contain one frame (either positive, neutral, or negative). This is dominant for supportive and critical involvement and articles without claim. Articles with a call for action contain the highest percentage of neutral framing (see above) and do contain the highest amount of articles with two different frames either positive and negative, positive and neutral, or neutral and negative. That means calls for action do indeed lead to the most differentiated framing. The representations of different forms of involvement are interpreted and discussed in the following chapters in detail.

Table 16 – Claim and Framing of Actor (in Percent)

		Criticism (n=183)	Call for action (n=93)	Support (n=63)	No message (n=61)
Actor positive[1]	Yes	12	47	**57**	33
	No	88	53	43	67
Actor neutral[2]	Yes	5	12	6	21
	No	95	88	94	79
Actor negative[3]	Yes	**68**	32	17	49
	No	32	68	83	51

[1] is $\chi^2(3, N400) = 63.125, p = .000$;
[2] is $\chi^2(3, N400) = 14.678, p = .002$;
[3] is $\chi^2(3, N400) = 62.804, p = .000$

The distribution within the newspapers of the involvement is significantly different ($p = .032$, see Figure 13). However, these differences are only significant between Haaretz

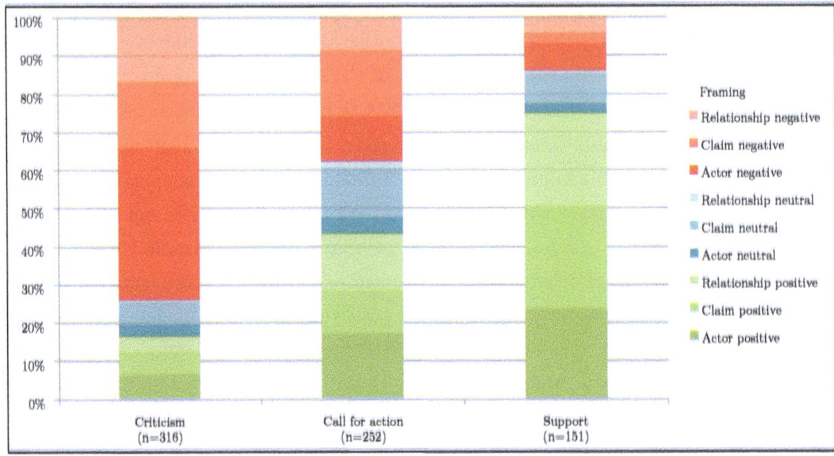

Figure 11 – Framing of Central Claims

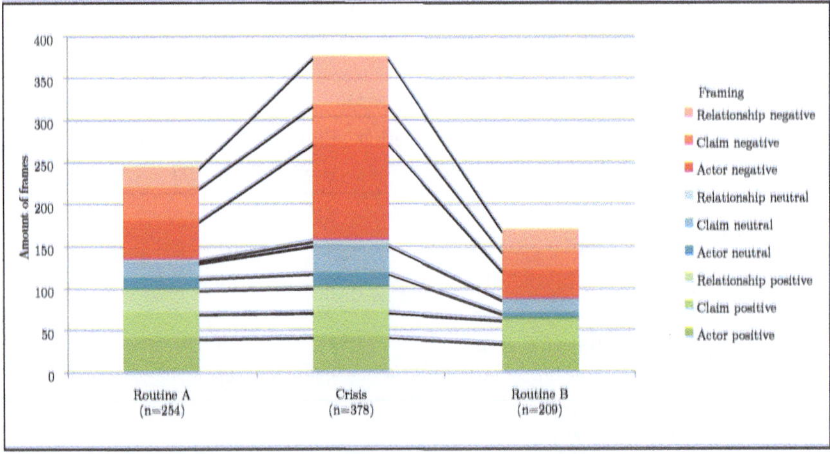

Figure 12 – Framing in Analyzed Periods

Table 17 – Claim and Framing of Relationship (in Percent)

		Criticism (n=183)	Call for action (n=93)	Support (N=63)	No message (n=61)
Relationship positive[1]	Yes	7	40	**59**	36
	No	93	60	41	64
Relationship neutral[2]	Yes	1	4	2	3
	No	99	96	98	97
Relationship negative[3]	Yes	29	23	10	**44**
	No	71	77	90	56

[1] is $\chi^2(3, N400) = 78.721, p = .000$;
[2] is $\chi^2(3, N400) = 3.312, p = .346$;
[3] is $\chi^2(3, N400) = 20.370, p = .000$

Table 18 – Differentiated Framing of Claims (in Percent)

	Criticism (n=183)	Call for action (n=93)	Support (n=63)	No message (n=61)
No frames (n=16)	4	4	3	3
One frame (n=238)	**72**	36	67	53
Two frames (n=54) (incl.neutral)	9	**23**	14	12
Two frames+ (n=92) (positive and negative)	15	**38**	16	33
Total	100	101[1]	100	101[1]

$\chi^2(9, N = 400) = 108.225, p = .000$ [1] rounding error

and the other newspapers and not among them[45]. In Haaretz more articles than in the other newspapers are about calls for action (19%) and less articles than in Maariv and Yediot Aheronot are about critical involvement (40%). In Maariv and Yediot Aheronot more than half the articles (52% and 57%) contain critical claims. Israel Hayom has the least amount of critical articles with 37%, but most articles with supportive involvement (24%). No other newspaper has more than 15% supportive involvement.

There are no significant differences regarding the *topics* the articles relate to ($p = .065$). Maariv and Yediot Aheronot concentrate more on the Gaza flotilla (40% and 42%) and thus have a higher concentration of articles in the period of crisis than the other newspapers. Israel Hayom publishes an almost equal amount of articles on the flotilla, the conflict, and the relationship (35%, 30%, and 36%), whereas Haaretz also has each 30% of the articles on the flotilla and the relationship to the international actor, yet most articles pertain to

---

[45] χ^2 on Israel Hayom, Yediot Aheronot, Maariv excl. Haaretz is $\chi^2(5, N = 300) = 12,439, p = .053$

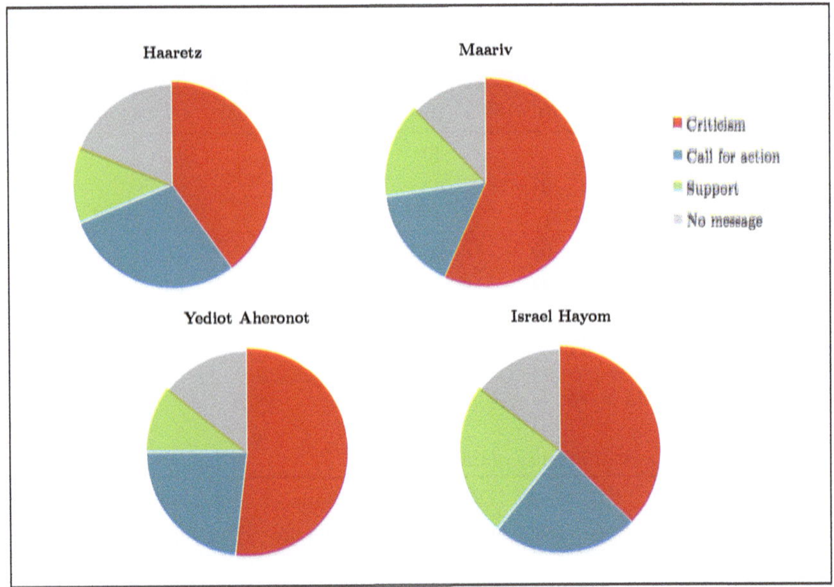

Figure 13 – Involvement in the four Analyzed Newspapers

the Israeli-Palestinian conflict. Interestingly, only 20% of the articles in Yediot Aheronot relate to the conflict.

The positive and negative *framing of the involvement* does not differ significantly between the newspapers (positive framing of the claim: $p = .402$; negative framing of the claim: $p = .455$). In general, the four newspapers rarely frame the claim positively. Still, Haaretz as the liberal newspaper contains slightly more positive frames on the claim than the other newspapers (in 26% of the articles) and Maariv contains the least (in 16% of Maariv's articles). Also the differences in negative framing of the claim are minor Haaretz has the least number of negative frames on the claim (in 22% of the articles) and Yediot Aheronot the highest amount of negative frames on the claim in 32% of the articles.

The neutral framing of the involvement differs significantly ($p = .007$). Articles in Haaretz have a significantly higher numbers of neutral frames on the claim (in 27% of the articles) than the other newspapers which have no significant differences among them[46]. In Haaretz, every third article contains neutral frames on the claim, in the other papers much less (Israel Hayom 18%, the others 11%).

As the previous chapter shows, the actors appear in the newspapers without significant differences, they are however ascribed different claims. These claims are not framed

---

[46]χ^2 on Israel Hayom, Yediot Aheronot, Maariv excl. Haaretz is $\chi^2(2, N = 300) = 3,347, p = .188$

     © Frank & Timme   Verlag für wissenschaftliche Literatur

differently, apart from in Haaretz where there are more neutral frames regarding the claims than in the other newspapers.

6.2 Critical Involvement – "We Strongly Condemn..."

Critical claims regarding Israel's actions are the most common form of involvement by the actors in the mediated reality of the newspapers. Almost half of the articles (46%) are based on critical claims by international actors.

Criticism is crisis related Half of the articles with critical involvement are related to the Gaza flotilla raid (51%) and only every fifth article relates to the Israeli-Palestinian conflict (24%) or the relationship between Israel and the actor (25%). The Gaza flotilla raid is debated centrally during the crisis period, therefore the majority of the critical claims are found in the crisis period (64%) and less than one fifth (18% to 19%) are found in the routine periods.

Criticism is the dominant form of involvement for all actors except the USA

Although the crisis actors appear with more critical claims than the routine actors in Israeli newspapers, all except the USA are presented with critical involvement in at least two thirds of the articles. GFP are represented as being the most critical with 75%, the other crisis actors unspecified Western actors and Turkey criticize in 64% of the articles. Again, this criticism is almost completely related to the events on the Gaza flotilla.

Examples: The GFP are rarely quoted but when their intention to breach the naval blockade on Gaza is mentioned in the article it is coded as a critical claim as it opposes Israeli policies. Criticism by different unspecified Western actors is often subsumed in one article, for example in Israel Hayom: "The world already passed the judgment". The article collects examples of international media on the flotilla raid, for example: "Israel is a pirate state" (Libération), or "Israel is accused of state terror" (Guardian). Turkish Deputy Prime Minister Arinç "accuses Israel of piracy" following the raid of the flotilla (HA_2010_06_04_07b). The coverage of Turkey shows critical involvement regarding the relationship. For example President Gül warns: "If Israel does not apologize, we will cut the relationship off" (MA_2010_06_13_05). This example indicates debate of the relationship with Turkey (see also Chapter 5.5).

The routine actors United Nations and Europe appear with critical involvement in 59% and 60% of the articles. Only the USA differs significantly from all the other actors: in only 14% of the articles does it appear as criticizing. The critical involvement of the "routine" actors is hardly ever related to the Gaza flotilla raid and mostly concentrates on the Israeli-Palestinian conflict in general (USA and UN) or the relationship to Israel

(Europe). That does not mean that there are no articles on the reactions of European, UN and US-actors, but rather that those are represented in articles on "the world".

The results illustrate that in mediated reality of Israeli newspapers all the international actors appear predominantly critical. Only the USA stands out. This unambiguous character of international involvement explains the prominent perception in Jewish Israeli society of being alone in a hostile world (see siege mentality 3.1.4).

Delegitimizing the critical actor is in the focus of the mediated representation
In general, the representation is very unambiguous – the amount of frames is with 1.7 per article very low. The results show that most critical articles contain one either positive or neutral or negative contextualization. Accordingly, there is little room for debate or ambiguity. The representation is predominantly negative and focuses on the actors rather than on the claim or relationship. This is a classical *ad hominem* mechanism, by which traits and characteristics of an actor are attacked in an attempt to undermine the argument. This is the case in two of three articles with critical involvement framing the actor negatively (68%). Roughly every third critical actor is described as attacker (34%) or antisemite/anti-Israeli (29%). An example on European criticism framed as attacker and anti-Israeli:

> Europeans are regular critics of Israel involving themselves [...]. Experience teaches that it is advisable to prepare for an attack of European pressure [...]. So even if the anti-Israeli sentiment in the European public is occasionally reducing, the overall wave continuously grows. (YA_2010_05_10_32)

Mainly GFP and also Turkey are framed as attacking when criticizing. The declaration of critical actors as antisemites or anti-Israeli is evenly distributed between all actors except the UN and the USA. Concentration on the characteristics of the critical actors rather than on their criticism reduces the need to debate their point of criticism itself, since it cannot be legitimate. These patterns of delegitimization are discussed in chapter 7.

The criticism itself is the focus of 29% of the frames. The most frequent argument is that different behavior would negate Israel's policies, followed by framing the criticism as illegitimate or unacceptable. A less frequent argument is "the claim is counterproductive on the path to peace". Positive frames on negative involvements are rare. In 13 articles the authors admit that the criticism is justified, in four they emphasize the importance of the criticism. In every tenth article the criticism is outlined in detail, which is coded as neutral framing. It is considered a way to create distance when the point of criticism itself is elaborated on. The relationship itself is the weakest focus of frames (21%), mostly it is described as worsening, usually related to Turkey or Europe.

Critical actors receive different framing   While all the actors are rarely framed positively or neutrally when criticizing, the focus of the negative frame differs. In 60% of the rare critical involvement by the USA the claim itself is framed. An example is found in an article in Haaretz on US-criticism on the planned Israeli settlement construction within Palestinian land (MA_2010_06_22_06): "The US is furious on the decision [...]". While the author first underlines that the Israeli plan is "in law and order": "According to the plan the Palestinian families [that will be evicted for the planned Israeli garden] will receive exchange buildings for their houses, others were anyway constructed illegally". The author defends Israeli policies as just and law abiding, and the Palestinians' as "illegal" construction[47]. However, he continues to outline US-worries: "That is exactly the kind of measures that hurt the trust so necessary for progress in the peace process". Furthermore the author chooses to quote several Palestinian officials condemning the plan and explaining the consequences for Palestinians: "Instead of having a house, mine and my son's building will be destroyed." An Israeli official from the left-wing party Meretz is quoted supporting US-criticism: "We will pay a very high price in relations with the US and particularly with the Palestinians." This article illustrates framing of US-criticism. There are no frames regarding personal traits of US-actors. First the content of the claim is framed negatively as negating Israeli policies (that are described as legal), but then several actors are quoted that support and enhance the content of the critical US-claim. Therefore, there is also positive framing of the claim that is implied as justified.

For comparison, the criticism of Europe or UN is framed in 30% to 40%, the criticism of the crisis actors receive is framed in less than 30%. The example illustrates and the numbers show that critical involvement by the USA is considered different from critical involvement by other actors. This different representation of the same form of involvement may be rooted in several causes: The relationship with the USA is perceived very differently to the relationships with the other analyzed actors (see Chapter5). Whereas the USA is perceived as friend, partner, as being "with Israel", the UN and European actors are represented as more ambivalent, partially as friends and partners, but also as not trustworthy, irrelevant, in short: ambivalent and changing. Turkey, the GFP, and in the crisis period unspecified Western actors in general are perceived as being clearly against Israel to varying degrees. The perceived relationship to the actor seems to be decisive. Another possibility is the character of the interaction. The USA "expresses worries", argues with the negative consequences for the peace process, and is among others described as "furious". There is no condemnation, no expression of strong opposition towards Israel. Both the perceived different relationship and the different formulation and representation of the criticism are possibilities for the different representation.

Criticism is average in its formal appearance Critical claims appear on rear pages compared to calls for action. The observation that critical involvement is found on inside

---

[47]Palestinian houses are mostly demolished for "administrative" reasons in the West Bank and Gaza. Houses considered "illegal" by Israel are built without permit. Palestinians can build in 13% of East Jerusalem and in 1% of Area C in the West bank, both areas are already crowded and over 94% of the Palestinian permit applications were rejected. Therefore buildings are often constructed without permit (Schaeffer, Halper and Epshtain 2012).

pages of the newspaper is supported by Dor (2004, 2005). Dor claims the first pages contain information that is perceived as "hard facts" and opposing voices on the rear pages are perceived as "opinion" (ibid.). The length of the articles (on average 371 words) ranks average among the forms of involvement. The amount of articles containing quotes is also average, 43% of the articles with critical involvement contain quotes of an actor in the article. That means, criticism by international actors is neither represented as prominent nor debated in long articles.

In sum, criticism is the most frequent form of involvement by international actors as mediated in Israeli newspapers. Most critical are Gaza flotilla participants, but all actors except the USA are shown to be critical in more than every second article. There are differences between routine and crisis actors: While routine actors' criticism is related to the relationship or the Israeli-Palestinian conflict, crisis actors relate predominantly to the events of the flotilla, and Turkey also appears criticizing the relationship. Articles with critical involvement are average in their formal characteristics and the amount of quotes by the actors. The representation of critical involvement is predominantly negative. The message is frequently rejected by an *ad hominem* mechanism that discredits the claim by attributing negative traits to the international actor. Representing the international actor as attacking deflects responsibility from the own group that can be seen as merely reacting. Frames that regard the claims themselves reject them as either against Israel's policies or counterproductive for peace. Both arguments reject tha claim as inacceptable. These forms of representation are discussed in more detail in the next chapter.

6.3 Calling for Action – "Israel has to ... Immediately"

The second most frequent form of involvement is actors calling for a certain action – namely claims with focus on the future. Call for action is a form of involvement that focuses on future events and policies the actor demands from Israel. A total of 93 items (23%) fall into this category. Most of those articles (66%) neither criticize nor support. An example is "the leaders of the world set a clear demand: an investigation" (YA_2010_06_07_002). The article describes the "pressure on Prime Minister Netanyahu to open an investigation on the events of the Turkish flotilla." The central claim hereby is neither criticism nor support, but their call for an action – here investigation. In nearly one third of the articles, the call by the international actor implies criticism on Israel's policies or actions. An example are calls to end the Gaza blockade or: "President of Turkey: 'Israel has to apologize and pay compensation – otherwise we will consider cutting the diplomatic relations'" (IH_2010_06_13_7). In this article, the Turkish call is based on the assumption that Israel's behavior was wrong. In very rare cases the calls for future actions are based on support (7 articles, 8% of the articles with calls). One example is an article on American calls for investigation: "The American government promotes a committee that includes international representatives, to strengthen its conclusions" (HA_2010_06_04_03), as reads a subhead of an article in Haaretz. The "proposal" to include international members is here bound to support for an Israeli investigation. Calls for action are a form of involvement that differs from the other claims in its focus on future events rather than evaluation of past or present policies. The next subsections introduce further characteristics of the representation of this claim.

Call for action is an US-domain   Two third of all the calls (65%) are made by the USA. This comprises 40% of the total US-involvement. The other third is shared by UN (32% of its involvement) and unspecified Western actors (21% of its involvement) and Europe (14% of its involvement). Two examples illustrate the representation of this US-involvement: The demand of the Obama administration for an investigation of the events of the Gaza flotilla are represented as proposal. The first lines of the article emphasize the process of bargaining between Israel and US-administration, numerous phone calls, cooperative work on both the Israeli and American "trying to avoid a crisis" and the proposed investigation is displayed as positive for Israel since it will not have personal consequences (YA_2010_06_03_002; YA_2010_06_02_009). In the conversations, Prime Minister Netanyahu "explains" to President Obama why Israel "had to use power when boarding the vessel", the USA call for the end of the blockade on Gaza but "understand" that this depends on the freeing of Gilad Shalit (YA_2010_06_02_009).

Another article discusses the expectation of President Obama calling for an end of the blockade two weeks ahead of a meeting with Prime Minister Netanyahu. The author outlines what will be unacceptable for Obama: "The reality in which more than a million and half citizen live. The president is particularly infuriated by the denial of free movement out of the Gaza strip, which he considers 'collective punishment'" (YA_2010_06_27_004). The author describes exactly what is seen negative "from outside" and does not frame it further, but adds that "Diplomatic sources indicate that Netanyahu avoided last year to change the situation" and that he is now under "international pressure" to act on US demands – the author outlines the US-argument in detail and strengthens it by implying Netanyahu's responsibility and emphasizing the international pressures (YA_2010_06_27_004). The examples illustrate a form of interaction that is characterized by a pressuring call, by bargaining, and consideration of the claim itself.

Articles with calls for action contain the highest and most balanced amount of frames   Articles with calls for actions are framed positively in 43% and negatively in 37%. That means, positive and negative framing is balanced. Calls for actions also receive higher amounts of neutral framing (19%) than the other articles. For comparison: Articles with critical claims contain predominantly negative frames (in 74% of the frames), articles with supportive claims contain positive frames (also in 74% of the frames). In articles without claims 60% of the frames are negative. In articles with calls for action the focus of these positive, neutral, and negative frames relates to the claim itself in 42% of the articles which is higher than the other forms of involvement (see Chapter 6.1). The actor is the focus of the frame in 34% and the relationship in 25% of the articles. Supportive claims are also framed with a balanced focus on actor, relationship and claim but criticism focuses on the actor (50% of the frames) and articles without claims on the relationship (69% of the frames). That means, both the character of the framing (positive, neutral, balanced) and the focus of the frames (claim, relationship, actor) are more balanced than in articles with other forms of involvement.

Furthermore, an article with a claim calling for action contains on average 2,7 frames. That is the highest amount of all the claims (see Chapter 6.1). A high amount of frames indicates the possibility for debate (which is not possible when the article contains only one frame, e.g., the actor is described positive; or the actor is described negative). As the results illustrate, articles with calls for action contain more and more balanced framing. These articles contain significantly more diversity of representation than any other analyzed form of involvement.

Compared to the US-calls for investigations, calls by other international actors are represented in a different light, yet the focus is on the calls themselves. For example an article in Israel Hayom titles "Turkey will not give up on an international investigation – that is the fear in Jerusalem" (IH_2010_06_13_007). The article concentrates on Israeli efforts to convince other states of an investigation proposed by Israel. The call for an investigation by the UN is perceived as a threat. An article in Yediot Aheronot starts with the headline: "The fear: The UN will not give up an international investigation" (YA_2010_06_15_003) and twice emphasizes the former Goldstone report initiated by the UN following the Gaza war in 2008-09 that is perceived as a very negative memory of an unjust international treatment of Israeli society. This is intensified by repeated vocabulary such as "threatens" and "fear" of an investigation. Again the focus is on Israel's main efforts to convince "friendly states" (and named the US and Great Britain) to support the Israeli investigation against the Turkish or UN proposal. International demands for investigations are described as "pressure on Prime minister Netanyahu to open an investigation on the events of the Turkish flotilla" (YA_2010_06_07_002). These examples and the results indicate that, although the USA is the dominant actor represented involving itself with calls for action other actors are also framed in a balanced manner when involving themselves in the same way.

Articles with calls for action appear prominently and continuously These articles appear on average on page 7, other forms of involvement on page 9 to 11 on average. As mentioned above, this supports Dor's claim that in Israeli newspapers material on the first pages is considered "fact" and opposing information or criticism is found on rear pages and are perceived as subjective (Dor 2004, 2005). Moreover, articles are longer than those on critical or supportive involvement. The amount of articles with quote from the actor is average (46%). Calls for action are not related to crisis they appear continuously. Nearly two third of the articles (60%) are related to the Israeli-Palestinian conflict and only one third to the Gaza flotilla (30%). The distribution between the periods is almost even (Routine A and Crisis: 38% each; Routine B: 25%). These results show that the representation of calls for action is prominent, not dependent on crisis or routine phases and debated in comparably long articles.

In sum, calls for action predominantly refrain from evaluations in a supportive or critical manner. This form of involvement is strongest in articles covering US-involvement. It appears continuously throughout the analyzed periods and is independent from the crisis. Those articles are represented prominently, on early pages that are considered more trustworthy, in long articles but with average amount of quote. Most striking is the high amount and comparably balanced character of the frames between concentration on the claim, the actor, and the relationship in positive, negative and neutral manner. Articles with a call for action contain several forms of frames that may be contradicting (e.g., positive and negative frames within one article).

The differences in the representation of calls for action from other claims could arguably be based on the fact that the majority of the calls are sent by the US. However, the majority of supportive claims are also attributed to the US and as the next chapter shows, the representation is less prominent, less balanced and differentiated. These findings are relevant for hypothesis H_2 that assumes supportive involvement has the highest potential for positive and prominent representation. As the next chapter shows, the representation is indeed positive, but not prominent. On the contrary, calls for action are represented most prominent and differentiating.

6.4 Supporting Involvement – "We Support Israel's Right to..."

Support is a less frequent form of involvement than a call for action or criticism – only in 15% of all articles (63 of 400) are supportive. Support is generally expressed in routine times. Only 22% of the support was reported in the crisis period, but 41% in Routine A and 37% in routine B. Therefore, the topic of supportive claims is rarely the Gaza flotilla (10%) – a central topic during the crisis – but commonly the relationship (62%).

Support is an US-domain 73% of the supportive claims are covered in articles on the USA, which is nearly one third of the total US-involvement. The crisis actors are the least supportive: unspecified Western actors in 8% of their claims, Turkey in 6% and Gaza flotilla participants in none. An example for support in Europe is found in Yediot Aheronot (YA_2010_06_24_03): "In Paris and Rome: Identification with Gilad." Gilad Shalit is an Israeli soldier who was kidnapped by Hamas and held hostage for several years, which lead to international support demonstrations. In another article, support by US-actors is represented prominently in a two-page article following a meeting between Prime Minister Netanyahu and President Obama. The article contains numerous quotes by Obama that build confidence in Netanyahu (IH_2010_07_07_02a): "I believe that Netanyahu wants peace and is ready to take risks for peace. Now is the time to do this." Also, the "bond between the US and Israel is not loosening." Note that in this article the support is expressed centrally for Netanyahu as a person and not for Israel in general. It suits the agenda of the newspaper Israel Hayom to support the Prime Minister. In a meeting with Israeli Defense Minister Ehud Barak, Obama "reaffirmed the unwavering commitment to Israel's security and our [US] determination to achieve a comprehensive peace in the Middle East, including the two-state solution with a Jewish state of Israel living in peace alongside an independent viable Palestinian state" (HA_2010_04_27_04).

Supportive involvement is not represented prominently The articles are the shortest with 360 words and appear on average on page 10, like articles without claim. But support is frequently expressed with quotes – in 65% of the articles, which is the highest amount of all forms of involvement. Quotes enhance the personal "interaction" and trustworthiness of the involvement. As mentioned above, quotes are considered a tool for estrangement from official narratives. Evidently however, quotes are also used most frequently to express international support in Israeli newspapers.

Support is framed in almost exact opposite to criticism Just as criticism is predominantly framed negatively, supportive involvement is almost completely framed positively (74% positive, 11% neutral, 14% negative). The framing is very balanced between actor, claim, and relationship. Framing of supportive claims is described as in agreement with Israel's policies (38%), important (26%) and helpful on the path to peace (15%). An example for positive framing as "in agreement with Israel's policies" is found in an article on former Spanish President "enthusiastically supporting Israel" (HA_2010_06_18_2c): "Israel is our first line of defense in an area full of turmoil, constant danger and deteriorating into absolute chaos [...]. If Israel falls we all fall." He continues defending the Israeli behavior on the Gaza flotilla, describing it as "an impossible situation for Israel in which it had to choose between giving up its security policy and the naval blockade, and between exposing itself to the outrage of the world". The former president fully supports the Israeli understanding of the situation.

The supporting actor is contextualized as important in every third article, half of the times as understanding Israel, or as legitimate. In more than 20%, the actor is declared a pro-Israeli or supporter of Israel. This framing also indicates a separation of international actors within a world view of "with or against Israel". An article in Israel Hayom describes a new international petition "for support of Israel." The article emphasizes the important position of the "Israel supporters" and outlines: "The petition supports Israel's right to exist and defend itself." A former Israeli ambassador is quoted considering the petition a "call for war against the delegitimization of Israel" (IH_2010_06_20_15). This example illustrates the fight for supporters in a "war" for legitimization and against international delegitimization.

The relationship is described similarly. Most frequent is its framing as positive, improving, as partnership (each ca. 30%), or as friendship and cooperation (each 22%). In addition, the relationship is in every third article described as complex – usually when covering the USA (see Chapter 5.2). An example for the framing of the relationship is found in Yediot Aheronot. The author discusses a new tone between Israel and the USA after the US just approved to financially support the Israeli Iron Drome project: "Pressures were replaced by caresses, and the chilled relationship between Israel and the US gains warmth. This is due to several meetings between officials and financial US backing for the Iron Dome project" (YA_2010_05_27_04). The amount of frames is comparably high with an average of 2.4 frames per article. As illustrated above, most of the framing is positive but it is balanced in its focus. That indicates that when actors appear supportive, the actors themselves, their claims and the relationship to them is framed positive.

In sum, support is also a form of involvement predominantly found in articles on the USA and when discussing the relationship. Support appears in routine times rather than during crisis times and is hence rarely expressed by crisis actors. Supportive articles are short but often contain quotes. The representation of supportive claims is almost the opposite of representation of critical involvement: the articles are short, often contain quotes and the framing is predominantly positive. There is a high amount of frames per article which indicates that supportive actors are considered positive on all three analyzed levels: the relationship to them, the actors themselves, and the claim naturally. As the examples also indicate, supportive involvement serves as external reassurance one's own policies. These findings support the hypothesis H_2 stating that supportive involvement has the highest potential for positive representation. It indeed does, although it is not represented prominently. However, the difference between the USA and the other actors is again striking.

6.5 Speechless Involvement – "..."

The fourth possibility, no claim at all, is the option chosen when the actor is not represented as taking an active part and no claim or action is found in the analyzed article. Those articles predominantly speak of the relationship between the actor (61%) and in 30% of the flotilla. As there is no central claim by the actors these articles rarely contain quotes by the actor (in 26%) within the articles. Articles without claims are a clear crisis phenomenon, as more than half of the articles appear in the crisis period (53%) and only 26% and 21% in the routine periods. There is a slight dominance of crisis actors: Turkey and Gaza flotilla participants are represented in this manner without a claim in 21% of their articles, unspecified Western actors rarely appear without a claim. Of the three routine actors USA, European actors, and UN only the USA are published in 15% of their articles without any claim. For example, in a column in Israel Hayom the "price of Obama's weakness" for the relationship is discussed (IH_2010_05_30_007b):

> There is the heavy feeling Obama failed again [...]. For several weeks Netanyahu and chosen ministers work in cooperation with the Americans to avoid an anti-Israeli decision at the Council [in which Israel would be forced to disarm nuclear power] The Israelis were optimistic, the Americans promised determination.

As the Council decided anyway against nuclear facilities the journalist regards Obama as responsible:

> The main reason for the attack on Dimona [the place of the Israeli nuclear facility] is the American weakness that is not reduced to the Middle East. Obama has an innocent vision and does not understand that the Americans will lose its status with the Arab states that fear Iranian nuclear power more than Israel. (IH_2010_05_30_007b)

In this whole article the USA does not appear with any claim. There is positive framing of the relationship in the emphasis on the cooperation. However, there is also negative framing of the actor Obama in particular is described as weak and as lacking understanding for the Middle East.

Another example is an article on the Gaza flotilla participants two days ahead of their arrival in Maariv. The participants are described as diverse (left-wing activists, diplomats, members of the European parliament and journalists) but following the GFP remain the "object" of the article that illustrates in detail the different steps Israeli security forces will take to stop the flotilla, to detain and interrogate the GFP and to later deport them from Israel (MA_2010_05_28_04). The GFP remain distant and passive but are framed as the chaos that Israeli security forces will respond to with "law and order". Not ascribing the GFP a claim, intention, and voice in general aides to keep the distance. In half the cases (49%) articles without claim are framed negatively but also often positively (35%) and sometimes neutrally (16%). These numbers are almost equal to the framing of calls for action. An article without claim by the actor contains on average two frames, one on the relationship, and one on the actor.

In sum, articles often lack any claim when either the relationship is discussed (with the USA or Turkey) or when the Gaza flotilla members are covered without them containing a claim. Since there is no central claim there is rarely a quote. This form of coverage with lacking involvement appears in times of crisis. Since the actor without a claim remains passive the evaluation and contextualization relies merely on the judgment of the journalist. As the example illustrated, describing interaction with the actors without ascribing any claim to them may serve as tool to keep a distance to the voice- and faceless actors. That leaves more room for the interpretations of the journalist.

6.6 Conclusion

As illustrated in the above chapters, the involvement is represented differently. The four main findings are:

1) International involvement is mostly critical in mediated reality. All actors except the United States are represented predominantly with critical claims in Israeli newspapers . The United States appear more often calling for actions or with supportive claims.

2) There is "crisis" and "routine" involvement. As shown in Chapter 5 there are "crisis actors", who are involved predominantly critical. Another form of crisis coverage on international actors are articles without claims. Supportive involvement is a clear form of "routine" involvement. Calls for action appear continuously and independent from the period.

3) The involvement is represented differently. Critical involvement is predominantly contextualized within negative frames on the involving actors. That means, in most cases the critical claim itself is not debated but denied through delegitimization of the critic (see Chapter 7). In the rare cases of critical US-involvement, the claims are framed twice as much as those by other actors. That indicates that the USA is represented differently not solely based on the form of involvement but on the relationship that is represented as stronger and closer than to the other actors (see Chapter 5.2). The USA is the only actor that is perceived as being "with Israel" (see Chapter 7.3). Supportive involvement is contextualized within positive frames on the involvement itself, the actor, and the relationship. Calls for actions appear most prominent in longer articles on earlier pages and with a balanced positive, neutral, and negative framing of the relationship, actor, and claim. Calls for actions and support are predominantly US-involvement, but the claim's representation is similar to the rare cases of Europe, unspecified Western actors or others involving themselves in this manner.

4) There are only some significant differences between the newspapers. As illustrated in Chapter 5, there are no significant differences in the actors appearances, but their representation differs significantly. In Haaretz, actors appear with different claims to the other newspapers that do not vary significantly in the claims by the actors. While Maariv, Yediot Aheronot represent actors predominantly critical and Israel Hayom more frequently supportive, Haaretz covers actors with calls for action more frequently. The contextualization of the involvement does not differ significantly between the four analyzed newspapers, only Haaretz frames involvement more frequently neutrally than the other three newspapers. These findings indicate that significant results are found regarding the involvement and its representation are found only between Haaretz and the other newspapers.

This corresponds with the differences found in the representation of the actors in the previous chapter. Maariv and Yediot Aheronot emphasize critical involvement and represent actors negatively. Those newspapers rely more heavily on street sales than the others. The results indicate that they emphasize drama. Israel Hayom, as the newspaper supporting the governing party Likud, does not differ significantly. Yet it covers international actors with supportive involvement more than the other newspapers, because support ultimately can be considered as reassurance of Prime Minister Netanyahu. All three newspapers frame the actors predominantly negatively without significant differences among them.

The results so far indicate that Haaretz represents international involvement different unlike the other newspapers. As the liberal, intellectual newspaper, it focuses the least on crisis involvement but more on calls for action with a emphasis on the Israeli-Palestinian conflict. Haaretz frames actors less frequently negatively than the other three newspapers and more frequently positive and neutral. In sum, the differences between the newspapers so far are largely between Haaretz and the other three newspapers that rarely vary significantly.

5) The consequences for H_2, H_4, and H_5. As outlined above, it is not in the scope and interest of this research to "verify" the reality mediated through Israeli newspapers. However, in Israeli newspapers' mediated reality the Western world is indeed predominantly critical towards Israel. International involvement is predominantly critical. Moreover, during crisis times there is even more critical involvement.

The hypothesis H_2 stating that the claims are represented differently is partly supported by the results. The analysis shows that the appearance of the claims and their contextualizations differ. Except for the USA, all the actors are predominantly involved critically and the representations of those actors (not so much the claims) are negative. The USA is involved either supportive or as calling for action. Support is represented in opposite ways from critical involvement in the newspapers. When supporting, the actor, the claim, and the relationship are framed positive. However, calls for action are more promising than supportive involvement. The representation is balanced and prominent. The question why calls for action are more promising will be answered in chapter 8. However, two decisive factors seem clear already:

1) Calling for an action requires a certain amount of direct commitment from the calling actor. For example, calling for an investigation requires the readiness to participate and invest in that investigation. Calling for an end of the Gaza blockade requires willingness to outline consequences if nothing changes. Calling for Israel to apologize requires willingness

to improve the relationship in case Israel apologizes. Condemning or supporting an action may be a verbal act that has no consequences.

2) Calling for an action is future-oriented, therefore pro-active and forward looking instead of judging past and present. Thereby calling for action has a stronger potential for an equal relationship than criticism and support does.

The hypothesis H_4 stating that representations differ in routine and conflict times is fully supported by the findings. Just as the chapter on the actors illustrates that there are "crisis actors" and "routine actors" (see Chapter 5), this chapter shows that there is crisis and routine involvement. Criticism is expressed in most cases during the crisis period, whereas support is expressed predominantly during the routine periods. Just calls for action appear continuously. The findings also show that the representations differ in times of routine and crisis, in particular criticism is represented in a way that focuses on the delegitimization of the actors in crisis.

The hypothesis H_5 stating that the newspaper representations differ is partially supported by the findings of this chapter as outlined above. There are no significant differences in the appearance of the actors, but their claims differ significantly between Haaretz and the other three newspapers. The framing of the claims however is predominantly similar, just neutral framing of the claim is more frequent in Haaretz than in other three newspapers. So far, most of the significant differences are found between Haaretz and the other three newspapers. Yediot Aheronot, Maariv and Israel Hayom rarely vary in their representations. This is the case in the contextualization of the actors. The overall mediated reality is predominantly negative and critical of Israel, which may support convictions of siege mentality (see Chapter 3.1.4 and 7.3).

7 The Representation of Involvement and Actors

As the chapters above indicate the representation of the international actors and their involvement in the Israeli-Palestinian conflict is characterized by several framing patterns. Most of them are not bound to either one kind of involvement or group of actors. This chapter introduces and discusses the frequent and dominant narratives arising from framing patterns used when representing actors and their involvement in Israeli newspapers. These regard different aspects of the representation.

A constant throughout the analyzed articles is the focus on the beliefs about the justness of the Israeli side. Narratives emphasizing Israeli justness are considered as basic assumptions that underlie other narratives. As the following chapter 7.2 shows, this conviction may contain, besides the self-revelation, a consequential allegation against the external actor and opponent depicted as unjust. Yet another pattern used frequently in the contextualization of the analyzed actors is their categorization regarding their alleged attitude towards Israel as friendly or hostile (7.3). While the focus on friendliness is restricted to US-actors, there are several different patterns categorizing the other actors as hostile. A crisis phenomenon is the categorization of the world as hostile towards Israel.

Another pattern found in the representations regards the amounts of personalization and closeness attributed to involved actors and hence the construction of closeness versus distance to certain actors (7.4). Further, the attribution of orderly versus disorderly behavior appears as a prominent mechanism of contextualization in the representation of the actors (7.5). A last general pattern of representation is the varying complexity of the representations (7.6). First the results are introduced briefly, followed by the different patterns of representation, which are illustrated and interpreted based on the findings.

7.1 The Results in Short

Many of the results that are relevant for this chapter have already been introduced in Chapter 5.1 and 6.1. In this section the appearance of societal beliefs of the ethos of conflict and two further significant framing patterns are outlined: the "law and order versus chaos" frame, and siege mentality.

Ethos of conflict Not all beliefs appear with the same frequency. In general four of the eight beliefs appear in at least every fifth article (see Tables 19, 20, 21, 22): the beliefs about the justness one's own goals (in 41% of the articles), beliefs about the delegitimization of the opponent (25%), beliefs about victimization (23%), and beliefs about security (21%). The other beliefs rarely play a role in media representations: beliefs about patriotism (2%), peace (8%), a positive collective self-image (8%), and unity (0%).

Table 19 – The Beliefs of the Ethos of Conflict and the Represented Actors (in Percent)

		Europe (n=57)	UN (n=22)	USA (n=151)	Turkey (n=63)	GFP (n=60)	Unsp. (n=47)
Delegitimization[1]	Yes	30	32	9	25	**57**	23
	No	70	68	91	75	33	77
Victimization[2]	Yes	28	36	7	16	40	**49**
	No	72	64	97	84	60	51
Security[3]	Yes	21	18	21	3	**45**	15
	No	79	82	79	97	55	85
Justness[4]	Yes	46	41	41	32	42	45
	No	54	59	59	68	58	55
Unity	Yes	–	–	–	–	–	–
	No	100	100	100	100	100	100
Patriotism[6]	Yes	3	4	1	–	–	4
	No	97	96	99	100	100	96
Peace[7]	Yes	–	4	19	2	2	–
	No	100	96	81	98	98	100
Positive Ingroup[8]	Yes	11	–	6	6	10	15
	No	89	100	94	94	90	85

[1] is $\chi^2(5, N = 400) = 53,680, p = .000$
[2] is $\chi^2(5, N = 400) = 53.553, p = .000$
[3] is $\chi^2(5, N = 400) = 34,367, p = .000$
[4] is $\chi^2(5, N = 400) = 3,002, p = .700$
[6] is $\chi^2(5, N = 400) = 5,119, p = .401$
[7] is $\chi^2(5, N = 400) = 41,950, p = .000$
[8] is $\chi^2(5, N = 400) = 6,181, p = .289$

The most frequent *beliefs about the justness of one's own side* is continuously found in articles. There is no significant difference between the actors ($p = .700$) nor in the

Table 20 – The Beliefs of the Ethos of Conflict and the Claims(in Percent)

		Criticism (n=183)	Call for action (n=93)	Support (n=63)	No msg. (n=61)
Delegitimization[1]	Yes (n=99)	**43**	6	2	23
	No	105	94	98	77
Victimization[2]	Yes (n=92)	**36**	15	6	15
	No	64	85	94	85
Security[3]	Yes (n=83)	19	26	19	21
	No	81	74	81	79
Justness[4]	Yes (n=163)	43	38	**52**	26
	No	57	62	48	74
Unity	Yes (n=0)	–	–	–	–
	No	100	100	100	100
Patriotism[6]	Yes (n=8)	1	1	8	2
	No	99	99	92	98
Peace[7]	Yes (n=32)	1	13	21	8
	No	99	87	79	92
Positive Ingroup[8]	Yes (n=33)	8	5	13	8
	No	92	95	87	92

[1] is $\chi^2(3, N = 400) = 66.362, p = .000$
[2] is $\chi^2(3, N = 400) = 31,715, p = .000$
[3] is $\chi^2(3, N = 400) = 2,093, p = .553$
[4] is $\chi^2(3, N = 400) = 9,674, p = .022$
[6] is $\chi^2(3, N = 400) = 13,747, p = .003$
[7] is $\chi^2(3, N = 400) = 28,568, p = .000$
[8] is $\chi^2(3, N = 400) = 2,662, p = .447$

time periods of crisis and routine ($p = .107$). There is a significant difference between the forms of involvement ($p = .022$) and the appearance of the beliefs about justness.. Beliefs about the justness appear in every second supportive article, and less on other claims (but still at least in every fourth article). Furthermore, there is a significant difference between the newspapers ($p = .000$): In Haaretz, the beliefs about justness appear only in 25% of the articles. The belief in one's own side's justness is most frequent in Israel Hayom and Maariv (in 51% of their articles each) and in 37% of the articles of Yediot Aheronot. There is no significant difference between the three newspapers Israel Hayom, Yediot Aheronot and Maariv[48].

The other beliefs have significant differences in their distributions in the periods, on different actors and forms of involvement. *Beliefs about the delegitimization of the opponent are used mostly in articles about GFP* (57% of the articles about them) and the least in

---

[48] χ^2 on Israel Hayom, Yediot Aheronot, Maariv excluding Haaretz and the beliefs about justness is $\chi^2(2, N = 300) = 5,746, p = .057$

Table 21 – The Central Beliefs of the Ethos of Conflict in the Analyzed Periods (in Percent)

		Routine A (n=109)	Crisis (n=198)	Routine B (n=93)
Delegitimization[1]	Yes	17	**69**	13
	No	92	129	80
Victimization[2]	Yes	16	**61**	15
	No	93	137	78
Security[3]	Yes	26	**43**	14
	No	83	155	79
Justness[4]	Yes	47	71	45
	No	62	127	48

[1] is $\chi^2(5, N = 400) = 21,539, p = .000$
[2] is $\chi^2(5, N = 400) = 13,557, p = .001$
[3] is $\chi^2(5, N = 400) = 2,586, p = .274$
[4] is $\chi^2(5, N = 400) = 4,462, p = .107$

articles about US-actors (9%, $p = .000$). The beliefs in delegitimization are crisis-related (70%, $p = .000$). Furthermore, the appearance of delegitimization is strongly related to critical involvement (78%, $p = .000$). There is a significant difference in the appearance of delegitimization between the four analyzed newspapers ($p = .040$). These beliefs appear in every third article in Yediot Aheronot and Maariv, but only in half as many articles of Haaretz. Again, the significant difference is only found between Haaretz and the other three newspapers and not between them[49].

The *beliefs about victimization* appear almost similarly to beliefs delegitimizing the other. However, victimizing beliefs appear more often in articles about unspecified Western actors (49%) and somewhat less than delegitimization in articles about GFP (40%, $p = .000$). Victimization appears predominantly during the crisis period (66%, $p = .000$) and mostly in articles with critical involvement (70%, $p = .000$). Moreover, victimization appears significantly different in the four newspapers ($p = .002$), strongest in Yediot Aheronot (34%) and weakest in Haaretz (11%). Also here, the significant difference is caused by Haaretz, as the other three newspapers are similar in the appearance of the beliefs about delegitimization[50].

Also the *beliefs about security* appear significantly different between the actors ($p = .000$). They appears more frequent than delegitimization and victimization in articles about European or US-involvement (in 21%) and the UN (18%) and in almost half of the articles on the GFP (45%). Concurrently, the security beliefs are not restricted to crisis periods

---

[49] χ^2 on Israel Hayom, Yediot Aheronot, Maariv excluding Haaretz and the beliefs about delegitimization is $\chi^2(2, N = 300) = 18, p = .991$

[50] χ^2 on Israel Hayom, Yediot Aheronot, Maariv excluding Haaretz and the beliefs about victimization is $\chi^2(2, N = 300) = 3,680, p = .159$

Table 22 – The Central Beliefs of the Ethos of Conflict in the Newspapers (in Percent)

		Haaretz (n=100)	Israel Hayom (n=115)	Yediot Aherhonot (n=104)	Maariv (n=81)
Delegitimization[1]	Yes	14	**33**	29	23
	No	86	82	75	58
Victimization[2]	Yes	11	26	**35**	20
	No	89	89	69	61
Security[3]	Yes	14	21	28	20
	No	86	94	76	61
Justness[4]	Yes	25	**59**	38	41
	No	75	56	66	40

[1] is $\chi^2(5, N = 400) = 8,293, p = .040$
[2] is $\chi^2(5, N = 400) = 14,937, p = .002$
[3] is $\chi^2(5, N = 400) = 6,379, p = .095$
[4] is $\chi^2(5, N = 400) = 19,610, p = .000$

but are distributed evenly throughout the periods (p=.274) and the different forms of involvement (p=.394). There is also no significant difference in its appearance in the four newspapers (p=.095).

The *beliefs about unity* do not appear at all in this investigation, the beliefs about peace appear several times in articles with supportive involvement and calls for action, particularly in articles on the USA. The beliefs about a positive collective self-image appear also rarely, but in supportive articles.

The frame of *law and order versus chaos* is a frame used in 43% of the articles on the GFP, and very rarely on other actors (in 0-6%, $\chi^2(5, N = 400) = 117,527, p = .000$). There is no significant difference between the four newspapers ($\chi^2(3, N = 400) = 1,479, p = .687$).

Siege mentality appears in more than every second article (53%) on unspecified Western actors and in every fourth article on Europe and the UN ($\chi^2(5, N = 400) = 54,179, p = .000$). Siege mentality appears in 28% of all the articles with critical involvement, and between 13% to 8% of the other forms of involvement ($\chi^2(3, N = 400) = 19,021, p = .000$), in total it appears in 19% of the articles. There is a difference between the newspapers, while siege mentality appears in 20% to 25% of the articles in Yediot Aheronot, Maariv, and Israel Hayom, it appears only in 7% of the articles in Haaretz ($\chi^2(3, N = 400) = 13,025, p = .005$). This difference as well is caused by Haaretz, as the other three newspapers do not differ in their contextualization using siege mentality[51].

---

[51] χ^2 on Israel Hayom, Yediot Aheronot, Maariv excluding Haaretz and siege mentality is $\chi^2(2, N = 300) = 818, p = .664$

7.2 Defense of one's own Justness

Describing the own actions as moral and justified has an aspect of self-revelation that underlies and precedes the representation and perception of the other as different and wrong. Therefore the results of this reseach indicate that this belief is most prevalent among the societal beliefs of the ethos of conflict and serves as a framework for the understanding of the other beliefs.

The belief in the justness of one's own goals appears very frequently (40% of all the articles) and independently from factors such as actor and period of appearance. It appears strongest in articles with supportive involvement and in Israel Hayom. In general, the beliefs in the justness of one's own goals appear in 40% up to 70% of most categories. Only in Haaretz and articles on unspecified Western actors it appears less, but still 25%. Hence, the belief in the justness of Israeli goals and actions can be regarded as a continuum of representation of international involvement and relations.

An example for the use of justness in a routine phase is found in an article titled "Netanyahu to Obama: We will continue to build in [East-]Jerusalem" (IH_2010_04_21_05). The article is mainly an assembly of responses by Prime Minister Netanyahu to an unspecified request "from the Americans" to stop the construction of settlements in East-Jerusalem (Palestinian territories). Netanyahu is reported to refuse adamantly, not only since these constructions are conducted by all Israeli Prime Ministers but also because he considers the areas have been Jewish: "The request to stop all Jewish construction in Jewish areas of Jerusalem is not acceptable, explicitly since it stops the peace process". The construction of settlements is regarded legitimate, and even necessary for peace. The superior justness is defended with an imagined comparison to other states: "If something like this was requested from London, New York or Paris, people would rise up" (IH_2010_04_21_05). The article ends with a quote of the Chairman of the Knesset, Rivlin: "We will not be sorry for the occupation of Qatamon, Yafo or Zfat, not for the liberation of Hebron nor for the construction in Jerusalem, our capital." The message is very clear: Israel is willing to pay a high price for peace, but these requests cannot be justified. The construction in East Jerusalem is represented as just, right and no doubt or alternative narration is voiced in the article. There is, for example, no mention that the areas in discussion are not Jewish Israeli areas by international law. The emphasis and defense of the justness of one's own side's actions and goals underlie several other narratives. Some of them appeared centrally in this investigation and are introduced below.

"We" are Just – hence "They" are Wrong

A striking example for the emphasis on the own righteousness as basis for other beliefs is the description of the Israeli Defense Forces and their actions regarding the Gaza flotilla. A day after the raid on the flotilla an article titled "Our Wonderful Boys" aims at uniting the readers around the fundamental justness of Israel's actions and existence. The article starts: "Israel is a moral state. The hardship in Gaza stems exclusively from Hamas' regime". The author continues to defend the blockade on Gaza as necessary and due to Hamas' actions. In this context, the IDF soldiers and their role in the raid on the flotilla is described as very positive. The young combat fighters, titled "the best of our sons" entered a ship "full of violent people". While themselves hardly carrying weapons, they entered "in the most silent possible manner" and were met by what the author describes as a

> wild terror cell, armed and murderous, attempting to lynch[...]. The soldiers had no choice but to defend themselves fiercely and under impossible conditions. They heroically succeeded in meeting the goal of the operation and to keep the minimum amount of death for the other side. Yes, nine deaths in such a dangerous situation is much less than what would have happened if any other military power of any state had encountered the same situation. (YA_2010_06_01_019)

The author continues by criticizing Israelis for asking self-critical questions instead of being proud of the soldiers that overpowered the attackers without one death on the own side. The article illustrates that the belief in justness of the Israeli goals is intertwined with other beliefs. The just goals (uphold the blockade, defend it) are based on a self-attribution of positive traits (moral army, soldiers are the salt of the country that merely and defend with heroism and restraint). These claims are intertwined with a consequential attribution and delegitimization of the Other. Hence, if the own side is declared to be moral and its goals are just, it must be the other side itself that is responsible for its potential suffering under the blockade of Gaza. Noteworthy is the one-sidedness of the attribution of responsibility. The increased self-perception as positive is evident in the heroization of the soldiers. They are considered the essence of the Israeli state and the Israeli military is described as more moral than any other army could possibly be. Consequently, it is the Israeli army that responds in restraint to the violent attack of the illegitimate opponent.

The Opponent Attacked, the Opponent is Responsible

These are the most frequent forms of negative framing of actors. Blaming the Other as the responsible provocateur and attacker may delegitimize the actor but also holds strong information on the Self as victims defending themselves and their just goals. The justified self-defense exonerates from guilt (Bandura 2002: 110). This overall narrative is mostly used against the "crisis actors": Gaza flotilla participants, Western actors and Turkey. Most frequent are the references to the attempted lynch by the Gaza flotilla participants on the Israeli soldiers boarding the ship (e.g., MA_2010_06_03_05: "This was a boat of hate, there was an attempted lynch"; YA_2010_06_02_11 describes in detail how international media is hiding the images of the "lynch"). This is a typical strategy of delegitimization as outlined by Rinnawi (2007): The own violence is described as response to the violence of the opponent, which is in turn dramatized and exaggerated.

The chosen term "lynch" serves as an example for this exaggeration, since apparently none of the soldiers but only Turkish flotilla participants were killed. It can be assumed with certainty that the term "lynch" evokes the images of the Ramallah lynch in 2000: a man in white shirt waving blood stained hands from a police station window to a crowd outside. This crowd killed and mutilated reservists of the Israeli army. With that perspective in mind, the Israeli soldiers have not killed nine people but averted a lynch to themselves in a helpless situation. In this perspective, the killed Turkish flotilla participants remain invisible and impersonal. Blaming the victim and repeated description of the violence against the security forces are a sign of defending the exaggerated force used. The forces are thereby equalized in their power and violent reactions are legitimized (Liebes 1997). Wolfsfeld, Frosh and Awabdy (2008) describe this as "defense mode", a coverage in which the own violence is rationalized and justified.

"What about Syria?"

This narrative distracts the attention to other atrocities or in general other actors worthy of criticism. The own justness and morality is defended or restored through comparison with the alleged immorality of other, possibly unrelated actors. The act of contextualizing the own actions within atrocities considered worse downplays the relative immorality of the particular action. It also aims at displaying Israel in an exceptionally moral light and its violence as insignificant compared to that of others (Bar-Tal 2013: 191). On another level, this framing contains a blame of the critic itself: Why is Israel criticized and not Syria, or North Korea, Iran, or Turkey? While this is in general a legitimate question worth discussing, it implies an attribution of hypocrisy to the critic. Hence, the distraction to other atrocities may contain a self-attribution of justness and victimization in light of the implied hypocrisy of the critic. Bandura (2002) as well as McAlister, Bandura and Owen (2006) declares contrasting own atrocities with "worse atrocities" as an "exonerating social comparison" performed by creating an assumed advantage: "The more flagrant the contrasting inhumanities, the more likely it is that one's own destructive conduct will appear benevolent" (Bandura 2002: 105).

Two examples to illustrate this narrative: 1) Germany, when criticizing Israel for its conduct during the raid of the Gaza flotilla and calling for an investigation, is delegitimized as hypocritical by a journalist. The journalist questions the "sudden unit" of the whole German government" to criticize Israel while "it cannot unite to condemn the systematic genocide and persecution of Kurds by the Turkish government, Syria and Iran, and the genocide in Darfur" (YA_2010_07_13_24b). 2) Erdogans role in the Gaza flotilla is questioned in Haaretz: "This man, the representative of a state that carried out a genocide on the Armenians and now persecutes the Kurds, preaches to Israel that it should behave humanely" (HA_2010_06_07_15). 3) Israel Hayom goes further and devotes a whole article to four professors calling for the recognition of the "Armenian Holocaust"

(IH_2010_06_09_007). This is an interesting step, since a strong characteristic of Israeli official remembrance of the Holocaust relies of the emphasis on its uniqueness and singularity. Therefore, this is a remarkable call for equalization of the genocide with the Holocaust. They argue that "Turkey is a hypocrite" and therefore the Israeli Prime Minister should request the end of "the Turkish occupation of Cyprus" (IH_2010_06_09_007) in return.

In sum, the frequent appearance of the belief about the justness of one's own goals in articles on all actors, regarding all kinds of involvement and in all three periods indicates that these beliefs are a continuum in media representation. This chapter illustrates that beliefs in the justness of one's own goals may contain a message of self-revelation that is connected to a judgment of the opponent. One frequent direction regards the opponent as attacker, responsible and ultimately worthy of negative attributions, while the own side is described as just, reacting and merely defending one's own goals. Another prominent perspective upholds the justness of one's own goals by diversion of attention to other atrocities (and to the hypocrisy of the actor who judged Israel instead of other atrocities). The results of this investigation indicate that the beliefs in justness underlie further beliefs and narratives and that they are connected to other beliefs as the next chapters illustrate.

7.3 Friend or Foe

Several forms of representation can be subsumed under a master pattern that categorizes actors according to their alleged position towards Israel. Dowty (1999) assumes that the "two camp thesis" guides Zionist leaders dividing British leaders into "Pro-Zionist" versus "Pro-Arab" even during the times of the British Mandate and continued guiding the evaluation of European and US-leaders.

A leading argument of the present investigation suggests that also in newspaper representation today, the two-camp thesis is a guiding principle in the evaluation of actors that polarizes and may preempt and prevent considering the actor's claim. This is the central part of the assumed mutual polarization (see Chapter 3.1 and 4). It is hence considered a basic contextualization, like the categorization of the Self as just. In the following paragraphs several framing strategies are illuminated and discussed.

Focus on Friendliness

Positive traits are largely attributed to the USA, with 74% of all positive relationship contextualizations and 60% of all positive actor contextualizations. As shown above, the USA are represented very differently from all the other actors (see Chapter 5). The two-camp thesis of polarization suggests that these frames mainly highlight the pro-Israeli standpoint of the USA. About 40% of the positive framings of actors describe them as supporter, less as pro-Israeli. The relationship is also in 40% of these articles described as partnership, a little less as friendship (25%). But the most frequent positive contextualization (50%) of the USA is the framing of actor and relationship as important.

Clearly the USA are strongly represented from a "with Israel" and "friendliness" perspective and accordingly differ from the other actors that are hardly ever described using these frames. Concurrently, the slightly stronger emphasis on the importance of the USA and the relationship indicates a pragmatic perspective. However, the relation of dependence remains unclear: is the relationship to the USA considered important, since it is regarded the only friend and partner, or is the relationship above all important and the emphasis on friendship and cooperation a subordinated rhetoric tool? This investigation illustrates that the USA is represented very positively and closely, but not in an idealized fashion, especially the relationship with President Obama is perceived as complicated (see Chapter 5.2).

Ad hominem. Attacking the Critic prior to the Criticism

In general, this investigation shows that most frames relate to the actor (42%) or the relationship (27%). This is based on the high amount of articles on critical involvement. In those, 50% of the frames focus on the actor and only a quarter on the relationship or the claim itself. Thereby the actor is almost exclusively (80%) framed negatively. This means that the most frequent form of handling criticism is the delegitimization of the critics themselves. This is an *ad hominem* mechanism which diverts the attention from the argument made by the international actors by questioning of the legitimacy of the actors or attribution of negative characterizations on them. Questioning the credibility of the actors themselves, their argument loses credibility and the need to debate its implications are diminished. Therefore, ad hominem is an efficient tool of persuasion and diversion of attention. As the next sections illustrate this is done strongly through delegitimization.

The Actor is Antisemitic or Anti-Israeli

These are the second most frequent forms of delegitimization (only topped by framing the actor as an attacker, see below). Anti-Israelism and antisemitism relate to different issues, however these terms are often mixed up and represented in the media with the same implications, therefore they are coded in one category. Cohen et al. (2009: 302) show, based on several studies that antisemitism evokes anti-Israeli sentiments and vice versa, while the latter can occur without antisemitism. Both are frequently mistaken as being the same: "anti-Israelism" is seen by mainstream Israeli narrative as "the new antisemitism", as for example prominently declared by former Foreign Minister Avigdor Liebermann in 2001 (Zuckermann 2010: pp.40). This equalization of both terms is comprehensible from a perspective of Zionist self-conception of Israel as the homeland for all Jews (ibid. 2010:

119). As these conditions remain unfulfilled, these terms are not necessarily interrelated[52]. In the context of this work however, it is not relevant to verify antisemitic or anti-Israeli motivation by the actors or whether they are intertwined or not. This should not imply that the author of this work denies that antisemitism is a frequent underlying motivation to act "against" Israel in international actors, nor that antisemitism and anti-Israelism are indeed one and the same.

In the representation of the actors, the terms imply either the hostility towards Jews or towards the state of Israel and therefore a total rejection of the essence of Jewish and/or Israeli existence. Both terms therefore indicate a complete rejection of the legitimacy of the actor in Israeli perspective. Consequently, claims made by actors that are represented as antisemites or anti-Israeli can be avoided as irrelevant. Remarkable for this investigation is that, in the mediated representation in Israeli newspapers all actors except the USA are framed as antisemites or anti-Israelis in almost every forth article. Why are references to antisemitism/anti-Israeli sentiments so frequent?

First and foremost, antisemitism and anti-Israelism are an internationally common motivation for involvement in the Israeli-Palestinian conflict. As illustrated in chapter 3.1, Israel suffers from a very negative image and it is often not easy to separate legitimate criticism from anti-Israelism and anti-Israelism from antisemitism. This is one part of international polarization of Israel and in particular of the reasons leading to it (see Chapter 3.1 and in particular Chapter 3.1.1).

Nevertheless, the categorization of actors as anti-Israeli/antisemites is not frequent in all the articles but mostly in articles with critical involvement (79%). This indicates that the actors are not generally and predominantly considered antisemites, but whenever Israel is criticized, antisemitism serves as the primary explanation.

Some examples to illustrate: 1) When an US-General criticized Israel for not controlling settler violence against Palestinians, the sub-head reads: "The settlers are furious: The Americans crossed all the lines" (YA_2010_05_13_07). While quoting official approval in brief, the article pays most attention to settlers' angry response, particularly one settler stating: "I do not feel the need to comment on every hiccup of an antisemite". The criticism by the US-General is regarded illegitimate, and the author chooses to give voice mainly to settlers calling it illegitimate, hypocritical and antisemitic (YA_2010_05_13_07). 2) The European antisemitism is the topic in YA_2010_05_10_32, where the author hopes that the rising economical crisis will lead Europeans, "regular critics of Israel", to concentrate on their own problems rather than to "complicate the situation in the Middle East". Especially Germany has "for years been in denial of old and new anti-Israelism" and while people claim anti-Israelism and antisemitism are impossible in Germany, their

---

[52]Zuckermann (2010: 121) illustrates various possible constellations: Antisemites may be Anti-Zionists, but also may wish for all Jews to be in one state. Anti-Israelis or anti-Zionists may be antisemites but not necessarily (they could be anti-Israeli orthodox Jews). Criticism towards Israel may or may not be motivated by antisemitism or by anti-Israelism or by Zionist sympathies.

statements refute those claims". Yet Spain, "still considered by many Israelis as one of the most anti-Israeli states in Europe", established noteworthy institutions to fight lacking knowledge about Israel and Jews. 3) In another article on the international involvement in the Gaza situation, the author outlines, how costly Israel's care for Gaza is, yet the world shouts "'Siege! Starvation! Apartheid!' and antisemites all over the world respond and prepare a blockade – on us" (YA_2010_06_07_024). Israel is seen as the victim of injustice on two fronts: First it is a victim of having to deal with Gaza and the high sacrifices it necessitates. Second, it is a victim of the international injustice caused by antisemitism despite Israeli efforts. The journalist concludes with the following advice: "Israel should stop helping Gaza and let Turkey take care of it."

Why is antisemitism such a frequently chosen explanation for criticism on Israeli policies? First, there is great awareness and alertness towards international antisemitism and anti-Israelism in Israel, it has continuous high news value and every incident is covered in the news. antisemitism is always an obtrusive explanation. As Pardo (2009: pp.79) shows, there is a widespread understanding in many sectors of Israeli society, especially among politicians, that antisemitism is deeply rooted in Europe and permeates Israel-related policies. This perception is apparent in the representation of Europe but also the UN, which is characterized by the ambivalence between perceptions of hostility and intense interactions in politics, economics, science, and culture (see Chapter 5).

Second, claims of antisemitism are assumed to have a strong effect. antisemitism and the Holocaust are a personal experience, history and trauma of many Jewish Israeli families. and a central part in Jewish Israeli collective memory. Hence, this memory is likely to cause a very unambiguous and emotional reaction in the recipients. The actors are, whether justified or not, excluded from the circle of legitimacy. Concurrently, the emphasis on anti-Israeli/antisemite predispositions reinforces the conviction of siege mentality (see below and 3.1) and victimization (see Chapter 2.2).

A third answer is offered by a broader perspective regarding the connection of the state of Israel and Jewish history of persecution. As examined in chapter 3.1.4, the Jewish history is shaped by persecution, discrimination and attempts of annihilation. This corresponds to the biblical belief in *Amalek*, the eternal enemy willing to destroy the Jewish nation and changing its shape in every generation. Modern antisemitism and the Holocaust can be regarded as one phase in this endless line of Amaleks. The Zionist movement arose from the understanding that the persecution of Jews would never end while Jews went on living in the Diaspora. Zuckermann sums up the direct connection to the state of Israel: " it is born of antisemitism" (2010: 13, translated by the author) and arose from the understanding that the only way to emancipation, liberation, independence, and freedom from persecution was to establish a new state, a homeland for Jews (see Chapter 3.1.4). The Holocaust accelerated the foundation of the state of Israel that is still regarded as the answer to the Holocaust. Zuckermann outlines the consequent paradoxon: "The claim of Zionism to overcome antisemitism made the conservation of antisemitism in the world necessary" (Zuckermann 2010: 14, translated by the author), as long as its raison d'être to be the homeland of the Jews is not achieved. Eventually, the Holocaust is an essential pillar of Jewish Israeli identity building (Diner 2000: 66) and as Segev (1993: 11) puts it: "The Israelis' vision of the Holocaust has shaped their idea of themselves, just as their changing sense of self has altered their view of the Holocaust and their understanding of its meaning". As Zuckermann, Diner and Segev indicate, the remembrance of the Holocaust serves not only itself but is essential for Israeli identity. The functionalization of the narratives of the Holocaust and its usage as an argument for other means instrumentalizes the Holocaust. When the Holocaust is utilized to legitimize actions, to defame opponents, and in general as a political knockout argument, this bears the danger of mythologizing instead of remembering the Holocaust (Thiel 2006: 80). By using the Holocaust and antisemitism for political, diplomatic, and economic means, as proof of the necessity of a Jewish state, as an argument for or against policies, and to explain the Israeli-Palestinian conflict, the Holocaust and antisemitism are used, polemized, and trivialized (On instrumentalization see: Joggerst 2002; Mueller 2009; Ofer 2000, 2009; Porat 2008; Segev 1993; Zertal and Lemke 2001; Zuckermann 1998, 2009, 2010). The instrumentalization of the Holocaust in the Israeli political discourse serves to demonize unfavored decisions and actors. Zertal (2005) reasons the possibility of instrumentalization with the impossibility, and indescribability of Auschwitz that in a distorted way enabled it to become an empty rhetoric figure, easily available for use and misuse (Zertal 2005: 27 quoted in Mueller 2009).

In sum, the framing of critical actors as antisemites can be a very efficient tool to delegitimize the actor. Consequently, this framing strategy prevents the journalist and recipient from the necessity to examine the critic's worthiness. (Orgad 2009) also finds this strategy of delegitimization of critical international actors, describing it as "another version of Israel hatred and antisemitism", in her study on Israeli television treatment of international coverage on the Gaza war 2008-09. The contextualization of actors as antisemites or as anti-Israelis is frequent due to their real and frequent appearance in societies internationally. However, other reasons are based in the strong resonance in collective trauma and memory. Another possible explanation can be sought in the interrelatedness between antisemitism and Zionism and also the instrumentalization of Holocaust and antisemitism for political means.

The Actor is Biased and a Hypocrite

Both those frames are found in articles on all analyzed actors, mostly when they are represented criticizing Israel. Contextualizing actors as biased towards Israel or as hypocritical in their intentions serves as a less of an absolute delegitimization than "antisemitism" or "anti-Israeli". However, the consequences are alike: Hypocritical actors are only pretending to seek justice, while being blind to their own or other actors' injustice. Biased actors have a distorted, hostile predisposition towards Israel. In both cases the actor is delegitimized and the attention diverted from their actual claim. Besides delegitimizing the actor on the level of self-revelation it victimizes the target of biased and hypocritical involvement. A frequent variation of exposing the actors as hypocritical is the reference to other atrocities (see Chapter 7.2).

The Actor is a Terrorist

This frame is used in every third article about the Gaza flotilla participants. Again, the actors are described as having a hostile predisposition towards Israel. The terrorist frame not only delegitimizes the actor but also indicates a security threat. Defining terrorism is not easy and the coined phrase "one man's terrorist is the other man's freedom fighter" holds also for the Gaza flotilla participants. The understanding changes between different countries and actors (Roberts 2015; Ruby 2002). The connection of some of the Gaza flotilla participants to terrorism is discussed earlier (see Chapter 3.4), yet it is questionable whether this term is suitable for the flotilla in general and whether it is suitable for describing violence against combatant forces (the IDF). However, terrorism, especially in Jewish Israeli society, which has suffered from terrorist attacks of various kinds for several decades, evokes strong and negative connotations.

The World – against Israel in Crisis

> The whole world is against us. This is a very ancient tune. Which was taught to us by our Fathers. The whole world is against us. Do not worry we will overcome. They do not care about us. Do not worry we will manage. We too, about them, Do not give (a damn) anymore.
>
> — Kol HaOlam Negdeinu, Lyrics by Yoram Taharlev, translation hebrewsongs.com

The distinction between Israel on one hand and "the world" on the other hand is clearly a prominent crisis phenomenon in media representation of international involvement. In the coding process, the actor category was established for the frequent articles covering the international community involving itself in the conflict (see Chapter 5.7).

Where does this polarization "Israel versus the world" stem from? As discussed earlier, siege mentality (see Chapter 3.1), the sense of a "People that dwells alone", still permeates Jewish Israeli identity, as "in traditional Jewish perceptions no distinction is more fundamental than that between Jews and non-Jews" (Dowty 1999: 8). The concept of segregation from other nations is one of the foundations of Judaism. It guaranteed the survival of the Jewish traditions and the religion through 2000 years of Diaspora. Simultaneously, it is based until today on the hostility of other nations (Mueller 2009: 2).

The sense of siege mentality may be escalated by "survival anxiety" – fear for the very existence of the state of Israel, based on repeated real and perceived threats to the state of Israel and the Jewish people. A comment in Yediot Aheronot illustrates this perception well. It starts: "When we examine the subtext of the flotilla affair, existential anxiety[53] appears. Rightly so. The impression that the world hates us even more than we thought is definitely part of that"(YA_2010_06_15_033). The "existential anxiety" touches a very sensitive subject in Israel. It regards the state's "right to exist" and is a central issue of the Israeli-Palestinian conflict, as this right is not recognized by many Palestinians (for example Hamas and other actors). It is likewise not taken for granted by its citizens. Jewish Israeli citizen fear for the existence of the state of Israel and opponents are often seen as existential threats. A collective state of mind in which the very existence of the collective as a nation-state is perceived as under constant threat (with changing sources) leads to anxiety. This fear is shaped by the collective memory and identity (Andriani 2013; Shinar 2005). This collective anxiety may explain the urgency of narratives in which the "world hates Israel" and "even more than we thought" (see above). Not only is the Jewish Israeli society under numerous existential threats, it is also utterly alone in a hostile world that will not come to save it.

These anxieties seem to have been triggered in the aftermath of the Gaza flotilla raid. It is expressed in titles like "The world already passed the sentence" (IH_2010_06_02_15), "The world was quick to condemn – worldwide anger" (MA_2010_06_01_20) or "The protests against the events of the flotilla do not calm down – the rest of the world against Israel" (MA_2010_06_06_12). The latter article lists different protests on diplomatic and cultural levels and on the streets:

> The demonstrations on the streets of the world against Israel also continued. More than 10.000 participated in a big demonstration in Paris, amongst them political leaders and professional organizations. They waved Turkish flags [...] and Palestinian and Hamas flags. The protesters called to destroy the terrorist state of Israel and called on the French government to 'announce war' on Israel. (MA_2010_06_06_12)

The author continues listing other countries protesting. The emphasis is clearly anti-Israeli. There are several articles (11% of all the articles) that are based on the distinction of "the world" versus Israel. The representation of these actors is described in 5.7. The existence of an actor category for "the World" is certainly remarkable. However, it is not a continuous strategy representing multiple Western actors but a phenomenon of the crisis period (70% of the articles on western actors appear in crisis). The existence of a category for "the world" versus Israel and the frequent appearance of the belief about victimization in those articles supports the suggested conviction of siege mentality in Israeli representation of international involvement. However, its reduction to crisis phases also supports the temporary character of siege mentality. In crisis, the society pulls together

---

[53]It can be translated as "anxiety over the own existence" or "fear of annihilation" and it is considered a central fear in Jewish Israeli society.

against "the rest of the world". Anxieties, assumptions, and fears seem reassured and are brought up extensively to explain the situation. But after the crisis, these lose relevance for a while until the next crisis. This is what Dowty (1999: 8) calls a behavior of "an interrupted society".

Reporting what international media says about Israel

Some of the articles about "the world" versus Israel emphasize international media reactions and representations of Israel. Orgad (2011) regards coverage of Israeli politics through the lens of the Other as an opportunity for estrangement. International media can offer perspectives, narratives, and vocabulary independent from the "national" narrative and the boundaries set by media institutions that are part of society. This alternative perspective may broaden the recipients' understanding.

However, the opportunity for estrangement is rarely used in the proposed manner. Articles on international media coverage of the flotilla events concentrate on international media bias ("distorted image", YA_2010_06_02_11), their negative vocabulary, the anti-Israeli coverage, and their unfair judgment against Israel. Just as Orgad (2009: 10) shows in her study, international coverage is rather used to "reassert commonsensical conceptions of 'us' versus 'them', and to reproduce attachment to a dominant narrative of self-righteousness" .

Figure 14 – Cartoon in Israel Hayom on Hasbara and International Public Opinion
"Hasbara" (on the rubber bullet) "International Public Opinion" (under the waving arms)
Shlomo Cohen's Daily Cartoon. June 2, 2010 in Israel Hayom

Fights over narratives – debate on hasbara

One important part of the "with or against Israel" perspective is the battlefield of narratives in the international arena over sympathies. As already stated, the battlefield over narrative "supremacy" may at times be as important as the battle on the ground. In conflict and rebellion, the challengers strive towards a frame of "injustice" whereas the authorities want to implement the frame of "law and order" (Wolfsfeld 1997; Wolfsfeld, Avraham and Aburaiya 2000). As outlined in chapter 3.1.5, there is a widespread conviction in Israel that its image would be better if it were able to explain itself and its policies correctly. Hence, following critical events like the Gaza flotilla raid, the international debate is also observed with regards to the battlefield over support by the actors, in order to find out which side would win the media war. It is the role of the "hasbara apparatus" to shape Israel's international image. Therefore, the success or failure of Israeli hasbara is a repeated issue. The cartoon in Figure 14 illustrates the perception of Israeli hasbara in a hostile battlefield of narratives. The abseiling Israeli [54] is armed poorly and inadequately with a rubber bullet that symbolizes Israeli hasbara landing into a hostile crowd equipped with sticks that symbolizes the international public opinion. The image resembles the images of Israeli soldiers abseiling aboard the Mavi Marmara.

Several reasons for the poor hasbara are given in the newspaper representations: Israel is losing the battle since it has failed to utilize hasbara efforts in a timely and smart manner, while the Gaza flotilla participants' intention is to hurt Israel's image through publicity. Especially before the raid several articles describe the Gaza flotilla as a PR threat and a potential source of "media damage", but this also explains how Israel is prepared to deal with it "possibly through disruption of broadcasting on the ship" (HA_2010_05_30_02d). Later, the failure of the operation is mainly seen in the late and hesitant hasbara by Israel, video proof is published too late and "precious" hours are lost. The term "lynch" (allegedly attempted on the IDF soldiers) has been introduced "too late" and the "wrong" spokespeople are chosen (HA_2010_05_30_02d). The self-critical attitude of "had we just explained ourselves right" is what Neiger, Zandberg and Meyers (2008) call approving criticism on a strategic level: the general action is approved, but strategic questions appear critical.

In sum, this chapter illuminates several framing strategies that promote a "with or against" Israel perspective when representing international actors' involvement. As Dowty (1999: 8) argues:

> this focus on 'friendliness' or 'hostility' towards Jewish Israelis leads to an extraordinary focus on the attributes of specific foreign leaders rather than on impersonal forces driving policy. Friendly or unfriendly acts by foreign leaders are attributed to their like or dislike of Jews as a group. (Dowty 1999: 8)

---

[54] Note that he is wearing a "kova tembel" hat, a national Israeli symbol of a typical Israeli. *Tembel* means silly or fool.

The "with Israel" narrative is reserved for US-involvement. The USA are represented in Israeli newspapers frequently and continuously, positively, in a personalized manner, as important, supporters and friends. Critical involvement is mostly contextualized through delegitimization of the critics themselves. Thereby "critical involvement" comes frequently from actors considered as hostile towards Israel. The narratives contextualize them as antisemites/anti-Israeli, terrorists, hypocrites, or, most frequently attackers. Also the narrative of "the world versus Israel" is used in times of crisis. As Orgad (2011: 412) puts it,

> The potential self-distancing opened up by exposing criticisms of Israel from around the world, was contained and suppressed by the interpretation of this international criticism within the Israeli society's siege mentality [...] and the familiar 'the world is against us' narrative. Orgad (2011: 412)

It is however noteworthy that these narratives are no invention of Israeli media and are based on real antisemitism, real existing hypocrisy and real existing unproportional criticism. Therefore Rosner's (2014) comment on the international reactions to the Gaza war in 2014 is of high relevance:

> Understanding that the world is not on Israel's side, and that powerful forces work to delegitimize Israel, is essential for Israel's self-preservation. However, wallowing in self-pity and basking in a comforting sense of righteousness is counterproductive and dangerous." (Rosner 2014)

He argues that this attitude leads not only to blindness for legitimate and helpful criticism, it also hinders self-improvement, opportunities to take a positive impact, and ultimately possibilities to counter the hatred of Israel. In general, the importance of categorizing actors into friendly or hostile camps supports the hypothesis of polarization of actors. Further, the appearance of several frames, especially when the actor had been covered as criticizing, supports the hypothesis of the different framings of involvement. The appearance of societal beliefs of the ethos of conflict in this framing strategy is very apparent, especially in delegitimization, victimization, and justness.

7.4 Personalization versus Depersonalization

The formal presentation of the actors differs drastically in the amount of knowledge that is provided about them. This investigation focuses on two central indicators for personalization: First, is the actor quoted? Second, is an institutional background described? This indicates whether there is a possibility for the recipient to get any amount of information to understand the actor. One side of the spectrum are certainly US-actors who are covered. They are often described as members of the government and administration. Quotes are frequent and chosen by the author. These facilitate a sense of direct communication from the actor to the recipient that, although framed by the author, leaves a certain freedom to the recipient to understand and contextualize the actors. In general, the representation of US-involvement contains personal stories (e.g., visits, phone calls) that intend to convey a human touch to the relations, shorten distances and enable a sense of familiarity and empathy.

The opposite characterizes the representation of the Gaza flotilla participants. Often, their origin is not specified, also not their institutional background and they are rarely quoted. Thus they remain unknown, impersonal and hence a projection surface for contextualization and interpretations of various kinds. They do not speak for themselves and consequently their motivation, intentions, actions, and calls are solely ascribed to them by the author. Liebes (1997: 73) refers to "excising" of the enemy as one of the mechanisms of media coverage in conflicts. While the own side (here the actors perceived as "with Israel") are presented in a personal manner, the other side is hardly apparent: The victims are hardly named, described, or even referred to. The Other remains anonymous and silent and hence minimal, and is thus mystified. Excizing the enemy and sanitizing the consequences of the harm committed by the Own is a mechanism of moral disengagement (Bandura 2002; McAlister, Bandura and Owen 2006). This enables the victimization of the own side (since there are no "visible" or personal victims on the other side) and the equalization of powers and consequences of the violent events (Liebes 1997: 73).

7.5 Law and Order Versus Chaos

The focus on security is dominant in two central framing mechanisms relevant to this investigation. On the one hand, there is the security aspect in the relationship to the routine actors, and in particular to the USA, on the other , there is the security threat (and security answer to it) by the Gaza flotilla participants.

The relationship between Israel and the USA is based on several foundations, one of which is the US-commitment to Israeli security: "The president repeated the commitments [...] of the United States on Israels security" (YA_2010_04_27_06). The relationship is based on the "right of Israel to defend itself" which is reassured when Israel is in a violent crisis with an opponent, and is based on the fundamental "right to exist" of the state of Israel. These commitments are not taken for granted but are reassured and repeated. Especially in times of different concepts of suitable ways for peace in the region, these "common grounds" need to be emphasized. However, the commitment to Israeli security has strong practical and financial implications (see Chapter 5.2) and thus the security frame implies safety.

Very different is the security framing regarding the Gaza flotilla participants. As already outlined above, they are presented as attackers and in an impersonal manner. This indicates that they are not given space nor voice to discuss their own motivation or perspective, but are framed within what Wolfsfeld and colleagues introduced as the "law and order" frame, a key contextualization for conflict and rebellion (Wolfsfeld, Avraham and Aburaiya 2000;

Wolfsfeld 1997). The (own) Israeli side is described with great emphasis on lawful and orderly behavior that is disrupted by "chaotic" rebellion of impersonal attackers. This perspective is common in covering the Gaza flotilla participants who are seen as a danger to "law and order". Some articles describe in great detail how order will be upheld by the own forces and how the danger of a clash that leads to a "publicity disaster" will be avoided. For example, two exceptionally long articles (700-900 words) before the raid outline the explicit steps the security sector is planning to take during the raid, the instructions to the soldiers, the detailed procedures of dealing with the flotilla participants after the raid. Everything shall appear lawful, organized and structured. There is a structured plan to reply to any possible "chaos" scenario the passengers could force on the authorities (HA_2010_05_28_02, YA_2010_05_28_03).

In this setting the Israeli actors are presented as lawful and legitimate and opposed to a faceless, voiceless group that intends to disturb and to create chaos. It is therefore only natural that the latter are framed as the attackers the authorities are defending themselves against. In this framing strategy the attacking, mobbing and lynching group is opposed to lawful Israeli soldiers who are restricted in their response since they have to stick to rules and cannot behave as they wish. The own violence is not only legitimized but also equalized as being on the same level with the opponents.

7.6 Simplification Versus Complexity

One strategy of framing concerns the manner in which involvement is represented. Are the frames used unambiguously and clearly to categorize the actor and involvement or is there room for debate and ambiguity?

Simplistic representation The results suggest that both critical involvement and actors perceived as opponents are represented in a very simple manner. The Gaza flotilla participants are framed on average 1.4 times, critical involvement in general has an average of 1,7 frames. As the chapters above illustrated, both criticism and the Gaza flotilla participants in particular, are often repelled in strong and simple ways. As outlined above (see Chapter 5 and 6), in articles containing one frame there is no potential for diverse representation that either focuses on different aspects (the claim, the actor, or the relationship) and/or contains different evaluations (positive, neutral, or negative). Only articles that have more than one frame can entail diversity of opinions and perspectives. Therefore, the representation of the Gaza flotilla participants leaves little room for debate whether parts of the arguments might be based on certain true facts. On the contrary, the framing is predominantly simple and based on either the actor, the claim, or the relationship that is considered as positive or negative.

Calls for actions are debated   Very different is the representation of the United States, with 2.6 different frames per article on average. This means that either there are contextualizations of the actor, relationship, and the claim, or one of those is contextualized both positively and negatively. Thia indicates a less unambiguous and simplistic contextualization. As illustrated in chapter 5.2 and 7.3 the USA are represented differently from all the other actors: More positively, prominently and including intense debate on the relationship that is not described as only positive, but also as complex, improving, or in crisis.

The highest average numbers of frames are found in articles on supportive claims and calls for action. Both are predominantly used in articles about the USA (in 65 and 73% of these involvements). Supporting involvement is framed on average 2.4 times, calls for action on average 2.7 times. Articles with calls for action appear continuously throughout crisis and routine times, support is a routine involvement. As such, supportive involvement is not represented prominently, the articles are short and on rear pages, and they contain predominantly positive frames on the actors, the relationship and the claims. Supportive involvement contains a high amount of quotes. The supporting actor is given a voice. Calls for action are represented differently. They are published prominently and the framing is more balanced than for any other form of involvement. There is a comparably high number of neutral frames, articles contain different frames (positive and negative, or positive and neutral, or negative and positive) that are balanced in their focus on the claim, actor, and relationship.

This indicates that supportive involvement is likely to be quoted, but on rear pages in short articles and both the actor, relationship and claim might be contextualized positively (see Chapter 6). However, actors calling for a certain action are likely to be presented more prominently, and their claim, relationship and the actor are likely to be contextualized in a more differentiated manner than other forms of involvement.

Self-critical coverage   There are articles that contain criticism on the Israeli policies and the official reactions to international involvement. There are in total 23 articles in which authors discuss the claim itself and admit to misconduct, most of them about the Gaza flotilla participants and in Haaretz. An example is the criticism of Netanyahu's conduct in the Israeli-Palestinian peace process: "Instead of continuing the senseless cycle of symbolic steps taken because of US-pressure and then taking the steps back again, Netanyahu has to decide and take an initiative" (HA_2010_04_25_13), and: "Netanyahu seems to see the peace process as an Israeli gesture to the Americans, and not as an attempt to compromise with the Palestinians" (ibid.). The criticism of Israeli hasbara following the Gaza flotilla has been presented above. Yet general criticism on policy decisions is found for example a day before the raid in Haaretz, titled "also the Israeli government seeks confrontation" (HA_2010_05_30_02d). The authors explain that the delays of the flotilla remain temporary so far, argue that the IDF proposal to accompany the ships will likely be refused and there will be confrontation at sea.

> However, paradoxically, it seems that the Islamist activists and leftist organizers of the flotilla with the clear encouragement of the Turkish government are not the only ones looking for confrontation. The Israeli government has turned stopping the flotilla into a virtually critical matter through the importance it attributes to the not very effective blockade on Gaza. (HA_2010_05_30_02d)

The authors furhter question whether the flotilla organizers' best interest is solely the Gaza citizen. They regard their central goal as "portraying Israel as a cruel state that hurts innocent Palestinians" (HA_2010_05_30_02d). The authors also assume that international media will not recognize the amounts of goods Israel sells to Gaza daily: Yet they conclude

> The problem, as mentioned, is that the government has helped glorifying the flotilla. It is hard to understand why no other solutions were carefully considered, like stopping, searching and permitting them to enter. Even if hundreds of Muslim and European activists and one Knesset member entered Gaza, this is not comparable to the harmful image of an exchange of blows between the naval commando and unarmed civilians in front of the cameras. But it seems to late: It looks like stopping the flotilla became a test of Israel's power. (HA_2010_05_30_02d)

The authors do not take the position of the flotilla activists. Their judgment about them is not different. However, they offer an alternative narration through their critical questioning of the basic decisions – why stop the flotilla? Their central goal is avoiding negative images and harmful media coverage. They also they anticipate that international media will not cover "the whole story" and be biased. But the solution they propose is different: They do not argue for more or better campaigning of Israel's image or for better and faster explaining of the Israeli standpoint. They argue for a policy decision that takes its media and public diplomacy consequences into consideration and weighs the greater loss according to that. In short, while their assessment of the situation is the same as in many of the other articles, they take the international bias and the questionable motivation of the Gaza flotilla participants into account to argue for a smarter policy rather than stopping at the point of complaining about injustice.

7.7 The Representations in the four Analyzed Newspapers

The findings of this analysis indicate that the four newspapers vary in their representations of international involvement. However, in most of the analyzed variables Haaretz is different from Israel Hayom, Maariv and Yediot Aheronot, whereas these three newspapers do not vary in their representations.

The actors appear in all four newspapers with similar frequency ($p = .169$). The USA appears sightly more in Israel Hayom and Haaretz than in the other two newspapers.

There are significant differences in the appearance of claims among the four newspapers ($p = .032$): There is more critical involvement in Maariv and Yediot Aheronot and the least criticism but highest amount of supportive claims in Israel Hayom. But only Haaretz is significantly different, as it covers call for action appears more than the others and less critical involvement. The topics of the claims do not differ significantly ($p = .065$).

The representations of international involvement do not vary significantly. This means, there is no significant difference in the framing of the actor, the claim or the relationship. The one significant exception is that in Haaretz' articles there is more neutral framing.

The appearance of the ethos of conflict is different again between Haaretz and the other three newspapers: The belief in the justness of one's own goals appears less in Haaretz than in the other newspapers, especially Israel Hayom and Maariv. Also the belief in victimization and delegitimization appears least in Haaretz and most in Yediot Aheronot. The appearance of the beliefs about security is similar, as they appear in articles on USA, Europe, UN, and the GFP.

The results regarding the representation indicate two findings: 1) The Israeli newspaper representation of international involvement is in large parts univocal. The appearance and the representation of the involvement hardly varies between the four newspapers. 2) However, when there are significant differences, these are mostly between Haaretz and the other three newspapers. Haaretz represents the actors with different claims, frames claims more frequently neutral, actors less frequently negative than the others. In Haaretz, there is significantly less appearance of the societal beliefs of the ethos of conflict. The only two cases in which the three other newspapers significantly vary are positive and neutral framing of the actors. Israel Hayom contextualizes international actors only rarely positively, and Maariv and Israel Hayom only rarely contextualize them neutrally. Three types of newspapers emerge from the findings:

1) Yediot Aheronot and Maariv are newspapers sold on the street, struggling for their position against the power of the freely distributed Israel Hayom. They emphasize drama, report most intensively on the Gaza flotilla, critical involvement. Both newspapers have the highest amounts of negative framing. Both differ in one aspect: in Yediot Aheronot the belief in victimization is slightly more apparent, in Maariv the belief in justness is slightly more frequent. Within the little amount of differences between the newspapers these two most frequently follow a dramatizing agenda.

2) Israel Hayom is freely distributed and following only a political agenda instead of an economic one. A major goal is the support of the Likud Party, particularly Prime Minister Netanyahu. Therefore, it fits that the USA appears strongly, and in Israel Hayom there are the most supportive articles of all newspapers. Also the belief in justness of one's own goals appears strongest. A frequent coverage of critical international involvement would not suit the agenda, therefore it is not surprising that supportive claims are emphasized the most. The latter serve as a means to external legitimization of internal policies. However,

the differences between Israel Hayom and Maariv and Yediot Aheronot are minor and not significant.

3) Haaretz differs from the other three papers in its striving for balance. The USA and the UN appear more frequently, calls for actions are most frequent, and the Israeli-Palestinian conflict is the central topic. The beliefs of the ethos of conflict appear rarely. In covering the same issues as the other newspapers Haaretz gives less room to drama and societal beliefs of the ethos of conflict. As introduced in chapter 3.3, Haaretz has a low circulation, but its leadership comprises the elites, intelligentsia and highly educated, largely Ashkenasi populations. The results indicate that this very specific readership receives a significantly different representation of international involvement than others. The other three newspapers which cover larger populations offer an univocal representation of international involvement. The three newspapers Israel Hayom, Maariv and Yediot Aheronot constitute a newspaper sphere that hardly offers alternative narratives and leaves consumers little room for interpretation and ambiguity.

7.8 Conclusion

This previous chapter illustrates that the prominent narratives of the representation are frequently based on more than one belief of the ethos of conflict. Likewise one belief can appear in several framing patterns. This interdependency is displayed in Figure 15.

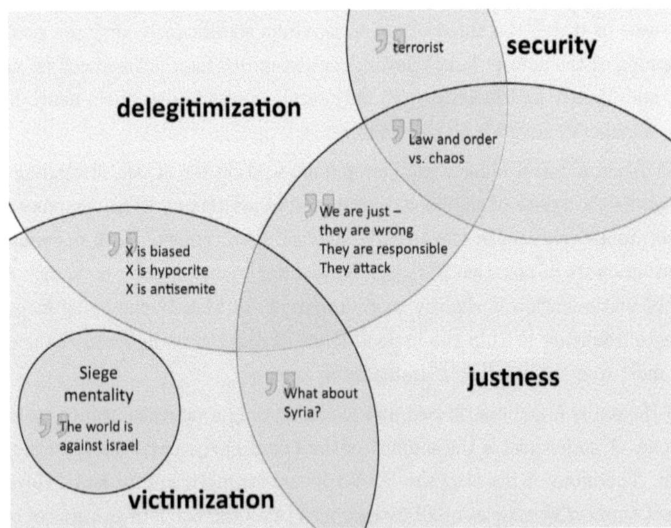

Figure 15 – Narratives and Societal Beliefs of the Ethos of Conflict

The figure considers the four frequent societal beliefs of the ethos of conflict and shows both their connection and the narratives that are based on them. The beliefs about the justness of Israel's goals are considered a continuum as they appear largely independent from the analyzed factors and in almost half the articles. Narratives based on these beliefs contain a message of self-revelation and a consequential attribution of characteristics of the Other. Central are narratives that describe one's own side as just and opposing a wrongful opponent who is the attacker and therefore responsible for any consequences of an event. This belief is based both on delegitimization of the Other and justification of one's own side.

The narratives that describe the opponent as source of chaos and one's own side as restoring law and order contain three societal beliefs: the other side is delegitimized in their goals that are regarded illegitimate and solely creating chaos, and as threat to one's own side. The own Israeli side is considered just and using security means to deal with the threat. The security perspective on opponents enables a distant narration in which their claims and reasons are not relevant. Another narrative focuses solely on the opponent as terrorist, which is both a delegitimization of the actor and frames him as security threat.

Further narratives found in articles with critical involvement pass the attention on to other conflicts. Asking why the international actor cares for Israel and not for other conflicts contains two self-revelations: the own side is regarded just and the therefore as victim of disproportionate and hypocritical attacks.

A narrative that is strongly crisis related is siege mentality, the perception of a hostile world. It is a form of victimization of the own Jewish Israeli society which is considered as treated unjustly by the whole world. This perception derives from narratives that consider the actor as biased, hypocritical, antisemite. Those narratives both delegitimize the actor and victimize the own group that is judged by actors that in their predisposition are against the own group. Therefore the own group again is victim of unjust treatment. Apart from the beliefs in the justness of one's own goals that is continuously important in media representation, most of these beliefs and narratives are crisis related or appear when the actors appear in mediated reality as criticizing.

8 Discussion – Ending a Journey

"Coming back to where you started is not the same
as never leaving."

— Terry Pratchett

The journey of this investigation started with the question how international involvement
is represented in the media of a conflict society and laid out a plan to explore this
question within the case of Jewish Israeli society. As a point of departure, the theoretical
backgrounds were investigated. The socio-psychological consequences for societies in
conflict were considered and particular reference was given to introducing the ethos of
conflict and the impact of conflict beliefs on the present. These were set in relation to
narratives. In order to explore how narratives and beliefs could find themselves in media
representation, the relationship of media actors within the societal and political system
was examined. These relations are explained with reference to the concept of mediatization
and particular emphasis on the mediatization of conflicts.

Thereafter, the specific case of this investigation was introduced. A central part was
dedicated to the exploration of what is considered a mutual polarization between the
international community and Jewish Israelis. Central questions included: Why does the
world pay so much attention to the Israeli-Palestinian conflict, and vice versa? Why is
bias or alleged bias an issue in interaction? Furthermore, the theoretical considerations of
the ethos of conflict were applied to Jewish Israeli society. In preparation for the concrete
analysis, both characteristics of the Israeli media landscape and the raid on the Gaza
flotilla were presented. In the last chapter of this section, all the knowledge gained so
far was connected, clear research questions and hypotheses were drawn from it for the
empirical investigation, and the research design for the empirical investigation was outlined.
A central component of the methodology was the creation of an instrument for the analysis.
In the second part of this investigation, the results of the content analysis are introduced
and discussed. The results are split into three sections: the involved actors, the actors'
involvement, and the patterns of representation. Each of those three chapters starts with
a brief introduction of the central results and then elaborates on them in detail.

Reaching the end of the journey, this final chapter draws conclusions on the questions
asked and the hypotheses stated in chapter 4.3. At first, the major findings regarding the
five hypotheses are introduced and contextualized. Some of these results were expected,

others surprising. Subsequently, the general findings and consequences are discussed. This journey ends with a brief glance at the limitations but also at the benefits and contributions of the investigation.

8.1 The Major Findings

Hypothesis 1 – The Actors are Mostly Represented in a Polarizing Manner

This hypothesis investigated whether actors are represented differently and in a polarizing manner. The examination revealed numerous aspects that supported the hypothesis while not at all times and all circumstances.

The first part of the hypothesis regarding a difference in the repesentations of the actors can be fully supported. The findings, introduced especially in chapter 5, indicate that there is a central distinction between actors appearing continuously (USA, Europe, UN) and those appearing solely during crisis periods (Turkey, GFP, unspecified Western actors) in Israeli media. The second part is supported partially. There is a distinction between actors categorized as "with or against Israel", however it is not a continuous pattern. As it turns out, the USA are the only actor considered to be "with" Israel, whereas all other actors are represented at times as "against" Israel, but not continuously. During the crisis period, the polarization as being "against" Israel is particularly present in mediated reality regarding all actors except the USA. This is true also for articles reporting critical involvement.

In detail: In mediated reality, the USA plays an important role, as its actors appear three times more frequently than any other actor. The USA is portrayed as partner, friend and close associate. Regarding the content, the articles on the USA comprise intense debates on the relationship between Israel and the USA based on any interaction, be it phone calls or vacation trips of members of the administration. Through emphasis on personal interaction, debate on trivial issues and numerous comments and speculations on the complicated relations between Prime Minister Netanyahu and President Obama, a sense of closeness is constituted that is not comparable to any other investigated group of actors. The intense debate on the relationship also shows that the relationship is not without complications. Especially Obama and Netanyahu undertake several bumpy attempts to put the partnership first in spite of strong differences. The results indicate that Israeli newspapers portray Obama's political line with scepticism, through repeated framing of him as weak and lacking understanding.

European actors as well as the institutions and actors of the United Nations are considered and displayed with ambivalence. The relationship is represented as more pragmatic and sober than with the USA, and is rarely described as a "friendship" or "partnership". Concurrently, the United Nations and European actors play a continuous role in mediated reality (although the UN appears only rarely in total). The outlined analyses show the ambivalence of the relations in spite of pragmatic contact. Whenever the actors involve themselves critically, a central part of representation is to judge them as biased and hostile towards Israel. The strong reaction to criticism by European and UN actors is based on the longstanding trauma of shared history and on central assumptions of an international hostility that remain under the surface in phases of pragmatic relationship, but may be evoked at any time as patterns of orientation. This implies that criticism evokes an initial reaction that not only questions the legitimacy of the international actor but also displays the fragility of the relationship and the lack of trust for each other.

The representations of those actors that appear in Israeli media differ solely during the crisis period. It can be assumed that they are not considered relevant continuously for Israel. The representations of Turkey are dominated by the motif of a pragmatic partnership breaking apart. The events of the Gaza flotilla catapult the disintegrating relationship into a serious crisis. The media representation holds Turkey responsible for the events on the flotilla and the crisis. Thus, the crisis is not considered a result of joint failure but solely of Turkey's changing foreign policy interests by Turkey. The representation of Turkey is negative, its motifs are seen as hypocritical. However, in spite of the obvious resentments against Turkish actors, particularly Premier Erdogan, the relationship between Israel and Turkey is repeatedly discussed and its strategic relevance for Israel emphasized.

Less ambiguous is the representation of the Gaza flotilla participants (GFP). They are clearly displayed as opponents. The representation bears, more strongly than the representation of other actors, characteristics of conflict coverage. The actors are depersonalized, as are their victims. They are rarely described in terms of their intention or origin, nor are they quoted. The GFP remain strangers and thus can be framed more strongly: as an aggressive crowd that aims to lynch Israeli soldiers, as terrorists and a danger for Israel. The GFP are delegitimized, the softest frame considers them a group motivated by gaining publicity to hurt Israel's image.

During crisis period the perspective of "with or against Israel" is especially present in the appearance of the unspecified Western actors, i.e. the "world". Those articles deal with the international community and its attitude towards Israel, which is often considered hostile and hypocritical. They use and spur on a perception of "a whole world against Israel" and are permeated by siege mentality.

A third category includes Russia and the Quartet on the Middle East, which do not appear in the investigated periods more than five times. This indicates a very low importance ascribed to those actors in mediated reality.

The results support the assumed polarization of the analyzed actors, but with the limitation that the categorization of actors as friend or foe takes place especially during the crisis periods or when the actors are portrayed as criticizing, which is the case in most articles.

Were these results expected? As discussed in chapter 7.3, Dowty (1999) argues for a „two camp thesis", guiding the Israeli perspective on international actors and their relation to them as friendly or hostile. The results coincide with the assumed mutual polarization as outlined in Chapter 3.1 and 4. US-actors are at times represented as "with Israel", the others in crisis and when criticizing are described as "against Israel". At the same time, the mediated representations of the actors and their representations correspond with the relevant literature (see Chapter 5).

What does that mean? The representations of international actors are not univocal. The varying manners of representation on the analyzed actor groups reflect on the relationships between them. Therefore broadly assumed perception of Israeli newspapers representing merely "a world that is against Israel" cannot be supported. The media representations of international actors are more diverse and complex than that; there are articles covering the United States critically, emphasizing on the importance of Europe for Israel, articles that argue for keeping the important relationship with Turkey, etc. However, in a phase of crisis, of perceived emergency, the diversity of opinions shrinks and popular available narratives serving as explanation patterns are consulted to contextualize the complex reality. Especially in crisis, when orientation is of particular importance, these very accessible narratives and societal beliefs of the ethos of conflict ("we are just", "we are victims of unjustified attacks by illegitimate enemies") but also collective memories (particularly of the Holocaust, or general convictions like siege mentality) contribute close and clear answers. However, also in routine times criticizing actors are frequently contextualized with these narratives (see next hypothesis).

Hypothesis 2 – The Claims are Represented in a Polarizing Manner, Except for Calls for Action

This hypothesis investigated whether claims by the actors are represented differently. The claims were expected to be supportive or critical and represented in a positive or negative way. The examination revealed a more complicated picture, namely that supportive involvement is represented positively but not prominently, and critical involvement is represented very negatively. However, a new category emerged: calls for concrete actions that are represented in a balanced and prominent manner.

The claims appear differently in Israeli newspapers and their contextualization differs. All the actors except for the USA involve themselves predominantly critically in mediated reality. This leads to a negative representation of the actors. The USA is different. Its involvement is either supportive or calling for concrete actions in the future. These forms of engagement are contextualized in a more balanced and positive way and the claim itself is discussed.

In detail. In mediated reality, Israel is predominantly criticized by international actors. Almost every second article analyzed contains criticism. Moreover, this result supports the early assumption of mutual polarization – in Israeli media, international actors appear mainly as critics of past events and policies. Especially high is the amount of criticism during the crisis period and in relation to the events of the Gaza flotilla raid.

Both the claims ascribed to the involved actors and their representations are highly polarizing. Criticism is predominantly refused by criticizing and delegitimizing the critical actor. This simple *ad hominem* mechanism efficiently focuses on the actors. Not only do they lose the moral grounds to criticize, the criticism itself becomes irrelevant. In general, the representation of articles on critical involvement is simple, there are not many possibly contradicting frames. This leads to the conclusion that criticism is not a very promising form of involvement in a conflict setting where the goal is to initiate a debate.

Calls for action can be considered as an US-centered version of criticism, although other actors also choose this claim at times. The representation differs substantially in that there is a high average amount of frames compared to other forms of involvement. Articles contain diverse frames. This indicates that the representation of calls for action is multi-faceted and not reduced to one judgment of one category. The frames are balanced and articles are longer and appear more prominent than others.

Besides, supportive claims are found mainly by US-actors. Those articles are usually short, and contain the highest amount of quotes by supportive actors. The framing of actor, claim, and relationship is positive. Supportive involvement is perceived positively and represented as legitimization of the current policies. Therefore, it does not evoke debate.

Undoubtedly, claims calling for action receive a more balanced media representation than critical claims. The results indicate that claims calling for action are more successful in evoking balanced media representation than critical or supportive forms of involvement.

What does that mean? Calling for action is a form of involvement that requires a certain amount of commitment to the conflict society. A call has to be concrete to propose a certain goal that is seen as advisable to the conflict society by the external actor. Therefore the question arises whether calling for action is a predominantly American form of involvement due to the USA's commitment to Israel or whether it is merely represented differently in the analyzed articles, as the relationship to the USA is perceived differently and hence also its claims are considered more thoroughly. An indicator for the latter perspective is that in the rare cases of US-criticism it is represented more positively than criticism by other actors. However, the combination of a commitment to the conflict society that is perceived as a partnership certainly has a positive impact on the perception of the involvement by this external actor in media representation.

Supportive involvement is perceived as a legitimization of current policies and is therefore helpful for the relationship. However, it also does not promote any change due to its backward looking focus. The high amount of critical involvement in mediated representation supports the assumption of mutual polarization, especially during crisis periods. The recipients of Israeli newspapers encounter a mostly criticizing world, which supports assumptions of siege mentality. The critical claims are rarely considered or debated but rather denied through a focus on the actors.

An involvement that is perceived as merely criticizing past events and decisions of the conflict society is in several ways counterproductive: 1) The actors themselves are questioned in their legitimacy and therefore their ability to take constructive influence is at risk. 2) Within the conflict society itself the increased and concentrated international criticisms intensify already existing assumptions on being alone and isolated in the world, irrespective of how the economic and political relationship is structured in reality. 3) This perception can lead to a conflict society's fatigue affront the international community and the increasing turn of the societal focus inwards. In this case, the society would stop to long for the acknowledgement of international actors. Such a position is dangerous, since it can lead to an increasing spiral of isolation in which the conflict actors behave increasingly as if they were right, which leads to increasing international criticism and gradually to chosen isolation by the conflict society.

Hypothesis 3 – The Ethos of Conflict in Israeli Newspapers

This hypothesis investigated whether the newspaper representation is permeated by beliefs of the ethos of conflict found in narratives. The examination revealed that four core beliefs of the ethos of conflict play a central role in newspaper representations of international involvement, whereas the other four do not.

Some of the beliefs of the ethos of conflict play an important role in the media representations of international involvement. These four out of eight beliefs are found in narratives, as Figure 15 illustrates. The narratives frequently found within the representations each are connected to more than one belief of the ethos of conflict.

In detail: Only four out of eight beliefs of the ethos of conflict appear frequently in this investigation, namely: beliefs about the justness of one's own goals, beliefs about the delegitimization of the Other, beliefs about victimization, and the beliefs about security. The other four beliefs about unity, peace, patriotism, and a positive collective self-image rarely play a role in the media representations.

The beliefs about the justness of Israel's goals appear continuously in routine and crisis periods, in articles on different actors. It appears in all forms of involvement, but strongest in articles on supportive claims. This belief serves as strong, independent basis for the other societal beliefs. It is also a basis for mobilization and justification of one's own actions. It is therefore not surprising that this particular belief is a continuum in media representation as it preempts the perception on the Self and the Other in different contexts.

The beliefs about the delegitimization of the opponent appear predominantly in the crisis period and as a reaction to critical claims. As mentioned above, the delegitimization of the actor prevents conflict societies from having to deal with the point of criticism. The violence committed by one's own group is regarded as defense to what is considered an illegitimate attack by an illegitimate actor. The act of moral disengagement from the harm done to an actor considered inhumane legitimizes one's own actions.

The beliefs about the victimization of Israel correspond with the other beliefs. As the attacks are considered illegitimate, Israel must thus be considered a victim of them. This regards both the physical attack by the Gaza Flotilla participants and the verbal attacks by the international actors. The beliefs in the victimization of one's own side resemble deeply rooted understandings of the Jewish people as eternal victims of persecution, trauma and instrumentalization during the Holocaust, as well as siege mentality. In the context of this collective memory and trauma, international criticism must seem unfair and unjustified, especially if the "world" is perceived as having lost moral grounds to criticize Israel. A central part of this conviction is convincing the international community of one's own victim position. However, when this status is not granted, this attitude leads to resentment. The appearance of this belief in the representation of critical involvement suits the interpretation of it in terms of siege mentality and is frequently connected to beliefs of collective memory, such as the Holocaust.

The beliefs about security also appear continuously in Israel media representation since they entail two different perspectives relevant in this investigation. 1) The USA guarantees Israel's security. This supportive statement and its reassurance is a frequent issue in the relationship. 2) The Gaza flotilla participants pose a security threat to Israel. The emphasis in both of these views lies on the importance and urgence of security, the means needed to reestablish security which may lead to preemptive strikes, especially when the society is used to catastrophic thinking (see Chapter 2.2; Eidelson and Eidelson 2003). The latter is the case for Israel as a society filled with traumatic experiences and experiences of genocidal initiatives. It may lead to fear of annihilation, which explains the importance of security to prevent perceived vulnerability. The emphasis on security legitimizes actions, mobilizes and supports conformism for decisions taken.

Was this outcome expected? Exactly three of those beliefs that are important in the media representations of this investigation are identified as core beliefs of the ethos of conflict by Bar Tal, Halperin and Oren (2010; 2007*b*). They are considered as conflict specific, whereas the other five beliefs are considered as general societal beliefs adapted to the conflict environment. Additionally, the core beliefs are the mirror beliefs conflict societies hold on themselves and the respective other. These factors support the appearance of particularly those beliefs. The belief in security is not part of those core beliefs, yet appeared frequently in the present investigation. This corresponds with earlier investigations on societal beliefs in school textbooks which identify security as the belief relied upon the strongest (Bar-Tal

1998*a*,*b*; Podeh 2002). However, a stronger appearance of beliefs in peace as motivation or defense of policies or the beliefs in unity in spite of the critical world were expected. Also Oren (2009) did not find the belief unity in her investigations.

What does that mean? The combined appearance of the beliefs in justness and victimization of Israel and the delegitimization of the Other is strong and risky. In the context of international involvement it bears the above mentioned risk of a chosen disconnection and a circle of isolation. This risk is further amplified as the international community at times holds opposing perspectives on particular events and developments, which adds to the enlarging gap. Only four of the eight beliefs of the ethos of conflict appear frequently. The remaining question is that of whether this can be traced to the specific focus of this investigation on particular aspects of media coverage. This question can only be answered by further empirical analysis on media content that is not related to specific external actor groups.

Hypothesis 4 – Routine and Crisis have an Impact on the Representations

This hypothesis investigated whether the representations differ in routine and conflict times. It is fully supported by the findings. The presence or absence of acute crisis has an effect on the appearance of the actors, the forms of involvement, and the representations of both.

In detail: There are crisis and routine actors. As discussed above, the actors appearing continuously throughout the crisis and routine periods are the USA, Europe and the UN. The actors appearing solely or predominantly during the crisis period are the GFP, Turkey, and unspecified Western actors.

There is crisis and routine involvement. Critical claims, while generally being the most dominant form of involvement, clearly appear strongest during the crisis period surrounding the events on the Gaza flotilla. On the contrary, supportive claims appear mainly during routine times. Only calls for action appear continuously throughout the analyzed periods.

There is crisis and routine representation. During the crisis period, the beliefs of the ethos of conflict are used more frequently to contextualize international involvement and the involving actors are framed more negatively than in routine times. Moreover, siege mentality is a crisis phenomenon.

Was this outcome expected? These results suit the expectations. The crisis period causes the appearance of directly and indirectly involved crisis actors while at the same time the events of the Gaza flotilla raid cause strong international reactions. The numerous international reactions increase a sense of a hostile world, as the investigation shows during the crisis period. The results are compatible with literature on media coverage during crisis periods and mediatization of conflicts (Rinnawi 2007; Wolfsfeld 1997, 2001, 2003; Wolfsfeld, Frosh and Awabdy 2008). The media is mobilized in defense modus (Rinnawi 2007) and only rarely are there articles that differ from the hegemonial narrative. The dominant narratives entail the demonization (Liebes 1997) of the rival. The activists are described as terrorists and a threat to the existence of Israel. The violence by the rivals is exaggerated and dramatized (as lynch) and covered prominently, whereas their victims are depersonalized and marginalized. One's own violence is described as legitimate defense and self protection. Therefore the enemies themselves are blamed for their victims. In this modus, the military and governmental information is treated as facts and international actors are contesting those. The Gaza Flotilla members remain voiceless and faceless. All these patterns suit what Wolfsfeld calls an "ethnocentric control over the flow of information" (Wolfsfeld 2003; Wolfsfeld, Frosh and Awabdy 2008: 403).

What does that mean? In crisis, there is both: a high amount of international criticism but also a low tolerance for it in conflict societies. In this sense, the need for orientation outplays the need for information, as the media within a crisis society is both dependent on official sources and chooses to uphold societal conflict beliefs and narratives. Thus, during the crisis when information is most needed, it is the least likely that balanced information can be obtained.

Hypothesis 5 – The Newspapers are more alike than Assumed, Except for Haaretz

This hypothesis investigated whether the representations differ amongst the various newspapers analyzed. The examination revealed that the newspapers' representation of international involvement is largely similar among Israel Hayom, Maariv, and Yediot Aheronot, whereas Haaretz differs from them in various variables.

In detail: The appearance of actors, the topics they relate to, and the framing of the claims and relationship do not differ significantly. However, there are also differences. The actors appear in all four newspapers in similar frequency, but they are contextualized differently. Yediot Aheronot, Maariv, and Israel Hayom frame actors predominantly negatively, Haaretz significantly less. Haaretz contextualizes actors more frequently positively or neutrally than the other newspapers. However, the contextualizations of the actors are the only variables in which also Yediot Aheronot, Maariv, and Israel Hayom vary significantly. Israel Hayom rarely contextualizes actors positively and Yediot Aheronot more frequently contextualizes them neutrally than the others.

Also the forms of involvement differ significantly between Haaretz and the other newspapers. Haaretz represents the actors with more supportive involvement or calls for action, also Israel Hayom also represents slightly more supportive involvement than the other two newspapers. The involvement is contextualized in similar manner among the four newspapers, only Haaretz contextualizes it more frequently neutrally. Except for Haaretz all three newspapers strongly contextualize the involvement within societal beliefs of the ethos of conflict.

As introduced above, the findings illustrate that Israel Hayom and Maariv strive towards dramatic and crisis-oriented coverage and therefore put the strongest emphasis on international criticism and the events of the Gaza flotilla. Moreover, Israel Hayom, following its agenda to support the Likud-government and Prime Minister Netanyahu, emphasizes supportive involvement as a means to legitimize current policies slightly stronger than the others. All three newspapers emphasize the societal beliefs of the ethos of conflict. Israel Hayom in particular emphasizes the justness of one's own goals.

These results indicate that Haaretz, the liberal newspaper, offers different representations than the other three newspapers in several critical aspects: it emphasizes societal beliefs of the ethos of conflict to a lesser extent and apparently the same actors are represented less critical but more frequently as they call for action or express support. The actors themselves are represented more positively and neutrally than in the other three newspapers. The three other newspapers are fairly univocal in their representations of international involvement.

Was this outcome expected? The results illustrate that significant differences are found only between Haaretz and the other three newspapers which are not very different from each other. The three newspapers Israel Hayom, Maariv, and Yediot Aheronot target wide audiences of Jewish Israelis and may be considered "mainstream". For these readers, the range of opinions and perspectives offered by the three newspapers is limited. These findings are not surprising when taking into account the small population of the country as a total. The political and hence also the media sphere is very limited. As discussed in chapter 3.3, the Israeli media landscape is characterized by a practical independence of the media but also several constraining regulations. Institutions such as military censorship restrain the journalists' independence, particularly during crisis time. Another implication of a small media landscape is the pseudo-pluralism. There is a limited number of companies that hold cross-ownership of the media formats. Consequentially, journalists have only a limited amount of alternative employers to choose once disgraced at a place.

Furthermore, the pressure may be very personal and comparable to an old boys' network. Most journalists and politicians used to serve in the Israeli military and reserve and the boundaries between the sectors blur (Liebes 1997). Moreover, as Orgad (2009) points out, national media actors are under a different pressure than international media actors and cannot afford too much freedom in their role as they need to connect community members and to convey a sense of belonging. This prevents them from reporting outside of the communities' narrative. That is seen as the main reason why international involvement is not used as a tool for estrangement as suggested in the introduction. However, more differences would be expected due to the competition over audiences between the three newspapers. This may indicate furthermore that there is a low range of legitimate viewpoints to be expressed by political and social elites (Bennett 1990) and a high level of elite consensus (Wolfsfeld 1997, 2004) on issues regarding international actors.

Haaretz is in its appearance and its target group different from the other three newspapers. It is in spite of its low distribution internationally renowned and influential due to its sophisticated readership that comprises Israeli elites and intellectuals. As such, Haaretz is in its essence different from the other three newspapers. Therefore, differences from the other three newspapers were to be expected. This position of a "privileged outcast" apparently allows for a greater range of perspectives differing from the dominant narratives, e.g societal beliefs of the ethos of conflict. Following Orgad's argumentation, Haaretz is reporting outside the community's narrative. However, the elite readership of Haaretz indicates that Haaretz reports inside *its own* community's narrative, just the community itself is different from the other three newspapers.

In this environment, Haaretz constitutes a different space, and a separation between the representation for Jewish Israeli elites and for the overall Jewish population. In such an environment Haaretz, as a newspaper that is in its essence different from the other newspapers may appear to use more freedom

What does that mean? The lack of differences between the three newspapers indicates that there is not much diversity in media representation except for Haaretz. The consumers of "mainstream" newspapers gain little contradictory information and alternative narratives. On the contrary, the similar coverage and representation enhances each paper's credibility as the narratives remain largely unchallenged. This amplifies the possible effect of an univocal voice and representation. Haaretz constitutes a "privileged outcast" both in its audience and in its coverage. The existence of an "outcast" newspaper further validates the pseudo-pluralism and hence the credibility of the "mainstream" newspapers as democratic and free. It is however questionable whether Haaretz poses a legitimate challenge to the mainstream narratives or whether its coverage is considered "outcast narrative" and therefore ignored by most members of Jewish Israeli society

Arguing in agreement with Orgad (2009) that both the "mainstream" and the "outcast" newspapers connect their community members and convey a sense of belonging leads to the conclusion that there are different audience communities. While Haaretz connects a small group of local intellectuals and elites of the country, the three "mainstream" newspapers target the larger populations with a largely univocal content and representations. When focusing merely on these four Israeli newspapers these findings indicate a gap between two different groups within the Jewish Israeli society: an elitist liberal minority and the vast majority who identifies with a conflict-supportive narrative and the ethos of conflict. This investigation has focused only on the newspapers in Israel. Hence its results do not supply conclusions on the whole Israeli media sphere. However, when taking into account the interrelatedness of ownership in print, TV, Radio, and online media (see Chapter 3.3) the conclusion of a lack of diversity can be extrapolated to other means of communication as well.

In sum, the five hypotheses are each at least partly supported by the results of this investigation. In most cases, the results present a mediated reality more complex than implied by the hypothesis. There is polarization of the actors as friends or foes, but only in crisis and when criticized and not in general. The international involvement is polarizing and mostly critical, but there are also calls for action that lead to a less polarizing representation than claims merely criticizing or supporting existent or past events and policies. The representations do emphasize societal beliefs of the ethos of conflict, but mostly during crisis times and not all of them. In general, everything shows different results in routine and crisis times: the actors and their involvement, the representation, the societal beliefs. The representations of the mainstream newspapers are largely univocal. but the representations in Haaretz provide a different contextualization than in the other three newspapers.

8.2 The Limitations

Exploring a new field on a quest for answers to questions considered striking is a process that seems to include numerous encounters with trial and error. Another central encounter is the deep understanding of human and time limitations as to how much can be answered and what can not be answered. 1) This investigation is limited to Hebrew-language newspapers that address Jewish Israeli society. That means Palestinian media are not analyzed, due to language barriers and a lack of resources, although Palestinian Israelis comprise more than 20% of the Israeli society. The narratives are expected to differ vastly, existing research even suggests mirroring beliefs and a comparison is recommended for further research. 2) The author is not a native Hebrew speaker. Yet, the analysis was conducted on Hebrew newspapers. To ensure valid results, four native Hebrew speakers were asked to re-code the same articles for comparison. The results were identical. The creation of the codebook through a pretest could be considered as limitation for a non-native speaker. Therefore, it was created in close cooperation with native speakers. Still, despite all these precautions and the thorough analysis and frequent debate, reassurance and discussion with native speakers, it is not possible to completely rule out mistakes. The created instrument itself proved efficient and suitable for the investigation. However, as explained above, its creation was part of a long process and this investigation its first real test. In the next section, some adjustments are recommended for further research. 3) The case of this study is a very unique incident in which international groups involve themselves actively in the course of the conflict. This leads to the legitimate question whether the results can be generalized. To preempt this possible weakness, a rapid qualitative analysis of the representation of international involvement during the 2014 Gaza war was conducted. It is briefly introduced in the next section.

8.3 The Contributions of this Investigation

After answering the hypotheses and acknowledging the limitations of this investigation, what are its contributions? This section distills those wider implications of the findings.

Is there a mutual polarization between Jewish Israeli society and the international community? In central parts of this investigation, the assumed polarization in media representation is supported by the results. In mediated reality:

- The international community polarizes Israel in a predominantly negative fashion by criticizing its policies, events, and actions.
- The international community is categorized as "with or against Israel" during crisis and when criticizing Israel.
- Israel sees itself isolated against a strong group of opponents and ambivalent or unreliable partners.
- The crisis perspective is simple: the ambivalent partners like European actors and UN show their opportunistic and partially their anti-Israeli attitudes. There are many direct and indirect opponents attacking Israel.
- In crisis periods, fears of siege mentality seem to reaffirm themselves.
- In crisis periods there is little room and longing for self-critical representation.

In short, in mediated reality, there is largely polarizing involvement that is represented in a polarizing manner, particularly in crisis times. The mediated polarization, both of international actors and in the representation of them, is particularly strong during crisis times and less dominant in routine times, leaving more space and openness for less polarizing and more differentiated representation. Those results suggest that critical involvement during a crisis time will lead to a very polarizing contextualization.

Advisable involvement – how (not to) involve oneself in a conflict society As this investigation focuses solely on the mediated representation of international involvement and not its political impact, its possible implications for policymakers are also limited. Taking this into account, several suggestions can be drawn from this investigation:

Criticizing a conflict society is not useful but counterproductive. The criticism, while it might be justified or regarded necessary, does not reach far and – at least in its media representation – is even counterproductive. 1) The criticism itself is rarely considered and debated. It is far more likely that the involving actor in response is attributed with negative traits questioning his or her moral grounds to judge the conflict society. 2) This process can endanger the relationship and the ability of the involving actor to take a constructive position in attempts to conflict resolution – as its moral grounds to judge the conflict setting are questioned. 3) Furthermore, the critical involvement may consolidate convictions of the conflict society to be isolated from the international community. Especially when a society is criticized intensively by a lot of international actors, this criticism is perceived as unfair and evokes beliefs of victimization by the criticized actors. It is unlikely for a society criticized by everyone – based on these grounds – to reconsider and reconcile.

It is an illusion that threatening to isolate a conflict society if its behavior does not change will have a positive impact. This investigation and especially its focus on socio-psychological aspects of conflict settings shows that it is more likely the society in question will – convinced of its own justness – dig into convictions of collective victimization against the illegitimate and unjust "world".

Support is reassuring but not productive. Supportive involvement appears especially in the newspaper with the most hawkish perspective on the conflict. It is used as a means of external approval and legitimization to "be on the right track". However, these supportive claims are not considered important enough to appear on front pages or in long articles. It therefore does not seem to be a suitable tool to build trust or a constructive relationship.

Calling for concrete action has potential. The main difference between calls for action and supportive or critical involvement is the focus on the future rather than on past or present. This implies activity rather than reactivity and offers a chance for improvement rather than just excoriating the conflict society for misbehavior. Therefore, the representation is more prominent, the articles are longer, contain more and more diverse representation – both positive and negative frames – thereby indicating a debate by the journalists. The call itself is debated and not only the involving actor. Calling for an action requires commitment by the international actor = otherwise the call remains empty and useless and might be ignored the next time. The action called for needs to be within the range of acceptability for the conflict society. When the demands exceed this range they are represented just like in the case of critical involvement (see Chapter 7.3).

The ethos of conflict, narratives, and media   Just as indicated in answering the hypotheses, this first known empirical analysis on ethos of conflicts in media representation supports the assumption that media is an important transmitter and amplifier of the ethos of conflict. However, as only four of the eight beliefs show frequent appearance, it is advisable to conduct further research not related to a particular actor group on Israeli newspapers. The investigation so far indicates that in the representation of international involvement, only half of the ethos of conflict is relevant. This responds to research indicating that those are the core and frequent beliefs (see above).

Moreover, this investigation illustrates that the societal beliefs of the ethos of conflicts feed narratives as Figure 15 indicates. These are not used constantly but are available to be used when triggered. The results also show that the ethos of conflict as well as attached narratives explain and contextualize the crisis to make it understandable. Again, this indicates that international involvement is rarely used as a tool for estrangement. Quite the contrary: in the newspapers' coverage of the world's relation to Israel, moral disengagement is promoted, which renders the crisis bearable on a personal and societal level. However, it also amplifies the incomprehension between the international community and Israel. It may lead to a deepening of the division if Israeli recipients perceive international criticism as unfair and unjustified or if international actors see Israeli actions as unjust and both sides cannot understand the rationale of the Other.

The research instrument   The instrument created for this investigation proves to be efficient and gives clear and distinctive results. This codebook can be easily adapted to the overall conflict and other phases. Moreover, it can easily be adapted to other conflict settings (for example the Serbia and Kosovo conflict, the Turkey and Kurds conflict, Tamils and Hindus in Sri Lanka, Muslims and Serbs in Bosnia-Herzegovina, and many others).

Several adaptations need to be made for the analysis in another conflict setting: change of the period (Question 03), the newspaper (Q04), the main actors (Q07), extraction of question 08 on the Gaza flotilla members, change of topic of the item (Q10), and changes of the sub-categories of framing (Q12a to 14d). For both the identification of relevant topics (Q10) and the sub-categories of framing (Q12a to 14d) it is advisable to conduct a pretest to identify which are the central topics of international involvement and which are the central positive, neutral or negative frames of the actors, claims, and relationships.

Not all of the questions have proven to be efficient. In the section on mechanisms of framing (Q15 to Q17) only Q17 had significant results. The other two questions on the contextualization of the claims and the enhancement or softening of their impact did not lead to distinct results. It might be different in another setting. However, the investigation has shown that Q16 can be analyzed in various ways. Is the enhancement of a claim's impact – the dramatization – a good or a bad thing? It can be both. Standing for itself, this information does not tell anything and can be chosen in very different cases.

The section on the societal beliefs of the ethos of conflict (Q18 to Q25) proves to give very distinct results. There are scales on the ethos of conflict with more items (See for a 16 item scale Bar-Tal et al. 2012: 14; and for a 48-item scale in Gopher's thesis see Bar-Tal 2013: 201; Oren 2009: 14). Since the codebook is already long, it exceeded the scope of this investigation to choose a scale with more than eight items without employing research assistants. Therefore, this part of the investigation solely gives results on the appearance of the beliefs of the ethos of conflict, and not on more detail.

Transferability of the results onto other contexts   A central question when discussing the results remains: are these results specific to the period surrounding the Gaza flotilla raid? The event was unique; does that mean the results are too? The recent Gaza conflict in 2014 and its newspaper coverage indicate that the representation of international involvement is alike in other crisis phases. A brief analysis was conducted during and after the crisis on Israeli newspapers and some examples are illustrated in Appendix D. They illustrate that media representation of international involvement is similar in the Gaza crisis in 2014 to the investigation period of the present study.

Although these are merely excerpts of a brief examination and not of an empirical content analysis, the scanned content suggests that in a crisis between Israel and Gaza that lasts several weeks and is characterized by bombing and high amounts of casualties, the appearance of narratives and the ethos of conflict is stronger than in the analyzed crisis times. There is a very strong focus on "the world" being "with or against Israel". Criticism is often denied as hypocritical and biased. The ongoing conflict harshens the perspectives and also the judgment on international criticism. In mediated reality, Israel increasingly sees itself as alone in a fight over its existence. The world supposedly lacks understanding for the truth and biased against Israel and fully sympathetic to Palestinian terrorists. Investigating on media representation in this period is highly recommended for further analysis.

Another central question is that of whether the results of this analysis are specific for the analyzed conflict setting. This question should be explored in further research. However, the beliefs of the ethos of conflict have been found in various conflict societies. There are more conflicts in which societies might feel isolated and mistreated by the international community. Therefore, it can be assumed that similar results can be found in other conflict settings.

In sum, the findings of the present investigation indicate a cycle of polarization in Israeli media representations. While international actors predominantly appear as criticizing Israeli policies, they are also represented negatively in Israeli media. Thus, the portrayal relies on the core societal conflict beliefs and narratives as explanation patterns. The cycle is especially polarizing in crisis times. Israel finds itself isolated in face of its numerous critics. The findings also suggest forms of involvement that escape this cycle. While criticism provokes negative representation and support provokes self-affirmation, calling for an action may trigger concrete debate about the claim.

The results of this investigation relate to a specific period in 2010 surrounding the raid of the Gaza flotilla. However, the sample representation of the Gaza crisis coverage in 2014 indicates that similar results can be expected for other periods. For following investigations within the Israeli-Palestinian conflict and especially on other conflict societies, the developed instrument can be used with small proposed revisions.

Reaching this point in the journey it seems fair to come back to the preliminary assumption often stated in jest by Israelis of various political affiliations that in Israeli media "the whole world is against Israel." After a comprehensive methodological investigation, it appears that these popular assumptions regarding the Israeli media are not entirely far from what the results reveal. The reality mediated in Israeli newspapers indeed portrays an image of a world that is in large parts critical or even hostile towards the state of Israel, its actions and policies. Regardless of whether these portrayals correspond with a truth, media representations contribute to the perpetuation of such popular beliefs and sentiments, and in doing so may affect the conflict realities themselves.

Bibliography

Abarbach, Li-Or. 2012. "TGI Polls: Maariv rises in distribution for the first time in years." Globes. July 25. (in Hebrew).

Abraham, A.J. 2012. *The eternal war: a psychological perspective on the Arab-Israeli conflict.* Lanham, Md.: University Press of America.

Anderson, Benedict. 2006. *Imagined communities: reflections on the origin and spread of nationalism.* Rev. ed. ed. London; New York: Verso.

Andriani, Cristina. 2013. "Swords or plowshares? Holocaust collective memories and the Palestinian-Israeli conflict." Clark University. PhD thesis.

Anholt, Simon. 2006. "Israel's International image. Special Report." Anholt Nations Brand Index. Q 3 Report.

Arakelyan, Liana. 2013. "The underlying reasons of deterioration of Turkish-Israeli relations in the aftermath of the Gaza blockade and the flotilla incident." Armenian University of Armenia. PhD thesis.

Archibald, David and Mitchell Miller. 2012. "Full-spectacle dominance? An analysis of the Israeli state's attempts to control media images of the 2010 Gaza flotilla." *Journal of War & Culture Studies* 5(2):189–201.

Arian, Alan. 1995. *Security threatened: surveying Israeli opinion on peace and war.* Cambridge; New York: Cambridge University Press.

Asseburg, Muriel. 2003. "The EU and the Middle East Conflict: Tackling the Main Obstacle to Euro-Mediterranean Partnership." *Mediterranean Politics* 8(2-3):174–193.

Associated Press. 2012. "Israel looks to gays to improve image." Ynet News. February 2.

Atteslander, Peter. 2003. *Methoden der empirischen Sozialforschung.* Berlin: Walter de Gruyter.

Azar, Edward E. 1990. *The management of protracted social conflict: theory and cases.* Aldershot, Hampshire, England: Dartmouth Publishing Company.

Azar, Edward E., Paul Jureidini and Ronald McLaurin. 1978. "Protracted Social Conflict; Theory and Practice in the Middle East." *Journal of Palestine Studies* 8(1):41–60.

Bandura, Albert. 2002. "Selective moral disengagement in the exercise of moral agency." *Journal of moral education* 31(2):101–119.

Bapat, Navin A. 2011. "Transnational terrorism, US military aid, and the incentive to misrepresent." *Journal of Peace Research* 48(3):303–318.

Bibliography

Bar-Tal, Daniel. 1998*a*. "Societal Beliefs in Times of Intractable Conflict: The Case of Israel." *International Journal of Conflict Management* 9(1):22–50.

Bar-Tal, Daniel. 1998*b*. "The Rocky Road Toward Peace: Beliefs on Conflict in Israeli Textbooks." *Journal of Peace Research* 35(6):723–742.

Bar-Tal, Daniel. 2007*a*. *Living with the Conflict: Socio-psychological Analysis of the Jewish Society in Israel.* Jerusalem: Carmel. (in Hebrew).

Bar-Tal, Daniel. 2007*b*. "Sociopsychological Foundations of Intractable Conflicts." *American Behavioral Scientist* 50(11):1430–1453.

Bar-Tal, Daniel. 2013. *Intractable Conflicts: Socio-psychological Foundations and Dynamics.* Cambridge; New York: Cambridge University Press.

Bar-Tal, Daniel, Alona Raviv, Alona Raviv and Adi Dgani-Hirsh. 2008. "The Influence of the Ethos of Conflict on Israeli Jews' Interpretation of Jewish–Palestinian Encounters." 53(1):94–118.

Bar-Tal, Daniel and Dik Antebi. 1992*a*. "Beliefs about Negative Intentions of the World: A Study of the Israeli Siege Mentality." *Political Psychology* 13(4):633–645.

Bar-Tal, Daniel and Dikla Antebi. 1992*b*. "Siege mentality in Israel." *International Journal of Intercultural Relations* 16(3):251–275.

Bar-Tal, Daniel and Eran Halperin. 2011. Socio-psychological Barriers to Conflict Resolution. In *Intergroup conflicts and their resolution: A social psychological perspective*, ed. Daniel Bar-Tal. Psychology Press pp. 217–240.

Bar-Tal, Daniel, Eran Halperin and Joseph de Rivera. 2007. "Collective Emotions in Conflict Situations: Societal Implications." *Journal of Social Issues* 63(2):441–460.

Bar-Tal, Daniel, Eran Halperin and Neta Oren. 2010. "Socio-Psychological Barriers to Peace Making: The Case of the Israeli Jewish Society." *Social Issues and Policy Review* 4(1):63–109.

Bar-Tal, Daniel, Eran Halperin and Ruthie Pliskin. 2015. Why Is It So Difficult to Resolve Intractable Conflicts Peacefully? A Sociopsychological Explanation. In *Handbook of International Negotiation*, ed. Mauro Galluccio. Springer International Publishing pp. 73–92.

Bar-Tal, Daniel and Keren Sharvit. 2009. The Influence of the Threatening Transitional Context on Israeli Jews' Reactions to Al Aqsa Intifada. In *Explaining the Breakdown of Ethnic Relations: Why Neighbors Kill*, ed. Victoria M. Esses and Richard A. Vernon. Oxford, UK: Blackwell Publishing Ltd. pp. 147–170.

Bar-Tal, Daniel, Keren Sharvit, Eran Halperin and Anat Zafran. 2012. "Ethos of conflict: The concept and its measurement." *Peace and Conflict: Journal of Peace Psychology* 18(1):40–61.

Bar-Tal, Daniel, Lily Chernyak-Hai, Noa Schori and Ayelet Gundar. 2009. "A sense of self-perceived collective victimhood in intractable conflicts." *International Review of the Red Cross* 91(874):229–254.

Bar-Tal, Daniel, Neta Oren and Rafi Nets-Zehngut. 2014. "Sociopsychological analysis of conflict-supporting narratives: A general framework." *Journal of Peace Research* 51(5):662–675.

Bar-Tal, Daniel and Phillip Hammack. 2012. Conflict, Delegitimization, and Violence. In *The Oxford handbook of intergroup conflict*, ed. Linda R. Tropp. Oxford library of psychology New York: Oxford University Press pp. 29–52.

Barkho, Leon. 2008. "The BBC's Discursive Strategy and Practices vis-a-vis the Palestinian Israeli Conflict." *Journalism Studies* 9(2):278–294.

Becker, Raphael N., Arye L. Hillman, Niklas Potrafke and Alexander H. Schwemmer. 2015. "The preoccupation of the United Nations with Israel: Evidence and theory." *The Review of International Organizations* pp. 1–25. March 4.

Beinart, Peter. 2015. "Sorry, Bibi: Iran is bad, but it is no Amalek, Haman or even Nazi Germany." Haaretz. March 4.

Benn, Aluf. 2006. "U.S. backs Israel on aid for humanitarian groups, not Hamas." Haaretz. February 16.

Bennett, W. Lance. 1990. "Toward a Theory of Press-State Relations in the United States." *Journal of Communication* 40(2):103–127.

Benvenisti, Eyal. 2012. *The International Law of Occupation.* 2nd ed ed. Oxford: Oxford University Press.

Berelson, Bernard. 1952. *Content analysis in communications research.* Illinois: Glencoe.

Bland, Byron, Brenna Powell and Lee Ross. 2012. Barriers to Dispute Resolution. Reflections on Peacemaking and Relationships between Adversaries. In *Understanding Social Action, Promoting Human Rights*, ed. Andrew K. Woods Ryan Goodman, Derek Jinks. pp. 265–291.

Bohrer, Ashley. 2014. "Against the pinkwashing of Israel." AlJazeera. August 9.

Bruner, Jerome S. 1992. *Acts of Meaning. Feour Lectures on Mind and Culture.* Vol. 21 Cambridge MA: Harvard University Press.

Buchan, Russell. 2011. "The International Law of Naval Blockade and Israel's Interception of the Mavi Marmara." *Netherlands International Law Review* 58(02):209–41.

Buchan, Russell. 2012. "The Palmer Report and the Legality of Israel's Naval Blockade of Gaza." *ICLQ* 61(01):264–273.

Caspi, Dan. 2011. "A revised look at online journalism in Israel: entrenching the old hegemony." *Israel Affairs* 17(3):341–363.

Caspi, Dan and Yehiel Limor. 1992. "The Mediators: The Mass Media in Israel 1948-1990." *Tel Aviv: Am Oved* .

Bibliography

Caspi, Dan and Yehiel Limor. 1999. *The In/Outsiders: the Media in Israel.* Cresskill: Hampton Press.

Central Bureau of Statistics. State of Israel. 2010. "Social Survey 2009: Jewish Tradition Observance and Changes in Religiosity of the Jewish population in Israel.". http://www.cbs.gov.il/hodaot2010n/19_10_211e.pdf.

Central Bureau of Statistics. State of Israel. 2012. "Press Release. Selected Data from the New Statistical Abstract of Israel No.63-2012.". http://www1.cbs.gov.il/www/hodaot2012n/11_12_239e.pdf.

Cheung-Blunden, Violet and Bill Blunden. 2008. "The emotional construal of war: Anger, fear, and other negative emotions." *Peace and Conflict: Journal of Peace Psychology* 14(2):123–149.

Cohen, Florette, Lee Jussim, Kent D Harber and Gautam Bhasin. 2009. "Modern anti-Semitism and anti-Israeli attitudes." *Journal of personality and social psychology* 97:290–306.

Cottle, Simon. 2006. *Mediatized Conflict: Developments in Media and Conflict Studies.* Issues in cultural and media studies Maidenhead: Open University Press.

Council of the European Union. 2010. "Council conclusions on Gaza. 3023rd Foreign Affairs Council meeting." Luxembourg. June 14.

Craig, Alan Ian Henry. 2011. "The struggle for legitimacy: a study of military lawyers in Israel." University of Leeds. PhD thesis.

Dag, Haluk. 2013. "Peace journalism or war journalism? A comparative analysis of the coverage of Israeli and Turkish newspapers during the Gaza flotilla crisis." Concordia University. Master thesis.

David, Steven R. 2012. "Existential threats to Israel: learning from the ancient past." *Israel Affairs* 18(4):503–525.

Deprez, A. and K. Raeymaeckers. 2010. "Bias in the News? The Representation of Palestinians and Israelis in the Coverage of the First and Second Intifada." *International Communication Gazette* 72(1):91–109.

Deprez, Annelore and Karin Raeymaeckers. 2011. "Bottlenecks in the coverage of the Israeli-Palestinian conflict: the coverage of the first and second intifada in the Flemish press." *Media, War & Conflict* 4(2):185–202.

Deutsch, Morton. 2005. Mediation and difficult conflict. In *Handbook of Mediation: Bridging Theory, Research and Practice*, ed. Margaret Hermann. Oxford, UK: Basil Blackwell pp. 335–374.

Deutsche Welle. 2010. "EU demands inquiry after Israeli raid on ships, Turkey outraged.". http://www.dw.de/eu-demands-inquiry-after-israeli-raid-on-ships-turkey-outraged/a-5633390.

Diner, Dan. 2000. "Deutschland" als Chiffre im israelischen Selbstverständnis. In *Israelis und Deutsche. Die Ambivalenz der Normalität.* Friedrich-Ebert-Stiftung pp. 65–71.

Dominikowski, Thomas. 2004. Massenmedien und Massenkrieg. Historische Annäherungen an eine unfriedliche Symbiose. In *Krieg als Medienereignis II. Krisenkommunikation im 21.Jahrhundert,* ed. Martin Löffelholz. VS Verlag fuer Sozialwissenschaften pp. 59–81.

Dor, Daniel. 2004. *Intifada hits the headlines : how the Israeli press misreported the outbreak of the second Palestinian uprising.* Bloomington: Indiana University.

Dor, Daniel. 2005. *The suppression of guilt the Israeli media and the reoccupation of the West Bank.* London: Pluto Press.

Doron, Gideon. 1998. "The Politics of Mass Communication in Israel." *The ANNALS of the American Academy of Political and Social Science* 555(1):163–179.

Downey, John, David Deacon, Peter Golding, B. Oldfield and Dominic Wring. 2006. *The BBC's reporting of the Israeli-Palestinian conflict, for the BBC Board of Governors.* Loughborough: Communications Research Centre, Loughbororough University.

Dowty, Alan. 1999. "Israeli foreign policy and the jewish question." *Middle East* 3(1):2.

Dreher, Axel. 2014. "KOF Index of Globalization 2014.". http://globalization.kof.ethz.ch/media/filer_public/2014/04/15/rankings_2014.pdf.

Eichner, Itamar. 2010. "Israelis recruited to PR Corps." Ynet News. February 21.

Eidelson, Roy J and Judy I. Eidelson. 2003. "Dangerous ideas. Five beliefs that propel groups toward conflict." *The American psychologist* 58(3):182–192.

Entman, Robert. 2003. "Cascading Activation: Contesting the White House's Frame After 9/11." *Political Communication* 20(4):415–432.

Entman, Robert. 2004. *Projections of power: framing news, public opinion, and U.S. foreign policy.* Studies in communication, media, and public opinion Chicago: University of Chicago Press.

Entman, Robert. 2007. "Framing Bias: Media in the Distribution of Power." *Journal of Communication* 57(1):163–173.

Entman, Robert. 2008. "Theorizing Mediated Public Diplomacy: The U.S. Case." *The International Journal of Press/Politics* 13(2):87–102.

Epstein, A. L. 1978. *Ethos and Identity: Three Studies in Ethnicity.* Chicago: Aldine Publishing.

Erdem, Burcu Kaya. 2011. "The Place of Public Diplomacy in the Asymmetric Media Conflict: The 'Hasbara Example' in the Hezbollah - Israel Media War." *International Journal of Humanities and Social Science* I(16):210 – 222.

FPA Israel. 2014. "The Foreigh Press Association - Who we are and what we do.". http://www.fpa.org.il/?categoryId=74684.

Franck, Thomas M. 1984. "Of Gnats and Camels: Is There a Double Standard at the United Nations?" *American Journal of International Law* 78(4):811–833.

Freedman, Rosa. 2013. *The United Nations Human Rights Council: a critique and early assessment.* London: Routledge.

Früh, Werner. 2007. *Inhaltsanalyse : Theorie und Praxis.* Konstanz: UVK Verlagsgesellschaft.

Früh, Werner. 2011. *Inhaltsanalyse: Theorie und Praxis.* Konstanz: UVK Verlagsgesellschaft.

Fuxman, Shai. 2012. "Learning the Past, Interpreting the Present, Shaping the Future: Israeli Adolescents' Narratives of the Israeli-Palestinian Conflict." Harvard University. PhD thesis.

Galtung, J. and M. H. Ruge. 1965. "The Structure of Foreign News: The Presentation of the Congo, Cuba and Cyprus Crises in Four Norwegian Newspapers." *Journal of Peace Research* 2(1):64–90.

Gans, Herbert J. 1980. *Deciding what's news: a study of CBS Evening News, NBC Nightly News, Newsweek and Time.* Evanston III.: Northwestern University Press.

Gayer, Corinna. 2012. *Gendered intractability: national identity constructions and gender in the Israeli-Palestinian conflict.* [Baden-Baden]: Nomos Verlagsgesellschaft.

Ghareeb, Edmund. 1983. *Split vision: the portrayal of Arabs in the American media.* Rev. and expanded ed ed. Washington, DC: American-Arab Affairs Council.

Gilboa, Eitan. 2001. "Diplomacy in the media age: Three models of uses and effects." *Diplomacy & Statecraft* 12(2):1–28.

Gilboa, Eitan. 2006. "Public Diplomacy: The Missing Component in Israel's Foreign Policy." *Israel Affairs* 12(4):715–747.

Gilboa, Eitan. 2008*a*. "Searching for a Theory of Public Diplomacy." *The ANNALS of the American Academy of Political and Social Science* 616(1):55–77.

Gilboa, Eitan. 2008*b*. "The evolution of Israeli media." *Middle East Review of International Affairs* 12(3):88–101.

Gill, Rosalind. 2007. *Gender and the Media.* Cambridge: Polity Press.

Globescan, Pipa. 2014. "Country Ratings Poll." BBC World Service Poll. http://downloads.bbc.co.uk/mediacentre/country-rating-poll.pdf.

Goertz, Gary and Paul F. Diehl. 1995. "The Initiation and Termination of Enduring Rivalries: The Impact of Political Shocks." *American Journal of Political Science* 39(1):30.

Gray, Barbara, Peter T. Coleman and Linda L. Putnam. 2007. "Introduction: Intractable Conflict: New Perspectives on the Causes and Conditions for Change." *American Behavioral Scientist* 50(11):1415–1429.

Greenfield, Shivi. 2012. "Israeli Hasbara: Myths and Facts. A Report on the Israeli Hasbara Apparatus 2012." Molad the center for the renewal of Israeli democracy. Report. http://www.molad.org/images/upload/files/49381451033828.pdf.

Gross, James J., Eran Halperin and Roni Porat. 2013. "Emotion regulation in intractable conflicts." *Current Directions in Psychological Science* 22(6):423–429.

Hadjipavlou, M. 2007. "The Cyprus Conflict: Root Causes and Implications for Peace-building." *Journal of Peace Research* 44(3):349–365.

Hahn, Oliver, Julia Loennendonker and Roland Schroeder, eds. 2008. *Deutsche Auslandskorrespondenten: ein Handbuch.* Konstanz: UVk Verlagsgesellschaft.

Hall, Stuart. 1997. *Representation: Cultural Representations and Signifying Practices.* University of Essex: Sage Publications.

Hallin, Daniel. 1986. *The "uncensored war": the media and Vietnam.* New York: Oxford University Press.

Halperin, Eran and Daniel Bar-Tal. 2011. "Socio-psychological barriers to peace making: An empirical examination within the Israeli Jewish Society." *Journal of Peace Research* 48(5):637–651.

Halperin, Eran, Daniel Bar-Tal, Keren Sharvit, Nimrod Rosler and Amiram Raviv. 2010. "Socio-psychological implications for an occupying society: The case of Israel." *Journal of Peace Research* 47(1):59–70.

Halperin, Eran and Ruthie Pliskin. 2015. "Emotions and Emotion Regulation in Intractable Conflict: Studying Emotional Processes Within a Unique Context." *Political Psychology* 36(S1):119–150.

Hameiri, Boaz, Daniel Bar-Tal and Eran Halperin. 2014. "Challenges for Peacemakers: How to Overcome Socio-Psychological Barriers." *Policy Insights from the Behavioral and Brain Sciences* 1(1):164–171.

Hammack, Phillip. 2014. Mind, Story, Society: The Political Psychology of Narrative. In *Warring with Words: Narrative and Metapor in Domestic and International Politics*, ed. Michael Hanne, William D. Crano and Jeffery Scott Mio. New York: Psychology Press pp. 51–77.

Hammack, Phillip and Andrew Pilecki. 2012. "Narrative as a Root Metaphor for Political Psychology." *Political Psychology* 33(1):75–103.

Harpaz, Guy and Asaf Shamis. 2010. "Normative Power Europe and the State of Israel: An Illegitimate EUtopia?" *JCMS: Journal of Common Market Studies* 48(3):579–616.

Herman, Edward and Noam Chomsky. 2002. *Manufacturing Consent : the Political Economy of the Mass Media.* New York: Pantheon Books.

Hershkovitz, S. 2011. "Masbirim Israel: Israel's PR Campaign as Glocalized and Grobalized Political Prosumption." *American Behavioral Scientist* 20(10):1–20.

Hug, Simon and Richard Lukács. 2014. "Preferences or blocs? Voting in the United Nations human rights council." *The Review of International Organizations* 9(1):83–106.

Ibrahim, Dina. 2003. "Individual Perceptions of International Correspondents in the Middle East: An Obstacle to Fair News?" *International Communication Gazette* 65(1):87–101.

International Institute of Humanitarian Law. 1995. *San Remo Manual on International Law Applicable to Armed Conflict at Sea.* Vol. 35 Cambridge ; New York: Cambridge University Press.

Israel Ministry of Foreign Affairs. 2010. "Statement by Prime Minister Netanyahu "No Love Boat".". http://www.mfa.gov.il/MFA/PressRoom/2010/Pages/Statement_PM_Netanyahu_2-Jun-2010.aspx.

It Is Apartheid. 2014. "List of International Law Violations by the State of Israel.". http://itisapartheid.org/Documents_pdf_etc/IsraelViolationsInternationalLaw.pdf.

Jansezian, Nicole. 2011. "Pastors, Hollywood celebrities tour Israel." Jerusalem Post. December 13, http://www.jpost.com/Travel/Travel-News/Pastors-Hollywood-celebrities-tour-Israel.

Joggerst, Karin. 2002. *Getrennte Welten-getrennte Geschichte (n)?: zur politischen Bedeutung von Erinnerungskultur im israelisch-palästinensischen Konflikt.* Vol. 6 of *Schriftenreihe Konfrontation und Kooperation im Vorderen Orient* Münster: Lit.

Johnson, Stephan and Nathan Mack. 2014. "The United Nations Institutions: A Critical Analysis of Their Ability to Promote and Protect International Human Rights." *NUCB journal of language culture and communication* 15(2):5–13.

Jost, John T., Mahzarin R. Banaji and Brian A. Nosek. 2004. "A Decade of System Justification Theory: Accumulated Evidence of Conscious and Unconscious Bolstering of the Status Quo." *Political Psychology* 25(6):881–919.

Kalb, M. and C. Saivetz. 2007. "The Israeli–Hezbollah War of 2006: The Media as a Weapon in Asymmetrical Conflict." *The Harvard International Journal of Press/Politics* 12(3):43–66.

Katz, Alexander. 2011. "Earthquake in the newspaper world - Israel Hayom catched Yediot.". July 28 (in Hebrew).

Keane, David and Valentina Azarov. 2012. "UNESCO, Palestine and Archaeology in Conflict." *Denver Journal of International Law and Policy* 41:309.

Kelman, Herbert. 2007. Social Psychological Dimensions of International Conflict. In *Peacemaking in international conflict: Methods & Techniques*, ed. I.W. Zartman. Washington, DC: U.S. Institute of Peace pp. 61–107.

Kelner, Gil. 2014. "Severe blow to Maariv and Haaretz: they are not anymore part of the three popular newspapers.". April 12.

Kepplinger, Hans Mathias. 2002. "Mediatization of Politics: Theory and Data." *Journal of Communication* 52(4):972–986.

Kershner, Isabel. 2012. "Concentration and Politics Hinder Israel Newspapers." The New York Times. October 4.

Khalidi, Rashid. 2009. *Sowing Crisis: The Cold War and American Hegemony in the Middle East.* Boston: Beacon Press.

Koch, Carmen. 2012. *Religion in den Medien: eine quantitative Inhaltsanalyse von Medien in der Schweiz.* Konstanz: UVK Verlagsgesellschaft.

Kriesberg, Louis. 2001. "Mediation and the Transformation of the Israeli-Palestinian Conflict." *Journal of Peace Research* 38(3):373–392.

Kriesberg, Louis. 2005. Nature, dynamics, and phases of intractability. In *Grasping the Nettle. Analyzing Cases of Intractable Conflict,* ed. Chester A. Crocker, Fen Osler Hampson and Pamela Aall. Washington, DC: United States Institute of Peace Press pp. 65–98.

Landerer, Nino. 2013. "Rethinking the logics: A conceptual framework for the mediatization of politics." *Communication Theory* 23(3):239–258.

Langenbucher, Wolfgang R. and Guni Yasin. 2009. Produziert die Logik des Journalismus Anti-Israelismus? Von den Schwierigkeiten, aus Israel zu berichten. In *Wissenschaft mit Wirkung. BeitrÃ€ge zu Journalismus- und Medienwirkungsforschung,* ed. Christina Holtz-Bacha, Gunter Reus and Lee B. Becker. VS Verlag für Sozialwissenschaften pp. 257–277.

Leo, Rebekah and Sarah Terlizzi. 2014. "The (D)evolution of the Security Council: A Three-Part Case Study on the post-Cold War Use of the Veto." Proceedings of The National Conference On Undergraduate Research (NCUR). University of Kentucky, Lexington. http://www.ncurproceedings.org/ojs/index.php/NCUR2014/article/view/1086/592.

Lieber, Robert J. 1998. "U.S.-Israel Reations Since 1948." *Middle East* 2(3):12.

Liebes, Tamar. 1997. *Reporting the Arab-Israeli conflict : how Hegemony Works.* London; New York: Routledge.

Liebes, Tamar and Zohar Kampf. 2004. The PR of terror: how new-Style Wars Give Voice to Terrorists. In *Reporting War: Journalism in Wartime,* ed. Stuart Allan and Barbie Zelizer. London, New York: Routledge pp. 77–96.

Lipson, Nathan and Mayan Cohen. 2008. "Ynet is the leading Israeli Internet portal." Haaretz. June 23.

Little, Douglas. 2008. *American orientalism: the United States and the Middle East since 1945.* University of North Carolina Press.

Livingston, Steven and W. Lance Bennett. 2003. "Gatekeeping, Indexing, and Live-Event News: Is Technology Altering the Construction of News?" *Political Communication* 20(4):363–380.

Livneh, Neri. 2010. "The new campaign of the Ministry of Information asks us to sell an imaginary Israel to Goys (Hebrew)." Haaretz.

Luhmann, Niklas. 1974. Soziologie des politischen Systems. In *Soziologische Aufklärung. Aufsätze zur Theorie sozialer Systeme.* 4 ed. Opladen: Westdeutscher Verlag pp. 154–177.

Lundby, Knut. 2009. *Mediatization: Concept, Changes, Consequences.* New York: Peter Lang.

Luyendijk, Joris and Anne Fritz Middelhoek. 2014. *Von Bildern und Luegen in Zeiten des Krieges: aus dem Leben eines Kriegsberichterstatters.* Stuttgart: Tropen-Verlag.

MacDonald, David Bruce. 2002. *Balkan holocausts? Serbian and Croatian victim-centred propaganda and the war in Yugoslavia.* New approaches to conflict analysis Manchester, New York: Manchester University Press.

Mack, Andrew. 1975. "Why big nations lose small wars: The politics of asymmetric conflict." *World Politics* 27(02):175–200.

Manheim, Jarol B. 1994. Strategic Public Diplomacy. Managing Kuwait's Image During the Gulf Conflict. Chicago: University of Chicago Press pp. 131–148.

Mansel, Tim (Producer). 2014. "Media and the Middle East [Audio Podcast]." BBC World Service. The Documentary. September 28. http://www.bbc.co.uk/programmes/p0270hwx.

Maoz, Ifat, Andrew Ward, Michael Katz and Lee Ross. 2002. "Reactive devaluation of an 'Israeli' versus 'Palestinian' peace proposal." *Journal of Conflict Resolution* 46(4):515–546.

Maoz, Zeev and Ben. D. Mor. 1996. "Enduring Rivalries: The Early Years." 17(2):141–160.

Maslow, Abraham H. and Robert Frager. 1987. *Motivation and personality.* 3rd ed ed. New York: Harper and Row.

Mauro, Danilo Di. 2011. *The UN and the Arab-Israeli conflict: American hegemony and UN intervention since 1947.* Abingdon, Oxon; New York, NY: Routledge.

Mazmudar, B. Theo. 2012. "Shifting Blame on the High Seas... and on YouTube: The Narrative Failure of Israel's Flotilla Cyber Diplomacy." *Global Media Journal* 11(21).

Mazzoleni, Gianpietro and Winfried Schulz. 1999. "'Mediatization' of Politics: A Challenge for Democracy?" *Political Communication* 16(3):247–261.

McAlister, Alfred L., Albert Bandura and Steven V. Owen. 2006. "Mechanisms of moral disengagement in support of military force: The impact of Sept. 11." *Journal of Social and Clinical Psychology* 25(2):141–165.

Mcclosky, Herbert and John Zaller. 1987. *American ethos: public attitudes toward capitalism & democracy.* Cambridge: Harvard University Press.

McQuail, Denis. 2006. "On the Mediatization of War: A Review Article." *International Communication Gazette* 68(2):107–118.

Mearsheimer, John J. and Stephen M. Walt. 2006. "The Israel Lobby and U.S. Foreign Policy." *Middle East Policy* 13(3):29–87.

Medjedovic, Janko and Boban Petrovic. 2013. "Predictors of party evaluation in post-conflict society: The case of Serbia." *Psihologija* 46(1):27–43.

Merom, Gil. 1999. "Israel's National Security and the Myth of Exceptionalism." *Political Science Quarterly* 114(3):409–434.

Merten, Klaus. 1983. *Inhaltsanalyse : Einführung in Theorie, Methode und Praxis.* Opladen: Westdeutscher Verlag.

Meyers, Oren and Jonathan Cohen. 2011. "A Self-portrait of Israeli Journalists: Characteristics, Values, and Attitudes." Maryland University. The Joseph and Alma Gildenhorn Institute for Israel Studies. Research Paper.

Migdalovitz, Carol. 2010. *Israel's Blockade of Gaza, the Mavi Marmara Incident, and Its Aftermath.* CRS Report for Congress Washington, DC: Congressional Research Service.

Ministry of Foreign Affairs. 2010*a*. "Documents and Materials of the Russian MFA .". http://www.mid.ru/bdomp/brp_4.nsf/english!OpenView&Start=5.779& Count=30&Expand=5#5.

Ministry of Foreign Affairs. 2010*b*. "MFA of Russia. Incident with "Humanitarian Convoy" for Gaza.". May 31. http://www.mid.ru/Brp_4.nsf/arh/D383242A209FAA29C325773500293C15?

Mitchell, C. R. 1991. "Classifying Conflicts: Asymmetry and Resolution." *The ANNALS of the American Academy of Political and Social Science* 518(1):23–38.

Mor, Ben D. 2006. "Public Diplomacy in Grand Strategy." *Foreign Policy Analysis* 2(2):157–176.

Mueller, Margret. 2009. "Das Deutschlandbild israelischer Deutschlerner." TU Dresden. Master thesis.

Nasie, Meytal and Daniel Bar-Tal. 2012. "Sociopsychological infrastructure of an intractable conflict through the eyes of palestinian children and adolescents." *Peace and Conflict: Journal of Peace Psychology* 18(1):3–20.

Neiger, Motti, Eyal Zandberg and Oren Meyers. 2008. *The Rhetoric of Criticism: Challenging Criticism, Reaffirming Criticism, and Israeli Journalism during the Second Lebanon War.* The Media in the Lebanon War Series Tel Aviv: The Rothschild Caesarea School of Communication.

Nossek, Hillel. 2009. "On the future of journalism as a professional practice and the case of journalism in Israel." *Journalism* 10(3):358–361.

Nye, J. S. 2008. "Public Diplomacy and Soft Power." *The ANNALS of the American Academy of Political and Social Science* 616(1):94–109.

OCHA. 2010. "The Humanitarian Monitor April 2010." The Humanitarian Bulletin (Monthly). April. http://www.ochaopt.org/documents/ocha_opt_the_humanitarian_monitor_ 2010_04_english.pdf.

O'Donnell, Clara Marina. 2008. "The EU, Israel and Hamas." Centre for European Reform. Working Paper.

Oehmer, Franziska. 2010. "Aggressor or victim? Hew the antagonists of the Lebanon War 2006 are constructed in the German newspapers." *conflict & communication online* 9(1).

Ofer, Dalia. 2000. "The strength of remembrance: Commemorating the holocaust during the first decade of Israel." *Jewish Social Studies* 6(2):24–55.

Ofer, Dalia. 2009. "The past that does not pass: Israelis and Holocaust memory." *Israel Studies* 14(1):1–35.
URL: *http://muse.jhu.edu/journals/is/summary/v014/14.1.ofer.html*

Office of the Quartet Representative. 2010. "Latest News | Office of the Quartet Representative." Statements by the office of the Quartet Representative. http://www.tonyblairoffice.org/quartet/news/P110/.

Olmert, Ehud. 2009. "PM Olmert's Statement after the Cabinet Meeting." The Prime Minister's Office. Archive. January 17, http://www.pmo.gov.il/English/MediaCenter/Speeches/Pages/ speechcabinet170109.aspx.

Oren, Neta. 2009. "The Israeli Ethos of Conflict 1967-2006." *Institute for Conflict Analysis and Resolution* 27:1–26.

Oren, Neta and Daniel Bar-Tal. 2006. "Ethos and identity: Expressions and changes in the Israeli Jewish society Ethos e identidad: expresiones y cambio en la sociedad judía israelí." *Estudios de Psicología* 27(3):293–316.

Oren, Neta, Daniel Bar-Tal and Ohad David. 2004. Conflict, Identity and Ethos: The Israeli-Palestinian Case. In *The Psychology of Ethnic and Cultural Conflict (Psychological Dimensions to War and Peace)*, ed. Yueh-Ting Lee, Clark McCauley, Fathali M. Moghaddam and Stephen Worchel. Greenwood Publishing Group pp. 133–154.

Oren, Neta, Rafi Nets-Zehngut and Daniel Bar-Tal. 2015. "Construction of the Israeli-Jewish Conflict-Supportive Narrative and the Struggle Over Its Dominance." *Political Psychology* 36(2):215–230.

Orgad, Shani. 2009. "Watching How Others Watch Us: The Israeli Media's Treatment of International Coverage of the Gaza War." *The Communication Review* 12:250–261.

Orgad, Shani. 2011. "Proper Distance from Ourselves: The potential for Estrangement in the Mediapolis." *International Journal of Cultural Studies* 14(4):401–421.

Orgad, Shani. 2012. *Media Representation and the Global Imagination.* Global media and communication Cambridge; Malden, MA: Polity Press.

Palmer, Sir Geoffrey, Alvaro Uribe, Joseph Ciechanover Itzhar and Süleyman Özdem Sanberk. 2011. "Report of the Secretary-General's Panel of Inquiry on the 31 May 2010 Flotilla Incident." United Nations Report. http://www.un.org/News/dh/infocus/middle_east/Gaza_Flotilla_ Panel_Report.pdf.

Papadakis, Yiannis. 1998. "Greek Cypriot Narratives of History and Collective Identity: Nationalism as a Contested Process." *American Ethnologist* 25(2):149–165.

Papadakis, Yiannis. 2008. "Narrative, Memory and History Education in Divided Cyprus: A Comparison of Schoolbooks on the 'History of Cyprus'." *History & Memory* 20(2):128–148.

Pardo, Sharon. 2009. "Going West: Guidelines for Israel's Integration into the European Union." *Israel Journal of Foreign Affairs* 3(2):51–62.

Pardo, Sharon and Joel Peters. 2010. *Uneasy neighbors: Israel and the European Union.* Lanham, Md: Lexington Books.

Peleg, Anat and Bryna Bogoch. 2014. "Mediatization, Legal Logic and the Coverage of Israeli Politicians on Trial." *Journalism Practice* 8(3):311–325.

Peri, Yoram, Gadi Baltiansky, Akiva Eldar and Ben Caspit. 2005. 'No One to Talk To' A Critical Look at the Linkage Between Politics and the Media. Tel Aviv University: The Herzog Institute for Media, Politics and Society.

Pfeffer, Anshel. 2012. "Israel is more focused on 'hasbara' than it is on policy." Haaretz. March 2.

Pfetsch, Barbara and Eva Mayerhöffer. 2006. "Politische Kommunikation in der modernen Demokratie." *Öffentlichkeit & Politische Kommunikation* 1:1–36.

Pfetsch, Barbara and Silke Adam. 2008. Die Akteursperspektive in der politischen Kommunikationsforschung. Fragestellungen, Forschungsparadigmen und Problemlagen. In *Massenmedien als politische Akteure. Konzepte und Analysen,* ed. Barbara Pfetsch and Silke Adam. Wiesbaden: VS Verlag für Sozialwissenschaften pp. 9–26.

Philo, Greg and Mike Berry. 2004. *Bad news from Israel.* London: Pluto Press.

Philo, Greg and Mike Berry. 2011. *More bad news from Israel.* London: Pluto Press.

Podeh, Elie. 2002. *The Arab-Israeli conflict in Israeli history textbooks, 1948-2000.* Westport, CT: Bergin & Garvey.

Porat, Dina. 2008. *Israeli society, the Holocaust and its survivors.* London ; Portland, OR: Vallentine Mitchell.

Porat, Roni, Eran Halperin and Daniel Bar-Tal. 2015. "The Effect of Sociopsychological Barriers on the Processing of New Information about Peace Opportunities." *Journal of Conflict Resolution* 59(1):93–119.

Rada, Moran. 2008. "Netanyahu paid, what do you want from him?" The Seventh Eye. 9 July (in Hebrew). http://www.the7eye.org.il/26965.

Ravid, Barak. 2010. "The Ministry of Foreign Affairs will use Straw Companies for Hasbara Purposes." Haaretz.

Richardson, John E. and Leon Barkho. 2009. "Reporting Israel/Palestine: Ethnographic insights into the verbal and visual rhetoric of BBC journalism." *Journalism Studies* 10(5):594–622.

Rinnawi, Khalil. 2007. "De-legitimization of Media Mechanisms: Israeli Press Coverage of the Al Aqsa Intifada." *International Communication Gazette* 69(2):149–178.

Roberts, Adam. 2015. "Terrorism Research:Past, Present, and Future." *Studies in Conflict & Terrorism* 38(1):62–74.

Robinson, Piers. 2001. "Theorizing the Influence of Media on World Politics Models of Media Influence on Foreign Policy." *European Journal of Communication* 16(4):523–544.

Robinson, Piers. 2004. Researching US Media-State Relations and Twenty-First Century Wars. Taylor & Francis pp. 96–112.

Rosner, Shmuel. 2014. "Israel and a Hostile World." New York Times. October 8.

Rössler, Patrick. 2005. *Inhaltsanalyse*. Stuttgart: UVK-Verlagsgesellschaft.

Ruby, Charles L. 2002. "The Definition of Terrorism." *Analyses of Social Issues and Public Policy* 2:9–14.

Rudoren, Jodi. 2014. "In Gaza, Epithets Are Fired and Euphemisms Give Shelter." The New York Times. July 20.

Saad, Lydia. 2015. "Seven in 10 Americans Continue to View Israel Favorably." Gallup Poll Social Series. February. http://www.gallup.com/poll/181652/seven-americans-continue-view-israel-favorably.aspx.

Sacharoff, Justin. 2011. "'Love' for Israel winning Twitter war." The Jerusalem Post. May 12.

Sarcinelli, Ulrich. 1991. "Massenmedien und Politikvermittlung - eine Problem- und Forschungsskizze." *Rundfunk und Fernsehen* 39:469–486.

Schaeffer, Emily, Jeff Halper and Itay Epshtain. 2012. "Israel's Policy of Demolishing Palestinian Homes must end: A Submission to the UN Human Rights ." Council by the Israeli Committee Against House Demolitions ICAHD. Report. http://www.icahd.org/node/458.

Schori-Eyal, Noa, Eran Halperin and Daniel Bar-Tal. 2014. "Three layers of collective victimhood: effects of multileveled victimhood on intergroup conflicts in the Israeli-Arab context: Three layers of collective victimhood." *Journal of Applied Social Psychology* 44:778–794.

Schulz, Winfried. 1976. *Die Konstruktion von Realität in den Nachrichtenmedien. Analyse der aktuellen Berichterstattung*. Alber-Borschur Kommunikation 1 ed. Muenchen: Alber.

Schulz, Winfried. 2008. *Politische Kommunikation theoretische Ansätze und Ergebnisse empirischer Forschung*. 2. ed. Wiesbaden: VS Verlag für Sozialwissenschaften.

Security Council of the United Nations. 1967. "Resolution 242.".

Segev, Elad. 2010. "Mapping the International: Global and Local Salience and News-Links Between Countries in Popular Nesw Sites Worldwide." *International Journal of Interne Science* 5(1):48–71.

Segev, Elad and Menahem Blondheim. 2013. "Online News About Israel and Palestine." *Digital Journalism* 1(3):386–398.

Segev, Elad and Regula Miesch. 2011. "A Systematic Procedure for Detecting News Biases: The Case of Israel in European News Sites." *International Journal of Communication* 5(0):20.

Segev, Tom. 1993. *The Seventh Million: The Israelis and the Holocaust.* New York: Henry Holt.

Shamir, Jacob and Khalil Shikaki. 2006. "Joint Palestinian-Israeli Public Opinion Poll." Harry S. Truman Research Institute for the Advancement of Peace; Center for Policy and Survey Research. http://truman.huji.ac.il/.upload/Polls 2006 2007.pdf.

Sharon, Assaf, Shivi Greenfield, Mikhael Manekin, Oded Naaman, Jesse Rothman and Dahlia Shaham. 2013. "Alliance in Crisis: Israel's Standing in the World and the Question of Isolation." Molad the center for the renewal of Israeli democracy. Jerusalem.

Sharp, Jeremy M. 2009. "US foreign aid to Israel." Congressional Research Service. CRS Report for Congress. DIANE Publishing.

Sharvit, Keren and Daniel Bar-Tal. 2007. Ethos of Conflict in the Israeli Media during the Period of the Violent Confrontation. In *The Israeli-Palestinian Conflict: From Conflict Resolution to Conflict Management,* ed. Yaacov Bar-Siman-Tov. New York: Palgrave Macmillan pp. 203–232.

Sheafer, Tamir and Itay Gabay. 2009. "Mediated Public Diplomacy: A Strategic Contest over International Agenda Building and Frame Building." *Political Communication* 26(4):447–467.

Sheafer, Tamir, Shaul R. Shenhav, Janet Takens and Wouter van Atteveldt. 2014. "Relative Political and Value Proximity in Mediated Public Diplomacy: The Effect of State-Level Homophily on International Frame Building." *Political Communication* 31(1):149–167.

Sheafer, Tamir and Shaul Shenhav. 2009. "Mediated Public Diplomacy in a New Era of Warfare." *The Communication Review* 12:272–283.

Sheffer, Bridget Reynolds. 2014. "Mediated Public Diplomacy and Political Dialectics: 2010 Free Gaza Flotilla." *Journal of Intercultural Communication Research* 43(2):134–150.

Shefler, Gil. 2012. "Edelstein: Israel-Diaspora dynamic a two-way street." The Jerusalem Post. January 17.

Sheizaf, Noam. 2010. "The political line of Israeli papers (a reader's guide)." +972 Magazine. October 26.

Sheizaf, Noam. 2012. "Maariv daily paper purchased by ultra-rightist publisher." +972 Magazine. September 7.

Shenhav, Shaul, Tamir Sheafer and Itay Gabay. 2010. "Incoherent Narrator: Israeli Public Diplomacy During the Disengagement and the Elections in the Palestinian Authority." *Israel Studies* 15(3):143–162.

Sherman, Martin. 2012. "Into the Fray: a Study in Impotence." The Jerusalem Post. January 27.

Shinar, Dov. 2005. Constructing Collective Identities and Democratic Media in a Globalizing World: Israel as a Test Case. In *Democratizing Global Media. One World, many Struggles*, ed. Robert A. Hackett and Yuezhi Zhao. Lanham, Md: Rowman & Littlefield pp. 165–183.

Shoemaker, Pamela J. and Stephen D. Reese. 1996. *Mediating the message: theories of influences on mass media content.* 2nd ed. White Plains, N.Y: Longman.

Slocum-Bradley, Nikki R. 2008. Discursive Production of Conflict in Rwanda. In *Global Conflict Resolution Through Positioning Analysis*, ed. Fathali M. Moghaddam, Rom Harré and Naomi Lee. Peace Psychology Book Series Springer New York pp. 207–226.

Smith, Charles D. 2001. *Palestine and the Arab-Israeli conflict.* 4th ed. Boston: Bedford St. Martin's.

Smooha, Sammy. 2008. "The mass immigrations to Israel: A comparison of the failure of the Mizrahi immigrants of the 1950s with the success of the Russian immigrants of the 1990s." *Journal of Israeli History* 27(1):1–27.

Sofer, Ronny. 2006. "Hamas sworn in - Israel to cut off funds." Ynet News. February 2.

Sofer, Sasson. 2004. "Towards distant frontiers: the course of Israeli diplomacy." *Israel Affairs* 10(1-2):1–9.

Sørensen, Majken Jul and Brian Martin. 2014. "The Dilemma Action: Analysis of an Activist Technique." *Peace & Change* 39(1):73–100.

Spelman, Elizabeth. 2013. "The Legality of the Israeli Naval Blockade of the Gaza Strip." *Web Journal of Current Legal Issues* 19(1).

Spiegel, Steven L. 2014. *The Other Arab-Israeli Conflict: Making America's Middle East Policy, from Truman to Reagan.* University of Chicago Press.

Staub, Erwin and Daniel Bar-Tal. 2003. Genocide, mass killing and intractable conflict: Roots, evolution, prevention and reconciliation. In *Oxford Handbook of Political Psychology*, ed. David Sears, Leonie Huddy and Robert Jervis Adlai. Oxford: Oxford University Press pp. 710–751.

Strand, Trude. 2015. ""Meeting with a Dietician": Israel's Institutionalized Impoverishment of Gaza." *Theory & Event* 18.

Straughen, Harriet. 2011. "Image is everything: The importance of public diplomacy in the Israeli-Palestinian conflict." *MIFTAH Special Studies* .

Strömbäck, Jesper and Daniela V. Dimitrova. 2011. "Mediatization and Media Interventionism: A Comparative Analysis of Sweden and the United States." *The International Journal of Press/Politics* 16(1):30–49.

Teitelbaum, Joshua and Michael Segall. 2012. "The Iranian Leadership's Continuing Declarations of Intent to Destroy Israel.". Report. http://www.phibetaiota.net/wp-content/uploads/2012/06/Israeli-Compilation-of-Iranian-Declarations-Against-Israel.pdf.

Tenenboim-Weinblatt, K. 2014. "Producing Protest News: An Inquiry into Journalist-sŃarratives." *The International Journal of Press/Politics* 19(4):410–429.

The Telegraph. 2010. "Gaza aid flotilla attack: David Cameron calls Israel's assault 'unacceptable'." The Telegraph.

The White House. 2010. "Readout of the President's Call with Prime Minister Netanyahu of Israel.". http://www.whitehouse.gov/the-press-office/readout-presidents-call-with-prime-minister-netanyahu-israel.

Thiel, Thorsten. 2006. "Von der Staatsgründung zu den 'neuen Historikern'." *hamburg review of social sciences* 1(1):64–104.

Tint, Barbara. 2010. "History, memory, and intractable conflict." *Conflict Resolution Quarterly* 27(3):239–256.

Triandis, Harry C. 1996. "The psychological measurement of cultural syndromes." *American Psychologist* 51(4):407–415.

Turkish National Commission of Inquiry. 2011. "Report on The Israeli Attack on the Humanitarian Aid Convoy to Gaza on 31 May 2010.".

Uluğ, Melis and Christopher Cohrs. 2014. "Laypeople's Representations of the Kurdish Conflict." *Manuscript submitted for publication* .

Ulutaş, Ufuk. 2010*a*. "Turkey and Israel in the Aftermath of the Flotilla Crisis." *SETA Policy Brief* 43.

Ulutaş, Ufuk. 2010*b*. "Turkey-Israel: A fluctuating alliance." *SETA Policy Brief* 42.

UN Watch. 2013. "2013 at the UN: 21 resolutions against Israel, 4 on rest of the world, a View from Geneva.". http://blog.unwatch.org/index.php/2013/11/25/this-years-22-unga-resolutions-against-israel-4-on-rest-of-world/.

United Nations Security Council. 2010. "Statement by the President of the Security Council.". June 1. http://www.un.org/en/ga/search/view_doc.asp?symbol=S/PRST/2010/9.

VAP. 2014. "Herzlich willkommen beim Verein der ausländischen Presse.". www.vap-berlin.de.

Video, CNN. 2010. "U.S. condemns Israeli flotilla raid - Statement Hillary Clinton.". May 31. http://www.cnn.com/video/ http://edition.cnn.com/video/data/2.0/video/politics/2010/06/01/bts.clinton.israel.gaza.flotilla.cnn.html.

Volkan, Vamik D. 1999. "Psychoanalysis and Diplomacy: Part I. Individual and Large Group Identity." *Journal of Applied Psychoanalytic Studies* 1(1):29–55.

Vowe, Gerhard. 2006. "Mediatisierung der Politik?" *Publizistik* 51(4):437–455.

Waxman, Dov. 2012. "The Real Problem in U.S.-Israeli Relations." *The Washington Quarterly* 35(2):71–87.

Bibliography

Werder, Olaf and Guy Golan. 2002. "Sharon wins: News coverage and framing of the 2001 Israeli Prime Minister election in ten Western print media." *Global Media Journal* 1(1).

Witzthum, David. 2002. The Israeli-Palestinian Conflict: The Role of the Media. Bonn: .

Wolfsfeld, Gadi. 1997. *Media and Political Conflict: News from the Middle East*. Cambridge; New York: Cambridge University Press.

Wolfsfeld, Gadi. 2001. "The News Media and the Second Intifada: Some Initial Lessons." *The Harvard International Journal of Press/Politics* 6(4):113–118.

Wolfsfeld, Gadi. 2003. "The News Media and the Second Intifada." *Palestine-Israel Journal of Politics, Economics and Culture* 10(2).

Wolfsfeld, Gadi. 2004. *Media and the Path to Peace*. Communication, society, and politics Cambridge; New York: Cambridge University Press.

Wolfsfeld, Gadi, Eli Avraham and Issam Aburaiya. 2000. "When Prophesy Always Fails: Israeli Press Coverage of the Arab Minority's Land Day Protests." *Political Communication* 17:115–131.

Wolfsfeld, Gadi, Paul Frosh and Maurice T. Awabdy. 2008. "Covering Death in Conflicts: Coverage of the Second Intifada on Israeli and Palestinian Television." *Journal of Peace Research* 45(3):401–417.

Wolfsfeld, Gadi and Tamir Sheafer. 2006. "Competing Actors and the Construction of Political News: The Contest Over Waves in Israel." *Political Communication* 23(3):333–354.

Yaar, Ephraim and Tamar Hermann. 2000. "Peace Index November." The Tami Steinmetz Center for Peace Research. http://www.peaceindex.org/files/peaceindex2000_11_3.pdf.

Yaar, Ephraim and Tamar Hermann. 2007. "Peace Index October." The Tami Steinmetz Center for Peace Research. http://www.peaceindex.org/files/peaceindex2007_10_3.pdf.

Yaar, Ephraim and Tamar Hermann. 2008a. "Peace Index March." The Tami Steinmetz Center for Peace Research. http://www.peaceindex.org/files/peaceindex2008_3_3.pdf.

Yaar, Ephraim and Tamar Hermann. 2008b. "War and Peace Index November." The Tami Steinmetz Center for Peace Research. http://www.peaceindex.org/files/peaceindex2008_11_3.pdf.

Yaar, Ephraim and Tamar Hermann. 2009a. "War and Peace Index April." The Tami Steinmetz Center for Peace Research. http://www.peaceindex.org/files/peaceindex2009_4_3.pdf.

Yaar, Ephraim and Tamar Hermann. 2009b. "War and Peace Index June." The Tami Steinmetz Center for Peace Research. http://www.peaceindex.org/files/peaceindex2009_6_3.pdf.

Yaar, Ephraim and Tamar Hermann. 2010a. "Peace Index August." The Israel Democracy Institute. http://www.peaceindex.org/files/Peace Index-August-trans.pdf.

Yaar, Ephraim and Tamar Hermann. 2010*b*. "Peace Index December." The Israel Democracy Institute. http://www.peaceindex.org/files/Peace Index-December-trans(1).pdf.

Zelizer, Barbie, David Park and David Gudelunas. 2002. "How bias shapes the news: Challenging The New York Times' status as a newspaper of record on the Middle East." *Journalism* 3(3):283–307.

Zertal, Idith and M Lemke. 2001. *Nation und Tod. Der Holocaust in der israelischen Öffentlichkeit.* Göttingen: Wallstein Verlag.

Zuckermann, Moshe. 1998. *Zweierlei Holocaust: der Holocaust in den politischen Kulturen Israels und Deutschlands.* Göttingen: Wallstein.

Zuckermann, Moshe. 2009. *Sechzig Jahre Israel: die Genesis einer politischen Krise des Zionismus.* Bonn: Pahl-Rugenstein.

Zuckermann, Moshe. 2010. *"Antisemit!": ein Vorwurf als Herrschaftsinstrument.* Wien: Promedia.

Zuckermann, Moshe. 2012. *Wider den Zeitgeist. Aufsaetze und Gespraeche ueber Juden, Deutsche, den Nahostkonflikt und Antisemitismus.* Vol. 1 Hamburg: Laika-Verl.

A Tables

Table 23 – Actors' Appearance in Analyzed Periods

	Routine A	Crisis	Routine B	Total
Europe	17	17	23	57
United Nations	10	6	6	22
USA	66	45	40	151
Turkey	3	43	17	63
Gaza flotilla participants	6	54	–	60
Unspecified Western actors	7	33	7	47
Total	109	198	93	N=400

$\chi^2(10, N = 400) = 109,368, p = .000$

Table 24 – Framing of Actors (in Percent)

Framing		Europe (n=57)	UN (n=22)	USA (n=151)	Turkey (n=63)	GFP (n=60)	Unsp. (n=47)
Actor positive[1]	yes	23	14	**49**	17	13	28
	no	77	86	51	83	87	72
Actor neutral[2]	yes	7	14	11	3	**18**	4
	no	93	86	89	97	82	96
Actor negative[3]	yes	40	68	32	60	**75**	55
	no	60	32	68	40	25	48

[1] is $\chi^2(5, N = 400) = 42,514, p = .000$
[2] is $\chi^2(5, N = 400) = 10,938, p = .053$
[3] is $\chi^2(5, N = 400) = 41,706, p = .000$

Table 25 – Framing of the Relationship to the Actors (in Percent)

		Europe (n=57)	UN (n=22)	USA (n=151)	Turkey (n=63)	GFP (n=60)	Unsp. (n=47)
Relationship positive[1]	yes	23	4	**54**	22	–	–
	no	77	96	46	78	100	100
Relationship neutral[2]	yes	4	5	4	–	–	–
	no	96	95	96	100	100	100
Relationship negative[3]	yes	28	31	17	**63**	12	23
	no	72	68	83	37	88	77

[1] is $\chi^2(5, N = 400) = 100,227, p = .000$
[2] is $\chi^2(5, N = 400) = 6,890, p = .229$
[3] is $\chi^2(5, N = 400) = 57,980, p = .000$

Table 26 – The Actors' Involvement (In Percent)

	Europe (n=57)	UN (n=22)	USA (n=151)	Turkey (n=63)	GFP (n=60)	Unspecified (n=47)
Criticism	**60**	**59**	14	**64**	**75**	**64**
Call for action	14	32	**40**	10	3	21
Support	16	–	31	6	–	9
No message	11	9	16	21	22	6
Total	101[1]	100	101[1]	101[1]	100	100

$\chi^2(15, N = 400) = 136.922, p = .000$ [1] rounding error

Table 27 – Framing of the Claim (in Percent)

		Criticism (n=183)	Call for action (n=93)	Support (n=63)	No message (n=61)
Claim positive[1]	Yes	9	30	**63**	2
	No	91	70	37	98
Claim neutral[2]	Yes	10	**35**	19	2
	No	90	65	81	98
Claim negative[3]	Yes	30	**47**	6	5
	No	70	53	94	95

[1] is $\chi^2(5, N400) = 100.326, p = .000$;
[2] is $\chi^2(5, N400) = 3.100, p = .000$;
[3] is $\chi^2(5, N400) = 49.589, p = .000$

B Abstract

Since its outbreak, the Israeli-Palestinian conflict has been shaped by international involvement. These external engagements in the conflict are primarily transmitted to Jewish Israelis through the Israeli mass media. These media portrayals shape not only perceptions of the "global" attitudes towards the conflict, but in so doing they also influence and legitimize domestic political debates and decisions. It is argued that these media representations are categorizing and polarizing international actors and thereby creating dichotomies according to their alleged position towards Israel.

This research is guided by the question how Israeli newspapers represent international involvement in the Israeli-Palestinian conflict. 1) How is the involvement contextualized and how qualified? 2) Do societal constructs and beliefs shape the media representations and if so, in which manner? 3) Do media representations differ in times of crisis and routine? These questions were explored in a content analysis of the four general daily Israeli newspapers. The Gaza flotilla raid in May, 2010 was chosen for the case study of crisis coverage and was compared to one month of routine before and after the crisis respectively.

Intractable conflicts have a strong impact on the societies entangled in them. On a socio-psychological level, societies adapt by forming beliefs about themselves, the conflict reality and the opponent. They comprise the ethos of conflict and serve as bases for narratives that contextualize events of the past and present.. Narratives can be identified in media representations through frames, i.e. perspectives taken on a certain aspect that shape the contextualization of international involvement.

The findings suggest that the representations vary according to the perceived relationship with the international actors. The USA stands out from European actors and the United Nations, which are represented in an ambivalent manner, and from other actors classified as opponents. In the reality mediated by Israeli newspapers, all international actors – with the exception of the United States – predominantly involve themselves critically in Israeli policies. While criticism is contextualized by delegitimizing the actors involved, supportive involvement is represented as a reassurance of current Israeli policies. In contrast, calls for concrete actions are debated and represented in a balanced manner. The representations are permeated by core beliefs of the ethos of conflict, particularly beliefs about the justness of one's own goals, delegitimization, victimization, and security. These are found in several conflict-supportive narratives that dominate the representations, especially in times of crisis and in articles reporting critical involvement. The representations in the Israeli newspapers Maariv, Yediot Aheronot and Israel Hayom are largely congruent, whereas Haaretz differs from them in various variables. This indicates a lack of diversity in the newspaper landscape. The findings support the assumed polarization of international actors and their involvement, particularly in crisis periods. They further indicate advisable forms of involvement in a conflict society and show that core societal conflict beliefs are crucial in the perception and representation of international involvement.

Der israelisch-palästinensische Konflikt ist seit seinem Ausbruch stark von externer Einmischung geprägt. Dieses internationale Engagement wird jüdischen Israelis vor allem durch israelische Medien vermittelt. Dadurch werden nicht nur Wahrnehmungen zu Einstellungen der „Welt" zum Konflikt geprägt, sondern auch innenpolitische Debatten und Entscheidungen beeinflusst oder legitimiert. Daher wird angenommen, dass die medialen Darstellungen internationale Akteure entsprechend des wahrgenommenen Standpunktes zu Israel dichotom kategorisieren und polarisieren.

Die Dissertation wird von der Frage geleitet, wie israelische Medien internationale Einmischungen in den israelisch-palästinensischen Konflikt repräsentieren. 1) In welche Kontexte werden diese gesetzt und wie werden sie bewertet? 2) Bedienen sich die medialen Repräsentationen gesellschaftlicher Konstrukte und Überzeugungen? Inwiefern? 3) Unterscheidet sich die Berichterstattung internationaler Meinungen in Phasen der Routine und Zeiten der Krise? Diesen Fragen wurde in einer Inhaltsanalyse der vier allgemeinen israelischen Tageszeitungen nachgegangen. Die Krisenphase um den Ship-to-Gaza-Zwischenfall im Jahr 2010 wurde als Fallbeispiel ausgewählt und mit je einem Monat relativer Routine vor und nach der Krise verglichen.

Andauernde Konflikte haben starke Auswirkungen auf die in ihnen verstrickten Gesellschaften. Auf der sozialpsychologischen Ebene passen sich Gruppen in Überzeugungen über ihr Selbst, die Konflikt-Realität und den Gegner an. Diese umfassen den *ethos of conflict* und bilden die Basis für Narrative, die Ereignisse der Gegenwart und Vergangenheit einordnen. Narrative finden sich in medialen Darstellungen in *frames*, den Perspektiven, die zu einem Thema gewählt werden und die Kontextualisierungen internationaler Einmischungen prägen.

Die Ergebnisse legen nahe, dass die Darstellungen je nach Wahrnehmung der Beziehungen zu den internationalen Akteuren variieren. Die USA heben sich von europäischen Akteuren und den Vereinten Nationen ab, deren Einordnung ambivalent bleibt, und von anderen Akteuren, die als Gegner eingeordnet werden. In der medialisierten Realität israelischer Zeitungen erscheinen alle internationalen Akteure außer den USA hauptsächlich als Kritiker israelischer Politiken. Diese Kritiken werden oftmals durch Delegitimisierung der Akteure selbst eingeordnet. Unterstützende Einmischungen hingegen werden als Versicherung der eigenen Politik dargestellt. Im Kontrast dazu werden Aufrufe zu konkreten Aktionen debattiert und ausgewogen dargestellt. Die Darstellungen sind durchdrungen von den zentralen Überzeugungen des ethos of conflict, vor allem derer zur Gerechtigkeit eigener Ziele, zur Delegitimisierung des Gegners, Viktimisierung und Sicherheit. Sie finden sich in konflikt-stützenden Narrativen, die vor allem im Krisenzeitraum und in Artikeln mit kritischer Einmischung präsent sind. Die Darstellungen der drei Zeitungen Maariv, Yediot Aheronot und Israel Hayom ähneln sich stark, während Haaretz sich in mehreren Variablen unterscheidet. Dies deutet auf eine mangelnde Vielfalt in der Zeitungslandschaft hin. Die Ergebnisse stützen die angenommenen Polarisierungen internationaler Akteure und ihrer

B Abstract

Einmischungen, vor allem in Krisenzeiträumen. Zudem deuten sie an, welche Formen des Engagements empfehlenswert sind und zeigen, dass die zentralen gesellschaftlichen Konfliktüberzeugungen wesentlich in der Wahrnehmung und Darstellung internationaler Einmischungen sind.

C The Codebook

See next page

Coding Scheme August 12, 2013

Instructions

1. **Read the article**
2. **Check if the article is relevant**
   - Is the article referring to an international actor? (United States, United Nations, Russia, Europe/an Union, Turkey, Gaza Flotilla Members)
   - Is the actor addressing an issue of the Israeli-Palestinian conflict OR Israeli Policies? OR is the article discussing the relationship between the actor and Israel?
   - Is this actor named in the headlines OR subtitle OR first subsection of the article?
   →If you cannot answer these questions with yes, please consult me.
3. **Answer the following questions. And note the answers with the number of the question.**
4. **If you have any question or are not sure how to answer the questions below, please contact me before you continue coding. Thank you very much for your help**

Nr.	Category	Code	Explanation
01	ID of the Article	[File name]	(NP_YYYY_MM_DD_PAG/a,b)
02	Coder	[your Name] 01 Margret 02	
03	Period	□ 01 Period A □ 02 Period BA □ 03 Period BB □ 04 Period C	15.04.2010 – 14.05.2010 15.05.2010 – 30.05.2010 31.05.2010 – 14.06.2010 15.06.2010 – 14.07.2010
03b	Month	[Number]	04 OR05 OR 06 OR 07
03c	Day	[Number]	01 to 31
04	Newspaper	□ 01 Haaretz □ 02 Israel Hayom □ 03 Yediot Aheronot □ 04 Maariv	

05	Page	[Number]	01 to 50
05b	**Words** [Number]		*articles in Haaretz and Yediot Aheronot – count with Word* *articles in Israel Hayom or printed – count the average word in line – and then the lines – use the approximate result*
06	**Article Format** *What is the genre of the article?* *NOTE: only one answer can be given* □ 01 News article, analysis □ 02 Comment, Opinion □ 03 Editorial	The item presents an event and answers the W-Questions (What? When? Who? Where? How? Why?) The article is mainly informing. The author presents his/her opinion on a certain event or process. The editors write about trends, developments and represent thereby the line of the paper.	
07	**Main Actor in the article** *Main actor is the international actor given the greatest coverage in the article according to the volume of space and order of their presentation. If this is still* *unclear choose the actor mentioned more clearly in the headline or first subsection.* □ 01 European Union/Europe □ 02 Russia □ 03 Turkey □ 04 United Nations □ 05 United States □ 06 Unspecified □ 07 Middle East Quartet □ 08 None of the above	□ [Country] Code the country in next section (Country) Includes all the bodies of the UN includes actor is "the World" OR an unspecified group of countries, OR for example Gaza flotilla members without clear description of origin in this case, please consult me	
07b	**Country (if coded Europe/United Nations OR Unspecified in section above)** □ [Name]	Europe: Country or European Union Unspecified: World OR various countries UN: institution within the UN	

07c	**What is the institution of the actor?**	
	□ 01 President and Administration	Includes heads of the respective government or institution/organization, Ministers, Heads of Defense, Security, Army AND whenever only the country is named ("Turkey did x and y")
	□ 02 Elites of Governments Coalition	Members of Coalition/Parliament of the governing parties, experts and foreign officials (f.ex.Embassadors) and staff of the ministries (except Ministers →01)
	□ 03 Member of the Opposition	Includes members of the opposing parties
	□ 04 Media	Includes TV, Radio, Newspaper and Online-Magazines
	□ 05 NGO	Includes all the organization funded independently from the state
	□ 06 Unclassified individuals	Individuals that are not grouped to any of the above, may include: demonstrators, musicians, all citizen not affiliated with any institution
	□ 07 not specified	
08	**Is the main actor member of a flotilla bound to Gaza?** *If the articles main international actors are Gaza flotilla members choose "yes" and choose the actors main origin in question 7 as presented in the article* "Activists from several European Countries" →Europe // "The Turkish flotilla" →Turkey// "The flotilla members" [no origin mentioned] →Unspecified	□ 01 Yes □ 02 No
09	**Is the actor quoted?**	□ 01 Yes □ 02 No
10	**What is the main topic/event of the item?** *Please choose one of the four categories.*	
	□ 01 Gaza Flotilla	Includes intentions, expectations, preparations events, outcomes, aftermath of the raid
	□ 02 Israeli-Palestinian Conflict	Includes all aspects of the conflict, e.g., settlements, negotiations, nuclear weapons, the gaza blockade, terror attacks
	□ 03 Relationship Israel and Actor	Discussion of actors relationship with Israel and Israels standing or image
	□ 04 Other	Please discuss with me or clarify
10b	**specify topic in max 5 words (this is only for me and you)** **for example Existing options: (you can add more)**	
	Gaza flotilla:	expectations/preparations/intentions/violent outcomes/aftermath/…
	Israeli politics:	in general/existence/nuclear arms/ peace negotiations/…
	Relationship:	Discussion of Israel's image/ Discussion of relation to actor/…

11	**Evaluation of the actors main claim/action** *Judge whether the action/claim by the actor is affirmative or critical of Israeli politics from an Israeli standpoint.* *NOTE: Not every article contains an action/message by the actor or evaluative content.*	
	□ 01 Criticism/Condemnation	Includes all items in which main actors action/claim is critical towards Israeli policy/existence/standpoints or condemning it *"Actor X criticizes the Israeli settlement policy"* *"Actor X condemns Israel in general"*
	□ 02 Balanced (equal positive/negative)	Includes criticism/call for/support equally for all the sides, also: unwillingness to take part/ one side/ responsibility *"Actor X calls for Israel and Turkey to reconcile"*
	□ 03 Support/ Affirmation	Includes all claims/actions of support of Israels policies and actions. *"Actor X supports Israel's right to defend itself"*
	□ 04 No message/No evaluative content	Includes articles on the relationships with the actor and the perceived attitudes towards Israel
11b	**specify the claim/action in max 5 words (this is only for me and you)** **For exampleExisting options: (you can add more)** Support Call for Condemnation	Complete support for Israel, condemnation of rivals, Defense of Israel's right to exist investigation/ Call for end, easening of Gaza blockade/ Call for peace negotiation of Israeli action/ Condemnation of Israel/ Criticism of Israeli actions
11c	**Direction of the Claim** *Judge whether the main claim is focused on a action/behavior/policy in the past and/or present or in the future* □ 01 Focus on past/ present □ 01 Focus on the future	Includes all items in which the main actor relates to issues that are already passed or ongoing Includes all items in which the main actor calls/proposes/requests a certain action/behavior/policy in the future *"Actor X calls for investigation/peace negotiation"*

FRAMING OF CLAIM/ACTOR/ RELATIONSHIP

12	**How is the claim/action framed?** *Please judge if there is framing/description of the claim or action. Does the journalist describe or classify the claim/action in any way? If yes, in a positive OR neutral OR negative way? If the description of the claim/action uses any of the mentioned sub-categories, mark them.* *NOTE: More than one answer/framing is possible. This includes framing undertaken by the author of the article as well as by the people the author chose to cite.*	
	POSITIVE	**01 Yes (if possible specify in next lines)** **02 No (Go to Q12b)**
12a	In sense with Israel's policies　　　(includes: approval of claim)	□ 01 Yes □ 02 No
	Helpful on path to peace	□ 01 Yes □ 02 No
	Important	□ 01 Yes □ 02 No
	Other________________	Please specify
	NEUTRAL	**01 Yes (if possible specify in next lines)** **02 No (Go to Q12c)**
12b	Worth a discussion	□ 01 Yes □ 02 No
	Unbiased/balanced	□ 01 Yes □ 02 No
	Other________________	□ 01 Yes □ 02 No
	NEGATIVE	**01 Yes (if possible specify in next lines)** **02 No (Go to Q 13)**
12c	negating Israels policies　　　(includes: fighting parts of Israel's policies)	□ 01 Yes □ 02 No
	Illegitimate/unacceptable	□ 01 Yes □ 02 No
	Counterproductive on path to peace (includes: not use/helpful)	□ 01 Yes □ 02 No
	not important/relevant	□ 01 Yes □ 02 No
	Exaggerated	□ 01 Yes □ 02 No
	other________________	Please specify

13	**How is the actor framed?** *Please judge if there is framing/description of the actor. Does the journalist describe or classify the actor in any way? If yes, in a positive/neutral or negative way? Then, if the description of the actor uses any of the mentioned sub-categories, mark them. It is possible that an actor is described in more than one way. For example the description could be:* "The actor is Pro-Israeli, but he lacks understanding for Israel" → Code: Positive & Pro-Israeli and Negative & lacks understanding for Israel *NOTE: several framings are possible*	
	01 Positive	**01 Yes (if possible specify in next lines)** **02 No (Go to Q13b)**
13a	understands Israel	□ 01 Yes □ 02 No
	legitimate	□ 01 Yes □ 02 No
	Pro-Israeli	□ 01 Yes □ 02 No
	supporter (includes: active cooperation/help)	□ 01 Yes □ 02 No
	important	□ 01 Yes □ 02 No
	other___	Please specify
	02 Neutral	**01 Yes (if possible specify in next lines)** **02 No (Go to Q13c)**
13b	unbiased/balanced	□ 01 Yes □ 02 No
	nonpartisan	□ 01 Yes □ 02 No
	uncommitted	□ 01 Yes □ 02 No
	description of diversity	□ 01 Yes □ 02 No
	Other___	Please specify
	03 Negative	**01 Yes (if possible specify in next lines)** **02 No (Go to Q14)**
13c	Lacks understanding for Israel	□ 01 Yes □ 02 No
	biased	□ 01 Yes □ 02 No
	hypocrite	□ 01 Yes □ 02 No
	illegitimate	□ 01 Yes □ 02 No
	Terrorist	□ 01 Yes □ 02 No
	Anti-Israeli/Anti-Semite	□ 01 Yes □ 02 No
	Not important/ not relevant (includes: is weak)	□ 01 Yes □ 02 No
	responsible for the course events took and its outcomes	□ 01 Yes □ 02 No
	attack Israel (includes: wants to lynch/ provocates/wants media war/ wants to hurt/delegitimize Israel)	□ 01 Yes □ 02 No
	Other___	Please specify

How is the relationship framed?

Please judge if there is framing/description of the relationship. Does the journalist describe or classify the relationship in any way? If yes, in a positive/neutral or negative way? Then, if the description of the actor uses any of the mentioned sub-categories, mark them.
NOTE: several framings are possible

			01 Yes (if possible specify in next lines) 02 No (Go to Q14b)
14a	**01 Positive**		
	friend		□ 01 Yes □ 02 No
	partner		□ 01 Yes □ 02 No
	cooperation		□ 01 Yes □ 02 No
	important		□ 01 Yes □ 02 No
	relationship improved		□ 01 Yes □ 02 No
	relationship is stable/strong		□ 01 Yes □ 02 No
	Other		□ 01 Yes □ 02 No
			Please specify
14b	**02 Neutral**		01 Yes (if possible specify in next lines) 02 No (Go to Q14c)
	nonpartisan		□ 01 Yes □ 02 No
	uncommitted		□ 01 Yes □ 02 No
	Other		□ 01 Yes □ 02 No
			Please specify
14c	**03 Negative**		01 Yes (if possible specify in next lines) 02 No (Go to Q15)
	Enemy		□ 01 Yes □ 02 No
	No partner	(includes: Actor supports rival)	□ 01 Yes □ 02 No
	Confrontation	(includes: refuse to cooperate)	□ 01 Yes □ 02 No
	Not important/relevant		□ 01 Yes □ 02 No
	Relationship in crisis/worsened		□ 01 Yes □ 02 No
	Other		□ 01 Yes □ 02 No
			Please specify
14d	**Relationship is complex**		□ 01 Yes □ 02 No

MECHANISMS OF FRAMING		
15	**How does the author contextualize the claims/actions?** *Does the article concentrate on details of an action or claim or does it explain backgrounds, causes, developments, interfering factors* □ 01 Embedding in wider contexts □ 02 Concentration on details □ 03 No contextualization	Explanation of the context (causes, events, developments) leading to and shaping the incident/situation described Detailed description of parts of an incident/situation without description of its context
16	**Is the impact of the claim/action enhanced or softened?** □ 01 Enhancing of impact □ 02 Softening of claim's impact □ 03 No enhancing or softening of impact	Enhancing/Dramatization of impact can be achieved through: repetition of argument, comparison of the action/message with other events, emphasis on the events/actors/claims significance Downgrading of the significance of impact by concentrating on the positive facts for Israel, emphasizing that worse outcomes were possible, and the current is the favorable *"this option is the lesser evil"*
17	**FURTHER MECHANISMS OF FRAMING** law and order versus chaos	Framing of the OTHER as destroying the order, and of the OWN as responding to it with order and structure	□ 01 Yes □ 02 No
	Siege mentality	Framing the OTHER as constantly attacking/oppressing the OWN, meaning the OWN is isolated in case of emergency	□ 01 Yes □ 02 No
	with or against us	Framing claim or action of OTHER within the framework of those possible options	□ 01 Yes □ 02 No
	personalization of the OTHER	Framing of the rival with naming, description of intentions, citations	□ 01 Yes □ 02 No

POSSIBLE USE OF ETHOS OF CONFLICT IN REPRESENTATION OF MESSAGE/ACTION BY INTERNATIONAL ACTOR

Is the narration of the international involvement/actor permeated by one or more of the following beliefs?

18	**Delegitimization of the other/ the others message**	Includes negative and inhuman description and characterization of the actor or Palestinians including their intentions, the representations of their acts	☐ 01 Yes ☐ 02 No
19	**Victimization of the own group**	Includes references to harsh unjust experiences that Jewish Israelis encounter as individuals and/or collectives throughout the conflict as a result of Palestinian or international maltreatment, including harsh criticism, accusations, condemnation of Israel's policies or mere existence; killing, injuries, destruction, power, etc. Includes also the belief that the world is hostile towards Israel.	☐ 01 Yes ☐ 02 No
20	**Security**	Includes referring to threats to Israeli security, military actions carried out by Israelis, conditions and actions that are necessary to secure the life of Jewish Israelis.	☐ 01 Yes ☐ 02 No
21	**Justness of own goals**	Includes justifying of Jewish Israelis' goals, denies Actors or Palestinian's goals; means to achieve these goals are justified, including violence against actors or Palestinians or Above all, includes Israel's right to exist and to settle in Israel.	☐ 01 Yes ☐ 02 No
22	**National Unity**	This includes reference to descriptions of society's unity, the necessity of supporting the leaders and the conflict goals, and the high cost that society might pay if unity is impaired. In addition, this theme refers to the importance of solidarity against the external threat and the need for consensus.	☐ 01 Yes ☐ 02 No
23	**Patriotism**	Includes expressions of belonging, love, pride, loyalty, and commitment to homeland and people of Israel and the need for self-sacrifice.	☐ 01 Yes ☐ 02 No
24	**Peace**	Refers to nature of peace, devotion, longing for peace, and the endeavors to solve the conflict in peaceful ways.	☐ 01 Yes ☐ 02 No
25	**Positive ingroup image**	Includes positive self-collective characterization with traits, intentions or behaviors.	☐ 01 Yes ☐ 02 No

D Gaza Crisis 2014

Examples of Brief Analysis of Media Representation of International Involvement in Gaza Conflict 2014

The opponent, the Gazan population and their suffering are invisible in the majority of the newspapers throughout the conflict period. Only Haaretz frequently shows images of destruction and counts numbers of deaths prominently.

Delegitimization and Victimization: International support diminishes as the crisis continues. Israeli newspapers discuss the lack of international media sympathy and blame it to be hypocritical and biased. Another factor is seen in the Palestinian lack of respect for humans: "Palestinians do everything to get as many Jewish and Palestinian victims, however they win the media war" (MA_2014_07_13_20).

Polarization as friend or foe: A central issue is the question whether international actors are with or against Israel and why. In the days of the outbreak of the conflict articles on international support are frequent "US: We support Israel's right to defend itself" (IH_2014_07_09_19); "Merkel: Israel has the right to defend itself" (MA_2014_07_20_15); "They stand with us: Demonstrations of support in the USA and London" (IH_2014_07_20_25) are titles of articles. Note the emphasis on security and defense. "US and Europe on Israel's side" (YA_2014_07_10_08). The latter headline is an example for a perspective splitting international actors into "with or against Israel". "The leaders of the world show understanding" (IH_2014_07_13_11). This first long article on international opinions after the outbreak concludes that, while international media "does not like Israel", the world leaders surprisingly support Israel since now they understand the realities of Europe.

The media battle: As the conflict continues, international support diminishes. *Maariv* evaluates why international media sympathy is with the Gazan population: "The more successful Iron Dome [the Israeli rocket defense system], the less sympathy the world will have for a state under rocket attack" (MA_2014_07_13_10). He continues: "There would be more sympathy for Israel if Hamas succeeded to reach its goal and kill a high number of Jews". Another author argues that the game for international sympathy is unfair as "Palestinians do everything to get as many Jewish and Palestinian victims, however they win the media war" (MA_2014_07_13_20). The international media is blamed to be hypocritical and biased and to ignore Israeli suffering in the conflict: They "emphasize suffering of Palestinians and not on the threat of live on millions of Israelis". International media counts the Palestinian deaths "and not the suffering of Israeli kids that have a difficult summer holiday" (MA_2014_07_14_04). Haaretz also criticizes the focus on Palestinian over Israeli suffering (HA_2014_07_15_5). An article in *Maariv* analyzes the international media coverage of the beginning ground operation by the Israeli army in Gaza and concludes that it was balanced in the beginning, but increasingly focuses on the amount of killed: "The death toll is based on data by Hamas and it is not clear who is civilian. However, for the normal recipient around the world the image is clear: they see the body of a child or a woman and Israel is the one powerfully attacking innocent civilian Palestinians which is in no way comparable to the attacks of Hamas on Israeli cities" (MA_2014_21_07_16). The author concludes that most international politicians agree with Israel, silently or in public, however the international public has this understanding. An author in *Maariv* addresses the worries within the Israeli political establishment that Israel will lose international sympathies and sums the perception up: "Israel is losing at the scene of hasbara of Protective Edge" (name of the Gaza war 2014) (MA_2014_07_15_07). However, an author in Israel Hayom concludes: "Israel gets hit for its ground operation from international media, but it is worth it" with focus on the justness of one's own goals that are worth the international image loss (IH_2014_07_20_23).

The world and Israel: A week into the conflict international criticism rises and is covered in articles summing up various demonstrations worldwide and condemnations of international leaders. "Condemnations in the world on Israeli attacks". The world appears again as actor group: "How do we look in the world after a week. As usually not very good. The world is still against us, but a little less" (YA_2014_07_15_06). Another article, titled "The European streets are recruited for Gaza" focuses on European Leftists, Green parties and Muslims uniting against Israel (IH_2014_07_20_23). This emphasizes both on an image of "everyone is against Israel" and on their alleged hypocrisy as two groups that do not belong together unite in their opposition to Israel.

The world against Israel: International demonstrations are centrally framed as violent and antisemitic. "The echoes of the war reached Europe and antisemitism already raises its head" (IH_2014_07_14_13). Another article titled "the new antisemites" claims "the facts are not important and Gaza is just an excuse for the rise of antisemitism. Europe should understand that in the global fight against terror we are part of the solution" (IH_2014_07_28_19). Israel Hayom sums the criticism up: "whatever is going on, the world will attack Israel, so let the world wait (with cease fire), this is a war on our right to exist" (IH_2014_08_07_03).

Victimization: The perception as being victim to an international attack of hypocrisy only rises when Israel starts the ground operation after two weeks, international pressure and frustration over international opinion increases. A repeated allegation is that the "world" focuses solely on "images of Palestinian injuries" without caring if they are civilian or not.

(Note the emphasis on "images of injuries" as opposed to victims) (MA_2014_07_20_14). Yediot Aheronot titles: "Ongoing hypocrisy" and "the Secretary General of the UN insists on condemning Israel in particular" (YA_2014_08_07_02). As the UNHRC decides to investigate Israel for war crimes the reactions are univocal: Haaretz calls the institution "anyway against Israel" and criticizes the one-sidedness (HA_2014_07_24_5). *Maariv* suggests to ignore the UN and continue fighting: "They will always blame us". And: "They don't want democracy or human rights they just want to hurt Israel's ability to defend itself and its existence as Jewish democratic state" (MA_2014_07_25_29). Both the actors are delegitimized in their goals and one's own goals are explained as just. A commentator stresses the perceived injustice: "We do not get to rest. After four weeks of attacks by the Hamas, the UN opens the diplomatic artillery fire. The world is biased. We said that already." He argues, when Americans fire on Iraqi civilians, that is considered a decent mistake, whereas the same happening to Israel is considered a war crime. "Israel, as expected, gets criticized. Hamas, a terror organization, gets "discounts" and that is how the world encourages Hamas to use civilians." (IH_2014_08_07_05). The author did not only blame the world for its hypocrisy and the injustice of its judgment over Israel, also Hamas is blamed for the deaths. Israel Hayom emphasizes the UN's lack of importance (UM-Shoom) (IH_2014_07_24_07).

Rejection of involvement: Further international pressure, especially by President Obama is explained by his alleged lack of understanding for the Middle East (IH_2013_08_01_10) or as stabbing Israel in the back, or "With friends like this." (YA_2014_07_28_03). UN criticism is denied through referral to the position of the UN in Mogadishu, the conflict between the Russians and the Chechens, the war by the USA in Iraq and Afghanistan (YA_2014_08_07_02).

These examples illustrate that some of the patterns found in the present investigation were apparent in the newspaper representation of international involvement during the Gaza conflict in 2014. They cannot substitute an empirical analysis on this phase.

MEDIEN UND POLITISCHE KOMMUNIKATION – NAHER OSTEN UND ISLAMISCHE WELT / MEDIA AND POLITICAL COMMUNICATION – MIDDLE EAST AND ISLAM

Band 9 Carola Richter: Das Mediensystem in Libyen – Akteure und Entwicklungen. ISBN 3-89173-088-8

Band 10 Ines Braune: Die Journalistenverbände in Jordanien und im Libanon – ein Teil der Zivilgesellschaft? ISBN 3-89173-090-X

(Die Bände 1–10 sind beim Deutschen Orient-Institut, Hamburg erschienen und über dieses und den Buchhandel zu beziehen.)

Band 11 Jamal Nazzal: Das palästinensische Rundfunksystem und die deutsch-palästinensische Medienkooperation. 340 Seiten. ISBN 978-3-86596-058-0. ISBN 3-86596-058-8

Band 12 Aydin Nasseri: Internet und Gesellschaft in Iran. Mit einem Vorwort von Katajun Amirpur. 198 Seiten. ISBN 3-86596-116-9

Band 13 Maria Röder: Haremsdame, Opfer oder Extremistin? Muslimische Frauen im Nachrichtenmagazin Der Spiegel. 160 Seiten. ISBN 978-3-86596-143-3

Band 14 Antje Glück: Terror im Kopf. Terrorismusberichterstattung in der deutschen und arabischen Elitepresse. 206 Seiten. ISBN 978-386596-157-0

Band 15 Muhammad I. Ayish: The New Arab Public Sphere. 254 Seiten. ISBN 978-3-86596-168-6

Band 16 Susan Schenk: Das Islambild im internationalen Fernsehen. Ein Vergleich der Nachrichtensender *Al Jazeera English*, *BBC World* und *CNN International*. 176 Seiten. ISBN 978-3-86596-224-9

T Frank & Timme

MEDIEN UND POLITISCHE KOMMUNIKATION –
NAHER OSTEN UND ISLAMISCHE WELT /
MEDIA AND POLITICAL COMMUNICATION –
MIDDLE EAST AND ISLAM

Band 17   Jan Michael Schäfer: Protest in Ägypten. Wie Al-Jazeera und andere
Medien die Kifaya-Bewegung möglich machten. 150 Seiten.
ISBN 978-3-86596-219-5

Band 18   Sarah Jurkiewicz: Al-Jazeera vor Ort. Journalismus als ethische
Praxis. 140 Seiten. ISBN 978-3-86596-228-7

Band 19   Katharina Nötzold: Defining the Nation? Lebanese Television and
Political Elites, 1990–2005. 376 Seiten. ISBN 978-3-86596-242-3

Band 20   Kerstin Engelmann, Friederike Günther, Nele Heise, Florian
Hohmann, Ulrike Irrgang, Sabrina Schmidt: Muslimische Weblogs.
Der Islam im deutschsprachigen Internet. 282 Seiten.
ISBN 978-3-86596-239-3

Band 21   Carola Richter: Medienstrategien ägyptischer Islamisten im Kontext
von Demokratisierung. 354 Seiten. ISBN 978-3-86596-361-1

Band 22   Douglas Reynolds: Turkey, Greece, and the "Borders" of Europe.
Images of Nations in the West German Press 1950–1975. 558 Seiten.
ISBN 978-3-86596-441-0

Band 23   Kai Hafez (Hg.): Arabischer Frühling und deutsches Islambild.
Bildwandel durch ein Medienereignis? 154 Seiten.
ISBN 978-3-86596-497-7

Band 24   Almut Woller: Transformation der Geschlechterverhältnisse in den
Vereinigten Arabischen Emiraten. Eine feministische Diskursanalyse
der Arbeitsmarktintegration emiratischer Frauen. 234 Seiten.
ISBN 978-3-7329-0015-2

T Frank & Timme

MEDIEN UND POLITISCHE KOMMUNIKATION –
NAHER OSTEN UND ISLAMISCHE WELT /
MEDIA AND POLITICAL COMMUNICATION –
MIDDLE EAST AND ISLAM

Band 25   Margret Müller: The World According To Israeli Newspapers.
Representations of International Involvement in the
Israeli-Palestinian Conflict. 286 Seiten. ISBN 978-3-7329-0286-6

T Frank & Timme